CW01360030

*Britain, the United States
and the Transfer of Power in the Middle East,
1945–1962*

By the same author:

'Appeasement' and the English Speaking World: Britain, the United States, the Dominions and the Policy of 'Appeasement', 1937–1939 (1975)
The Origins of the Arab–Israeli Wars (1984). Second Edition (1992)
The Foreign Policy of the British Labour Governments, 1945–1951, editor (1984)
The English-Speaking Alliance: Britain, the United States, the Dominions and the Cold War 1945–1951 (1985)
Britain, the United States, and the End of the Palestine Mandate, 1942–1948 (1989)
The Longman Companion to the Middle East since 1914 (1992)
British Defence Policy since 1945: Documents in Contemporary History, editor (1994)

Britain, the United States, and the Transfer of Power in the Middle East, 1945–1962

RITCHIE OVENDALE

Leicester University Press
London and New York

Leicester University Press
A Cassell imprint
Wellington House, 125 Strand, London WC2R 0BB, England
127 West 24th Street, New York, NY 10011, USA.
First published 1996

© Ritchie Ovendale, 1996

Apart from any fair dealing for the purposes of research or private study, or criticism or review, as permitted under the Copyright, Designs and Patents Act 1988, this publication may not be reproduced, stored or transmitted, in any form or by any means or process, without the prior permission in writing of the copyright holders or their agents. Except for reproduction in accordance with the terms of licences issued by the Copyright Licensing Agency, photocopying of whole or part of this publication without the prior written permission of the copyright holders or their agents in single or multiple copies whether for gain or not is illegal and expressly forbidden. Please direct all enquiries concerning copyright to the publishers at the address above.

Ritchie Ovendale is hereby identified as the author of this work as provided for under Section 77 of the Copyright, Designs and Patents Act 1988.

British Library Cataloguing in Publication Data

A CIP catalogue record for this book is available from the British Library

ISBN 0 7185 1438 6

Library of Congress Cataloging-in-Publication Data

Ovendale, Ritchie.
    Britain, the United States, and the transfer of power in the Middle East, 1945–1962 / Ritchie Ovendale.
      p. cm.
    Includes bibliographical references (p.248) and index.
    ISBN 0-7185-1438-6
    1. Middle East–foreign relations–Great Britain. 2. Great Britain–foreign relations–Middle East. 3. Middle East–foreign relations–United States. 4. United States–foreign relations–Middle East. 5. Great Britain–foreign relations–United States. 6. United States–foreign relations–Great Britain. 7. Great Britain–foreign relations–1945– I. Title.
DS63.2.G7093   1996
327.41056–dc20   96-6321
                                                                                                    CIP

Typeset by BookEns Ltd, Royston, Herts.
Printed and bound in Great Britain by Biddles Ltd, Guildford and King's Lynn

Contents

Acknowledgements vii

1. British Paramountcy in the Middle East 1
2. The American Interest 24
3. Churchill and 'Getting the Americans In': Iran and Egypt 58
4. Churchill and 'Getting the Americans In': Saudi Arabia, Iraq, Jordan, Israel 84
5. Eden and the 'Flexing of British Muscles': The Baghdad Pact 108
6. Eden and the 'Flexing of British Muscles': The Suez Crisis 140
7. The American Involvement: The Eisenhower Doctrine 178
8. The Anglo-American Invasion of Jordan and Lebanon 198
9. The Defence of Kuwait 216
10. Conclusions 242

Bibliography 248
Index 259

Acknowledgements

Part of the research of this book was made possible by grants from the Nuffield Foundation, and from the British Academy and its Small Grants Fund in the Humanities, and a visiting research fellowship from the American Council of Learned Societies tenable at the University of Virginia, Charlottesville. The Australian National University, Canberra, kindly elected me a visiting research fellow in the Department of International Relations attached to the Research School of Pacific Studies.

I should like to thank the following for assistance: Professor Christopher Andrew, Sir Harold Beeley, Professor Inis Claude, Professor John Garnett, the late Professor Agnes Headlam-Morley, Professor Edward Ingram, Professor Ieuan John, Dr Clive Jones, James W. Leyerzapf, Professor Wm. Roger Louis, the late Professor J.D.B. Miller, Professor Ian Nish, the late Professor F.S. Northedge, Dr Alistair Parker, Professor James Piscatori, Sir Frank K. Roberts, Professor Keith Robbins, Professor Jack Spence, David Steeds, Professor Geoffrey Warner, and Professor D. Cameron Watt.

I am grateful to the library staffs of many institutions and archives for their expertise. In particular I should like to thank the following and, where appropriate, acknowledge permission to quote from collections in their custody: Church 1 College, Cambridge and the Earl Attlee for the Attlee Papers; the British Library for the Oliver Harvey Diaries; the British Library of Political and Economic Science for the Dalton Papers; the Western Manuscripts Department of the Bodleian Library, and the Master and Fellows of University College, Oxford for the Attlee Papers; the Guy W. Bailey Library, the University of Vermont, for the Warren R. Austin and Ernest Gibson Jr papers; the Eisenhower Library, Abilene, Kansas; the Aldeman Library, University of Virginia; the George C. Marshall Library, Virginia Military Institute, for George C. Marshall's papers and other collections housed there; Princeton University Library; the Harry S. Truman Library, Independence, Missouri; the Franklin D. Roosevelt Library; Georgetown University Library for the Robert F. Wagner Papers; the Library of Congress Manuscript Division; the National Archives in Washington together with the National Records Centre at Suitland, Maryland; the Australian Archives in Canberra; and the Australian National Library for the papers of Sir

Percy Spender and Sir Robert Menzies. The staff of the Public Record Office, London were always obliging and courteous; copyright material housed there appears by permission of Her Majesty's Stationery Office.

Some of the material used in this book originally appeared in *The English-Speaking Alliance: Britain, the United States, the Dominions and the Cold War 1945–1951*, published by George Allen and Unwin, in *The International History Review*, and in *Churchill and Britain's Place in the World*, edited by Alastair Parker and published by Brasseys. I appreciate permission from the respective editors to incorporate that work.

I should also like to thank Nicola Viinikka for allowing me an extension of contract.

1

British Paramountcy in the Middle East

In 1945 Britain was the paramount power in the Middle East. British influence had been established there in the aftermath of the First World War. At the San Remo Conference, in April 1920, British and French mandates were unceremoniously imposed on reluctant Arab populations, and Palestine was specifically excluded from the principle of self-determination. The Western powers carved up the area in their own domestic and imperial interests. The Arabs had little say. Lawrence of Arabia felt that he discharged his debts to those who had helped him during the desert campaign by establishing Feisal in Iraq and Abdullah in Transjordan. The Soviets had no real opportunity to penetrate the area. The French were preoccupied with problems in Syria and did not interfere with the British mandates.

In May 1945 the French, determined to crush Arab nationalism, tried to re-establish their influence in the Levant by bombing Damascus. To Britain this move seemed to threaten the security of the whole of the Middle East. The British Commander-in-Chief forced the French troops to withdraw to their barracks. General Charles de Gaulle complained that this humiliation both insulted the French and betrayed the West. Effectively, Britain forced France out of Syria and the Lebanon. Some Americans were worried that Britain was securing too large a share of the world's potential oil resources, and American commercial interests were established in Saudi Arabia, but at that time these did not seriously challenge British predominance.

For many public school products the Middle East remained an area in which they could apply Dr Thomas Arnold's principles of discipline and moral leadership. They were able to relate to the Arab leaders who had been chosen. They appreciated their courtesy. The Arab hierarchy responded in return: it sent its sons to Harrow and Sandhurst. A section of the British upper and upper-middle classes came to respect and admire the Arabs, and particularly the Bedouin. The desert seemed clean. On the whole the British administrative structure established in the Middle East showed at least a façade of equality to the governed. There was a liberal tradition and even an idealism. The social snobberies so prevalent in the Indian subcontinent were largely absent, except in Egypt. Above all, British policy in the Middle East appeared to be flexible, and to respond to local needs.

The principal challenge to British predominance came from the Zionists. To the Arabs it seemed that the British government had issued the Balfour declaration in 1917 favouring the establishment of a Jewish homeland in Palestine, and it was Britain that held the Palestine mandate and admitted the Jewish immigrants who took over Arab land. After the increase in Jewish immigration, following the rise of Adolf Hitler in Germany, the Arabs rebelled in 1936. The Balfour declaration had specifically stated that 'the civil and religious rights of existing non-Jewish communities in Palestine' should not be prejudiced. In the 1930s, as war seemed likely, Britain abandoned the policy sympathetic to Zionism which had been secured by the Zionist lobby. The Middle East was unlikely to be a secure base in time of rebellion. The British Empire contained many millions of Muslim subjects. They were concerned over Jewish immigration into Palestine, and opposed vehemently the creation of a Jewish state, which they regarded as a base for foreign influence in the Arab world. Britain was still the paramount power.

In May 1939 Britain issued a White Paper limiting Jewish immigration into Palestine. The Zionists changed their tactics. Instead of concentrating on the mandatory power, they focused on the United States. The new policy was accepted at the American Zionist Conference meeting at the Biltmore Hotel in New York in 1942. The Zionists threatened electoral punishment through the Zionist vote if the American administration failed to support a Jewish state. It was thought that the United States could force Britain to hand Palestine over to the Zionists. In the mandate itself the Zionists used new methods. A policy of attrition was waged against the administration. Violence and terrorism were aimed at wearing down British morale. Britain, rather than the Arabs, became the principal enemy. Palestine became an area of Anglo-American controversy at the time of the emergence of the Cold War.[1]

At the end of the Second World War the Middle East, to the British military mind, had an importance second only to the United Kingdom. The experience of Mons and Dunkirk lingered. British land armies should not again fight on the European continent. That was a job for the Europeans. Air and naval support might be possible, but that was all. Britain could not stop the advance of Soviet armies across the continent. Only the United States could do that. The security of the British Commonwealth depended on protecting the United Kingdom, maintaining vital sea communications and securing the Middle East as a defensive and striking base against the Soviet Union. The existence of the atomic bomb did not affect this strategy.[2]

As strategic planners began to assess the situation after the devastation of Hiroshima and Nagasaki, the British military presence in the Middle East was considerable. There were over 200,000 troops in the Canal Zone on the Suez base, occupying an area about the size of Wales and equipped with almost every facility needed for war. The Suez base was supported in the front line by the air installations at Lydda and a British naval presence at Haifa in the Palestine mandate. There were two further air bases at Habbaniya and Shaiba in Iraq. In Transjordan, the Arab Legion was led by a British officer, John Glubb. There were naval bases at Bahrain and Aden, and air and military installations at Khartoum in the Sudan. Britain had oil interests in Iraq, and particularly in Iran where the Abadan refinery was the largest in the world and produced, in 1945, more oil than the other Arab States together. In Iran the Anglo-Iranian Oil Company was staffed by what was virtually an autonomous British community which had vastly increased its oil production by 1950. The pipeline from the oilfields at Kirkuk in Iraq ended in Haifa where there was a large British refinery. But none of these areas was under permanent British sovereignty. Alternatives did exist: Cyrenaica, the eastern province of Libya, and Kenya. The island of Cyprus was the only British possession in the Middle East. It had 20 airfields, but only a small harbour, Famagusta, which was not a deep-water port. On 5 September 1945 the Chiefs of Staff recommended that British rule be maintained over Cyprus. 'Enosis', or union with Greece, had to be resisted.[3]

This strategic policy meant that the British Empire in the Middle East, acquired almost accidentally earlier in the century, had to be maintained and consolidated. As the British Commonwealth became the Commonwealth, the empire was wound up in Asia, and power began to be transferred on the African continent, the Middle East was the only large area over which British suzerainty could still be exerted. After 1947 even the United States acknowledged the need to maintain the British presence there. With the joining of the Cold War those two countries agreed that the Middle East was to be a British and Commonwealth area of responsibility.[4] Ernest Bevin, the Foreign Secretary, masterminded this British policy. He hoped for a relationship between Britain and the Arab states based on mutual interdependence and trust. British policy in the Middle East had to be broadened to secure the economic welfare of the inhabitants. Aware of the significance of the rise of a new generation of young Arabs, just as disenchanted with their own rulers as with any British presence, Bevin felt that this policy had to be based on peasants and not pashas.

Increasingly, Arabism was not just synonymous with Islam, the Arabic language and the geographic area of Arabia. The inhabitants of North Africa stressed their Arab identity. During the 1930s and 1940s Arab writers and thinkers developed the idea of the *ba'ath* or renaissance of the Arab nation. In 1942 Nuri al-Said and Abdullah developed the Greater Syria concept into the Fertile Crescent, which would be formed by the union of Transjordan, Palestine, the Lebanon and Syria, and finally to include Iraq and Saudi Arabia. Britain was disturbed by the likelihood of an adverse reaction to this by Egyptian nationalists and the obvious consequences for the British base in Egypt. The young generation's dislike of Western imperialism was partly fomented by a scorn for the defeat of France and the subsequent division between Gaullist and Vichy officers in the Levant, by the crushing of the Rashid Ali government in Iraq in

1941 with Anglo-Indian troops, and by Sir Miles Lampson (later Lord Killearn) forcing Farouk – with British tanks in the palace grounds – to appoint Mustafa al-Nahas as leader in Egypt on 4 February 1942.[5]

On 24 August 1945, Bevin notified the Foreign Office how he was anxious that Middle Eastern policy should not provide the Soviets with an opportunity to criticize it.[6] Six days later, Bevin suggested to the Cabinet a conference of British representatives in the Middle East to discuss general policy in the area. It was time to consider whether Britain should continue to assert its political predominance in the Middle East and its overriding responsibility for the area's defence, or whether on defence and manpower grounds Britain should ask for the assistance of other powers. In addition, an economic and social policy covering the Middle East was needed.[7]

The conference met in London during September. It decided that a British influence in the Middle East, which rested on military or political props, could not be enduring. Britain should broaden the base on which its influence rested, and develop an economic and social policy that would make for the prosperity and contentment of the area as a whole. But the Middle East was to remain largely a British sphere of influence: Britain 'should not make any concession that would assist American commercial penetration into a region which for generations has been an established British market'.[8]

The Palestine Committee of the Cabinet, however, took a more precise view of Britain's strategic position in the Middle East. It was a region of 'vital consequence' for Britain and the empire. It formed the nodal point in the communication system, by land, sea and air, linking Britain with India, Australia and the Far East. It was the empire's main reserve of oil. Within it lay the Suez Canal, and the principal naval bases in the eastern Mediterranean and at Alexandria. In this important region Cyprus was the only territory under full British sovereignty: Palestine, as a mandated territory, was subject to international agreement; all the other Middle Eastern countries were independent except Transjordan which was likely to achieve that status in the near future. Britain, therefore, depended on co-operation from these independent states. The attitude of the Arabs was of the first importance. British prestige, at that time, was 'immensely high' and relations with the various rulers was 'friendly and cordial'. Yet this could be transformed overnight if Britain took any action which the Arabs might construe as injurious to their interests: the Arabs were sensitive about the future of Palestine. The Arab League had been formed in March 1945, and that made the situation more difficult since individual Arab states might resist policies they did not like. If Britain enforced a policy in Palestine which the Arabs resented, especially if that policy could be called a breach of faith, that would undermine Britain's position in the Middle East. There would be widespread disturbances in the Arab countries, and the co-operation on which British imperial interests so largely depended would be withdrawn.[9]

The Cabinet discussed these reports on 4 October. Bevin said that he wanted to broaden the basis of British influence in the Middle East 'by developing an economic and social policy which would make for prosperity and contentment in the area as a whole'. Economic development and social reform could make for an easier solution of military and political problems, which included a threatening situation in Palestine, agitation in Egypt for the withdrawal of British forces and difficulties with France in the Levant. The Cabinet was interested in Britain's strategic position. The Chiefs of Staff were considering the feasibility of basing forces needed for the protection of the Middle East on British territory rather than in Egypt. It was hoped that there would be some joint agreement for the defence of that country leaving Britain with responsibility for the Suez Canal. Sir Alan Brooke, the Chief of the Imperial General Staff, agreed with the proposed policy for Egypt. The Mombasa areas was being considered, but while it was suitable as a base, it had difficulties in rail and road communications and port facilities. George Glenville Hall, the Secretary of State for the Colonies, asked for the strategic importance of Cyprus to be considered again. The Cabinet approved the new policy for the Middle East.[10]

In effect, British strategic policy for the Middle East was dependent on a British military presence in Palestine. On 24 January 1944, the Chiefs of Staff had pointed to the military disadvantages of dividing Palestine into separate states.[11] At the end of that year, the State Department warned that an expansion of Soviet influence in the Middle East had to be prevented. The area was of vital strategic importance to the United States. There were obvious difficulties for Britain: the Soviets might capitalize on Arab resentment of the United States to maintain its pre-eminence in the area. At that time President F.D. Roosevelt viewed the world with a different perspective: referring to difficulties with Britain, the President told his Cabinet on 16 March 1945, in a 'semi-jocular' way, that Britain was prepared for the United States to fight the Soviet Union at any time – 'to follow the British programme would be to proceed toward that end'.[12] A meeting of the Commanders-in-Chief and British officials near Cairo on 3 April 1945 agreed unanimously that the 'insane' idea of partition for Palestine should be abandoned. Lord Killearn, the ambassador in Egypt, thought that Britain should stay in Palestine indefinitely.[13] In August 1945, the Chiefs of Staff opposed partition: it would be drastic and irrevocable.[14] If partition had to be enforced they estimated that three additional divisions, including one airborne division, would have to be dispatched to the Middle East, as well as two infantry and one armoured brigade. A British division in India would be needed as an additional reserve. Furthermore, Indian troops should not be used to implement a policy in the Middle East that would arouse agitation in India. If that happened British requirements would be increased by one armoured division and a further two brigades.[15]

At this point President Harry S. Truman intervened. He had sent Earl G. Harrison to investigate the condition of displaced persons in Europe. Harrison recommended that Washington should, under existing laws, allow reasonable numbers of Jewish refugees into the United States. Truman, realizing that Congress would not relax the immigration quotas, chose instead to assign the responsibility to Britain. In doing this he overrode the advice of the State and War Departments. There was an election in New York, and the Jewish vote seemed crucial. Truman wrote to Clement Attlee, the British Prime Minister, on 31 August suggesting that the main solution lay in the quick evacuation of Jews to Palestine. Harrison had recommended that 100,000 be admitted. Bevin, unable to accept that Jews could not live in Europe, suggested to the Cabinet an Anglo-American commission to investigate the refugee problem. At a time when British soldiers were being killed by terrorists in Palestine, the American response was hesitant because of Zionist agitation in the New York election campaign. Bevin wanted to involve the United States. He was increasingly worried about Soviet advances in the Middle East, and saw the area as essential to Western security at a time of the emergence of the Cold War. To maintain its position, Britain had to negotiate treaties with the new Arab states. This would hardly be possible if Britain were seen as the sponsor of a Zionist state in Palestine, to be achieved through Jewish immigration. After the New York election was over – in which Truman's Democrat won a resounding victory – an Anglo-American commission was appointed that heard evidence in Washington, London, Europe and the Middle East, and reported in April 1946.[16]

In the meantime, the Chief of the Imperial General Staff toured the Middle East to assess the chances of implementing the new British policy in the area. In Egypt he saw the Prime Minister, Mahmud Fahmi al-Nuqrashi, King Farouk and the Chef-du-Cabinet, Sir Ahmed Hassanien Pasha. Nuqrashi was not impressed with arguments about the need for partnership in defence throughout those countries in the Middle East which had a common interest in its security. He responded that without real freedom and the removal of British forces from Egypt the internal conditions in that country would make it unsuitable for participating in defensive plans. Farouk, however, was worried about the Soviet Union: there would be war within a few years. Concrete action in the Middle East was desirable, and the king liked the idea of partnership. But political considerations might make that difficult. The king was not antagonistic to Britain, but he was pro-Egyptian before anything else, and after that pro-British. Farouk seemed to believe that in Europe only two great powers were left: Britain and the Soviet Union. He appeared to be frightened of the latter, and prepared to co-operate with the former. Hassanien Pasha confirmed this. Abdullah, then the Emir of Transjordan, was ready to fit into any form of defensive confederation. He was apprehensive as to Soviet intentions. At a conference in Iraq with the regent, the Prime Minister, the Finance and Defence Ministers, the British ambassador and the Commander-in Chief Middle East, it was clear that Baghdad wanted some form of Middle East defence confederation backed by Britain. It was felt that the partnership could be extended to include economic development. The Chief of the Imperial General Staff thought the conception of a Middle East Defensive Confederation, based on a partnership between those concerned, a promising line of approach, especially if Britain worked mainly through the rulers. This was pashas not peasants.[17]

The new Middle East policy was successfully implemented in Transjordan. Possibly with an eye to his Fertile Crescent scheme, Abdullah, early in 1946, was pleased to agree to a mutual defence pact with Britain: he willingly conceded Britain the right to station and train troops, insisted on by the Chiefs of Staff; Britain could develop the port of Aqaba, move troops across Jordan, establish a signal communications system and maintain air bases at Mafrak and Amman. In return Abdullah became king, and the British subsidy of £2 million a year continued. Under the treaty, signed on 22 March 1946, Transjordan was given 'full independence'. In London, Abdullah warned Attlee that the Soviet Union was playing a dangerous game: 'Russia is following a forward policy in Iran and Kurdistan, a policy which may well aim at expansion to the Gulf and the Mediterranean. Against this, it is desirable that a defensive front should be built up covering Turkey, Iran and Afghanistan by the fertile crescent of Arab countries stretching from Basra to Aqaba.'[18] Abdullah also told Bevin that British divisions in Iraq and Transjordan would have a salutary effect on the Middle East, especially on Egypt.[19]

Transjordan, however, was the only success. On 20 December 1945, Egypt asked for a revision of the Anglo-Egyptian treaty of 1936. The treaty gave Britain the right to station troops in the Suez Canal Zone and Sinai, and the right of reoccupation in the event of war. Early in 1946 Killearn was removed from Cairo, possibly as a result of another altercation with Farouk, possibly because of pressure from sections of the Labour Party to make changes in the staffing of the Foreign Office and diplomatic posts abroad. Killearn, apparently to his annoyance as it meant a considerable loss of salary, was made Special Commissioner for South-East Asia. He was replaced by someone thought to be more amenable to the Egyptians, Sir Ronald Campbell.[20]

Attlee argued that the strategic importance of the Middle East needed to be reconsidered. On 18 February he said it was useless to pretend that Britain could keep the Mediterranean route open in wartime. If this were accepted Britain could withdraw troops from Egypt, the rest of the Middle East and Greece. Britain could not defend Turkey, Iraq, or Iran against the pressure of the Soviet land masses. If India went its own way, as it had to, there would be even less point in thinking of lines of imperial communications through the Suez Canal. Britons should be prepared to travel around the Cape to Australia and New Zealand, but American interest in Middle Eastern oil could change the situation.

At the end of March, Attlee urged the Defence Committee to consider disengagement from areas where there was a risk of clashing with the Soviet Union. Britain should withdraw from the Middle East and concentrate on a line of defence across Africa from Lagos to Kenya. A large part of the British forces could be stationed in Kenya, while Commonwealth defence would be concentrated in Australia. The Arabs and the desert would form a barrier between the British and the Soviets. Bevin, however, thought that the Canal Zone should be the ultimate line of British withdrawal. The Foreign Secretary was attracted by the Lagos-Kenya idea, and spoke of building a road across Africa so that Britain could protect the mineral deposits in the Belgian Congo. He also envisaged a triangular ocean trade between East Africa, including Natal in South Africa, India and Australia.

Captain B.H. Liddell Hart, in a memorandum dated 20 March, debated whether British strategic policy should be based on the Middle East or Africa. He questioned the importance of the oil-fields of Iraq and Iran: they provided only a small fraction of Britain's national income. Oil could come from the United States, Venezuela and British Guiana, or synthetic oil was possible. Britain should retire from the Middle East with dignity and consolidate its position in Africa. The British disposition there would not be seriously disturbed even if the Soviet Union spread its influence to Egypt.[21]

The Egyptian ambassador in London warned Bevin about Soviet influence in Egypt. On 18 March he told the Foreign Secretary that the Egyptian government's investigations into the prevailing difficulties had revealed that the Wafd Party was responsible for part of the trouble, but a large proportion was due to the Soviets. There were 80 staff in the Soviet legation in Cairo. They had a cinema and plenty of money, and the voluminous literature coming into the country was being sent from Beirut and Palestine.[22]

On 2 April 1946, London announced that it had decided to send a delegation to Cairo. The Chiefs of Staff were prepared to compromise: fighting troops in the Canal Zone could go; British fighting squadrons and bomber bases had to stay.[23] Lord Stansgate, the Minister for Air, arrived in Cairo on 15 April, and had discussions with the Prime Minister, Ismail Sidky. Sidky immediately demanded the evacuation of all British forces. Stansgate advised that Britain give way on this. The Cabinet decided to concede, and the decision was made public. Sir Orme Sargent warned Campbell:

> It is true that as a matter of tactics we have decided to announce our willingness to clear out altogether if asked to do so but unless Egyptian leaders *are* made to realise what this entails, we shall be encouraging them to live in a fool's paradise, for the Alliance is just not going to be a guarantee of Egypt's independence in modern conditions of warfare if the evacuation now promised is to be the beginning and the end of the Treaty.

Sargent did not like the defeatist attitude of the delegation. He felt it was wrong not to tell the Egyptians what were the 'inevitable consequences' of Britain leaving Egypt to its own devices both in respect of Egypt's defence and the defence of the Middle East.[24] At the end of May, Bevin warned the Egyptians that steps had to be taken to defend the Canal Zone. Britain could not leave a vacuum. That would be a 'magnet of attraction' that could lead other countries to start a political and expansive aggression. While the Egyptian government had great nationalist claims on the Canal Zone, it also had international security obligations to meet because, by the mere accident of geography, its territory lay where it did. Britain might have to fall back on the treaty of 1936, and the negotiations would break down. That would be unfortunate since Britain hoped to weave the whole of the strategic area into an international security system.[25] In October, Sidky saw Bevin in London, but the worked-out arrangement foundered on Cairo's insistence on the unity of the Sudan with Egypt under the Egyptian Crown. At the end of January 1947, Bevin told the Cabinet that the negotiations had broken down: Britain had to ensure that the Sudanese would be able to sever their connection with Egypt on reaching self-government if they chose to do so.[26]

The negotiations with Egypt, and the discussions over Palestine, took place against the background of the conclusions of the Chiefs of Staff on 2 April 1946, namely that if Britain moved out of certain parts of the world in peacetime, the Soviets would move in. This would enable the Soviet Union to extend its influence, by all means short of war, to further strategic areas. It was imperative that Britain stay in the Mediterranean: first, to protect British access to Middle Eastern oil; secondly, to preserve political influence in southern Europe. If the Soviets secured control of the Egypt–Palestine area, they would have a ready-made base. It could be quickly built up by the short sea route from the Soviet Union. The Soviet Union would then be able to extend its influence westwards and southwards into Africa. The British position in both north-west Africa and the Indian Ocean would be prejudiced. It would be the first step in a direct threat to Britain's main support area of Southern Africa.[27] Attlee's scheme for retreating from the Middle East and standing on a line in Africa from Lagos to Kenya was rejected.

The Defence Committee of the Cabinet decided on 5 April that Britain's position as a 'World Power' should be maintained. Bevin was determined that Britain should remain as a 'great Power'.[28] He told the Commonwealth Prime Ministers meeting in London in April 1946: 'In my view it is essential that we should maintain our position in the Mediterranean and Red Sea. It is not only a question of preserving this life-line in time of war, but also the vital importance of acting in peace-time on the soft under-belly of Europe from the Mediterranean.'[29] Backed by arguments from General J.C. Smuts, the South African Prime Minister, Bevin resisted Soviet claims for a trusteeship over a former Italian colony in Africa at the Council of Foreign Ministers meeting in Paris in May. With the situations in Egypt and Palestine in mind, Bevin lodged a British claim for Cyrenaica – it could become a British strategic base.[30]

At this time the controversy over Palestine erupted. On 30 April, without consulting London, Truman endorsed the recommendation of the Anglo-American commission that 100,000 certificates be issued for Jewish immigrants to go to Palestine, and two other aspects favourable to Zionism. The British public was outraged: British soldiers had just been murdered by Zionist terrorists. Truman had succumbed again to Zionist pressure, and threats of electoral punishment in the forthcoming November congressional elections. The Chief of the Imperial General Staff, Viscount Alanbrooke (formerly Sir Alan Brooke), told the Dominion Prime Ministers meeting in London that, from the military angle, it was essential to seek the active assistance of the United States.[31] So far as the Chiefs of Staff were concerned the strategic importance of Palestine could not be questioned. On 24 May they concluded that Britain had to be able to place in Palestine any forces it considered necessary; Britain had to retain complete control of the organization of the defence of the area.[32] Their American colleagues agreed. On 21 June the Joint Chiefs of Staff insisted that no American armed forces should be used to implement the recommendations of the Anglo-American commission. There was the danger that the Middle East could 'fall into anarchy and become a breeding ground for world war'. The Soviet Union could replace Britain and the United States in influence and power throughout the area:

> As to the importance of a stable Middle East, friendly to the Western Powers, it is obvious that this area is the buffer between Russia and the British Mediterranean life line. If the peoples of the Middle East turn to the Soviet Union, this would have the same impact in many respects as would military conquest on this area by the Soviets. Under these conditions, even if Turkey maintains her internal political integrity, it is highly questionable that she could continue her stand on the Dardanelles and maintain her position as other than a satellite Russian state. Also, for very serious consideration from a military point of view is control of the oil of the Middle East. This is probably the one large undeveloped reserve in a world which may come to the limits of its oil resources within this generation without having any substitute. A great part of our military strength, as well as our standard of living is based on oil.[33]

Anglo-American differences over Palestine were temporarily resolved when delegates from both countries met in London in July 1946 and suggested a scheme of provincial autonomy. The Chiefs of Staff had reservations: Lord Tedder, the Chief of the Air Staff, again insisted that any future government of Palestine should give Britain power to control and co-ordinate the defence of that country, as well as maintaining forces and military facilities. The Chiefs wanted 'a certain airfield' in Arab territory. Above all, Britain should not alienate the Arab states.[34] In Palestine, Menachem Begin and the Irgun Zvai Leumi (National Military Organization), with the co-operation of the Haganah, blew up the King David Hotel, one wing of which was used as British army headquarters: 91 were killed. Zionist propaganda throughout the world publicized what was construed as an anti-Semitic statement by the British army commander, and, as a result, turned a terrorist outrage into a Zionist victory. Under the threat of Zionist electoral punishment, Truman withdrew his support from the provincial autonomy scheme.[35]

Britain tried to implement the provincial autonomy scheme on its own. A Palestine Conference met at Lancaster House on 2 October, but was adjourned until 16 December. The Arabs were worried that the Zionists would fill their state with immigrants from Europe, creating conditions which would warrant a demand for more *Lebensraum*.[36] Chaim Weizmann, a Zionist delegate, told

Bevin that there was no need for immediate partition: there could be a transitional period of two to three years. The Foreign Secretary warned him that he had never known such strong latent anti-Semitism in Britain: 'The destruction of the King David Hotel had burned deeply into the hearts of the British people.' Britain could not allow its young soldiers in Palestine to be slaughtered. Bevin also said he had to ensure that the rights and position of the other inhabitants of Palestine were not prejudiced: 'If a person's land and livelihood had to go in order to make room for another, his rights and position were certainly prejudiced.' Bevin was not prepared to force partition on the Arabs at the point of British bayonets. Instead he would hand the problem to the United Nations. Palestine was not the only home for the Jewish people: the Foreign Secretary hoped that they would be a great force in the reconstruction of the European continent. The Zionist leaders agreed to talk to the Colonial Office about administrative procedures and the release of detainees in Jerusalem, and then come back to Bevin. They made participation in the Palestine Conference dependent on the release of the detained members of the Jewish executive in Palestine. They hoped that the Jewish delegates could be brought into the conference even before the return of the Arab delegates.[37]

Truman ruined this hopeful prospect. The Zionists, working with Robert E. Hannegan, the chairman of the Democratic National Committee with an eye on a forthcoming election in New York and the presidential election of 1948, urged Truman to make an immediate statement in favour of partition. The State Department advised against this, as did the Joint Chiefs of Staff: partition might alienate the Arabs from the West. Attlee asked Truman to delay. But on 4 October, the eve of the Jewish day of atonement, Truman said that a solution along the lines of partition originally proposed by the Jewish Agency on 5 August would 'command the support of public opinion in the United States'.[38]

In December 1946 with British policy towards Palestine in a state of suspension, and the Egyptian negotiations breaking down, it was decided to move a further division from Egypt to Palestine, which would leave only administrative troops in Egypt, and by 1 April 1947 the numbers there would have been reduced to 32,000.[39] In December Attlee again suggested that Britain should withdraw from the Middle East. The Prime Minister wanted to hand over the mandate for Palestine.[40] He argued that Britain had 'either to offend the Arab States and probably Turkey and Persia as well or offend world Jewry with its powerful influence in the U.S.A.'[41] At this time British public opinion was aroused: in retaliation for the judicial caning of a convicted Zionist terrorist, too young to hang, Begin's Irgun kidnapped and flogged four British army officers. Britain gave way, and stopped using judicial corporal punishment in the mandate.[42]

Tedder warned that a solution to the Palestine problem which alienated Arab goodwill would be unacceptable. Britain would be denied freedom of movement through an essential area, and its wider interests in the Middle East would be endangered.[43] The Chiefs of Staff reiterated their insistence that Britain had to be able to station forces in Palestine. Air bases were needed for imperial communications. With Egypt being evacuated, apart from the Canal Zone, Palestine was the only area able to accommodate Britain's Middle East reserve.[44]

On 15 January Tedder told the Cabinet that there were three cardinal requirements for the future defence of the British Commonwealth: the defence of the United Kingdom and its development as a base for air offensive; the maintenance of sea communications; and the retention of Britain's existing position and influence in the Middle East. These were the three 'vital props' of Britain's defensive position. They were all interdependent and if any one were lost, 'the whole structure would be imperilled'. These fundamental principles would be unaffected by any change in the nature and use of weapons, or assumptions made about the potential enemy. It was essential for Britain's defence that it could fight from the Middle East in war. This meant that Britain had to maintain a foothold there in peace. Though lightly manned in peace, these bases could be used for the rapid deployment of greater force against a threat of war. India would no longer be available for such bases so the retention of those in the Middle East was essential.

Palestine was of special importance. In war Egypt would be Britain's key position in the Middle East. Palestine had to be held as a screen for the defence of Egypt. As Britain had undertaken to withdraw from Egypt, it had to be able to use Palestine as a base for the mobile reserve of troops needed to be kept ready to meet any emergency throughout the Middle East. The facilities in Transjordan were insufficient. If separate states were established in Palestine it would be necessary to secure the full use of ports, airfields and communications, and to obtain military facilities by treaty arrangements with both states. Provided such facilities were obtained, it was immaterial whether Palestine became one or two states. If one of the communities had to be antagonized, it was preferable that a solution be found which did not involve the continuing hostility of the Arabs. Arab hostility would mean difficulties for Britain throughout the Middle East.[45]

Tedder was supported by the Minister of Defence, A.V. Alexander: if the Arabs were alienated they would be supported by the Soviet Union which intended to undermine the influence of the British Commonwealth and the United States in the Gulf area. Alexander advised the Cabinet that Britain should look to its own strategic interests, and it was therefore vital to retain the goodwill of the Arab world.[46]

Bevin and the new Colonial Secretary, Arthur Creech Jones, who had been sympathetic towards Zionism, submitted a plan early in February which envisaged self-government in Palestine leading to independence after a transitional period of five years under trusteeship, and 100,000 Jewish immigrants over the following two years. The Chiefs of Staff did not like the suggestion that if neither the Arabs nor the Zionists would accede to the plan, Britain would have to submit the problem to the United Nations without making any positive recommendations. The Chiefs felt that such a step would almost certainly entail the loss of practically all British military rights in Palestine.

It was essential that Britain, during the interim period of trusteeship, retain these rights and ensure that they could be acquired when that ended. Five years was too short a time for trusteeship. It would not be long enough to establish a stable state with which Britain could negotiate a favourable treaty. The period should be left indefinite.[47]

Despite these warnings, on 14 February the Cabinet decided to submit the Palestine problem to the United Nations without any recommendation for a solution. On 3 April 1947 it agreed, solely for 'political considerations' (demands from the left wing of the Labour Party), to reduce the period of national service from 18 to 12 months. The Chief of the Imperial General Staff, Viscount B.L. Montgomery, felt that this was acceptable provided overseas commitments such as Palestine and India were liquidated by 1949 or 1950.[48] On 15 May the United Nations Special Committee on Palestine (UNSCOP) was established with broad powers of investigation. The Soviet Union insisted that the membership be increased from 7 to 11. In the Foreign Office, Harold Beeley surmized that the Soviet Union hoped to be associated with a joint trusteeship over Palestine.

During the UNSCOP inquiry British morale in Palestine was eroded. The *President Warfield*, renamed *Exodus*, arrived in Palestine with 4,493 illegal immigrants. These were returned to their French port of embarkation. In retaliation for the execution of Zionist terrorists, the Irgun hanged two British sergeants and booby-trapped their bodies. These were found on 31 July. The American consul in Jerusalem argued that the terrorist thinking was based on the premiss proclaimed by both the Irgun and Stern gang, that all of Palestine and Transjordan belonged to the Jewish people; the British were merely there to bring about the unchallenged Jewish occupation of those two states. The consul concluded: 'During the time of the Nazis it was a commonplace to hear the opinion that Hitler and his followers were deluded to the point where their sanity was questionable. If such generalizations are permissible, it may be well to question whether the Zionists, in their present emotional state, can be dealt with as rational human beings.'[49] There were outbreaks of anti-Semitism in Britain. As Bevin explained, Britain had no alternative other than to ship the refugees on the *President Warfield* back to Germany. This gave the Zionists the most notable propaganda success of the time. The British authorities in Hamburg complained of the attitude of the American press correspondents who witnessed the landing: they were 'unfriendly' towards the British and their reports were coloured and exaggerated.[50]

UNSCOP, in a majority report, recommended in effect the partition of Palestine and the creation of a separate Zionist state. In a memorandum of 18 September the Chiefs of Staff emphasized again that Britain's strategic position made it essential that the goodwill of the Arab states, and the Muslim world as a whole, was retained. If Palestine were handed to an authority containing a considerable Soviet element, Britain's interests would not be served. An American-dominated body would be comparatively acceptable. Control should therefore pass to a 'national or international authority friendly to us, and both willing and able to resist Russian encroachment'. Even American control would only afford temporary security.[51] Bevin told the Cabinet on 20 September that the UNSCOP proposals were unacceptable. The Minister of Defence merely explained that Britain would have to choose between ceasing to administer Palestine immediately and maintaining such order as was necessary to ensure the withdrawal of British forces and civilians, or attempting to maintain law and order throughout the whole of Palestine until the date announced for the ends of the British administration. The Prime Minister did not think it reasonable to ask the British administration to continue in the prevailing conditions. The Cabinet accepted the policy of withdrawal.[52] Hugh Dalton noted that this was a historic decision: Britain was withdrawing to the eastern Mediterranean.[53]

The original assessment by the British Directors of Plans and the Service Directors of Intelligence estimated that withdrawal from Palestine would lead to the total collapse of Britain's position in the Middle East. The final report of the Joint Planning Staff, dated 19 September, argued that Britain's position in the Middle East and the possibility of recovering some of the military requirements would depend on the extent to which the British withdrawal from Palestine could be made acceptable to the Arab world. If the Arabs were convinced that British withdrawal was dictated by a refusal to implement a solution unjust to the Arabs, Britain might regain Arab friendship and a part of its strategic requirements in the Middle East. If the Arabs could not be persuaded, British influence in Iraq would be undermined and hopes of renewing the treaty with that country on a friendly basis would disappear. All the other Arab states might be alienated. The situation could arise where Britain had no footing in the Middle East, apart from Cyprus, since the attainment of British requirements in Egypt was doubtful, and the future of Cyrenaica undecided. Britain would lose oil interests not only in Palestine but possibly also in the oil-fields themselves and at the Gulf terminals. All this could lead to Soviet infiltration, and the eventual establishment of Soviet domination in the area.[54]

Early in October the Joint Administrative Planning Staff said that withdrawal from Palestine could not be efficiently mounted without deploying troops to Cyrenaica and the Sudan.[55] The Foreign Office raised the future strategic position of Transjordan: Abdullah would want the Arab part of Palestine. The Mufti of Jerusalem, backed by Syria and Egypt, would not accept that. Transjordan would then be surrounded by three unfriendly states. The Foreign Office thought a friendly Transjordan of considerable strategic importance. Abdullah might want to use the Arab Legion to fight in Palestine. That would be awkward since Britain helped to pay for, and staff, the Legion.[56] Similarly, the Joint Planning Staff pointed to the strategic importance of Transjordan. The state was traversed by all the direct communications connecting Iran and Iraq with the vital central area, namely Egypt and Palestine. Transjordan lay either on, or adjacent to, the two main strategic lines of approach to Palestine and Egypt from the Near East. Transjordan was also the only remaining Arab state in which Britain, by treaty, enjoyed extensive freedom of movement. It was definitely pro-

British. If Britain were forced to evacuate Egypt and Palestine, it would still need to re-enter those countries in an emergency; without this facility Britain's Middle East strategy would collapse. Provided Britain could re-enter Palestine, the importance attached to Transjordan would not be affected.

The Joint Planning Staff envisaged the eventual development and unification of the military facilities Britain enjoyed in Transjordan, but inadequate communications made that impossible in the immediate future. Transjordan, without extensive development, could do little to ease the wider military problems consequent on British withdrawal from Palestine. The most serious threat to Transjordan's independence would be the spread of communist influence if the Soviet Union were allowed to participate in the administration of Palestine after the British withdrawal. Indeed, Bevin thought that the Soviet Union hoped for the establishment of a communist state in Palestine, or at least in the Zionist areas organized by indoctrinated illegal immigrants from Eastern Europe.[57]

Britain tried to secure its position in the Middle East through alliances with Arab states. On 9 October the Cabinet agreed to informal and secret talks with the regent and the government of Iraq about the revision of the Anglo-Iraqi treaty of alliance of 1930.[58] To avoid demands for the evacuation of the two British air bases in Iraq, Britain negotiated on the principle of sharing the bases and a Joint Defence Board to co-ordinate defence plans.[59] This seemed agreeable to an élite group of Iraqis at the end of the year, and on 15 January 1948 an Iraqi delegation signed the treaty of Portsmouth. The regent's strong men were in Britain. But the news of the treaty brought a political outburst in Iraq, and the regent had to repudiate the document within a week of it being signed. Against the background of their withdrawal from Palestine, Britain had difficulty in negotiating alliances with Arab states[60] – except Jordan. Neither country was dissatisfied with the treaty of 1946, but a new one was negotiated in January and February 1948 to give the appearance of an arrangement between equals. A joint defence board was established responsible for external and strategic planning. Before leaving London the Jordanian delegate, Tawfig, saw Bevin. Glubb recorded how Bevin said that Transjordan's intention of occupying the west bank in Palestine was 'the obvious thing to do'.[61]

At this point the Americans began to acknowledge to Britain the importance, for the West, of Britain's strategic position in the Middle East. Informal political and strategic talks were held in Washington between 16 October and 7 November between British and American officials. The reason for these meetings was the American fear of repercussions of the withdrawal of British troops from Greece. Bevin did not want a combined Anglo-American policy for the Middle East: the Foreign Secretary still saw this as an area primarily of strategic, political and economic interest to Britain. Both Truman and the British Cabinet endorsed the recommendations of the officials, though there was no formal agreement. The American participants recommended that their government strengthen the British strategic, political and economic position throughout the Middle East.

This would include American diplomatic support for Britain, and also the United Nations, over the retention of facilities in Egypt, Cyrenaica and Iraq. The United States also favoured the retention of Britain's strategic position in the Sudan, Gibraltar, Aden and Cyprus.[62]

On 26 September, Creech Jones told the United Nations that if the General Assembly recommended a policy not acceptable to the Arabs and Jews, Britain would not be able to implement it. The Soviet Union, on 13 October, 'mystified' Britain and the United States by announcing its support for the partition of Palestine. Bevin thought that the Soviet Union hoped to pour enough indoctrinated communist Jews into Palestine to turn it into a communist state in a short time. He observed: 'The New York Jews have been doing their work for them.'[63] The Chiefs of Staff became worried that a communist regime could be set up in Palestine after the British withdrawal on 15 May 1948, but Bevin insisted on a British attitude of neutrality in the United Nations. The calculation probably was that partition would not secure the necessary two-thirds majority. On 24 November Bevin dined with George Marshall, the American Secretary of State, and told him that Britain would abstain in the United Nations vote. 'This great issue' had been handled by the United States more with 'the electoral situation in New York City in mind than the large issues of foreign policy which were involved'. Before the murder of the two British sergeants, Bevin had felt that the situation in Palestine could be held. He told Marshall that Britain could not be committed to a position which might involve military action against the Arabs.[64]

On 29 November the General Assembly voted for partition. Prior to the vote, and particularly during the immediately preceding three days, the American Zionists exerted unprecedented pressure on the American administration, on both delegations to the United Nations and their governments, to secure the necessary majority. Senators belonging to the American Christian Palestine Committee petitioned wavering United Nations delegations: Haiti, Greece, Luxembourg, Argentina, Columbia, China, El Salvador, Ethiopia, Honduras, Mexico, the Philippines and Paraguay. The senators called attention to the 'gravest consequences' of those countries' relations with the United States if the partition resolution was not adopted.[65] The congressman, Emmanuel Celler, campaigned actively for partition at Lake Success. Some of his correspondence suggests that Truman himself might have intervened at the last minute.[66] Sol Bloom, another congressman and one time chairman of the house committee on foreign affairs, acknowledged his own role in changing the votes of the delegations of Liberia, the Philippines and Haiti.[67] Loy W. Henderson, the Director of the Office of Near East and African Affairs, recalled that David Niles, Truman's minority rights adviser, had telephoned Hershel Johnson, the American delegate on the United Nations Ad Hoc Committee on Palestine, and said that Truman had instructed him to say that 'by God, he wanted us to get busy and get all the votes that we possibly could, that there would be hell if the voting went the wrong way'. Johnson, apparently in tears, told Henderson that the delegation was working under terrific strain to carry out the President's orders.[68] Henderson refused to believe that the President had authorized Niles to give such a strong order.

Zafar Khan, the Pakistan delegate to the United Nations, claimed that had the partition vote been taken on Wednesday 26 November, it would have been 26 to 16 and thus defeated. Knowing this the Zionist leaders went directly to Truman and told him that the vote had to be delayed. The President is alleged to have then instructed Johnson to secure a delay of the vote at all costs – which was done.[69] Edward Stettinius, a former Secretary of State, instigated pressure from the Firestone Tire and Rubber Company on Liberia.[70] The State Department thought that the votes of Haiti and the Philippines, at least, had been secured by the unauthorized intervention of American citizens. It felt that the danger to the interests of the United States and the United Nations could only be averted by a presidential statement admitting the undue pressure and saying that in future offenders would be prosecuted and existing legislation would immediately be reviewed with that in mind.[71]

The situation in Palestine deteriorated. The Arab reaction was worse than Bevin had expected. On 17 December he warned Marshall that the Middle East could 'blow up'. There would be serious consequences, even for the United States. The Soviet Union might profit when the Zionists and Arabs started fighting. The Foreign Secretary thought, however, when the Soviet Union intervened it would be in Iraq and not Palestine.[72]

Early in 1948, the American Joint Chiefs of Staff warned that partition would lead to Arab hatred, the loss of oil, Soviet penetration in the area in the guise of enforcing the United Nations plan, and a call for American troops for Palestine. On 29 January George Kennan, the head of the American Policy Planning Staff, explained that British relations with the Arabs and the remaining British strategic positions in the Middle East were among the few 'real assets' the United States still had in the area. James Forrestal, the Secretary of Defence, said that without Middle Eastern oil the Marshall Plan could not succeed. The United States began to move away from partition. In Britain, the Chiefs of Staff were instructed to investigate accelerating the British withdrawal. Zionists working through Clark Clifford, Truman's electoral adviser, George M. Elsey, Clifford's assistant, and Max Lowenthal, a White House consultant with Jewish Agency connections, secured a reversal of American policy. Truman, concerned about the significance of the Zionist vote in the forthcoming presidential election, recognized Israel on 14 May.

At midnight HMS *Euryalus* left Palestinian waters with Sir Alan Gordon Cunningham, the High Commissioner, on board. Britain was no longer the paramount power over the Zionists. David Ben-Gurion proclaimed the State of Israel at 4 p.m. the same day. On 15 May various Arab armies entered Palestine. On 21 May the Policy Planning Staff advised that American policy threatened 'not only to place in jeopardy some of our most vital national interests in the Middle East and the Mediterranean but also to disrupt the Unity of the western world and to undermine our entire policy towards the Soviet Union'.[73]

During the First Arab–Israeli War, the Foreign Office was worried that the Soviet Union might benefit from an Anglo-American rift. The Arabs could become desperate, and the Soviet Union consequently might be able to get control of their oil. The Arabs were divided. On 1 December 1948, to the fury of Egypt and other Arab states, Abdullah organized a ceremonial conference at Jericho where Palestinian and Transjordanian delegates favoured the joining of Palestine and Transjordan as an indivisible Hashemite Kingdom of Jordan. When the Israelis invaded Egypt, and on 7 January 1949 shot down five Royal Air Force planes, Britain sent troops to Aqaba and alerted its Mediterranean ships. London reminded Washington of the Middle East talks of November 1947, and the implied support offered by the United States to maintain Britain's position in the Middle East. Robert A. Lovett, the Under-Secretary of State, warned that the position might arise whereby Britain would be arming one side in the dispute and the United States the other, with the Soviet Union the permanent beneficiary. Ben-Gurion, the Israeli Prime Minister, withdrew his offending troops. On 24 February an armistice was signed at Rhodes between the Egyptians and the Israelis. Agreements with other Arab states followed. Israel increased its territory by 21 per cent, but acquired insecure frontiers. In 1949 the legally certified number of Palestinian–Arab refugees was almost one million.[74]

Britain's overall position in the Middle East was assessed by the newly formed Permanent Under-Secretary's Committee under Sir William Strang in April 1949. This committee was the equivalent of the American Policy Planning Staff. Like Bevin's Middle East Conference of September 1945 it stressed the economic aspect. The Middle East, particularly the oil-producing countries and Egypt with its cotton, was seen as an area of cardinal importance in the economic recovery of Britain and Western Europe. It was hoped that, by 1951, some 82 per cent of Britain's oil supplied would come from there; in 1938 the figure had been 23 per cent. This would present the largest single factor in balancing Britain's overseas payments. If Britain failed to maintain its position in the Middle East, the plans for Britain's economic recovery and future prosperity would fail.

Policy towards the Middle East had to be viewed in the light of the extension of communism, in various parts of the world: China was largely communist; South-East Asia was in danger. If the Middle East were also to fall to the communists the cause of the democratic countries would suffer a crippling blow. The economic recovery of Britain and Western Europe would be seriously affected. The way would be open for the spread of communism into Africa; Turkey, Greece and Italy would be largely undermined. The Soviet Union's ability to wage a successful war against the West would be greatly enhanced. The defence of the United Kingdom in the event of war would be compromised. Many of the conditions which favoured the extension of communism in China existed in the Middle East. Britain had overseen the emergence of most of the Middle Eastern countries to independence and self-government. But the transition from centuries of Turkish misrule to self-government under modern world conditions was difficult. Corruption, inefficiency and poverty were endemic. The standard of living of the mass of the people was appallingly low, and the contrast with the wealth of the small and selfish ruling classes was glaring. In spite of the contradiction between the principles of Islam and of communism, there were almost classic opportunities for communist agitation by the exploitation of hardship, chaos and discontent. A major objective of British policy had to be the prevention of the Middle East from falling behind the Iron Curtain. It therefore merited a high priority in effort and contribution.

Strang's committee noted that Britain had treaties of alliance with Egypt (expiring in 1956), Iraq (expiring in 1957 with right of review in 1952) and Transjordan (expiring in 1968). These treaties provided for the stationing of certain minimum forces in peacetime, the right of entry in an apprehended emergency and the provision of facilities in wartime. The treaties were not permanent, and the treaties with Egypt and Iraq expired at dates which were particularly awkward in terms of Soviet preparedness. In the event of war, Britain had no alternative but to use Egypt as the main base. Cyrenaica and Transjordan 'can afford adjuncts but not a substitute'. Airfields in Iraq were important and desirable elsewhere, particularly in Saudi Arabia (there was an American airfield in Dhahran) and in Cyprus. Air warning facilities, and possibly airfield and port facilities, were desirable in Syria and the Lebanon. The Americans wanted a fighter base in Tripolitania or Cyrenaica. A Middle East pact, along the lines of the Atlantic pact, or alternatively new treaties or agreements, would help to prevent the Middle East falling under communist domination.

Israel was a new factor. The Arab countries were united in their dislike and fear of Israel. The Arabs considered the creation of an independent state of Israel against the wishes of the majority of the former inhabitants as a major injustice and as an example of Western imperial colonization on a grand scale. The creation of Israel was tending to promote Arab unity. Although Britain was criticized as being largely responsible for its creation, the Arab states were, for the moment, turning towards Britain as being the only country likely to oppose indefinite Israeli expansion. Israel would have considerable strategic importance in the event of war. It should also be prevented from becoming communist. It was hoped that Israel would turn towards the West and not the Soviet Union, and have friendly relations with Britain and the United States. The committee wanted all of the Middle East, Greece, Turkey, the Arab countries, Iran, the Gulf, Egypt and Cyrenaica, and Israel to be friendly towards Britain. But it stressed that if Britain were to secure the friendship of Israel at the expense of the Arab countries, Britain would lose economically and strategically more than it gained. Britain had to be friendly to Israel, but not at the cost of losing the friendship of the Arab world. Strategically, facilities in Israel would be no substitute for facilities in Egypt and the other Arab states.

The committee suggested that Britain needed to explore the possibility of a Near East and African pact. Dr D.F. Malan, the new Afrikaner Nationalist Prime

Minister of South Africa, had mentioned that South Africa would join the Atlantic pact if invited. Alternatively, Malan had ideas of an African pact including Britain, the United States, South Africa and the European countries with possessions in Africa. Strang's people, however, felt that the Middle East was the shield of Africa. Any African pact had to be accompanied or followed by a Middle East pact. South Africa could join a Middle East and African pact, which could be extended to include other African countries.

The Middle East was strategically as crucial to Britain as it had been in 1945. Strang's committee pointed out that it shielded Africa, it was a key centre of land and sea communications and contained large supplies of oil. Above all, however, in the event of an attack on the United Kingdom, it was one of the principal areas from which offensive air action could be taken against the aggressor. The strategic key to the area was Egypt; no alternative existed as a main base. If the Middle East were to be denied to an enemy in wartime, at least two conditions were necessary: certain peacetime facilities which included the maintenance of airfields and stores; and the goodwill of the inhabitants. It was also desirable that Britain should have the right of entry or reinforcement in case of apprehended emergency. Otherwise Britain might be obliged to enter or reinforce certain countries either 'without right' or too late. The security of the Middle East was vital to the security of the United Kingdom.

The committee recognized, however, that it would be impossible for the British government to hold the Middle East in a major war without the assistance of the United States. Britain and the United States could not be rivals in the area, and the two countries should have a common policy. Apart from Palestine, American policy had for some time been crystallizing on lines similar to those of Britain. There was a common approach to the problems of Greece, Turkey and Iran, to defence and to the promotion of social and economic advancement. Washington had undertaken to help London maintain its position in the Middle East.[75]

Notes

1. Ritchie Ovendale, *The Origins of the Arab–Israeli Wars*, (2nd edn, London, 1992), pp. 17–102; *Britain, the United States, and the End of the Palestine Mandate, 1942–1948* (Woodbridge, Suffolk, 1989).
2. Public Record Office, London, FO 800/452, fol. 46, Def/6, Tedder to Alexander giving details of DO(47)44, 2 February 1948.
3. Public Record Office, London, CAB 79/39, COS (45)215, 5 September 1945; Ritchie Ovendale (ed.), *British Defence Policy since 1945 Documents in Contemporary History* (Manchester, 1994), pp. 18–41; Wm. Roger Louis, *The British Empire in the Middle East* (Oxford, 1984), pp. 8–12, 205–25, 265–306, 307–44, 689.
4. Ritchie Ovendale, 'From British Commonwealth to Commonwealth: the English

speaking Holy Roman Empire', *Interstate*, **2**, (1978–9), pp. 12–15; 'The South African policy of the British Labour government, 1947–51', *International Affairs*, 59 (1983), pp. 41–58 at pp. 44–50.
5. Ovendale, *The Origins of the Arab–Israeli Wars*, p. 147.
6. FO 800/475, fos 17–19, Dixon to Sargent, 24 August 1945.
7. CAB 128/3, fol. 34, CM26(45)2, Secret, 30 August 1945.
8. CAB 129/2, fol. 91, CP(45)174, Memorandum on Middle East policy by Bevin, Secret, 17 September 1945.
9. CAB 129/2, fol. 20, CP(45)156, Great Britain's position in the Middle East, Secret, 8 September 1945.
10. CAB 128/1, fol. 81, CM28(45)6, Secret, 4 October 1945.
11. Llewelyn Woodward, *British Foreign Policy in the Second World War*, (London, 1975), vol. 4, pp. 366–8.
12. Princeton University Library, Forrestal Diaries, Box 1, vol. 2, fol. 230, 16 March 1945.
13. Public Record Office, London, FO 954/19A, fol. 80, Killearn to Eden, Telegram no. 813, Top Secret and Personal, 6 April 1945; T.E. Evans (ed.), *The Killearn Diaries 1934–46* (London, 1972), pp. 336–8, diary, 2 April 1945; 3 April 1945.
14. Public Record Office, London, FO 371/45379, E6405/15/31G, COS(45)543(0), Top Secret, 22 August 1945; G.H. Gater to Secretary, Chiefs of Staff, 21 August 1945.
15. FO 371/45379, E6622/15/31G, Minutes by Baxter, 23 August 1945, Howe, 24 August 1945; 1 September 1945; Beeley, 4 September 1945; Memorandum by Hall on future policy for Palestine, August 1945 (draft); Memorandum by Hall on summary for Palestine Committee, Top Secret; E6744/15/G, P(M)(45)10, Memorandum by Hall for Palestine Committee, Top Secret, 1 September 1945.
16. Ovendale, *Britain, the United States, and the End of the Palestine Mandate, 1942–1948*, pp. 41–140.
17. FO 800/457, fos 5–6, Eg/45/4, Brook to Bevin, Top Secret, 5 November 1945.
18. Public Record Office, London, CO 537/1847, Memorandum by Kirkbride, 14 March 1946. Quoted by Louis, *The British Empire in the Middle East*, p. 357.
19. Ibid., pp. 354–8.
20. FO 800/463, fol. 32, FO/46/3, Unsigned minute, 11 February 1946.
21. British Library of Economic and Political Science, London, Dalton Diaries, 34, fol. 3, 18 February 1946; fol. 12, 22 March 1946; Bodleian, Oxford, Attlee Papers, 5, Liddell Hart to Attlee, 10 May 1946; Memorandum on Africa or the Middle East, Reflections on strategic and peace policy by Liddell Hart, 20 March 1946.
22. FO 800/457, Eg/46/14, Bevin to Bowker, no. 213, 18 March 1946.
23. CAB 131/2, DO(46), 15 April 1946.
24. FO 800/457, fol. 37, Eg/46/17/A, Sargent to Campbell, Telegram no. 821, Secret, 30 April 1946.
25. FO 800/457, fol. 44, Eg/46/22, Bevin to Campbell, Telegram no. 393, 23 May 1946.
26. F.S. Northedge, 'Britain and the Middle East', in Ritchie Ovendale (ed.), *The Foreign Policy of the British Labour Governments*, (Leicester, 1984), pp. 166–9.
27. CAB 131/2, DO(46)47, Strategic position of the British Commonwealth, 2 April 1946.
28. CAB 131/1, DO(46)10, 5 April 1946.

29. CAB 129/9, CP(46)165, Memorandum by Bevin, 18 April 1946.
30. Louis, *The British Empire in the Middle East*, pp. 277–8.
31. Public Record Office, London, PREM 8/627, pt. 2, PMM(46)8, Top Secret, 30 April 1946.
32. FO 371/52527, E5065/4/31G, Minute by Howe, 25 May 1946; DO(46)67, Chiefs of Staff Conclusions, Top Secret, 24 May 1946.
33. *Foreign Relations of the United States* (hereafter cited as '*FRUS*') 1946(7), pp. 631–3, Memorandum by McFarland, 21 June 1946; Truman Library, Independence, Missouri, Truman Papers, Box 184, PSF, McFarland to State-War-Navy Co-ordinating Committee, Top Secret, 21 June 1946.
34. CAB 128/6, fol. 37, CM71(46), Secret, 22 July 1946; FO 371/52548, E7448/4/31G, COS (46)203(0), Chiefs of Staff Committee, Top Secret, 24 July 1946.
35. Ovendale, *Britain, the United States, and the End of the Palestine Mandate, 1942–1948*, pp. 141–64.
36. CAB 129/13, fos. 26–7, CP(46)358, Secret, 5 October 1946.
37. FO 371/52560, E10030/4/31, Minutes of meeting at Foreign Office, 1 October 1946; PREM 8/627, pt. 5, Note by G.H. Gater of interview between Bevin and Weizmann on 26 September 1946, 27 September 1946; *FRUS* 1946(7), pp. 700–1, Attlee to British Embassy Washington, 2 October 1946; CAB 129/13, fos. 26–7, CP(46)358, Secret, 5 October 1946.
38. Ovendale, *The Origins of the Arab–Israeli Wars*, pp. 96–7.
39. CAB 128/6, fol. 193, CM105(46)4, Secret, 12 December 1946.
40. FO 800/475, fos 65–9, ME/46/25, minutes by J.N. Henderson, 28 December 1946.
41. FO 800/476, fos 2–9, ME/47/1, Attlee to Bevin, Top Secret, 5 January 1947; Memorandum by Attlee on Near East policy.
42. Ovendale, *Britain, the United States, and the End of the Palestine Mandate, 1944–1948*, p. 184.
43. FO 371/61763, E463/46/G, COS(47)4, JP(47)1, 6 January 1947.
44. PREM 8/627, pt. 6, COS161/7, Top Secret, 6 February 1947.
45. CAB 128/11, fos 7–9, CM6(47)3, Confidential Annex, 15 January 1947.
46. CAB 128/11, fos 11–18, CM6(47)4, Confidential Annex, 15 January 1947.
47. PREM 8/627, pt. 6, COS16/17, Top Secret, 6 February 1947.
48. CAB 128/9, fol. 159, CM35(47)5, Secret, 3 April 1947.
49. National Archives, Washington, DC, RG 59, Decimal Files 1945–9, Box 6760, 867 N.01/8–447, Robert B. Macatee to Merriam, Top Secret, 4 August 1947; enclosing memorandum, Secret, 3 August 1947.
50. National Archives, Washington, DC, RG 59, Decimal Files 1945–9, Box 6760, 867 N.01/9–1347, R.S. Huestis, Consul Hamburg, to Marshall, no. 647, Confidential, 13 September 1947.
51. CAB 129/21, fos 120–9, CP(47)262, Memorandum by Alexander on military and strategic requirements, Top Secret, 18 September 1947.
52. CAB 128/10, fos 148–50, CM76(47)6, Secret, 20 September 1947.
53. British Library of Economic and Political Science, London, Dalton Diaries, 35, fol. 91, 20 September 1947.
54. FO 371/61789, E8913/46/G, Hayter to Warner, 20 September 1947; JP(47)131 (Final), Report by the Joint Planning Staff on the implications of withdrawal from Palestine, Top Secret, 19 September 1947.

55. FO 371/61791, E9562/46/G, JAP/P(47)39 Revised Draft, Top Secret, 8 October 1947.
56. FO 371/61790, E9411/9373/31, B.A.B. Burrows to D.C. Stapleton, 11 October 1947.
57. FO 371/61790, E10133/9373/G, JP(47)136, Report by the Joint Planning Staff, 24 October 1947; Minute by P. Garran, 5 November 1947.
58. CAB 128/10, fol. 165, CM79(43), Secret, 9 October 1947.
59. FO 800/476, fol. 233, E12234/3/G, Bevin to Busk, no. 414, 23 December 1947.
60. Louis, *The British Empire in the Middle East*, pp. 331–44.
61. Alan Bullock, *Ernest Bevin, Foreign Secretary 1945–1951* (London, 1983), pp. 508–9, *The British Empire in the Middle East*, pp. 366–72; John B. Glubb, *A Soldier with the Arabs* (London, 1957), pp. 63–6.
62. *FRUS* 1947(5), pp. 488–96, Department of State memorandum on exchanges of views leading up to the discussions with the British on the Middle East, Top Secret, undated; FO 371/61114, AN4017/3997/45/G, COS(47)144, Top Secret, 21 November 1947; AN3997/3997/45/G, Record of informal political and strategic talks in Washington on Middle East held from 16 October to 7 November 1947, Top Secret; AN4080/3997/45/G, Bevin to Inverchapel, 13 December 1947.
63. FO 800/509, Bevin to Hector McNeill, Confidential and Personal, 15 October 1947.
64. Ovendale, *The Origins of the Arab–Israeli Wars*, p. 118.
65. Georgetown University Library, Washington, DC, Robert F. Wagner Papers, Palestine Files, Box 3, File 47, Senators to United Nations Delegations of Haiti, Greece, Luxembourg, Argentina, Columbia, China, El Salvador, Ethiopia, Honduras, Mexico, the Philippines, and Paraguay, Telegram, 25 November 1947.
66. Truman Library, Independence, Missouri, Truman Papers, Box 773, OF 204-Misc., Celler to Truman, Telegram, 26 November 1947; Celler to Truman, 3 December 1947; Celler to Matthew Connelly, 3 December 1947.
67. Forrestal Diaries, Box 4, vol. 10, fos 2094–5, 22 February 1948.
68. Truman Library, Oral History Interview with Loy W. Henderson, fol. 138.
69. RG 59, Decimal Files 1945–9, Box 2183, 501. BB Palestine/12–547, Robert B. Memminger, Chargé d'Affaires Damascus to Marshall, no. 859, 5 December 1947.
70. Forrestal Diaries, Box 4, vol. 9, fol. 1956, Cabinet, 1 December 1947.
71. RG 59, Office of Near Eastern Affairs Palestine, Box 1, Merriam to Henderson, Top Secret, 11 December 1947.
72. *FRUS* 1947(5), pp. 815–16, Anglo-US-French conversations, British memorandum of conversation, Top Secret, 17 December 1947.
73. Ovendale, *Britain, the United States and the End of the Palestine Mandate, 1944–1948*, pp. 283–9.
74. Ibid., pp. 119–25; Louis, *The British Empire in the Middle East*, pp. 113, 532–71.
75. FO 800/455, fos 191–6, PUSC(19)Final, Near East, Top Secret, 30 April 1949.

2
The American Interest

Before the end of the Second World War, in the spring of 1944, Wallace Murray, the Director of the Near East Affairs desk at the State Department, discussed Anglo-American co-operation in the Middle East with Foreign Office officials. Following these talks, British and American missions in the Middle East, in April 1944, were instructed to conduct Anglo-American relations in the area in a spirit of co-operation, based on frankness and goodwill. With the emergence of the Cold War, Soviet moves forced the United States to take an increased interest in the defence of the Middle East, particularly Greece and Turkey. Against the background of Britain's withdrawal from the Palestine mandate at the end of 1947, at a time when the Middle East was one of the three cardinal pillars of British defence, the British place in the area was reinforced by an agreement between Washington and London. This came about following conversations in Washington that each country should try to strengthen the other's position through mutual respect and co-operation, and that they should not try to increase influence at one another's expense. As previously in 1944, early in 1948, British and American posts in the Middle East were alerted to this. On 24 November 1947, President Harry S. Truman endorsed the conclusion of the National Security Council that Soviet expansionist policies made the security of the Middle East vital to that of the United States. The Joint Chiefs of Staff, on 5 August 1948, emphasized that in the global strategy the security considerations of the United States' potential allies had to be considered, and particularly those of Britain, and that in the Middle East the interests of Washington and London were so inter-related that they had to be considered as a whole.[1]

In April 1949, at the time of the signing of the North Atlantic Treaty, Ernest Bevin, the British Foreign Secretary, told the American Secretary of State, Dean Acheson, that he had nothing against the Jews and was trying to hold the Arabs in line. Bevin thought that 100 million Muslims was one of the biggest potential forces in the world, and suggested that Britain was 'the best window toward this area'. While the Foreign Secretary did not want joint military pacts for this area, he did suggest that Britain and the United States should adopt a common line for the great potential resources needed for their own defence, and in particular oil. Acheson insisted that Truman was greatly interested in the development of the Middle East, something the President regarded as the other side of the coin of Western European recovery. Indeed in June 1949 the Policy Planning Staff considered whether the North Atlantic Treaty should be extended to include Middle Eastern countries. It was argued that while the primary security interests of the United States outside the Western hemisphere lay in the North Atlantic area, the political and territorial integrity of the Middle East was of such importance to American security as to justify strenuous efforts in the political, economic and military fields that were non-provocative.[2]

For Washington, Iran was of particular significance. But, as stated in October 1948, the American objective owing to the needs of Europe and the backwardness of Iran, was limited to merely making Iran sufficiently strong enough to prevent it from collapsing through Soviet penetration, or pressures short of war. In this regard, the State Department on 1 February 1949 observed that recently, when American encouragement and support had replaced British power and influence in the area, Iran found it possible to maintain an effective degree of national independence and to withstand Soviet threats. But Washington thought it necessary to co-ordinate its policy with London over any action Iran might take over a Soviet contention that Moscow had a right to take action in Iran under the Soviet–Iranian treaty of 1921.[3] Washington's interests in Syria were also limited to a concern that it could become a Soviet base for subversive activity in the Middle East. It appears that Washington, in 1949, was prepared to use the Central Intelligence Agency to change the Syrian leadership.[4] The preservation of Turkish independence and its status as a buffer against Soviet expansion into the Middle East was also considered of critical importance to American security. Furthermore, it was essential for the United States to maintain its friendly relations with Saudi Arabia as, in war, it was estimated that although the regaining of Middle East oil would not be vital, it would be highly desirable. Pakistan was considered a potential base for air operations against the Soviet Union as well as a staging post for the defence or recapture of Middle Eastern oil areas. Washington also hoped that improved British relations with Israel might make a common Anglo-American approach to that country possible.[5]

Some areas were considered by the Americans to be a peculiar British preserve. Indeed Washington saw Jordan as having been created by London out of the Syrian provinces of the Ottoman Empire. Though, in 1950, Jordan was still dependent on Britain for economic assistance and political support, Washington regarded the continuance of this 'special relationship' between London and the Hashemite Kingdom as being in its own interests. Washington and London had both approved of Abdullah's annexation of the West Bank, described by the State Department as 'Arab Palestine'. The United States, however, did not recognize the claims to sovereignty over Jerusalem of either Israel or Jordan. Jordan had no relations with the Soviet Union. Although

Palestinian representatives from the West Bank in the Jordanian parliament made the first ever anti-British statements there in 1950, Jordan could be viewed as a British bastion. Following the assassination of Abdullah on 20 July 1951, the assessment of the State Department was that Jordan was not a viable territorial unit, its existence as an independent state had been related to the personality of Abdullah, and that this might be an opportunity to correct an illogical situation. But, in the end, it recommended that the maintenance of the status quo was the least risky alternative, and that from the point of view of the British strategic position this was probably the best arrangement.[6]

Washington also acknowledged the special British position in Iraq, one which it was American policy not to undermine, and in January 1950 the American ambassador at Baghdad, Edward S. Crocker, advised that in furthering Iraq's economic and social development the American role should be an ancillary one. Iraq belonged to the sterling area. Britain controlled almost all of the oil concessions and British employees of the Iraqi government were able to ensure contracts for British manufacturers. A pro-British regent, Nuri al-Said, was head of state, and the king was at school in Britain. Many of those in office were used to working with Britain. Britain controlled two air bases and provided most of Iraq's military equipment as well as training its officers. Britain had been helped to maintain this position because the Iraqi ruling class felt threatened by the Soviet Union. On the issue of a union of Syria and Iraq, the State Department in April 1950 stated its neutrality between British enthusiasm and French opposition. It was concerned, however, that such a union might attenuate the British strategic position in that it could consolidate the anti-British elements in Syria and Iraq and lead to the elimination of the special facilities Britain enjoyed under the Anglo-Iraqi Treaty.[7]

The State Department was also conscious of the extent to which Yemen, since it had achieved its independence from Turkey in 1918, was dominated by British influence from Aden which controlled the bulk of Yemen's trade. Border disputes in 1949 resulted in meetings in London between August and October 1950 and the establishment of a fact-finding commission, but the State Department thought that this did little to allay Yemeni cynicism over British sincerity. Yemen had not joined in attacking the United States over its Palestine policy, and Washington hoped to retain and cultivate the friendship of what it saw as a primitive country needing development of all kinds.[8]

Washington's main interest in the Middle East at this time, however, was Saudi Arabia. Its king, Ibn Saud, courted the Americans. In May 1949, he spoke to the American ambassador, J. Rives Childs, about the cooling off of British interest as American interests in Saudi Arabia had increased and those of Britain had been deflected to Iraq and Transjordan. Ibn Saud wanted American arms and advice. He thought that Britain did not favour a tripartite pact between London, Washington and Jedda, but preferred a bilateral pact without Washington. Britain, the king argued, desired air bases, but he would refrain from making any commitments to London until he heard from Washington.

There were boundary disputes between Saudi Arabia and sheikhdoms on the Gulf which had treaties with Britain. In June 1949 Britain started negotiating with Ibn Saud over these and hoped that, in this connection, Washington would not encourage the Saudis to believe that they would enjoy American support. The American ambassador at Jedda, however, had already told the Saudis that Washington favoured direct negotiations between the parties concerned, and failing that the appointment of a neutral boundary commission to settle the question by arbitration. To pacify Saudi neurosis over fears of possible encirclement by unfriendly Arab states, some of which were seen as being under British influence, Childs assured Ibn Saud in December 1949 that London had been told about Washington's special relations with Saudi Arabia.[9]

Oil interests were at stake. The Petroleum Division in the State Department, in December 1949, pointed to the unrestricted increase of British controlled production in Iraq, Iran, Kuwait and Qatar. This increase could stalemate Saudi progress and jeopardize the unique friendship that existed between Washington and Jedda. There was concern that the 'Western orientation' of Saudi Arabia, evidenced by Jedda's blocking of Arab League sanctions against the Middle East oil industry during the First Arab–Israeli War, would suffer. Furthermore, there was the communist threat. Saudi Arabia was thought to have fewer communists than any other strategically located country. If the American-controlled oil company in that country, the Arabian–American Oil Company (ARAMCO), was economically healthy it could fight the advance of communism by providing the local populations with a livelihood, and health, education and sanitation programmes. The economy of Saudi Arabia was oil. Royalty payments from oil production over the previous few years had increased Saudi income from approximately $20 million to $80 million a year. American oil companies had invested around $390 million in concessions and employed about 5,000 American personnel. The most important American military air base in the Middle East was at Dhahran in Saudi Arabia. That same month, December 1949, London restricted American fuel oil and dollar gasoline imports into Britain and the dependent overseas territories. The Americans announced a corresponding reduction in their aid programme to Britain which London claimed would block its economic recovery. By March 1950, Saudi Arabian oil production was approximately 200,000 barrels per day below production schedules formulated the previous year, and 100,000 below 1949 levels.

A conversation between Saudi and American officials at Jedda on 19 March 1950 covered the extent to which Saudi Arabia had moved away from Britain, particularly in view of Britain's support of 'interests' that had become a menace to Saudi Arabia, and was looking more towards the United States for support. Ibn Saud insisted that he had offered the oil concession to the British, but they had refused it, and had then resented it being given to the Americans. His difficulties with the British had stemmed from this. Ibn Saud thought the British a people of 'but': they gave assurances, but always at the end there was 'but'. Solutions satisfactory to both parties were reached in May 1950, and again early in 1951, that involved the oil company in using its sterling to purchase British manufactured goods and equipment. But the incident alerted Washington to the issue of Saudi income. And this was at a time when, following the breakdown of conversations in October 1949 between Britain and Saudi Arabia over boundary disputes, both sides appeared to the Americans to be advancing more extreme claims over pieces of land. This land included islands, shoals and tidal flats, unprepossessing, but seemingly the drilling of a hole would produce a billion barrels of oil in any place in the area. Washington, officially, insisted on a policy of strict neutrality, as important American oil interests in Saudi Arabia, Bahrain, and the Trucial sheikhdoms would be adversely affected if it became involved.[10] With this increasing American interest in the Middle East, fostered by the joining of the Cold War, there were talks with the British about Anglo-American policy in the area. Often these emphasized the need for military and political co-ordination. On 1 June 1949, at Paris, Bevin asked Acheson whether it would be helpful for the Foreign Office's Middle Eastern expert, Michael Wright, to make a repeat visit to Washington. The State Department thought this would be helpful. His American counterpart, George McGhee, the Assistant Secretary of State for Near Eastern, South Asian and African Affairs, later recalled Wright as being not only knowledgeable and articulate, but also friendly and co-operative, and having wit and great charm. The two men developed a friendship over the years. There was a considerable age gap between the 39-year-old McGhee and most of the Britons with whom he had to deal. Indeed one referred to McGhee scathingly as an 'infant prodigy'. An oil geologist from Texas, McGhee won a Rhodes scholarship to Oxford and read for a doctorate at that university, where his moral tutor was Oliver Franks, the British ambassador at Washington between 1948 and 1952. He claimed that his stay there gave him a high regard for the British people and for Britain as a world power. McGhee, who was allowed considerable latitude by Acheson, described himself as an Anglophile. However, he acknowledged that his insistence on taking a line independent from Britain on Middle East policy, where Washington's interests diverged from those of London, was something that the British found hard to take in an area which had been their exclusive domain for so long. British officials thought his conduct indiscreet and tactless, and his opposite number as Assistant Under-Secretary in the Foreign Office, R.J. Bowker, saw him as 'becoming one of our heavier crosses'.

Another important British official was Bernard Burrows, who moved in January 1950 from being head of the Eastern Department of the Foreign Office to being the Middle Eastern expert at the embassy in Washington. On 15 September 1949, Burrows observed that Britain was still the major power in the Middle East, and if it moved out there would be a vacuum which would certainly be filled. British interests there, in Burrows's view were part of one interest, that of Western civilization to which Israel professed to belong.[11]

In October 1949 McGhee, pointing out that no high level consultations had taken place with Britain on Middle Eastern affairs since October–November

1947, thought there was a need to bring these talks up to date, both to coordinate Anglo-American policies in the Middle East, and to serve as background for a proposed meeting of American Chiefs of Mission in the area. McGhee wrote to his friend Wright ('My dear Michael') about this on 24 October, stating that while he had no precise agenda in mind, the State Department would prefer to avoid military and strategic problems and to focus on the Arab world and Israel. In a memorandum prepared for McGhee to use at this meeting, it was specifically stated that Washington had already undertaken, and should continue the co-ordination of, the handling of its common strategic interests in the area with the British. The political and military adviser of the Near Eastern Office emphasized that it would be unrealistic for Washington to undertake policies in the area unless the British maintained their strong strategic, political and economic position in the Middle East and Eastern Mediterranean, and both London and Washington followed parallel policies.[12]

The Anglo-American talks in Washington between 14 and 22 November avoided specific discussion of any increase in American military responsibility in the Middle East, and the meeting of American chiefs of mission in Istanbul between 25 and 29 November considered the conclusions of the panels discussing individual issues and countries to be more like descriptions of projects than plans and thought that in any case many of these were outdated. But the Washington talks, put by McGhee into the context of the intimate discussions that had become a normal aspect of Anglo-American relations, were especially significant in policy terms. As McGhee observed: 'for the United States to take an increased interest in the Middle East was the assumption of a new responsibility'.

Washington, however, did not want to compete with or hinder London in the area. Wright spoke in the context of the Cold War: London saw the Middle East as a key to the struggle with the Soviet Union; should Western influence go, Communism would fill the vacuum; such a development would irretrievably damage the British economy, affect London's relations with Asia, prejudice the future of Europe, and pave the way for Communist domination of Africa. Wright insisted that it was to the common advantage of London and Washington that the United States increasingly concern itself with the Middle East. This was, of course, a decision that had to be taken by Washington. But it was one that London would welcome. McGhee explained that the American approach was not just to ward off Communism, but to assist the peoples of the Middle East to improve their living standards and to acquire self respect and their proper place among the nations of the world. Although nationalism in the area was not necessarily friendly to British and American interests, Washington had found it advantageous to back nationalism. Wright agreed that nationalism should be converted into a friendly force (a view not wholly shared by France, Belgium and the Netherlands), but thought that it was not possible to fight nationalism and communism together. McGhee assured Wright that the conclusions of the 1947 Anglo-American talks on the Middle East, which had been endorsed by the

National Security Council, still held. In the discussion of long range developments it was agreed that the Middle East should not be parcelled out into 'spheres of influence' and that there was no feeling of reserve or antagonism on London's part to Washington taking a more prominent role.

Wright, in considering long-term economic development, even mentioned the possibility of creating an Anglo-American Middle East Office to replace the British Middle East Office, but he thought that such a move could lead to a charge of Anglo-American imperialism. American military requirements in Tripolitania, including the maintenance of present air base rights, were also mentioned.

The American meeting at Istanbul was in general agreement with the conclusions of the Anglo-American Washington talks, but stressed that it would be premature for Washington to consider associating itself with any regional grouping in the area. The American chiefs of mission emphasized the need for Washington to continue developing particularly close relations with Saudi Arabia and to reassure Ibn Saud who was beset with a complex that his country was being encircled.[13]

A further conference of American diplomatic and consular officials was held at Cairo between 7 and 11 March 1950. The delegates thought that Anglo-American relations throughout the Middle East were very satisfactory, and noted the increasing desire of British officials to collaborate with their American counterparts working in the same area. In this regard the delegates thought that there should be a concentration on points of agreement with the British and a minimizing of the points of difference. A potential area of disagreement was Iran. It was noted that while Iranian regard for the United States was high, they felt neglected by Washington. On the other hand, the Iranians disliked and feared the British. Although Tehran's relations with London were correct, they were handicapped by dissatisfaction over the Anglo-Iranian Oil Company concession issue, and also by Iranian claims to the Bahrain islands.[14]

At this time Anglo-American relations in the Middle East once again became the tool of the Zionist lobby in congress. Just as in 1946, when the Zionist lobby in the form of the American (Christian) Palestine Committee had demanded that Congress make the American loan to Britain subject to allowing Jewish refugees into Palestine, and again in 1947, when it had tried to insist that Washington should make Britain stay in Greece and pay for British troops there by an enforced withdrawal of British troops from Palestine,[15] so on 28 March 1950, Democratic representatives mainly from New York, Illinois and Pennsylvania, along with two Republican representatives from New York, told Acheson of a growing sentiment in the House that there would be an amendment to cut the recovery aid to Britain if Britain continued to arm the Arabs. Acheson explained that when the arms embargo had been lifted at the end of the First Arab–Israeli War in 1949, the American ambassador at the United Nations, Warren Austin, had stated that Washington did not want to see an arms race in the Middle East and would only permit the exportation to the Middle East of such arms as it thought necessary for internal security and legitimate self-defence.

The Secretary pointed the congressmen to the two problems involved: the Arab-Israeli relationship; and the defence of the Eastern Mediterranean, which was a matter of vital importance to both Britain and the United States and because of which Britain had a modest programme of providing the Near Eastern countries with arms to repel an attack. But the congressmen remained agitated. Acheson refused to divulge the categories of British arms being shipped to the Arabs, but gave the assurance that Britain was not sending the Arabs anything that the Americans had supplied. Another congressman wanted to know whether Britain was using American money to make arms to send to Egypt. Acheson did not reveal the specific details of a National Security Council paper discussing information from the British Chiefs of Staff about an envisaged British plan to strengthen the Egyptian army with British equipment, and in the end to draw the other Arab states and Israel into a projected Middle East defence arrangement, but he did tell the congressmen that the American military thought the British plans for a strong Egyptian army were desirable.

Early in April the Department of State drafted a plan to obtain British and French agreement to minimize the damage that shipments of arms to the Middle East could bring about. This idea was developed into the Tripartite Declaration of 25 May 1950 under which Britain, the United States, and France acknowledged that the Arab states and Israel needed to maintain a certain level of armed force for the purposes of legitimate self-defence of the area as a whole. The three powers agreed to consider all applications for arms or war materials by the countries of the Middle East in the light of these principles.[16]

On 7 June the British Chiefs of Staff submitted a paper entitled 'Defence Policy and Global Strategy', which though slightly revised in 1951, laid down the principles of British policy until 1952 when they were changed by the new Conservative administration. The Chiefs argued that it made no sense to think of British or Western European strategy as something individual or independent. Full collaboration with the United States in policy and method was vital. That truth was recognized 'in the most important area of conflict' by the North Atlantic Treaty. But the Cold War against Soviet communism was a global war, as a hot war would 'inevitably' be. After stabilization of the European front, the next most important objective should be to secure an agreed allied military strategy in the Middle East and East Asian theatres, and also the machinery to implement it. It was also necessary to obtain the fullest possible political, economic and military collaboration in the British Commonwealth as a whole – if possible including the countries of the Indian subcontinent, but if necessary without them.

The British Chiefs of Staff pointed out that Britain, itself, could not afford all the forces required for the Middle East, in addition to those required to defend itself and Western Europe. Additional forces had, therefore, to be found from other parts of the Commonwealth and the United States. In the event of a hot war, in the short term, it was not the American intention to send any forces initially to the Middle East, although the American Chiefs of Staff were understood to attach great strategic importance to that region, and might revise their existing policy when resources were available. Britain did not intend to send bomber reinforcements to the Middle East in the early stages of a war in order to conduct an offensive from that region. The Middle East, however, was viewed as 'a potentially important base for air action against Southern Russia'. It was British policy to send reinforcements of bomber aircraft to the Middle East as soon as it had the necessary resources. The primary burden for the defence of the Middle East would fall on the army, which should be in a position as soon as possible to have at its disposal a reserve for cold war emergencies. Second priorities in the Middle East were a share in the defence of the Egyptian base, and 'control of the Mediterranean sea-route for as long as possible in conjunction with the United States Navy and its denial to the enemy'.

There was no co-ordinated or agreed allied cold war strategy in relation to Asia. Furthermore, agreement had not been reached on allied military hot war strategy in the Middle East and east Asia. Agreement on these matters would be necessary before firm military arrangements could be made for the defence of these regions.[17]

By the next Anglo-American talks on the Middle East in Washington, at the end of July, it was evident that although Washington was prepared to cultivate a new interest in the Middle East and even to play a role there, this did not mean that it was willing to relieve Britain and the Commonwealth of what had already been agreed was a British and Commonwealth responsibility to defend for the West. Britain's position in Egypt was of strategic significance for Washington. American defence planners expected to use British airfields there to attack industrial and petroleum targets in the Soviet Union. American strategic planning depended on Britain maintaining a strong position in Egypt. In May 1950 the State Department was not enthusiastic about Foreign Office suggestions for a Middle East defence pact organized by Britain, Turkey and Egypt which would be linked to the North Atlantic Treaty Organization. But the Americans did inform the Egyptians that they supported Britain's maintenance of strategic facilities in Egypt. Following the outbreak of the Korean War at the end of June 1950 there was a new American fear that Britain might not be able to defend the Canal Zone against Soviet penetration, and on 26 July Truman spoke of his fears that the Soviet Union might advance into the Middle East to obtain the oil it needed to fight in Korea. Moscow, the President feared, could start trouble in Iran, and from there take over the whole Middle East.[18]

Anglo-American discussions on Iran in May suggested agreement over a diagnosis of the situation in Iran: the Americans placed emphasis on Britain making the terms of the oil agreement more palatable to the Iranians; Britain insisted that the concession should be on a fair commercial basis. The immediate disagreements between London and Tehran went back to 1948 when, against the background of a financial crisis, the British government had required all British companies to limit dividend payments. This had affected Iran's income as dividends paid to the Iranian government by the Anglo-Iranian Oil Company were reduced. Iranian nationalists were angered. In 1949 a new agreement between the Anglo-Iranian Oil Company and the Iranian government had been negotiated, doubling the payments stipulated in the 1933 schedule. But at the same time the Anglo-Iranian Oil Company's report for 1948 was published, showing that Britain had received $79 million in taxes from the Anglo-Iranian Oil Company while the Iranian government had received only $37.8 million in royalties. The Shah, in June 1950, appointed General Ali Razmara as Prime Minister in an attempt to secure ratification by the Majlis, the Iranian parliament, of the oil agreement. The State Department thought that London was not taking positive action over seeming intransigence on the part of the Anglo-Iranian Oil Company. The Company appeared content to let matters slide and to continue making royalty payments under the old arrangements. Washington viewed such a situation as inappropriate to prevailing internal conditions in Iran and the world situation generally in which a stable Iran was seen as essential to stop a potential Soviet advance.[19]

At the Anglo-American talks in Washington, between 20 and 24 July, an agreed conclusion was reached that a Soviet attack on Iran would raise an immediate question of general war. The American delegates, Ambassador Philip Jessup and General Omar Bradley, insisted that the defence of Iran was primarily a British responsibility. But they did concede that Washington and London should consult together as to how to meet this problem. Both the British representative and ambassador at Washington, Oliver Franks, and the Marshal of the Royal Air Force, Lord Tedder, did point out that given its existing forces Britain would have difficulty assisting in the defence of the outer ring of the Middle East, that is primarily the area covered by Iran and Turkey. In the event of general war, Britain would have to concentrate on defence of the inner core, centred in and around Egypt. Britain hoped for assistance from Australian, New Zealand and South African armed forces to do this.[20] At first Tedder and Franks shied away from any reiteration of the previous understanding that Britain had the primary responsibility in the Middle East. There was a candid discussion. The American view prevailed. The British delegates agreed it was understood that Washington could look to London to take the initiative with regard to any steps needed to be carried out in the Middle East. They hoped that the Americans would study whether they could not give Britain more support in the Middle East in case of need. The Americans did acknowledge that these talks had laid the groundwork for joint Anglo-American planning in the Middle East. Washington had moved further towards becoming more intimately involved in the defence of the Middle East.[21]

With the revelation at these talks that Britain could not really defend the outer ring in the Middle East, together with fears about potential Soviet moves with the war in Korea, Washington was forced to consider how it could contain the Soviet Union on its Southern frontier. Acheson developed the idea of a Northern Tier collective defence arrangement. In August 1950 the Secretary of State mentioned the possibility of involving an outer ring of Middle East countries, Turkey, Iran and Iraq, with an equivalent South Asian regional organization. The South Asian scheme, however, was complicated by bitterness between Pakistan and India: those two countries were blind to suggestions that the spread of communism might be a common threat to both of them. But the Pakistan leader, Liaquat Ali Khan, was eager that his country should join a Northern Tier collective defence arrangement, inspired by the United States, provided that Washington gave Pakistan as much weight as Turkey.[22]

Further Anglo-American talks on the Middle East took place in London in the middle of September, and there was agreement over the supply of arms to Turkey, co-operation with Israel, and the retention of the British bases in Egypt. More defence talks were scheduled for October, and in preparation for these the Chiefs of Staff, the Foreign Office and the Ministry of Defence recommended a policy based on the holding of the inner ring, defence of the Gulf oil fields, and an attempt to secure the essential co-operation of Egypt, Turkey and Israel, as well as an expansion of the Arab Legion. The American response was based on the insistence of the Joint Chiefs of Staff that they were opposed to any measures which might commit American forces to the Middle East in a global war. The Americans wanted Turkey as a member of the Atlantic Pact, but felt that might have to wait until the powers were strong enough to offer the country greater assistance than they could at present. Israel was an increasingly important component in the Anglo-America considerations. Washington did agree with the British assessment that Israel was moving towards the West.[23] In a conversation with State Department officials on 24 October, B.A.B Burrows, the Counsellor at the British embassy in Washington, argued that Washington would be more able to gain access to military facilities in Israel than London.

London and Washington, however, diverged on the strategic importance of the Middle East: Washington was not willing to make military sacrifices to retain the area within the Western orbit; Britain was even prepared to send a brigade to Iran to assist the achievement of Western Cold War objectives. London wanted to persuade Washington to give the Middle East a higher priority, particularly in the Cold War stage. McGhee, however, thought that the possibility of sending American forces to the Middle East was remote, and left Burrows protesting about the psychological benefits of American forces in that area as well as the importance of their presence there in time of war. Burrows thought that oil requirements in war would necessitate the defence of the outer ring, but McGhee explained that American plans assumed the oil fields would be neutralized by air bombardment.[24]

In discussions with their British counterparts in Washington between 23 and 16 October, the American Chiefs of Staff reiterated that they saw the Middle East as a British and Commonwealth responsibility: the United States could make no commitment of forces for the area, in the event of war, but its Strategic Air Command would strike targets to assist in the defence of the area. The American fleet in the Mediterranean was there primarily to cover action in Italy and southern Europe. Operations in the eastern Mediterranean would be a secondary task. The Americans thought that, in defending the Middle East, every effort should be made to hold a ring to include Turkey and to cover Middle East oil. Britain had probably underestimated the value of a properly equipped and trained Iranian army. There was to be a combined study of the position between the Commander-in-Chief, Middle East, with the Commander of the American Mediterranean Fleet and the heads of missions in Turkey and Iran. The Americans thought Middle East oil essential to the war effort. There had to be a new review of the role of Middle East oil in allied strategic plans. The Americans further agreed that Egypt was indispensable as a wartime base for forces defending the Middle East. There was also to be a study of the association of Greece and Turkey with NATO planning.[25]

Britain, a little reluctantly, was left with the main responsibility for the defence of the Middle East. In November, the State Department noted that Washington would expect London to assume the primary role in giving military assistance to Iraq.[26] But the British position in Egypt was reinforced by a report from the American ambassador at Cairo, Jefferson Caffery. A senior figure in the American service, and a descendant of the Arcadians expelled in 1755 by the British from Nova Scotia and who had gone to Louisiana, Caffery was viewed as Anglophobe, vain and aloof. At the end of November 1950, Caffery warned that the Americans had to keep the British in Egypt: British evacuation was 'out'; any alternative to the present situation had to allow for British and possibly even American bases in Egypt.[27]

British requests for American support in the Middle East were reinforced by McGhee. On 29 November 1950 he suggested studies that might help to co-ordinate Anglo-American planning and reorientate the American programmes in the Middle East. At the end of the year, in a memorandum to Acheson, McGhee argued the need for a review of American policy in the Middle East. American actions did not reflect the conclusions of the National Security Council that the defence of the Middle East was vital to the defence of the United States. Britain, left with the primary responsibility for the defence of the area, lacked the necessary manpower and resources, and had no plans for the defence of the oil fields in Saudi Arabia and the Dhahran air base. The attached State Department paper insisted that the prevailing plans to abandon the Middle East did not provide for American security interests. It was wishful thinking to 'follow the time-honoured assumption' that the Americans could rely on the British to defend the Middle East. Britain could not defend American interests in the area. Local governments in the Middle East were aware of Britain's military weakness, and this hindered Britain's attempts to negotiate defence facilities in the area. These governments would prefer American aid, or alternatively joint Anglo-American support.

The situation was complicated by internal debates in the United States as to whether the Middle East was 'vital' or 'critical' in strategic planning. The Department of Defence hoped that the lower American priority would force the

British to do more for the defence of the Middle East. Also there was the issue of inter-service rivalry: if the Middle East were deemed 'vital' and ground forces were committed to its defence, the Navy would need equipment and facilities to defend the sea and air lanes on which these ground forces would have to depend. This increase in the Navy's appropriations would be at the expense of the other service branches. Washington was engaged in an accelerated military build-up, and as part of this the State Department wanted a move away from the concept of primary British responsibility for the defence of the Middle East, and towards one of a combined Anglo-American responsibility and active co-operation between London and Washington in the development and implementation of plans. McGhee told the National Security Council on 29 December that he wanted a combined Anglo-American military command structure in the Middle East. This would lead to co-operation with the Arabs, and make the idea of a mutual defence pact more attractive to them.[28]

At the beginning of January 1951 McGhee furthered his campaign by conversations with members of the State and Defence Departments. Following these on 27 January Acheson wrote to George C. Marshall, the Secretary of Defence, about the continued insistence of the Joint Chiefs of Staff that Washington's main effort had to be in Western Europe, and because of commitments in the Far East, it could not be involved in a security pact in the Middle East, or the commitment of combat forces there. At the very least Acheson did want to improve the Western position in the Middle East 'through the coordination of American, British and indigenous efforts under a concept of the defense of the Middle East as a whole'. The view of the State Department was that Britain held a position of declining political influence in the area and even with Commonwealth support could not defend it. There was a danger that important Middle Eastern countries would swing towards the Soviet Union, and only direct American participation in building up the defences of the area as a whole could halt this trend. The State Department viewed Turkey as the keystone in the defence of the Middle East. It also endorsed the idea of the defence of the outer ring – the Turkish–Iranian mountain line, and thought that Pakistan might help in the defence of Iran. McGhee argued this case with the Joint Chiefs of Staff on 30 January. His colleague, Paul Nitze, in response to the Joint Chiefs' concern about involvement with the French, insisted that if the United States wanted an arrangement with Britain in the Middle East, it should not shy away from this because it worried the French. Despite an assertion that Britain had only 11,000 combat troops in the area and was planning only for the defence of the Suez Canal, the Chiefs remained unsympathetic to any assumption of American responsibility in the Middle East.

McGhee expostulated that his use of the term 'United States leadership' was not accurate; rather it was envisaged that the United States should fit into the picture in a subordinate role, and that Washington and London should form 'an interlocking base for a regional defense effort'. But the Chiefs were largely insensitive to arguments that this would only involve the United States in a small effort. They were exercised by the 'atrocious' act of the British ambassador in Greece talking about British responsibility there because Britain had some kind of general responsibility in the Middle East. Greece was a Balkan country. It was Washington's responsibility. And the same could be said of Western Turkey. When McGhee explained that, in terms of the conversations of September 1950, Britain was responsible in the event of war, some of the Chiefs denied even being a party to this agreement. General Omar Bradley complained of the lack of organization in the Mediterranean area, and said that General Dwight D. Eisenhower would have to decide the relationship between his European command and the Mediterranean theatre.[29]

In January 1951 London also gave considerable attention to the Middle East. At the time of the Commonwealth Prime Ministers' Conference in London that month, the Assistant Under Secretary for Middle Eastern Affairs in the Foreign Office, R.J. Bowker, offered the assessment of the Foreign Office and the views of the Chiefs of Staff on the area of British Commonwealth responsibility. British defence plans for the Middle East aimed to defend as much of the Middle East as possible, Egypt was the only base from which this could be done. It was also a 'platform' from which an attack could be launched against the Soviet Union's most vulnerable area, the oil fields in the Caucuses. The Middle East also had to be held as a barrier to Africa to deny that continent's rich resources to the Soviets. Egypt was the best for doing that as well. The Suez Canal was not of vital importance in wartime. But 'Suez remains of vast importance as the backdoor to Egypt and will no doubt be of great importance in the next war in servicing the vital Australian and New Zealand, and also South African, contributions to Middle East defence.'[30]

On 6 January Sir William Slim, the Chief of the Imperial General Staff, opened the special meeting of the Commonwealth conference on the Middle East and the defence of Africa confined to Britain, Canada, Australia, New Zealand, South Africa and Southern Rhodesia, with the observation that the allies could almost certainly lose a hot war by losing the Middle East, and could not win the war without regaining the Middle East. Besides its vital strategic importance for the allies, the Middle East remained one of the three basic pillars of strategy for the Commonwealth, the others being the security of the United Kingdom, as an essential base, and the maintenance of sea communications. The Americans had said that they could not contribute to the defence of the area for the first two years of a major war. The defence of the Middle East remained a Commonwealth responsibility, while that of the Pacific was mainly up to the Americans. In outlining possible lines of defence of the Middle East, Slim used ideas promulgated by the American Chiefs of Staff in October. The only satisfactory line from a military point of view was an 'outer ring'. That included a large part of Turkey, likely to be the soundest ally, and the oil-producing territories. It would keep the Soviets a long way from Egypt, and was a sound military line resting on mountain ranges with only a few passes. But it was a long line, would need a lot of troops and was a long way away from the position of allied troops in peacetime. The second alternative was an 'inner line'. This would mean abandoning the oil-producing territories and most of Turkey. It was a compromise. The third position, 'the Lebanon-Jordan line', would merely hold a position of the Mediterranean covering part of Jordan as well as Israel and Egypt.

The extent of the threat to the position in the Middle East depended on whether the Soviet attack started from the existing Soviet border, or whether the Soviets would first advance their position by an operation in part of Iran. Such an action could reduce by almost two months the time at which the Soviets were in position. Assuming that the Russians started from the existing borders, it was estimated they would reach the Iranian passes on the 'outer ring' in about 14 days, and after 80 days would have six divisions on the east bank of the Euphrates. Three or four months after the operation started, the Soviets would have three or four divisions advancing over the desert towards 'Northern Palestine' and the 'inner ring', and in four to five months they would have eight divisions through Turkey moving southwards from Alexandretta. They would then have 12 divisions in position after about four months.

All that Britain could provide to meet this threat on the basis of existing planning was one and one-third divisions already in the Middle East, another two divisions three months after operations started and another three and one-third divisions six months after operations started. To these could be added the Arab Legion which was a first-class force and suitable for operations in the Middle East, but amounting only to the strength of a single division. The total opposing the Soviets after four months would thus be between five and six divisions. According to the medium-term plan which would come into operation in 1954, there would be a little acceleration, and six divisions could be in the field rather more quickly.

Military conversations with various Commonwealth countries had indicated that one division could be expected from Australia, one division eventually, from New Zealand and one armoured division from South Africa. If those Commonwealth forces arrived in the Middle East in time, they would greatly affect the position, leaving the allied force only slightly inferior to the Soviets in size, while superior in equipment and fighting capacity.

The British Chiefs of Staff were satisfied that the objective should be to hold the 'outer line'. That would ensure close contact with Turkey who could produce 19 divisions which, together with air support, would be 'a source of great strength'. There was the possibility of two not very reliable divisions from Iraq which were 'weakly officered'. The Americans were training an army in Iran, but the Chiefs of Staff in London thought that the Americans overestimated the value of these troops. If Israel fought on the allied side, it could contribute one further division of 'real fighting value'. The Americans and British were due to start talks about holding the 'outer ring', or failing that, the 'inner ring'. The problem was the Egyptian base. From the beginning of a war it was essential that the allies should be able to use Egypt. Sir Arthur Sanders, the Chief of Staff for

Air, warned that the air force would not be able to protect even the 'inner ring' or the Lebanon–Jordan line. Britain wanted a larger Commonwealth contribution.

Bevin, at that time ill and with only a few months to live, offered what was virtually his swan-song on an area which he saw as crucial to Britain's very existence. Initially determined to work with the peasants and not pashas, Bevin had been left in the position where Britain's only hope of maintaining suzerainty over the Arabs lay in working with the old ruling houses. During his period of office, Bevin had successfully resisted moves from his Prime Minister to withdraw the British presence from the Middle East. Probably more than any other British statesman at the time Bevin was identified with the Middle East. The Foreign Secretary told the conference how the main difficulty in arranging a comprehensive plan for the defence of the Middle East was that Britain had to deal with a number of small countries which were politically and economically unstable. Turkey was the most stable country in the area. Geographically, however, it was in the wrong place. A defence plan could not be centred on it. There were only a few places where British forces could be placed in the Middle East in peacetime, and begin to plan an offensive defence in war. Even in Cyprus, Greece, from time to time, 'provoked activities for independence'. In the United Nations, Britain's friends had not been co-operative in the attempt to secure the necessary facilities in Cyrenaica. Britain had been faced with impossible obstacles in handling the former Italian colonies: a plan proposed for the partition of Eritrea which was sound both politically and ethnically had been rejected. Egypt, however, was still the principal problem. For 67 years Britain had been promising to leave the Canal Zone, but Britain was still there, and still trying to make arrangements by which it might stay. There was also the trouble with Egypt over the condominium of the Sudan. Britain's legal position on both these matters in the United Nations was weak. Egypt did not seem to realize that geography made it a magnet for attack in war. In 1947, Stalin had hinted to Bevin that he would not promote subversive agitation in Egypt while Britain remained, but would do this if the British tried to bring the Americans into Egypt. Britain had to look for military facilities elsewhere in the Middle East. Whatever accommodation might be reached with Egypt, Britain would have to leave in 1956. Because of this Bevin was working with the Chiefs of Staff on a scheme by which the Egyptians would be left with the responsibility for looking after the stores, workshops and communications in the Canal Zone on Britain's behalf. Egypt would look after the Suez base in peacetime; but in war Egypt should allow Britain all the facilities it might require. These included base facilities, as well as the necessary immunities for British and allied forces. Bevin hoped that the Egyptians would allow Britain to decide when there was an emergency likely to lead to war.

The Chiefs of Staff, however, had to find an alternative peacetime base for troops in the Middle East. Facilities were also necessary in Israel and Libya. Egypt and Israel would not co-operate. It was British policy to make the Middle

Eastern countries feel that they were equal partners in efforts to defend their territories. The Sudan problem would solve itself as the Sudanese achieved more self-government, but it might be necessary to have some loose connection between the Sudan and the Egyptian Crown.

Discussion suggested that, with the exception of Israel where it might be difficult to get facilities, there was no base like Egypt. It had a front door on the Mediterranean, and a back door to the Red Sea. This was particularly important for the Commonwealth forces from Australia and New Zealand. The Chiefs of Staff, however, thought that at least for the first few months of the war it would be possible to keep open a sea line of communication through the Mediterranean. There were doubts about the Egyptians' ability to maintain valuable equipment. But the Commonwealth Prime Ministers would not make firm commitments, and the Dominions were not committed to the defence of the Middle East after the Commonwealth Prime Ministers' Conference in January 1951.[31]

Britain tried again for greater American involvement in the Middle East. At a meeting of State Department and Foreign Office officials in London on 6 February, Bowker explained that General Sir Brian Robertson, the Commander-in-Chief Middle East Land Forces, was visiting countries in the Middle East to state defence problems in the area. These countries were demanding jet aircraft and modern tanks. The jets could not be supplied as the Cabinet had decided on 16 October 1950 to give priority to the needs of Britain, the Commonwealth, and NATO countries. In particular, Syria was complaining about the non-delivery of 14 Gloster Meteor aircraft which had been partly paid for. There were also representations from Iraq about the non-delivery of a wide range of weapons. The Foreign Office felt that this bare arms cupboard made it important to steady fears in the Middle East with political, psychological and other means. Bowker suggested that Washington might explain to the Arab states and Israel the American interest in the defence of the Middle East, that it had been agreed that Britain had primary responsibility in the area and that in carrying out this responsibility it had both Washington's support and assistance.[32]

These issues were taken up at a conference of the American Middle Eastern Chiefs of Mission held at Istanbul between 14 and 21 February. The delegates recommended that Washington should bolster London's position in the Middle East where this could effectively serve the American interest. This was particularly so with regard to Egypt. Britain's position, however, had weakened. Turkey wanted a security arrangement and there was a danger of that country veering towards a policy of neutralism if something were not done. Political considerations required that the same offer be made to Greece. The conference recommended adherence by Turkey and Greece to NATO.[33] The issue of the membership of Greece and Turkey exercised the NATO standing group, and British and American officials. In May 1951 it was agreed that Greece and Turkey would be invited to join as full partners, and at the same time negotiations commenced between Britain, the United States, France and Turkey about the establishment of a Middle East Command which would be extended to include Egypt and other Middle Eastern countries.[34]

Washington also looked increasingly at a possible role for Pakistan in the defence of the Middle East. By early March 1951 Washington knew that Pakistan would help to defend Iran and the Near East if the dispute with India over Kashmir could be settled or neutralized. London, however, felt that an approach to India and Pakistan over assistance in the defence of the Iranian–Iraqi sector would do more harm than good because of the Kashmir dispute. But the Joint Chiefs of Staff insisted that any opportunity should be seized.[35]

At this time London pursued hints that Israel might be prepared to make an arrangement covering co-operation in war, and possibly even in times of peace. Israel made friendly overtures. During Robertson's visit there, on 19 and 21 February, David Ben-Gurion, the Israeli Prime Minister spoke cordially to the British Commander-in-Chief Middle East Land Forces. Ben-Gurion wanted Israel to survive. There was a 'great danger to civilisation'. The situation called for the 'closest possible collaboration' between Israel and Britain. By this Ben-Gurion meant that 'in an emergency Israel should act "as if" she were part of the British Commonwealth and should be regarded by Britain in exactly the same way'. Ben-Gurion was not proposing that Israel should join the Commonwealth. He did, however, want Israel to play an active rather than a merely passive role in resisting the common enemy. Israel could be useful in placing its industrial capacity at Britain's disposal. If Britain were interested, it could help to develop it. Israel was worried that in a general war the Arab states would try to destroy it. Ben-Gurion, therefore, wanted peaceful relations with the Arab states, and particularly Egypt.

Herbert Morrison, Bevin's successor as Foreign Secretary, replied on 24 April that the development of a relationship between Israel and Britain should be a gradual process, 'taking account of the realities of the existing situation and our respective world interests'. The process had to come about naturally, as a result of continued contacts, exchanges of views and individual acts of co-operation. The best way to start could be practical co-operation in the military field, co-operation that would contribute to Israel's security and the safeguarding of Britain's vital interests in the Middle East. Israel, however, was not invited to join the envisaged Middle East defence organization. It was not thought possible for both sides on the Palestine dispute to belong to the same defence body. Any inclusion of Israel would prejudice Arab participation. And the Arabs were more important.[36]

It was over Saudi Arabia, however, that the real divergence of policy between Washington and London was emerging. At the end of January 1951, A.C. Trott, the British ambassador at Jedda pointed to this. His counsellor, Scott Fox, offered an analysis of the background of the remarkable penetration of American interests in the Hejaz, which Britain had liberated from the Turks during the First World War. Indeed, until the early 1930s, no other power had interests comparable to those of Britain in Arabia. The first indication of a change was when in 1933 the Standard Oil Company of New Jersey was granted an oil concession in the newly created Kingdom of Saudi Arabia, a concession which Ibn Saud insisted he had first offered to the British. Saudi Arabia's revenue, until then largely derived from pilgrim dues most of whom came from the British Empire and paid in sterling, moved to a reliance on what became the Arabian–American Oil Company (ARAMCO) and its pipeline to the Mediterranean, and its small American town of 5,000 inhabitants near the American air base at Dhahran, the only American military base in Western Asia. British influence predominated until 1942.

In 1943 Washington started to share the subsidy and supply programme to Saudi Arabia with London, and continued it in a 'spate of philanthropy' in anticipation of the gratitude of the Muslim world. Lord Moyne, the British Deputy Minister of State in Cairo, on 29 September 1944 commented that there was a serious risk of the Americans

> adopting an excessively paternal and patronising attitude to Saudi Arabia from a failure to understand that a fanatical Moslem population does not take the same view of the blessings of American civilisation as they do themselves. If the results of misguided American benevolence should be to undermine the independence of the country and make it a satellite of the United States of America it would have serious reactions throughout the Moslem world and gravely prejudice British interests.

After 1945 Saudi Arabia benefited from ARAMCO: mobility was improved with the building of piers, roads and railways and the development of air transport; electricity and water was supplied to the principal towns. By the end of 1950 American economic interests tended to predominate, and Scott feared that the prevailing approximate balance between British and American interests would be upset in favour of the Americans. There remained some British activities: in 1946 the joint Anglo-American team for the training of the Saudi Arabian army had been replaced by a British Military Mission; there had also been a British Civil Air Training Mission, though it was possible that Jedda would accept any tempting American offer for air assistance that could be offered in connection with the negotiations for the annual renewal of the lease of the Dhahran air base.

Trott felt that where British and American interests in Saudi Arabia conflicted or competed Britain should not give in 'at the first huff'. He singled out the frontier question, the training and provision of the Saudi Arabian military, the provision of agricultural, public health and financial advisers, and relations between British and American construction companies. Trott also referred to 'the generally rather excessively obsequious attitude of the Arabian American Oil Company towards the Saudi Arabian Government'. The ambassador argued that Washington and London needed to recognize their separate and mutual interests in the country, and prevent the Saudis from playing one off against the other.

The Foreign Office felt that Anglo-American co-operation over Saudi Arabia was less close than was desirable. For example, in 1949, both a British and an

American military reconnaissance party had visited Saudi Arabia. The recommendation of the British party over the building of an airfield was not pursued because the Chiefs of Staff gave a low strategic priority to Saudi Arabia. This information was passed to the Americans, but they did not reciprocate. Similarly the Americans had not passed on details over the negotiations to renew the lease of the Dhahran air field, and the Americans were keeping quiet about bargaining over military facilities. London had deferred to American wishes in not raising the question of their potential contribution to the Saudi Arabian air force. The British also feared that ARAMCO was behind the Saudi attitude evidenced over the frontier disputes. Furthermore London was exercised over the agreement that had been made between ARAMCO and the Saudi Arabian government that oil revenues should be shared between them on a 50:50 profit sharing basis. Neither the British government, nor British oil companies in the Middle East, had been consulted or even warned of this.

On 9 April 1951, however, Trott was advised by the Foreign Office that too much emphasis should not be placed on any local differences, lest they adversely affect the general Anglo-American collaboration which London wanted to maintain throughout the Middle East. Indeed the Foreign Office wanted Washington to increase its strategic commitment in the area. It was acknowledged, however, that Washington was inclined to deal with Arab countries in the light of Western standards and ideals, whereas London tried to reconcile its aims to changes necessitated by indigenous methods, outlook and capabilities.

The Foreign Office did ask whether, in the light of the Caltex Agreement concluded with certain American oil companies in July 1950, ARAMCO would be paying large amounts of sterling to the Saudi Arabian government, and consequently whether Jedda might have a greater interest in sources of supply in the sterling area. Trott thought not. American economic influence in a country which it considered as its foster child was likely to continue undiminished. Indeed the American role was more all-embracing than Britain's in Iran when the Anglo-Iranian Oil Company had that field to itself.

The principal factor was the massive presence of ARAMCO, followed by American financial aid, the influence of other American companies which tied Saudi Arabian business to American interests and standards, and the likely gift of arms in return for the lease at Dhahran with the implication of Americanization in that no other country need apply to be an arms supplier. American exports to Saudi Arabia had fallen from $84 million in 1948 and 1949 to under $40 million in 1950 and were likely to fall again in 1950. British exports fell from £3.4 million in 1949 to £2.8 million in 1950, but that excluded arms sales. This could be explained by the use of sterling for trade in other countries. But the British experience had been that the more extensive use of sterling by Saudi Arabia had not led to any acceptance of a greater British interest or influence in that country's affairs, and nothing comparable to the envisaged increase in American influence to be achieved by the appointment of an American financial adviser.

Trott, in a despatch which was his swan-song, referred to the 'quite unprecedented American invasion': Dhahran and the Tapline settlements were like towns in the United States. He doubted whether the 50:50 oil agreement would stabilize the situation 'in this grasping country, which lives on advances and always expects next year's revenue to be half as much again as the previous one's'. He predicted that the Americans would either have to yield a great part of their monopoly to the Saudi Arabians, or take control of the country themselves. When considering Anglo-American relations in Saudi Arabia he observed that he and his staff had made every effort to co-operate with the Americans. He referred to a lecture by Raymond A. Hare, his American counterpart, who even before he arrived spoke of the anachronistic nature of British arrangements in the Gulf, an area in which he had not served. Trott complained that other Americans were even more self-confident and certain that they knew the answers and the British did not: most of the members of the American embassy in Jedda seemed 'to have anti-British complexes in their very marrow'. It did not enter these American heads that there might be better ways of doing things than the American one.

The British ambassador disliked the American exclusiveness. He also warned that American policy in Saudi Arabia was not revealed through that country's diplomatic representatives, but through the enormously powerful oil interests. ARAMCO was constantly at work, often on policies that were at variance with official Washington policy. Trott cited three instances: the secret oil agreement of 1948 which kept British oil interests out of the Gulf and which the American embassy in Jedda claimed not to have received a copy; ARAMCO's drafting of the territorial waters decreed for the Saudi Arabian government which had led to objections from both Washington and London; and ARAMCO's activities in helping to establish claims for Jedda of large parts in the east which London insisted belonged to others.[37]

Although there was a real divergence of policy between Washington and London over Saudi Arabia, it was not as immediate or crucial as the open conflict between the two countries over Iran. As early as August 1950 Lewis Douglas, the American ambassador at London, reported that Bevin did not seem to appreciate the seriousness of the situation, and had referred to the Iranian propensity to keep opening their mouths wider. The Foreign Secretary's concern was that the Iranians would try to play off the United States against Britain. To ease the situation, London hoped for a joint arrangement with the United States to offer financial assistance to Iran. The American ambassador at Tehran from July 1950 to September 1951 was Henry F. Grady. Grady was recommended for this position by McGhee. An Irish–American, Grady's involvement in Greece, Palestine and India had led to a reputation for interference in British Empire affairs. Sympathetic to nationalist aspirations, Grady thought that the nationalists in Iran could modernize the economy and achieve real independence for Iran. His British counterpart, Sir Francis Shepherd, a bachelor who kept dachshunds and had his sister act as hostess, was hard working, intelligent, dry and one of the old school. Acheson, who never met Shepherd, referred to him as unimaginative, and a disciple of the 'whiff of grapeshot' school. When the British evacuated, Shepherd was chauffeur-driven through the streets of Tehran in an open car flying the Union Flag. Shepherd thought Grady temperamentally unsuited to dealing with Iranian deviousness and intrigue, and observed that he was plagued by 'an inflated and rather mediocre staff who listen credulously to every bazaar rumour and are sometimes individually anti-British'. On 31 October 1950 Grady reported to Acheson that Britain was 'bent on sabotaging our efforts to strengthen Iran in order to preserve its dubious supremacy and control here'. This was, in Grady's opinion, jeopardizing the global position of the Western democracies.[38]

In March 1951, after attempts by Razmara to secure concessions from the Anglo-Iranian Oil Company, the oil agreement negotiated in 1949 was submitted to the Majlis without amendment. Dr Muhammad Mossadeq, a veteran politician of aristocratic background, demanded that Iran recover assets that should never have been granted to a foreign company and that the oil industry be nationalized. Razmara was assassinated by a Muslim fanatic on 7 March 1951.

Following this, on 14 March, the National Security Council proposed a statement of policy that the United States should take all feasible steps to ensure that Iran did not fall to the Communists, and that because of American commitments in other areas, Washington should continue the understanding with London that Britain was responsible for taking the initiative for the military support of Iran. While on a tour of the Middle East, McGhee met Shepherd in Tehran on 17 March and upbraided the ambassador about the Anglo-Iranian's slowness in recognizing the new situation. McGhee complained that London, despite its controlling interest in Anglo-Iranian had allowed its chairman, Sir William Fraser, to dictate policy. McGhee dismissed complaints that the 50:50 profit-sharing agreement ARAMCO had made with Saudi Arabia had 'thrown a wrench into [the] Persian oil machinery'. After all, McGhee had warned Anglo-Iranian's board the previous September of the impending agreement that had been concluded in November 1950.

When McGhee was in London on 2 April the Treasury official, D.R. Serpell attempted to enlighten him on the effect that the loss of Iranian oil would have on Britain's balance of payments: if Britain had to acquire oil elsewhere that would cost £100 million a year, or one twenty-fifth of the whole balance of payments. This would affect both Britain's bargaining position and its armaments programme. McGhee saw Iran as the one 'real soft spot' on the Soviet periphery. The American insisted that 'nationalization' was an emotional concept in Iran and Britain had to accept that reality. He thought that a British concession to this was needed with Anglo-Iranian still retaining control of the oil operations. The British were, however, critical of his suggestion for joint Anglo-American support for the 50:50 profit sharing arrangement: competition between the oil companies of the Middle East would militate against any common adherence.

The British ambassador at Washington, Sir Oliver Franks, advised on 10 April that the Americans insisted there be 'some bow to nationalisation', and thought that the best Britain could hope for was a management contract with ownership of the assets vested in the Iranian government. The ambassador advised that the Americans recognized Britain's domestic difficulty in explaining why such an important asset should be transferred to a foreign company, particularly remembering the Royal Navy's dependence on Iranian oil. London decided not to tell Washington about its discussions with Iraq over the use of the Shaiba base for possible rescue operations from Abadan.[39]

On 29 April the Iranian Senate and Majlis named Mossadeq, the leader of the National Front (a loose grouping of parties that had come into existence in 1944), as Prime Minister. This was followed at the beginning of May by a decree nationalizing the Iranian oil industry, retroactive to 20 March. Britain contested this unilateral abrogation of the 1933 treaty. C.M. Woodhouse, a senior officer in British external intelligence, MI6, arrived in Tehran together with Robin Zaehner, an academic with extensive Iranian contacts from the Second World War. They formed a team in the British embassy under instructions from Morrison, later confirmed by Anthony Eden when he became Foreign Secretary, to arrange for the downfall of Mossadeq.

On 26 May 1951 Britain pleaded the case for arbitration to the International Court of Justice, and on 28 May Iran refused to recognize the International Court's jurisdiction.

At the end of that month the Chiefs of Staff reported to the Cabinet a proposal for invading the island of Abadan. Morrison was not only disturbed by the threat to the readiness of the Royal Navy, dependent on the Anglo-Iranian Company for 85 per cent of its furnace oil, but felt that if Iran succeeded in seizing Abadan the example might be followed by others including the Egyptians who might seize the Suez Canal. A hard line against Iran could have a salutary effect in the Middle East. At the end of June, HMS *Mauritius* moved towards Abadan. The National Front Party warned that the first shot fired would signal the start of World War Three.

Truman urged both sides to consider an interim operating agreement. The National Security Council advised that if British troops went into Iran, the Western world would be split and Tehran might look to Moscow for help. The Central Intelligence Agency warned that British intervention could invite a Soviet invasion of northern Iran. On 3 July the Anglo-Iranian Oil Company decided to transfer its field operations to Iranians and to send British personnel from fields in Abadan for possible evacuation. In effect this meant that all of Anglo-Iranian was on strike and that all oil exports from Iran would stop by the end of July.

Acheson scorned Morrison, and saw the British Foreign Secretary as a great expert on the government of London but knowing nothing of foreign affairs, and having no feeling for situations beyond the sound of Bow Bells. The American Secretary of State regarded his British opposite as being insecure and having a natural abrasiveness of temperament.

On American Independence Day, 1951, on Averell Harriman's verandah, Franks let the Americans know how angry the British government and public were over what was seen as 'the insolent defiance of decency, legality, and reason by a group of wild men in Iran who proposed to despoil Britain'. But there was the worry that armed intervention at Abadan would lead to Soviet intervention to support their oil concessions in Azerbaijan, Britain would lose the oil fields, and Washington and London would find themselves on opposite sides in the United Nations. It was proposed that Harriman should go to Tehran.[40]

Sir Pierson Dixon, a Deputy Under-Secretary of State at the Foreign Office insisted that although it might seem that Anglo-Iranian was to blame for the British predicament with its failure to bring their relations with Tehran up to date when there was time, there were more fundamental reasons: the Iranians knew that Britain did not have the strength to suppress their agitation; Britain could not use force because of its subscription to the principles of the United Nations. Dixon hoped that a closer Anglo-American understanding could hold the position in other Middle Eastern countries. At this time Franks reported that McGhee thought that the United States could not and would not be ready to take over Britain's position in the Middle East. On 30 July Britain sent a note to Tehran recognizing the nationalization of the Anglo-Iranian Oil Company on condition that the Iranians agreed to negotiations on the conditions suggested by Harriman to ensure the availability of oil from the fields in large quantities.

Richard Stokes, the Lord Privy Seal, left for Tehran on 3 August with an eight-point scheme. Stokes was a wealthy man and enjoyed eating at the club, White's. He was viewed as more pro-Arab than Bevin. His initial appointment as a minister had been seen as a bid by Attlee for Roman Catholic support. While Stokes was in Iran, Roger Makins, a Deputy Under-Secretary of State at the Foreign Office on 11 August offered ground for reassurance about the thrust of British foreign policy. The basis of this was that the resources and support of the United States were 'essential to the security of the United Kingdom and indeed to the free world'. The maintenance of the Anglo-American partnership was difficult because the power and resources of the United States were increasing at a rate much faster than those of Britain. But the Americans continued to regard Britain in a special way and this could be sustained provided Britain kept itself independent of economic aid and that it did not always expect the Americans to do things the way Britain wanted them done. The hard fact was that Britain needed American support to keep its end up in the Middle East. Makins recorded that the dispute with Iran had dealt a heavy blow to British prestige, and that Britain had brought this on itself by allowing the oil company too much freedom of action when vital national interests were at stake. In general, Makins referred to the need for a strength of national will and resolve behind a British policy which was the only feasible one to follow if Britain were to avoid sinking to the level of a second or third class power.[41]

The American negotiating team in Iran was taken on a tour of the oil fields in the south-west and shown the separate facilities and the better quarters provided for the British staff. There were drinking fountains labelled 'Not for Iranians'. Stokes returned on 23 August, and on 12 September the Iranian government sent Britain an ultimatum.

At the end of August Hugh Gaitskell, the Chancellor of the Exchequer, realized that Britain was approaching another sterling crisis as the trade gap reached record levels. Besides the cost of replacing Iranian oil there had been the rearmament programme, an increase in import prices and unusually heavy dollar expenditure by other members of the sterling area. On 4 September Gaitskell flew to Washington. Britain was in no position to defy Truman's objections to the use of force in Iran. On 5 September Mossadeq threatened to cancel the residence permits of British technicians if negotiations were not resumed within two weeks. Britain sent four warships to join the ten warships in the Gulf, and blocked Iranian holdings in the Bank of England.

From Tehran, on 11 September, Shepherd reported on the difficulties that existed between the American and British embassies there. He commented that Iran was a country where full sway was given to certain American characteristics: the Americans were suspicious of the colonialist and imperialist attributes of British policy and were inclined to be impressionable to Iranian complaints about this. The Americans were suspicious of the British, and although recognizing that Britain had more experience in Iran than themselves, they wanted to form their own opinions and were cagey about accepting advice from the British. The American personnel were 'ambitious of increasing American influence' in Iran and regarded Britain as their chief rival.

On 27 September the Iranian authorities occupied Abadan. The Cabinet discussed the possibility of seizing the island by force, but Law Officers advised that such action was illegal unless authorized by the Security Council. In Cabinet Morrison argued against 'scuttle and surrender'. Attlee conceded that the loss of Abadan would be humiliating, but he and the Cabinet agreed that Britain could not afford to break with the United States on this issue. Britain completed the evacuation of Abadan on 4 October 1951.[42]

Although divided over Saudi Arabia, and in open conflict on the Iranian question, Washington and London did succeed in reaching an agreement over policy towards Egypt and the attempt to form the Middle East Command.

On his tour around the Middle East McGhee visited Cairo between 29 March and 1 April 1951. There he met the leading British personnel, political and military, and sensed their 'traditional condescension' towards the Egyptians. McGhee gained the impression that the Americans were trying to undercut them in their negotiations with the Egyptians, and suspected that Washington wanted to control Egypt. In reality the Americans, at this stage, did not want to relieve Britain of their responsibilities in Egypt, and if anything wanted to establish ties with the Egyptians to help the British. At a meeting with the British ambassador at Cairo, Sir Ralph Stevenson, and Foreign Office officials in London, McGhee insisted that in his talks with the Egyptians he had vigorously defended the British point of view, and drawn attention to Soviet colonialism and contrasted it with Britain's move away from old-fashioned imperialism. McGhee feared an impasse in Anglo-Egyptian relations could result in a rapid deterioration of stability in the Arab world and affect its relations with the West. Britain should evacuate its forces over the next 18 months to two years. He intimated that the State Department was taking an increased interest in the Middle East and Britain could expect the United States to play a more active role in the politics and defence of that area even to the extent of making forces available and assuming a definite responsibility for the defence of the Middle East. This should be remembered in negotiations with the Egyptians as it might help them to accept a multinational arrangement for defence.[43]

But Bevin had been succeeded by his old enemy Herbert Morrison, as Foreign Secretary. Morrison, assisted by Emmanuel Shinwell, the Minister of Defence, shifted the basis of British policy towards Egypt. Bevin had accepted that the British would have to leave Egypt on Egyptian terms, but had hoped that the Egyptians might have been persuaded to accept a gradual British withdrawal and the right of British re-entry in the event of an emergency. Shinwell and Morrison fought for a firm British stand. The Cabinet agreed. New demands were made of the Egyptians: Britain would make a 'phased' withdrawal, but only after the conclusion of a new treaty. The Egyptian position on the Sudan was rejected. The Egyptians thought that what they received on 11 April looked like an ultimatum. Within two weeks they turned down the British proposals.[44]

The British position in Egypt, and in the Middle East generally, increasingly exercised the Americans. On 2 May McGhee, following his tour of the Middle East and his talks in London, discussed these issues with the Joint Chiefs of Staff. He warned that the Americans had to consider carefully whether they could support British policy in the Middle East. Britain was opposed to the rising tide of nationalism throughout the area, was increasingly unpopular and a liability to the United States. Indeed the liability was such that it could exceed the military value of co-operating with the British in the Middle East. McGhee pointed to the Egyptian rejection of the British proposals on withdrawal. The Egyptians were prepared to force the British out. The Middle East countries needed arms. Iraq and Israel wanted them, as did Syria although it was neutral. The Lebanese Prime Minister had said that Washington could use Lebanese bases in time of war provided that the French were not involved. There was a difficulty in that there was not a meeting of minds between the Joint Chiefs of Staff and the British Chiefs of Staff about division of responsibility in the area. Turkey would not accept the idea of British responsibility, and that concept was something the Iranians and Greeks were not even prepared to discuss. There was friction with Robertson over Saudi Arabia where Britain thought it had responsibility. The other Arab states and Israel had been a British sphere of influence. McGhee raised the question as to whom would have responsibility if both the United States and Britain provided arms.

Admiral Forrest Sherman thought that the problem resulted partly from the growth of national feelings, but also from a shrewd estimate by the countries of the Middle East that Britain was no longer a Great Power. He also insisted that Greece was in the Balkans and an American responsibility. At the end McGhee broadened the canvas and insisted that the Middle East could be defended without Pakistan.

A working group of State Department and Defence officials also considered these issues and pointed to the need to clarify the nature of American responsibility towards Saudi Arabia, and the respective responsibilities of Britain and the United States in the strengthening of several Arab states and Israel. It all, however, tied in closely with the settling of the Mediterranean Command question with the British and the French.

The American programme of aid to the Middle East which included an economic grant aid in excess of $100 million was discussed with Franks and members of the British Joint Services Mission in Washington on 17 May. McGhee emphasized that it was all designed to help, and not replace, British assistance and prestige in the area. Washington was worried by the trends towards neutrality on the part of certain Middle Eastern states, and McGhee cited in particular the voting of Egypt and Syria in the United Nations on Far Eastern issues. Britain might be doing a considerable amount in Iraq, Egypt and Jordan, but this was not enough. Washington did not envisage the same degree of co-operation with France: it regarded Britain as having the primary responsibility for the area, and did not want to give the French a position which they did not then occupy. It was necessary to discuss individual plans for each country and the command relationship. Although the United States intended to play a more positive role McGhee stressed that it was not going to make any military commitment. And, with regard to the Arab–Israeli question it intended to pursue a policy of impartiality within the framework of the Tripartite Declaration. Franks replied that there was no shadow of doubt about Britain's welcome of this positive interest of the United States in the Middle East, and that all both countries could do would still not be enough.

That same day Anthony Eden lunched with the American ambassador at London and impressed on him that the British and American positions in the Middle East were 'completely interlocked'. The ambassador thought that the Americans would be able to help but not take the lead. Franks explained to the Foreign Office that the initiative for the new American programme had come from the State Department. It recognized Britain's traditional and historical position in the Middle East and assumed an increased effort by Britain there. Should Britain not be able to sustain this there could be a serious deterioration in Anglo-American co-operation. The Americans were not insensitive to Arab taunts that they had prejudiced their reputation as missionaries and educators by associating closely with the older imperial powers. There was a feeling amongst many Americans 'possibly more subconscious than conscious, that it may be time to draw away from us and "go it alone" in the Middle East'. Franks thought that the temptation to do so would increase as Washington's military strength grew.

And the temptation would certainly grow if British efforts in the area showed signs of flagging, and if long standing disputes between Arab countries and Britain remained unresolved.[45]

At this time Britain had difficulties with the Americans over their proposals for command arrangements in the Middle East in time of war. It was evident that the post of Supreme Allied Commander in the Mediterranean which Britain had hoped to secure for itself as a political counterweight to the American Supreme Commander in the Atlantic was likely to disappear. There was an offer from the Americans of a British Supreme Allied Commander for the Middle East in time of war. The idea was floated for a Middle East Co-operative Defence Board: there would be an announcement by Britain, the United States, France and Turkey of their intention to establish the Board, and an invitation would be issued to the Middle East states to co-operate with it. Turkey and the Commonwealth countries should be consulted before the announcement was made. The Foreign Office thought that such a proposal could safeguard the British position, demonstrate a unified Anglo-American approach to Middle East defence, and encourage the Arabs who feared that Washington was leaving London to cope with a problem which it could not handle on its own. It was from this that the scheme for the Middle East Command developed.

Accordingly, the British Defence Policy and Global Strategy paper of 1951, prepared for the meeting of Commonwealth representatives in London between 21 and 26 June, emphasized that although the Americans still did not intend, in the short term, to send any forces to the Middle East in time of war, the British Chiefs of Staff understood that their American counterparts attached great strategic importance to that area and could revise their policy when they had the resources available. The Commonwealth representatives were told that the idea of a Middle East Command was taking shape. It was agreed that in any comprehensive command structure to be established in the Middle East, the contributing countries of the Commonwealth would be adequately represented. Washington pointed to the need for a more precise planning machinery to be set up between Britain and the United States to deal with Middle East affairs.[46]

In response to the accelerated American aid to the Middle East Britain expanded its British Middle East Office. Sir William Strang, at a Foreign Office meeting on 29 July 1951 emphasized the need for Britain to encourage economic development in the Middle East as a means of influencing the course of events there. Strang warned that it was important to understand what the Americans meant by partnership with the Middle East states: the Americans were prepared to take executive action under the cover of political arrangements in which local governments would participate as equals. This did not seem to the Americans to be colonialism.[47]

Britain pursued the idea of the Middle East Command. If Egypt were invited to join that could solve the problem of an allied presence on Egyptian soil which was considered essential by the Chiefs of Staff to hold the Middle East and Africa against the Soviets in the event of war. Britain resisted French pressure to be included in talks on the Middle East; France, after all, was making no contribution to the defence of the area. By the middle of July, British and American negotiators had reached agreement on several basic points of the Middle East Command. Britain submitted a paper on the subject to the Standing Group of NATO.

Britain authorized its new ambassador at Cairo, Sir Ralph Stevenson, to announce to Egypt details of a Middle East defence scheme in which it was proposed that Egypt would share as an equal partner with Britain and other nations. This would be a Middle East Command, and although at first a British commander would be in charge, later on any other competent commander of the new allied Middle East command would take over. Stevenson was told to put this proposition to the Egyptians just before the abrogation of the Anglo-Egyptian treaty of 1936.

The Pentagon agreed to this plan as this left Britain responsible for the defence of the Suez Canal, but noted Britain's declining capability to perform this mission. Australia agreed to accept an invitation to take part in discussions. New Zealand said that it would take part in the setting up of the command. South Africa was prepared to participate subject to the understanding that South Africa would not despatch troops to the Middle East 'until called upon to do so in interest [of] Union's obligations in event [of] war (sic)'. On 9 October Egypt denounced the Anglo-Egyptian treaty although it knew that the Middle East Command proposals were about to be presented. Cairo formally rejected the proposals on 16 October 1951.[48]

At the time of the fall of the second Labour government in October 1951 Britain could still be regarded as the paramount power in the Middle East. But its position was being steadily eroded. This was something of which British officials were acutely aware. The British Minister at Beirut, E.A. Chapman-Andrews, attributed this British decline to the British eagerness not to offend the United States who 'in turn, so far as Israel is concerned, is completely in the hands of American Jewry'. Chapman-Andrews complained that in the case of Syria, Britain had been supine in the face of French activity. Britain's leadership of the Arab world, secure since 1918, had, from 1945 been successfully challenged by the United States and France. Chapman-Andrews concluded: 'neither one nor the other is capable of taking our former place and both are largely for their own hand'. In the Foreign Office, G.W. Furlonge did not like this analysis: it was 'jejune', and did not merit a reasoned reply.[49]

This reaction reflects what at the time was a common dichotomy in the perception of British policy in the Middle East at the joining of the Cold War. Many of the officials in the field, along with some of those in London, did not get on with their American counterparts, and were suspicious of what they perceived as an American intention to replace Britain in a traditional British sphere of influence. But in September 1945 official British policy had moved away from the idea that other powers were, if possible, to be excluded from the area and American penetration, even commercial, was to be resisted. As the

Americans started to show an interest in the Middle East in the late 1940s, so the British, in response, welcomed what they increasingly saw as a necessary support for their position. Britain was left with responsibility for the area in war. This was something Britain tried to resist. In the military conversations with the Americans the British representatives tried initially to shy away from this obligation, which, given Britain's financial state and military preparedness it was impossible to meet. Australia, New Zealand and South Africa were reluctant to enter into definite commitments in the area as well. Britain was in a position where it had to do everything it could to encourage the American interest, and play down divergences of policy over Iran and Saudi Arabia. And Washington did support the British position in Egypt. In the United States the new interest in the Middle East revealed divisions between the State and Defence departments, and rivalries between the armed services. These slowed down the evolving policy. There was a political perception that British influence in the Middle East was declining, and that many countries in the area were looking more and more towards the United States. But the United States remained reluctant to commit forces there in time of war. It was willing to increase its economic stake, and London was aware that if it did not do the same the Americans might lose interest and Britain would be left in an impossible situation. After all, the Middle East, in 1951, remained one of the three cardinal pillars of Britain's defence.

Notes

1. *Foreign Relations of the United States* (hereafter cited as '*FRUS*') 1949(6), pp. 41–5, Memorandum by Merriam, Top Secret, 13 June 1950; 1950(5), pp. 123–5, Ranney to Labouisse, 30 January 1950; George McGhee, *Envoy to the Middle World: Adventures in Diplomacy* (New York, 1969), pp. 18–19.
2. *FRUS* 1949(6), pp. 50–5, Memorandum by Acheson, Top Secret, 4 April 1949; pp. 31–45, Memorandum by Merriam, Top Secret, 13 June 1949.
3. *FRUS* 1949(6), pp. 1–5, Jernegan to Thurston, Secret, 11 October 1948; pp. 474–5, Policy statement on Iran prepared in the Department of State, Secret, 1 February 1949; pp. 534–5, Desirable course of action relative to Soviet–Iranian treaty of 1921, 7 July 1949.
4. David W. Lesch, *Syria and the United States: Eisenhower's Cold War in the Middle East* (Boulder, Colorado, 1992), pp. 3–4; Miles Copeland, *The Game Player: Confessions of the CIA's original political operative* (London, 1989), pp. 88–109.
5. *FRUS* 1949(6), pp. 31–45, Memorandum by Merriam, Top Secret, 13 June 1949.
6. *FRUS* 1950(5), pp. 1094–9, Policy statement on Jordan prepared in the Department of State, Secret, 17 April 1950; Ilan Pappé, *Britain and the Arab–Israeli Conflict, 1948–51* (London, 1988), p. 113; *FRUS* 1951(5), pp. 985–9, Paper prepared in the Office of Near Eastern Affairs on the future of Jordan, Secret, 24 July 1951.
7. *FRUS* 1950(5), pp. 639–42, Crocker to McGhee, 30 January 1950; Daniel Silverfarb, *The Twilight of British Ascendancy in the Middle East. A case study of*

Iraq, 1941–1950 (New York, 1994), p. 227; *FRUS* 1950 (5), pp. 1206–10, Paper prepared in the Department of State on the political union of Syria and Iraq, 25 April 1950.
8. *FRUS* 1951(5), pp. 1192–8, Policy statement prepared in Department of State on Yemen, Secret, 8 February 1951.
9. *FRUS* 1949(6), pp. 1595–6, Childs to Acheson, 10 May 1949; pp. 136–7, Memorandum of conversation by Sanger, 21 June 1949; p. 1624, Editorial note.
10. *FRUS* 1950(5), pp. 9–10, Memorandum by Funkhouser for McGhee, Secret, 9 January 1950; pp. 10–11, Memorandum by Jackson to Labouisse, Secret, 10 January 1950; pp. 34–5, Memorandum by Wilkins and Funkhouser, 15 March 1950; pp. 1131–45, Memorandum of conversation on United States–Saudi Arabian relations, Secret, 19 March 1950; pp. 1146–7, Memorandum of conversation on United States–Saudi Arabian relations, 23 March 1950; McGhee, *Envoy*, pp. 193–9; Irvine H. Anderson, *ARAMCO. The United States and Saudi Arabia: A Study of the Dynamics of Foreign Oil Policy 1933–1950* (Princeton, NJ, 1981), pp. 185–6.
11. McGhee, *Envoy*, pp. xi–xix, 14–16, 334, 353, 380; James Cable, *Intervention at Abadan: Plan Buccaneer* (London, 1991), p. 33; Selwyn Lloyd, *Suez 1956: A Personal Account* (London, 1978), p. 6; Alex Danchev, *Oliver Franks Founding Father* (Oxford, 1993), pp. 108–35; Wm. Roger Louis, *The British Empire in the Middle East 1945–1951: Arab Nationalism, the United States, and Postwar Imperialism* (Oxford, 1984), p. 587.
12. *FRUS* 1949(6), pp. 165–7, Memorandum by McGhee to Webb, Top Secret, 7 October 1949; pp. 54–5, McGhee to Wright, Secret, 24 October 1949; pp. 56–9, Memorandum by Robertson on American strategic position in the Eastern Mediterranean and Middle East, Top Secret, 14 November 1949.
13. *FRUS* 1949(6), pp. 61–89, Memorandum by Hare to Rusk enclosing agreed record of Anglo-American meetings on Middle East held between 14 and 22 November 1949, Secret, 19 December 1949; pp. 168–75, Agreed conclusions of the conference of Near Eastern Chiefs of Mission held at Istanbul, 22–9 November 1949, Secret, Undated; Public Record Office, London, FO 371/81907, E1023/2/G, Minute by Wright, 12 December 1949; McGhee, *Envoy*, pp. 20–1.
14. *FRUS* 1950(5), pp. 2–8, Report of the Near East regional conference in Cairo, Secret, 16 March 1950.
15. See Ritchie Ovendale, *Britain, the United States, and the End of the Palestine Mandate 1942–1948* (Woodbridge, Suffolk, 1989) pp. 128, 204.
16. *FRUS* 1950(5), pp. 125–30, Memorandum by Acheson of conversation with various congressmen, Top Secret, 28 March 1950; pp. 130–5, Draft report by the National Security Council on American policy towards arms shipments to the Near East, Top Secret, 28 March 1950; pp. 135–6, Report prepared in the Department of State on arms shipments to Arab states and Israel, Top Secret, 20 April 1950; McGhee, *Envoy*, pp. 23, 205–12; Dean Acheson, *Present at the Creation* (London, 1970), pp. 395–6.
17. Ritchie Ovendale, *The English-Speaking Alliance: Britain, the United States, the Dominions and the Cold War 1945-1951* (London, 1985), pp. 122–3; (ed.), *British Defence Policy since 1945. Documents in Contemporary History* (Manchester, 1994), pp. 73–80.
18. Peter L. Hahn, 'Containment and Egyptian nationalism: the unsuccessful effort to establish the Middle East Command, 1950–53', *Diplomatic History*, XI (1987), pp.

23–40 at p. 25–7; *FRUS* 1950(5), pp. 289–92, Memorandum by Stabler to Berry on Anglo-Egyptian negotiations, Top Secret, 1 June 1950.
19. FO 371/81909, E1023/72/G, Minute by G.W. Furlonge on Anglo-American Bipartite Sub-Committee meeting on Iran, 10 May 1950; *FRUS* 1950(5), pp. 545–6, Webb to certain diplomatic offices, Secret, 17 May 1950; pp. 569–70, Acheson to embassy in United Kingdom, Secret, 14 July 1950.
20. For an account of Britain's negotiations with the Commonwealth countries over the defence of the Middle East and participation in the Middle East Command see Ovendale, *The English-Speaking Alliance*, pp. 118–42.
21. *FRUS* 1950(5), pp. 188–92, Memorandum by Jessup to Anderson and attachments, Top Secret, 25 July 1950; FO 371/124935, ZP/14/G, Commonwealth Relations Office to High Commissioners, Secret, 30 July 1950; McGhee, *Envoy*, p. 22.
22. Ayesha Jalal, 'Towards the Baghdad Pact: South Asia and Middle East Defence in the Cold War, 1947–1955', *The International History Review*, XI (1989), pp. 409–33 at p. 418; Hahn, p. 27.
23. For the case that Israel did not finally decide on a Western orientation until the mid-1950s see Uri Bialer, *Between East and West: Israel's Foreign Policy Orientation 1948–1956* (Cambridge, 1990).
24. FO 371/81912, E1023/152/G, Minute by Furlonge on review of Middle East policy and strategy, Top Secret, 22 September 1950; Furlonge to R.E. Barclay, Top Secret, 22 September 1950; *FRUS* 1950(5), p. 193, Record of informal Anglo-American discussions, Top Secret, 18 September 1950; pp. 217–21, Memorandum by McGhee to Jessup on British review of Middle East policy and strategy, Top Secret, 19 October 1950; pp. 230–3, Memorandum of conversation by Howard, Top Secret, 24 October 1950; McGhee, pp. 21–2; David R. Devereux, *The Formulation of British Defence Policy towards the Middle East, 1948–56* (London, 1990), pp. 40–1.
25. Ovendale, *The English-Speaking Alliance*, pp. 124–5.
26. *FRUS* 1950(5), pp. 651–7, Policy statement prepared in the Department of State on Iraq, Secret, 9 November 1950.
27. W. Scott Lucas, *Divided We Stand. Britain, the US and the Suez Crisis* (London, 1991), p. 12; Victor Rothwell, *Anthony Eden: A Political Biography 1931–57* (Manchester, 1992), p. 121; FRUS 1950(5), pp. 322–3, Caffery to Acheson, Top Secret, 22 November 1950.
28. *FRUS* 1951(5), pp. 1–3, Editorial note; pp. 4–11, Memorandum by McGhee to Acheson, Top Secret, 27 December 1950, and annex of re-evaluation by the State Department of American plans for the Middle East; Hahn, p. 29.
29. *FRUS* 1951(5), pp. 21–7, Acheson to Marshall, Top Secret, 27 January 1951, and annexed paper drafted in the Bureau of Near Eastern Affairs, Undated; pp. 27–42, Draft minutes of discussions at the State-Joint Chiefs of Staff meeting on 30 January 1951, Top Secret, 6 February 1951; McGhee, pp. 23–4; Acheson, p. 562.
30. FO 371/91219, E1192, Minute by Bowker, 10 January 1951.
31. Australian Archives, Canberra, A426, 845/20, 9/85/8-1st Mtg, The Middle East and the defence of Africa, Top Secret, 6 January 1951; FO 800/457, fol. 155, Eg/47/3, Bevin to Foreign Office, no. 344, Top Secret, 25 March 1947; for further details see Ovendale, *The English-Speaking Alliance*, pp. 126–31.
32. FO 371/91232, E1193, Minute by J.C. Wardrop on arms supplies for the Middle

East, 7 February 1951; *FRUS* 1951(5), pp. 43–4, Gifford to Department of State, Secret, 10 February 1951.
33. *FRUS* 1951(5), pp. 50–60, Agreed conclusions and recommendations of the conference of Middle Eastern Chiefs of Mission, Istanbul, 14–21 February 1951, Top Secret.
34. *FRUS* 1951(5), pp. 143–4, Editorial note; Hahn, p. 29; McGhee, *Envoy*, pp. 265–76.
35. *FRUS* 1951(5), Editorial note.
36. A426, 439/1/10 pt. 1, J.A.M. Marjoribanks to A.S. Brown, Top Secret, 21 May 1951; enclosing text of message from Morrison to Ben-Gurion delivered 24 April 1951; pt 2., MD 14 on Israel reaction to proposed Middle East Command, 29 October 1951; pt 3., C.J. Beaumont to Mr McKnight on British proposals for Middle East Defence Organisation, 1 September 1952.
37. FO 371/91759, fos 8–9, ES1022/2/G, 1054/1/51G, Trott to Bevin, Guard Secret, 30 January 1951; fos 10–15, Enclosure, Memorandum by David Scott Fox on British and American interests in Saudi Arabia, Secret Guard, 28 December 1951; fos 3–4, ES1022/1/G, Brief by L.A.C. Fry on Anglo-American relations in Saudi Arabia, 7 February 1951; fos 5–6, ES1022/2/G, Minute by H.A. Dudgeon, 6 March 1951; L.A.C. Fry to Alan Trott, Secret, 9 April 1951; ES1022/3/G, 1054/8/51G, A.C. Trott to Herbert Morrison, Guard Secret, 2 June 1951.
38. *FRUS* 1950(5), pp. 580–1, Douglas to Acheson, Secret, 12 August 1950; pp. 593–600, Record of informal Anglo-American discussions in London on 21 September 1950, Secret; pp. 612–3, Grady to Acheson, Secret, 31 October 1950; McGhee, *Envoy*, pp. 318–25; Louis, *The British Empire*, p, 653; Cable, *Intervention at Abadan*, pp. 17, 81; James A. Bill, 'America, Iran, and the politics of intervention, 1951–1953', in James A. Bill and Wm. Roger Louis (eds), *Mussadiq, Iranian Nationalism, and Oil* (London, 1988), pp. 261–95 at p. 268–9.
39. *FRUS* 1952–4(10), pp. 21–3, Draft statement of policy proposed by the National Security Council, Top Secret, 14 March 1951; McGhee, *Envoy*, pp. 332–6; FO 371/91470, EP1023/10/G, Record of Anglo-American meeting held in Foreign Office on 2 April 1951, Secret, 3 April 1951; EP1023/18, Franks to Foreign Office, Telegram no. 1081, Confidential, 10 April 1951 d(despatched) r(received) 11 April 1951; EP1023/21, Franks to Foreign Office, Telegram no. 1098, Confidential, 11 April 1951 recd. 12 April 1951; Cable, p. 14.
40. H.W. Brands, 'The Cairo-Tehran Connection in Anglo-American rivalry in the Middle East, 1951–1953', *The International History Review*, XI (1989), pp. 434–56 at pp. 438–9; Acheson, pp. 505–7.
41. FO 371/124968, ZP24/1/G, Minute by Dixon of conversation on international situation on 13 July 1951, Secret, 14 July 1951; McGhee, *Envoy*, pp. 385–7; Cable, *Intervention at Abadan*, p. 85; Louis, *The British Empire*, p. 678; FO 371/124968, ZP24/2, Some notes on British Foreign Policy by Roger Makins, Confidential, 11 August 1951.
42. Bill, 'America, Iran, and the politics of intervention, 1951–1953', pp. 261–95 at p. 271; Cable, *Intervention at Abadan*, pp. 93–4; Acheson, *Present at the Creation*, p. 509; FO 371/91473, EP1025/1, Shepherd to Sir William Strang, Personal and Secret, 11 September 1951; Brands, p. 440.
43. McGhee, *Envoy*, pp. 377–8; FO 371/90127, JE1024/1/G, Minutes of a meeting with McGhee at the Foreign Office on 3 April 1951, Secret.

44. Ovendale, *The English-Speaking Alliance*, pp. 131–2.
45. *FRUS* 1951(5), pp. 113–120, State Department draft minutes of discussions at the State-Joint Chiefs of Staff meeting on 2 May 1951, Top Secret; pp. 124–8, Memorandum prepared by the State-Defence working group established to discuss the implementation of NSC 47/5, Top Secret, Undated; pp. 134–41, Memorandum of conversation by Klopper, Top Secret, 17 May 1951; FO 317/91185, fol. 10, E1024/22/G, Barclay to Strang, 17 May 1951; fos 24–7, E1024/24/G, Franks to Morrison, Top Secret, 19 May 1951.
46. FO 371/91185, fos 102–4, Minute by H.A. Dudgeon on command arrangements in the Middle East, 29 May 1951; fos 106–9, Record by Dudgeon of a meeting at the Foreign Office on 30 May 1951, Top Secret, 31 May 1951; Devereux, pp. 52–5; Ovendale, *The English-Speaking Alliance*, pp. 133–8; FO 371/91182, E1022/7, H.A. Dudgeon to D.A Greenhill, Confidential, 18 June 1951.
47. FO 371/91185, fos 150–6, E1024/36, Record of meeting at Foreign Office on 29 June 1951, Top Secret.
48. Ovendale, *The English-Speaking Alliance*, pp. 138–9; Acheson, *Present at the Creation*, pp. 563–4; Hahn, 'Containment and Egyptian nationalism', pp. 30–7.
49. FO 371/124968, ZP 24/5, E.A. Chapman-Andrews to K.G. Younger, Guard, 17 September 1951; Minute by G.W. Furlonge, Undated.

3

Churchill and 'Getting the Americans In': Iran and Egypt

In October 1951, the British electorate returned a Conservative administration with Winston Churchill as Prime Minister to power. The general election was, in part, precipitated by the balance of payments crisis. Mossadeq's nationalization of the Anglo-Iranian Oil Company, in May 1951, had forced Britain to pay for oil in American dollars. In the second half of 1950, particularly with the deteriorating situation in Malaya and Indochina, British defence planners had placed increasing emphasis on South-East Asia. More forces were needed to stop the Communist threat. More money had to be spent on defence. On 25 January 1951 the Cabinet had accepted a huge increase in Britain's defence budget: £4,700 million was to be spent over the years 1951–54. R.A. Butler, the Chancellor of Exchequer of the new Conservative government, when examining the treasury accounts, decided that the British economy not only could not sustain the rearmament programme, but that the sterling crisis was also likely to challenge the nature of Britain's foreign and defence commitments, and, in effect, the position of Britain as a great power. Churchill gave his Minister of Defence, Field Marshal Sir Harold Alexander, the task of economizing on Britain's military commitments.

The Chiefs of Staff, in a paper dated 17 June 1952, revised Britain's global strategy. In the Defence Policy and Global Strategy Papers of 1950 and 1951 Britain's defence line had been extended from the Middle East and the United Kingdom to part of the European continent. The defence of the Middle East, in the years following the end of the Second World War, seen as being as important as defence of the United Kingdom itself, was reassessed in 1952. The allies were, in 1952, in a position to launch a devastating attack on the Soviet Union at the very outset of the war. In considering what preparations to make for a war, the Chiefs of Staff argued that it was necessary to take into account three major developments: the increased accuracy and power of atom bombing; the advent of the small bomb for tactical use; and the economic situation. The Chiefs of Staff decided that it was economically impossible to prepare and build up the necessary reserves for a prolonged war. Efforts had to be concentrated on producing forces and equipment for an intense, all-out conflict of short duration. In the view of the Chiefs of Staff in the Cold War period, the main effort had to be directed to the prevention of world war. In the Cold War, Europe had to be given top priority, with the Far East next, and after that the Middle East. In the hot war Europe should remain a top priority, but the Middle East should be given priority over the Far East owing to the importance of communications through the Middle East, its oil and the 'necessity to prevent Communism from spreading throughout Africa'. The 1952 Defence Policy and Global Strategy Paper outlined what the Chiefs of Staff regarded as 'reasonable' preparations for hot war. Their recommendations were undermined by the treasury under Butler who was concerned that the rearmament programme would reduce living standards in Britain.[1]

The new Conservative government reassessed British policy in the Middle East. On 4 December 1952 Anthony Eden, the Foreign Secretary, told a meeting of the Cabinet, attended by Commonwealth Prime Ministers, that the accession of Turkey to NATO had changed the whole problem. Eden hoped that Britain would conclude a treaty with Libya which would give Britain strategic facilities. It might be possible 'to devise a successful form of defence for the Middle East, based on Turkey, Cyprus and Libya'. Eden explained that it was proposed to move the British military headquarters from the Canal Zone, and that plans were being contemplated which envisaged the stationing of an armoured brigade in Libya, a brigade in Cyprus and possibly a brigade in Jordan.[2]

The successful test of the American hydrogen bomb in November 1952 also contributed significantly to another defence review which further undermined the 1952 Defence Policy and Global Strategy Paper. Churchill insisted that Britain needed a hydrogen bomb to remain a great power. Butler hoped that such a thermo-nuclear weapon would lessen expenditure on conventional forces. The Chiefs of Staff concluded that with thermo-nuclear weapons, provided the United States maintained its lead, another war was unlikely, but the Cold War would go on. The main British deterrent should be nuclear forces. This move towards a global strategy based upon the nuclear deterrent alongside conventional forces stationed in Europe, with a reduction of British forces in the Middle East was outlined in the February 1955 Statement on Defence.[3]

The problems of the Middle East changed with the development of the hydrogen bomb. Sir William Dickson, the Chief of the Air Staff, told the Cabinet on 2 June 1954:

> In view of the weight of atomic attack to which they would be subjected in the opening stages of a major war, the Russians were now less likely to be able to develop a substantial offensive through the Caucuses, and we had a better chance of holding them to the north-east of Iraq, possibly in the passes leading from Persia.[4]

The advent of thermo-nuclear weapons increased the vulnerability of concentrated base areas like the Canal base. With the formation of its military alliance in the Middle East, the Baghdad Pact, British defence policy moved towards a global strategy based upon the nuclear deterrent alongside conventional forces stationed in Europe. British forces in the Middle East were reduced.[5]

It was Winston Churchill's peacetime administration (1951–55) which oversaw the passing of British paramountcy in the Middle East.

Churchill had distinct views on the Middle East. It was Churchill as Colonial Secretary who had established the Middle East Department, persuaded T.E. Lawrence to join as an adviser on Arab affairs, effectively set up Feisal as King of Iraq in August 1921, and secured the agreement of the League of Nations to the provision of a local administration for Transjordan effectively separating it from Palestine. When Churchill visited Palestine in 1921 he rejected demands from the Arabs for the abolition of the principle of a national home for the Jews and the creation of a national government elected by those resident in Palestine before the war.

As Colonial Secretary, Churchill argued that the national home would be good for the Jews, the British Empire and the Arabs who dwelt in Palestine. Planting a tree on the site of the Hebrew university on Mount Scopus, Churchill said that personally his heart was full of sympathy for Zionism. The 1922 White Paper on Palestine which Churchill later referred to as his paper was a shrewd compromise: while suggesting continued support for Zionism it sought to reassure the Arabs and stated that Palestine would not constitute *the* national home, but merely *a* national home for the Jews with no subordination of the Arab population.[6]

Churchill frequently described himself as a Zionist. During the Second World War he fought the Foreign Office in an attempt to reverse British policy outlined in the May 1939 White Paper which effectively implied that Palestine would be controlled by the Arabs, and to secure a return to the policy of partition which would mean a separate Zionist state. Then, on 6 November 1944, Lord Moyne, the Minister Resident in the Middle East, was murdered in Cairo by the underground Zionist terrorist group, the Stern gang. Churchill told the House of Commons on 17 November that 'if our dreams for Zionism are to end in the smoke of assassins' pistols and our labours for its future to produce only a new set of gangsters worthy of Nazi Germany, many like myself will have to reconsider the position we have maintained so consistently in the past'. Plans for the future of Palestine could not be considered in such a climate: Churchill suspended British policy.[7]

On 6 July 1945, Churchill suggested that the United States should be invited to take over the Palestine mandate: 'I do not think we should take the responsibility upon ourselves of managing this very difficult place while the Americans sit back and criticize. ... I am not aware of the slightest advantage which has ever accrued to Great Britain from this painful and thankless task. Somebody else should have their turn now'. Indeed Ernest Bevin, as Foreign Secretary, in December 1946, wanted to pursue Churchill's suggestion and offer the mandate of Palestine to the United States before surrendering it to the

United Nations.[8] In March 1946 Churchill told Rabbi Abba Hillel Silver of the American Zionist Emergency Council that the only solution was for the United States to join Britain in maintaining a joint trusteeship over Palestine, in which both countries would share 'common responsibility'.

Churchill, however, did agree to support the Labour government's emergency measures in Palestine in the middle of 1946. This stand was again dictated by his dislike of terrorism. He wrote to the Prime Minister, Clement Attlee, that yielding to terrorism would be a disaster. But Churchill emphasized that he still felt bound by Britain's 'national pledges' to establish a Jewish national home in Palestine with immigration up to a limit of absorptive capacity of which the mandatory power would be the judge. It should be remembered that Churchill had wryly pointed out to President Roosevelt in August 1942 that an application of the Atlantic Charter to Asia and Africa could lead to claims by the Arab majority that they could expel the Jews from Palestine, and forbid further Jewish immigration.[9]

Following the blowing up of the King David Hotel on 22 July 1946 and Truman's prevarications over the provincial autonomy solution for Palestine, prevarications dictated by the Zionist lobby operating through the American Christian Palestine Committee and using the threat of punishment in the forthcoming congressional elections in November, Churchill thundered from the floor of the House of Commons on 1 August 1946:

> I think that the Government should say that if the United States will not come and share the burden of the Zionist cause, as defined or agreed, we should now give notice that we will return our Mandate to U.N.O. and that we will evacuate Palestine within a specified period.

Churchill said that the Zionists' claims now went beyond anything that had been agreed upon by Britain.[10] But, by the end of January 1947, Churchill was questioning the value of keeping 100,000 men in Palestine when they could be at home strengthening British industry; in August of that year he also criticized throwing away £30–40 million a year there.[11]

At the end of the First Arab–Israeli War Churchill was unimpressed with Bevin's warning in the House of Commons on 26 January 1949 that with over half a million Arabs being 'turned by the Jewish immigrants into homeless refugees without employment or resources', the tide of Arab nationalism was 'running high' and had bitten deep into the ordinary young Arab. Bevin commented: 'They consider that for the Arab population, which has been occupying Palestine for more than twenty centuries, to be turned out of their land and homes to make way for another race is a profound injustice', and wondered how the British people would feel if they had been asked to give up a slice of Scotland, Wales or Cornwall to another race. Churchill, in reply, argued that the coming into being of a Jewish state had to be seen in the perspective of 2,000 or even 3,000 years.[12]

As Prime Minister in the 1950s, Churchill very obviously preferred the Zionists and Israel to the Arabs. He was particularly scornful of the Egyptians who with the rise of the revolutionary Free Officers Movement had only recently discovered an Arab identity anyway. Churchill regarded the British presence in Egypt as a benevolent one. In the debate in the House of Commons on the 7 May 1946 over Attlee's statement that Britain was to withdraw all forces from Egyptian territory, Churchill accused Attlee of giving away the bargaining point at the outset. Rather than being suspicious he thought that the Egyptians should be grateful. Britain was throwing something away that had been built up with 'great labour'. The only way of ensuring that the Suez canal was kept open was to keep troops there.[13]

Churchill thought it 'of the utmost importance to get America in' to the Middle East. At the outset of his premiership he wrote to his friend, Lord Cherwell, that he found many unpleasant truths in the latter's observations that with India and Burma gone the Suez Canal was an international rather than a specifically British interest; with Middle Eastern oil falling into American hands was it not for the United States to defend it?; with the only reason for the defence of the Middle East being the need to prevent the Communists from gaining another large territory, did this not fall under the Truman doctrine and hence should it not be the United States rather than Britain that defended the Middle East?[14]

Churchill's Foreign Secretary, Anthony Eden, in the 1950s, like his master, based his reputation on having been seen to oppose Neville Chamberlain's policy for the 'appeasement' of Europe. He had resigned as Chamberlain's Foreign Secretary in February 1938 over relations with the United States. Eden, as he recorded in his memoirs, viewed the events of the 1950s through the spectacles of the 1930s. He was seen as being pro-Arab: in the late 1940s Zionist terrorists had sent him a letter bomb. At the end of the Second World War, Eden had thought it necessary to keep the Suez base, and had approved of British military bases in the area that became Libya. As Foreign Secretary in the 1950s, however, Eden's policy was to abandon exclusive British control of the Suez base, and to guide the Anglo-Egyptian condominium of the Sudan to self-determination. At this time he evidenced little liking for, or faith in, the United States. Sometimes he was worried about the possibility of the United States escaping again into isolationism; sometimes he feared that Washington's handling of the Cold War could precipitate actual war. He understood Britain's declining position and the growth of American power and influence, but, at times, had difficulty in accommodating to it emotionally. The assurance and even arrogance of some American leaders irritated Eden, particularly as he knew Britain to be financially dependent on the United States.

His relationship with the Republican Secretary of State, John Foster Dulles, was uneven. When the two men met on 13 November 1952, Eden agreed with Dulles' view that when the Western nations had to face non-Western problems such as those of Colonial Africa, Iran and China it was of the utmost importance that Washington, London and Paris should create a united position as contradictory policies would fail. Dulles recorded that their talk, on that occasion, was most cordial. Possibly alerted by Herbert Morrison to what was regarded as Dulles' duplicity over the apparent assurance that Japan would be able to recognize which Chinese government it wished, Eden was angry at the time of the Geneva conference of 1954 with what appeared to him as an American inability to realize that Britain had other allies, including Commonwealth partners, and felt that the United States seemed to be out to rule the world. On the other hand, in August 1956, he assured Dulles that he would go down in history as one of the great foreign ministers.[15]

Eden was assisted at the Foreign Office by Selwyn Lloyd as Minister of State, and by Anthony Nutting as the Parliamentary Under-Secretary of State for Foreign Affairs. When offered the post by Churchill, Lloyd, a barrister brought up as a Methodist and the son of a Welsh Liverpool dentist, reputedly described by Acheson as a 'crooked Welsh lawyer', told the Prime Minister that he did not like 'abroad' or foreigners, he had only been to foreign countries when serving in the army, and that he had never listened to a foreign affairs debate in the House of Commons. Churchill thought these positive advantages. Lloyd was 51 years old. Nutting, at thirty-five, good-looking and the heir to a baronetcy had served as Eden's Private Secretary in 1942 after being invalided out of the army, and was illustrated in *Punch* as a glove puppet called 'Eden's Eden'. Eden later supported him through his marital difficulties.[16]

With hindsight, Lloyd later recalled that the new Conservative government had to construct a policy for the Middle East. That policy was 'to preserve an anti-Soviet tier of defence, and behind it quietly and with honour and dignity reduce our commitments'. Evelyn Shuckburgh, Eden's Principal Private Secretary between 1951 and 1954, and then Assistant Under-Secretary at the Foreign Office until 1956, also later pointed to a Foreign Office view, shared to a point by Eden, that British interests in the Middle East, and Britain's increasing dependence on Middle Eastern oil, would have to be protected by agreements with Arab states rather than by holding onto positions of strength. It was necessary to eliminate irritants in Britain's relations with the Arab states. To defend the Middle East and its oil Britain needed to replace bilateral treaties with countries like Iraq and Jordan with multilateral mutual defence arrangements, arrangements that would seem less imperialistic to the Arabs and would help to spread the burden amongst the allies. To do this Britain needed to reach an agreement with Egypt allowing it to evacuate the Suez base. Egypt was especially important as it was seen to be the only Arab country 'with sufficient strength and detachment' to lead in efforts to secure a settlement between Israel and the Arab states that would offer Israel security and be guaranteed by the Great Powers.

It was Churchill's administration which negotiated an agreement with Egypt allowing evacuation of the Suez Canal base, a settlement with Iran which retrieved some of Britain's oil interests, and moved towards establishing a new defence agreement with Iraq which was incorporated into what became known as the Baghdad Pact in November 1955. Lloyd observed that during this period Britain's hope was to have a policy that would enable it to protect its oil interests and friends, and gradually establish, in Kuwait and elsewhere, governments that were viable and, hopefully, pro-British. There would be a continued British military presence but only in the Gulf at Bahrain, and in the Trucial States, but at comparatively small expense to Britain.[17]

On 29 October, Eden was presented with a review of Britain's position in the Middle East by the Eastern Department of the Foreign Office. In this paper, G.W. Furlonge argued that the situation in the Middle East was already serious and deteriorating. British influence had declined sharply in the recent past, and no other foreign influence had replaced it. As a result British and Western interests were threatened by xenophobic nationalism, and the inherent weaknesses of the states in the area and the strained relationships between them were creating conditions favourable to Soviet or Communist penetration. The Arab states, though at different stages of political development, were all politically immature. Parliamentary democracy, where it did exist, worked only imperfectly. Public opinion reflected the views of just the educated people in the towns. Power was in effect concentrated in a ruling élite, 'for the most part reactionary and corrupt and whose irresponsibility and personal rivalries create perpetual political instability and are responsible for a generally low standard of administration'. Though friendly to the West, the existing governments were confronted with extreme 'nationalist' elements, elements which lacked a national consciousness but who used catchwords like 'imperialism' and 'colonialism' to excite mob appeal. All this frustrated efforts to raise living standards, and it was 'only the influence of Islam, the absence of serious economic distress, and the generally patriarchal social structure' that had checked a drift to Communism which would otherwise have seemed inevitable. Iran suffered similar conditions, and there Mossadeq was indifferent to its economic future and wanted to remove foreign control of the oil industry. The stability of the British protected states in the Gulf was a welcome contrast, and Kuwait was rapidly becoming a major source of crude oil. Britain's relations with Israel, a country faced with grave economic troubles but saved by the determination and skill of its people, were good. Israel was moving towards the West. The Arab states, however, with nearly one million refugees, aimed at Israel's collapse and the British representatives in those countries agreed that pressure by the Western powers on Arab states would not achieve a settlement. The Arab states were divided amongst themselves.

Furlonge advised that the British withdrawals from India, and particularly from Palestine, had diminished the respect and influence Britain had formerly enjoyed throughout the Middle East. Jordan and Iraq still wanted close relations and looked to London for guidance. Israel wanted to cultivate a British connection. But because of Britain's still predominant position it attracted the forces of Arab and Iranian nationalism and xenophobia. Agitation for treaty revision in Iraq and Jordan was likely to develop into situations like the one prevailing in Egypt.

Although Washington had shown an increased interest in the Middle East the Eastern Department paper attributed this to the State Department's preoccupation with the possibility of Soviet penetration there. It suggested, however, that the American command of material resources had not resulted in a corresponding increase in Washington's influence: the Arab's resented the Palestine policy of the United States and its 'sometimes clumsy approach to the peoples and problems concerned'. Washington was determined to play a more important part in the Middle East in future, and this could only be 'beneficial to British interests provided that the somewhat exaggerated respect which they have hitherto tended to display towards Middle East nationalistic movements can be modified by experience so that undue encouragement is not given to their purely destructive aspects'.

France had cultural interests, wanted to preserve its crude oil supplies, re-establish as much as possible of their former political influence in Syria and the Lebanon, and stop developments in the Middle East from adversely influencing their position in North Africa. The Levant states and the Arab League, however, still suspected French interference in their affairs. The Soviet Union had paid comparatively little attention to the area.

Britain, faced with its financial straits, could not pursue alone the desired Western interests for the area of organizing its defence against Soviet aggression, promoting stable political and economic conditions in the Middle Eastern countries, and preserving economic interests, particularly oil. British policy in the area had to be closely co-ordinated with that of the United States, and, so far as possible, with France as well. To maintain a leading role in the Middle East, 'to which our experience and interests entitle us', and to preserve the area from the dangers threatening it, Britain had to match the incipient American efforts with renewed efforts of its own.[18]

Britain, however, did not have the money. The financial stringencies that forced a revised defence policy also led to a reduction of Britain's overseas commitments. In a Cabinet paper, dated 18 June 1952, Eden warned that rigorous maintenance of Britain's existing commitments placed a burden on the economy beyond Britain's resources. Britain could be faced with a choice between reducing its standard of living, or sinking to the level of a second class Power. Eden rejected the drastic and unilateral withdrawal from commitments: that could reflect a 'failure of will and relaxation of grip', and once a country's prestige started to slide there was no knowing where it would stop. The Foreign Secretary recommended that the only practical course was slowly to shed defence commitments in the Middle East and South-East Asia. This should be achieved by building up international defence organizations under the lead of the Americans.

When questioned by the Americans on 31 July 1952, Sir Oliver Franks, the British ambassador at Washington, explained that Britain could not set a definite time limit for the reduction of its forces in the Middle East; events as well as Britain's economic situation made that uncertain.

On 16 February 1953, Eden circulated a paper to the Cabinet in which he stated that in the second half of the twentieth century Britain could not hope to maintain its position in the Middle East by employing the methods used during the previous century. Commercial concessions, the benefits of which went to the Shahs and Pashas could no longer serve to strengthen British influence in those countries. Military occupation could be maintained by force, but this was of little use, say in Egypt, where the base needed to be staffed by local labour.

Eden went further:

> In most of the countries of the Middle East the social and economic aspirations of the common people are quickening and the tide of nationalism is rising fast. If we are to maintain our influence in this area, future policy must be designed to harness these movements rather than to struggle against them.

Britain's strategic purposes in the Middle East could no longer be served by arrangements which local nationalism would regard as military occupation by foreign troops. It did not matter from which country these troops came. It would be a delusion to suppose that in Egypt, or anywhere else in the Middle East, local opinion would 'tolerate occupation by American or French forces any more readily than the Egyptians tolerate the British garrison on the Canal'.

In his consideration of the redeployment of British forces in the Middle East, Churchill told the Cabinet, on 30 November 1953, that he thought the point of cardinal importance was to secure American agreement to a joint Anglo-American plan for the best disposition of forces in support of NATO. Eden, by January 1954, was moving towards a British policy in the Middle East based on close relations with Iraq and Jordan.[19]

There was also an American reassessment alongside that of the British. A paper, dated 27 December 1951, prepared by Henry S. Villard of the State Department's Policy Planning Staff for the National Security Council, offered an analysis of the Western dilemma in the Middle East similar to that which Eden presented to the Cabinet in March 1953. It too emphasized that Britain and the United States could not defend Western interests in the Middle East, an area where half the world's known oil reserves were located, in nineteenth-century fashion. Villard saw the threat to these interests as lying primarily within the Middle East states themselves, in hostility between the Arab states and Israel, and between the Arab states and the Western powers, particularly Britain, and also in the attitude of neutralism.

The declining ability of Britain to maintain and defend Western interests in the Middle East necessitated a review and restatement of American policy. The assumption of roles in Greece and Turkey were cited as instances of the transfer of major responsibility from Britain to the United States in the area. American influence had also largely replaced that of Britain in Saudi Arabia. But the

American ability was limited: it was in Washington's interest that Britain provide the forces to defend Western interests there. The declining ability of Britain to do this was not due to the inadequacy of British forces and Britain probably had sufficient troops in Cyprus, Egypt and Iraq to take local military action. Rather it was a complex phenomenon and could be explained partly in terms of Britain's decline as a world power. It was a measure of the nationalist aspirations of the Middle Eastern states intensified by what they believed was unjust exploitation, fostered by the United Nations charter and the independence of Pakistan, India and other Asiatic states which marked a new era in international affairs. Social and economic conditions in the Middle East had also lessened the grip of the ruling classes and the West's ability to maintain stability through them.

Whatever Washington could do to bolster Britain's power and prestige would help Britain to maintain stability in the Middle East and lessen the need for direct action by Washington or other allied powers. There was, however, the caveat that Western posture had to be regarded by the Middle Eastern states as being in their own interests. The Central Intelligence Agency identified anti-Western nationalism rather than Communism as the main threat to Western interests, and urged that Washington encourage the emergence of competent leaders well disposed towards the West. In May 1952, however, Britain's resources were seen as being inadequate for even the most minimal requirements in the Middle East. But divisions remained within the State Department and between the State Department and the Pentagon as to what Washington should do. Following a tour of the Middle East, Harold Hoskins of the Near Eastern Bureau, pointed also to a declining American influence in the Muslim world that derived from continued American support for Israel, and suggested that before the Americans adopted a more forward line in the Middle East they might try to build up 'areas of neutrality' there.[20]

When Dwight D. Eisenhower assumed the presidency at the beginning of 1953, he reassessed the Anglo-American relationship. Britain was no longer the special ally, and Eisenhower was determined that Washington should treat every country as a 'sovereign equal'. The Psychological Strategy Board, however, in a report dated 28 January 1953, pointed to Britain's influence as the leader of the British Commonwealth and Empire, combined with its remaining influence on the European continent, in the Middle East and other parts of the free world, as making it an 'invaluable ally' in securing acceptance in these areas for objectives important to Washington. A National Security Council Staff Study of 14 July 1953 stressed that in the Middle East it was in the security interest of America for Britain to 'continue to assume as much responsibility as is feasible under present conditions'. Although the trend was for American influence to replace that of Britain in the area as a whole, the British ability to 'aid in the preservation of Western security interests in the area should not be minimized'. But neither Washington nor London could either separately or together maintain and defend Western interests in the Middle East in the nineteenth-century fashion. With an eye to the Soviet Union, in trying to solve local problems in the Middle East,

Washington had to be careful not to worsen its relations with London. Washington should look forward to a regional defence organization in the Middle East in which it would participate, or with which it would be associated.

In January 1953 American intelligence offered the diagnosis that most Middle Eastern countries would remain determined to weaken if not abolish British influence and special privilege. Britain, however, for reasons of prestige, economic and military security could not relinquish its still substantial position. Too rapid an abandonment of the British position would leave a vacuum which Washington would find difficult to fill, and this would also encourage Soviet or local Communist exploitation. The difficulty for the Americans was that the Arabs feared Israeli aggression more than Soviet expansion, and suspected that a Western interest in defence was a camouflage for strengthening Western influence at the expense of Arab independence.

Some 18 months later, on 23 July 1954, the National Security Council offered a similar diagnosis, but with a greater emphasis on the need for American leadership. If the Middle East were to be preserved from communism the United States would need to increase its initiative, leadership and responsibility. To do this Washington would need to act in concert with London, while reserving its right to act with others, say France or Turkey, or alone. Although British and French influence had declined, Britain retained substantial interest, experience and security positions. But Washington had to convince the Arab states that it could act independently of other Western states and of Israel.[21]

Britain and the United States did discuss Middle East policy. Churchill, on his visit to Washington in January 1952, told Truman that close Anglo-American co-operation in the Middle East would 'divide the difficulties by ten'. The Prime Minister referred to the international task Britain was performing in the Canal Zone, and warned that Britain could not bear the burden indefinitely. Britain was not in the area to promote British imperialist interests. The United States should send a symbolic brigade to the Suez Canal area. Churchill reiterated these sentiments in his address to Congress, and warned that the danger in the Middle East was as great as that in Korea.

Churchill, however, was scornful of the supposed Soviet military threat to the Middle East. In April 1952 he wrote to Earl Alexander of Tunis, his Minister of Defence, that he did 'not understand how and when the anticipated Russian threat against the Middle East would eventuate'. Churchill thought that in any global war in 1952 and 1953 the Soviet armies would move swiftly to the ocean, subjugating the capitals of Western Europe within six weeks. But at the same time American atomic bombs would at least paralyse communications, apart from wireless messages, between the advancing Soviet armies and the central government. The Americans had explained to Churchill the effects of atomic bombing on Soviet industry, communications and oil fields. After all this Britain, if it survived, could take a new view of the matter. But Churchill could not see how an anticipated Soviet invasion of the Middle East and possibly North Africa fitted in: 'If Soviet Russia is shattered as an organic military force in the first three months of the War she will certainly not be in a position to cross the Sinai Peninsula and play about in the Western Desert.' Churchill argued that if the American atomic attack succeeded, it would be possible with conventional bombing to destroy the railway and other communications through Persia and Syria. It would not be easy for the Soviet Union to cross Turkey quickly. Churchill concluded:

> It is of course important to prevent infiltration into the Middle East in time of peace and to preserve the semblance at least of military power. But the idea of a heavy Russian invasion of the Middle East and across the Suez Canal into Egypt, Libya, Cyrenaica and Tripoli, is to my mind absurd. The best defence of the Middle East would be an overwhelming Air Force in Cyprus sustained by the necessary anti-submarine and air carrier forces. No surface fleet exists, even in imagination, for the American, British, French and Italian Navies to fight.[22]

There were occasions on which the Foreign Office noted the need to sit down and talk with the Americans, as at the beginning of 1954, when it seemed that the American plans for operating their forces in the Middle East were clashing with those of the Chiefs of Staff: both in the political and military fields American and British policy was not in tune. In June 1954, the Foreign Office warned that the Secretary of State, John Foster Dulles, had been convinced that American policy in the Middle East had been handicapped by a tendency to support British and French 'colonial' views, and this had meant that the United States was regarded as a colonial power by the peoples of the Middle East. Dulles thought that a result of this was that the Arab peoples were turning to the Soviet Union. Washington was likely to pursue a more independent policy in the Middle East and Africa. P.S. Falla, a counsellor in the Foreign Office, observed that Washington did not always realize that the chief guarantee of the security of the Middle East lay in the British garrison there and in Britain's treaty relations with Iraq and Jordan.[23]

In 1952 and 1953 British attempts to involved the Americans directly in the defence of the Middle East focused on what was called the Middle East Defence Organization (MEDO), a variation of the Middle East Command, proposed by British strategists on 22 January 1952. Seen as a planning, co-ordinating and liaison organization only, MEDO would be located in Cyprus, and not attached to NATO. American officials accepted this as a second best solution to the Middle East Command which had been rejected by the Egyptians. The overthrow of King Farouk in July 1952 delayed approaches to Cairo, and as Iraq, Syria and Lebanon in turn rejected the idea, the State Department cooled towards the scheme. By July 1953 the lack of Egyptian support had convinced Dulles that MEDO should be shelved.[24]

It was in Iran and Egypt that the traditional British position in the Middle East had been directly challenged. During Churchill's administration the situations were resolved. But the resolutions in both disputes involved the

United States, and Washington's involvement in the area increased as that of Britain declined.

For Churchill, the United States was central to any handling of the situation in Iran where Dr Muhammad Mossadeq, the Prime Minister, had challenged British paramountcy in the Middle East by nationalizing the Iranian oil industry, including the Anglo-Iranian Oil Company, on 2 May 1951. As officials of the Anglo-Iranian Oil Company prepared to evacuate the mainland fields and Abadan Island, Churchill told the then Prime Minister, Clement Attlee, that although he 'had never thought that the Persian oil-fields could be held by force', 'Abadan Island was quite another matter'.[25] Early in his career Churchill had helped to secure the change in the Royal Navy from coal to oil-fired ships. In the summer of 1914 Churchill personally had secured the largest share for the British government of the company operating the Persian (Iranian) concession so that the Royal Navy could be independent of Dutch and American firms who had control over the production and marketing of oil.[26] Churchill did not want the Americans to take over. Rather he envisaged common Anglo-American action in the face of the danger of a Soviet threat to the region between the Caspian Sea and the Persian Gulf.[27]

In the United States, *Time* magazine named Mossadeq the man of the year. Mossadeq's nationalization of the Anglo-Iranian Oil Company was referred to in terms of the ushering in of a new era: the pax Britannica was over and the United States had appeared in the Middle East as a sort of *deus ex machina*. *Time* reported that American correspondents in the area thought the British position hopeless. The United States had to make the West's policy in the Middle East or the inhabitants of the area would welcome communism.

Acheson pointed to the difference of his government's approach when he spoke to Eden on 4 November 1951. Acheson attributed this to the different information the two countries received from their embassies in Tehran. Britain seemed to think that Mossadeq might fall and be replaced by a more reasonable government. The advice he had was that the only alternative would be a communist regime. Some American policy makers might have been a little in awe of the British expertise and experience in Iran, but this did not include Acheson. He found Eden an improvement on Morrison with the exception of the Foreign Secretary's handling of the situation in Iran. Acheson believed that that policy largely derived from Sir Leslie Rowan, the Second Secretary at the treasury, a graduate of Queen's, Cambridge and described as being serious of purpose, but also having a rollicking sense of fun. Rowan, Acheson thought, had decreed that Mossadeq should be punished and this meant there could be no formula of retreat.

The new Conservative government considered the American proposals unacceptable: they would provide a wholly inadequate return on the capital Britain had invested in Iran and there was no assurance that the refinery at Abadan would be operated by British technicians.

Britain offered a proposal that the American oil companies should join in the operation of the refinery at Abadan, and, in return, grant Britain some share in the operation of their oil concessions in Saudi Arabia.[28] The joint appreciation from the American and British embassies in Tehran revealed an American view that nationalism in Iran was an overriding factor, whereas the British view was that nationalism could be controlled by firm handling. By the end of 1951, however, the Americans were coming around to the view that communism was not the only alternative to Mossadeq.

Churchill was angry at the thought that the Americans might give or lend money to Iran and 'prolong the present situation' to Britain's detriment. The British did not like American proposals put to Mossadeq while he was in the United States for medical treatment. They thought these endangered vital British interests and preferred a suggestion that the International Bank should try to make temporary arrangements for the operation of the Iranian oil industry pending a final settlement. On 6 January 1952 Churchill complained to Acheson that the Labour government had allowed 'Britain to be kicked out of Abadan in a most humiliating way'. Had he been Prime Minister, 'there might have been a splutter of musquetry, but Britain would have held firm'.

Truman did not increase aid to Tehran but he was under pressure: the new American ambassador in Tehran, Loy Henderson, warned of the possibility of Mossadeq developing closer relations with the Soviet Union, and the Joint Chiefs of Staff opined that Iran's orientation towards the United States was more important than Britain's position in the Middle East and Anglo-American collaboration in the area. After suspending military aid to Iran for four months, the United States agreed to resume that aid on 25 April 1952, Mossadeq resigned as a consequence of a dispute with the Shah over the right to appoint a War Minister. The Shah appointed Ahmad Qavam in Mossadeq's place, a man approved of by British officials. But Qavam was overthrown in riots, and Mossadeq reinstated.

In July 1952 C.M. Woodhouse of MI6 started flying arms from British air force bases in Iraq to Iran, in the hope of being able to strengthen tribesmen sympathetic to Britain. Then, on 22 July, the International Court of Justice ruled that it had no jurisdiction in the oil dispute. On 29 July Eden told the Cabinet that Mossadeq's position in Iran had been greatly strengthened, and that there was no early prospect of a favourable development in the oil dispute.[29] On 5 August 1952 Washington put forward a proposal including a grant of $10 million to Iran. Britain should agree to buy oil stored in Iran and Mossadeq should accept international arbitration to determine the compensation to be paid to the Anglo-Iranian Oil Company. Eden thought this constituted betrayal on the part of the Americans. Churchill suggested to Truman that the two leaders should send a joint telegram to Mossadeq; the alternative was that the United States would be blackmailed by Iran to the detriment of its 'greatest friend'. At first Truman refused: it would look too much like the 'two nations ganging up'. The Prime Minister responded that from Washington's point of view it would be an unprofitable course to pay Iran indefinite sums of money so that it did not become communist. Truman gave way.[30]

As the Americans pursued an independent policy, Churchill told the Cabinet on 30 September 1952 that Britain 'must do all in our power to maintain a joint Anglo-American pressure on the Persian Government, though in the last resort we had no means of preventing the United States Government from financing Dr. Mossadeq in the hope of preventing Persia from going Communist'.[31] On 22 October, Iran broke off diplomatic relations with Britain. Eden authorized Woodhouse to set up a joint operation with the American Central Intelligence Agency to overthrow Mossadeq. The proposals were put to the Central Intelligence Agency, and Kermit (Kim) Roosevelt, the head of that body's operations in the Middle East took charge of plans for the envisaged coup.[32]

An Anglo-American front emerged. On 20 February 1953 Washington and London proposed to Mossadeq a scheme under which Iran would control the country's oil industry provided that adequate compensation was paid to Anglo-Iranian, and the Americans would make available immediate loans that could be repaid with oil. Mossadeq rejected the plan. But he faced increasing internal difficulties. On 19 January 1953 the Majlis agreed to extend Mossadeq's dictatorial powers for one year. The Senate objected. Mossadeq won a referendum on the issue. Although still supported by the Tudeh Party and Soviet sponsors, Mossadeq found himself deserted by former allies particularly by Islamic leaders who were alienated by his schemes to nationalize businesses and enfranchise women.

On 6 March Eisenhower told Dulles and Eden that if the negotiations with Iran failed, there should be a new and imaginative approach to solve the oil dispute and keep Iran on the side of the West. While the British were prepared to wait, the Americans wanted action. The British, by April 1953, were in no hurry. Mossadeq should be left alone for 'quite a long time'. Anglo-Iranian had discovered new oil fields and there was increased refining capacity in Aden and Australia. Indeed it was debatable whether it was in Britain's interests to reach a settlement at all so long as Middle East oil was in surplus and tankers plentiful. The difficulty was the Americans and their concern about the prospect of cheap Iranian oil coming onto world markets as a result of the easing in the tanker and freight situation. This seemed to be more of a concern than the Communist bogey. It was necessary to convince Washington that its fears of cheap Iranian oil were exaggerated. Britain had, in the long term, to achieve a policy with which both American and British oil companies could be associated. In any case internal pressures might force the Iranians to seek a compromise.[33]

Although it was Herbert Morrison, the Labour Foreign Secretary, who initiated the overthrow of Mossadeq by covert means, it was Churchill who overrode the Foreign Office's attempts to curtail the conspiracy in February 1953, and authorized the operation to overthrow Mossadeq. At the end of June, Eisenhower approved the plan put forward by the Central Intelligence Agency. Kim Roosevelt took charge of the coup operations. The Shah hesitated to sign decrees dismissing Mossadeq and appointing General Fazullah Zahedi as Prime Minister. But he was convinced finally that the British and American governments supported the plan by codes inserted in a speech by Eisenhower, and in a Persian-language broadcast by the British Broadcasting Corporation. In August, Tudeh Party supporters demonstrated with anti-Royalist slogans. Provocateurs were used by Western intelligence to frighten Iranians into believing that a victory for Mossadeq would be against Islam and mean Soviet influence. At one point Zahedi took refuge in the American embassy compound, and the Shah flew to Rome. Roosevelt helped to organize the allies of the Shah, and on 19 August Mossadeq was deposed by troops. The Shah returned on 22 August 1953, and Zahedi became Prime Minister. On 5 September the United States announced aid to Iran of $45 million.[34]

Churchill, on 25 August 1953, warned the Cabinet about his fears of an American takeover in the area, and supported the arguments of Lord Salisbury, the Lord President, that Britain needed to give financial aid to the new Iranian government along with the United States, and find a solution to the oil dispute, or 'sacrifice all prospect of re-establishing British influence in Persia'. Churchill hoped that support of the new government would be undertaken on an Anglo-American basis. The Prime Minister warned: 'In present circumstances it would be easy for the Americans by the expenditure of a relatively small sum of money to reap all the benefit of many years of British work in Persia.'[35]

The Americans suggested the creation in Iran of a consortium of oil companies in which British and American companies would hold roughly equal interests. On 7 January 1954 Eden told the Cabinet that if American companies were given a share in the marketing of Iranian oil, there would be a corresponding reduction in oil production, mainly by American companies in other parts of the Middle East. This could apply to the oil field discovered near Buraimi. The Foreign Secretary thought that it would be to the general advantage if it could be arranged that both British and American companies were interested in the exploitation of oil in each of the oil-producing countries of the Middle East. The Iranians were adamant that the Anglo-Iranian Oil Company would not be allowed to return, and Britain acknowledged that the formation of an international group was the only way to achieve a solution.

The National Security Council decided that it would be in the interest of the United States for American companies to participate in a consortium for Iranian oil, and that companies should be free to sell oil in any market at any price. The Persia Committee of the Cabinet on 2 February 1954 agreed that American companies might be allowed 40 per cent, provided Anglo-Iranian also had 40 per cent and the remaining share, apart from a small percentage for the French, was taken by the Shell group controlled by the Dutch. Initially, Britain had wanted 50 per cent for Anglo-Iranian, but the Americans would not allow it. On 11 February 1954 the acting Secretary of State, Humphrey, told the National Security Council that the time had come for Washington to take firm action on a government-to-government basis to save the consortium plan.

Indeed, in the middle of March Dulles warned about the dangers to the Anglo-American working relationship in the Middle East and elsewhere of a failure to settle the Iranian oil dispute. The Secretary of State said that Washington had been trying: first to establish a country capable of resisting Communist penetration; secondly, to preserve foreign investors' rights against expropriation. It could prove necessary to concentrate on the former. Dulles went on to say that it had been his policy to work closely with Britain in the Middle East, to leave Britain in the lead, and generally to defer to Britain's judgement. But problems did not seem to get settled, and Washington had observed a tendency on London's part 'to overstay the market'. There was still no solution in Egypt. If London and Washington could not agree on the oil problem, the American administration 'would have more often to take their own line and rely on their own judgment in dealing with Middle Eastern countries and problems'. Dulles did not want to do this, and he realized the consequences for Anglo-American relations. But he thought that a turning point had been reached not only in the oil dispute, but in the policy of Anglo-American solidarity in Middle Eastern affairs. At a meeting of the Operations Coordinating Board Working Group of the National Security Council held on 18 March 1954, Judge Stanley N. Barnes warned that there had to be concrete action to support Dulles' warning: while the United States gave no indication of taking any action the British felt that time was playing into their hands.

In August Sir Roger Stevens, the British ambassador at Tehran, reported on the 'decisiveness, intelligence, realism and rectitude' shown by the Iranian delegation to the oil negotiations. On 5 August 1954, Iran reached an agreement with the Western oil companies. Under the new terms the Anglo-Iranian Oil Company, which had become British Petroleum, owned only 40 per cent of the assets of the new company. Initially the other 40 per cent was held by five American companies, 14 per cent by Royal Dutch Shell, and 6 per cent by the French Petroleum Company. The share of British capital invested in the oil industry of the Middle East dropped from 49 to 14 per cent, and the British share of oil production from 53 to 24 per cent. The American share increased from 44 to 58 per cent, and the American companies controlled 42 per cent of the capital.[36]

Churchill interfered with Middle East policy. He suspected the area's strategic value. But it was policy towards Egypt which particularly interested him, and which he was determined to control. The Prime Minister had his own ideas, and he fought his Foreign Secretary and suspected the advice of the Chiefs of Staff. At times Churchill wanted to work with the Americans over Egypt; at times he felt that they could be ignored.[37]

When he became Prime Minister, Churchill told the Cabinet on 30 October 1951 that it was the duty of the British government to keep the Suez Canal open to the shipping of the world, using force if necessary.[38] Churchill scorned the Egyptians. He resented their 'cheek', and in private told Eden to let them know if they continued in that vein, 'we shall set the Jews on them and drive them into the gutter, from which they should never have emerged'.[39] When Egyptian crowds ran riot in Cairo on 26 January 1952, burning Shepheards Hotel and the

BOAC offices, symbols of British imperialism, Churchill wrote to Eden that the 'horrible behaviour of the mob puts them lower than the most degraded savages now known'.[40] Churchill did not approve of the Foreign Office's attempts to negotiate with the new Egyptian government about the defence of the Canal Zone. The Prime Minister was in no hurry. He felt that Britain could negotiate from strength: Egypt had almost lost its place among civilized states; whereas Britain had remained firm, cool, resolute and immovable.[41]

In Cabinet, the Prime Minister opposed his Foreign Secretary. On 18 February 1952, Churchill objected to the proposal that the Suez base installations should be handed over to the Egyptian government as a preliminary to their being made available to the Allied Middle East Command, and insisted that British responsibility should be transferred directly to that command. Despite Eden's warnings, Churchill's amendment was approved.[42] Eden remonstrated with Churchill on 10 March 1952: without agreement Britain would have to leave in 1956 anyway; and, if Britain had to maintain its position in the Canal Zone by force there would be no troops available for the defence of the Middle East. Even Churchill viewed that as a difficult situation. Moreover, Eden insisted that the plain fact was that Britain was no longer in a position to impose its will on Egypt: 'If I cannot impose my will, I must negotiate.' Churchill started to consider what could be saved from the wreck. He could not understand why Britain was 'giving everything into Egypt's power and have nothing in return nor any means of securing the fulfilment of any understanding'.[43]

After the coup in Cairo on 22 July 1952, when a group of military officers seized power, Churchill did not like the idea of broaching the scheme for a Middle East Defence Organization with the new leader, Muhammad Neguib. The moment might be propitious, and Cairo wanted British military equipment, but Churchill thought this a dangerous bait. As an old Harrovian he wrote to the Etonian Eden: 'I believe it is an Eton custom to make parents of pupils pay for the birch.'[44] Eden had to remind his Prime Minister that failure to settle with Egypt could have serious consequences for the defence of the whole Middle East.[45]

While in the United States in January 1953 Churchill discussed the Middle East with the new American president, Eisenhower. It was Eisenhower who demoted Britain from being the special ally to just one among a number of allies, and the President hinted at this revision of the special relationship: while Britain and the United States should work together in the Middle East, there should be 'no collusion'.[46]

Churchill returned 'passionately interested' in the Egyptian situation. Furious at Eden's policy, he commented that he had 'not known that Munich was situated on the Nile', and John Colville, Churchill's private secretary, was left with the impression that Churchill would never give way over Egypt.[47] The Prime Minister explained the tactics he envisaged to his Foreign Secretary:

This military dictator is under the impression that he has only to kick us to make us run. I would like him to kick us and show him that we did not run. . . . Unless you can show that we have imposed our will upon Neguib you will find it very difficult to convince the Conservative Party that the evacuation of the Suez Canal Zone conforms with British interest or prestige.[48]

While Eden fought to secure American support for Britain's stand against Neguib in negotiating a new Anglo-Egyptian treaty, Churchill wanted Britain 'to go on alone' and was backed by Field Marshal Sir William Slim.[49] Early in April 1953, Eden fell ill and Churchill took over policy towards Egypt. Just before taking over, Churchill let Eden know that he did not like Britain being treated by the United States as if it were one of an equal crowd.[50] At this time Churchill was excited by a Foreign Office document on the validity of the Anglo-Egyptian treaty of 1936. It argued that as Egypt had denounced the treaty Egypt was no longer entitled to require negotiation for a revision. Pending revision, or unless both parties agreed to terminate the treaty it remained in full force. In 1956 the continued presence of the British troops could be dependent on whether Egypt was able to defend the canal, and that issue could be submitted by either parties to arbitration, in effect by the United Nations.[51]

It was against this background that talks between Britain and Egypt were opened in Cairo. Initially, the American attitude seemed unhelpful: there were fears that Washington was due to offer Cairo economic and military aid. Churchill drafted an angry note to Eisenhower reminding him of the Anglo-American agreement on the 'package': the Prime Minister had hoped for at least 'moral aid' from the United States. Eisenhower pleaded that he might not have understood the background. The President agreed to delay the whole matter until Dulles had seen Neguib. Churchill's initial response was blunt:

I should find it very difficult if our soldiers were killed and the massacre of our people as well perhaps as Americans were taking place in Cairo, to justify your support of the creation of an Egyptian army under the tutelage of Nazi criminals and furnished with American weapons.[52]

By the time Eden returned to the Foreign Office, Churchill had come around to the view that American help might be necessary. The Prime Minister was increasingly disturbed by the prospect of a back bench revolt: some government supporters were convinced that British troops should remain in Egypt to ensure the right of free transit through the Suez Canal. But Churchill did concede that the strategic importance of the base in peace and war was much less than it had been.

At the Bermuda conference in December 1953 the Americans did not give way to British demands. Eisenhower's relevant briefing paper for this conference pointed to the lack of agreement between Britain and the United States as to their respective roles in the Middle East, and argued that it was Britain's declining position that was at the heart of this matter. The British felt that they should be given a free hand in representing Western interests in the Middle East, that they had superior knowledge as a result of their long experience in the area, and that the Americans were amateurs. The paper did emphasize that Washington was not attempting to replace London in the Middle East or to vie with it on matters of prestige. Washington's interest derived from East–West tensions. The United States had, for generations, been content to look upon the Middle East as being in the British sphere of influence. But the existing state of affairs in that area was a threat to American security and Britain no longer had the ability to correct the situation. If Washington were to be effective in the Middle East it had at times to maintain an independent posture. Henry A. Byroade, the Assistant Secretary of State, presented Eden with a new formula which the Foreign Secretary thought inadequate as it gave no automatic right to return to the base even in the event of a United Nations decision. Churchill warned Eisenhower that although the Egyptian issue might seem petty to the Americans, it was one that could cause 'a deep and serious setback' to Anglo-American relations and that would be a disaster for all.[53]

Churchill faced increasing opposition to his Egyptian policy. In Egypt itself, at a time of disturbances in the Sudan early in March during which Churchill briefly contemplated a British occupation of Khartoum, the power base shifted from Neguib to Gamal Abdul Nasser. Britain had financial difficulties and only evacuation from the Canal Zone seemed to offer the prospect of substantial savings. This helped to convince Churchill of the need for a settlement with Egypt.[54] On 11 March Evelyn Shuckburgh, who had responsibility for Middle East policy, at a Foreign Office meeting suggested a new positive approach to Egypt: after all, the Egyptians had said they would allow Britain to re-enter the base if there were a threat of aggression against Turkey, and that really left only the issue of whether British technicians remaining on the base could wear uniforms and bear personal arms. Eden asked the Cabinet to consider whether essential installations on the base could not be maintained by civilian contract labour. He was supported by the Minister of Defence, Field Marshal Lord Alexander; the new proposal would enable Britain to remove all its troops from Egypt, reduce its overseas military expenditure, and redeploy forces in the Middle East to better advantage. Churchill, however, favoured an alternative policy: Britain should break off the defence negotiations with Egypt and start its programme of redeployment.[55]

Opposed by Eden, the Foreign Office and the military, Churchill would not give up Egypt. Early in April 1954 he reminded Eden of his 'constant interest' in the problem.[56] Churchill wanted American involvement, and approaches from Washington over the possibility of a collective defence organization for South-East Asia, led the Prime Minister to hope that the Americans might be persuaded to join the British in a similar assurance about the security of the Middle East and the Suez Canal. Eden, however, doubted whether the Americans could be persuaded.[57] The Cabinet debated the whole approach on 22 June 1954. It was emphasized that Britain's strategic needs had been radically changed by the development of thermo-nuclear weapons. It was no longer expedient to maintain so large a concentration of stores, equipment and men within the narrow confines of the Canal Zone. Churchill accepted the military argument for redeploying the British forces in the Middle East. But he remained impressed by the political disadvantages of abandoning the position Britain had held in Egypt since 1882. The Prime Minister felt that if the settlement could be presented as part of a comprehensive Anglo-American plan for building up a defensive front against Communist aggression throughout the world, it might become more acceptable to sections of the Conservative party.[58]

Churchill finally gave in to Eden. On 26 and 27 July 1954, in Washington, the Prime Minister and Foreign Secretary discussed the whole problem with Eisenhower and Dulles. Churchill specifically mentioned that initially he had thought it best that any agreement should be between Britain and the United States on one side, and Egypt on the other. But he acknowledged that the Americans would not participate unless invited to do so by the Egyptians.[59] Eden was able to tell the Cabinet on 7 July that Washington had gone as far as could be expected to meet British requirements. The provision of American economic aid to Egypt would be conditional on the Egyptian fulfilment of any agreement relating to the Canal Zone base, the United States would also support publicly the principal of free transit through the Suez Canal. Churchill confessed, that despite his earlier doubts, he was now satisfied that the withdrawal of British troops from Egypt could be justified fully on military grounds. British requirements in the Canal zone had been radically altered by Turkey's admission to NATO and the extension of a defensive Middle East front as far east as Pakistan. Thermo-nuclear weapons had increased the vulnerability of a concentrated base area and it would not be right to continue to keep 80,000 troops in Egypt who would be better placed elsewhere. Churchill was supported by Alexander, the Minister for Defence.[60] Churchill used these arguments against the Conservative 'Suez group' rebels in the House of Commons at the end of the month when 27 Conservatives voted against the government.[61]

The Secretary of State for War, Anthony Head, led the British delegation to Cairo to work out an agreement with the Egyptians along the lines agreed by the Cabinet. The new Minster of State, Anthony Nutting, finalized the arrangements early in October and the agreement was signed on 19 October 1954. The terms included: the maintenance of the base in peacetime by British and Egyptian civilian technicians; provision for placing the Suez base on a war footing if an attack took place on certain Arab states or Turkey; the withdrawal of British armed forces from Egypt within 20 months of the signature; and confirmation of the 1888 convention on freedom of navigation in the Suez Canal.[62]

Notes

1. Public Record Office, London, CAB 131/12, Annex 1, D(52)26, Report by the Chiefs of Staff for the Defence Committee of the Cabinet on Defence Policy and Global Strategy, Top Secret, 17 June 1952; Ritchie Ovendale (ed.), *British Defence Policy since 1945: Documents in Contemporary History* (Manchester, 1994), pp. 88–90; for an account of Britain's position in the world economy at this time see David Reynolds, *British Policy and World Power in the 20th Century* (London, 1991), pp. 206–10.
2. CAB 128/25, fos 344–5, CC102(52), Secret, 4 December 1952.
3. Ovendale (ed.), *British Defence Policy*, pp. 97–109; William Jackson and Lord Bramall, *The Chiefs: The Story of the United Kingdom Chiefs of Staff* (London, 1992), pp. 281–93.
4. CAB 128/27 pt. 1, fol. 284, CC37(54)3, Secret, 2 June 1954.
5. *Cmd. 9391, Statement of Defence 1955*, (London, February 1955). For accounts of British defence policy in the Middle East see: Wm. Roger Louis, *The British Empire in the Middle East 1945–1951* (Oxford, 1985), pp. 103–380; David R. Devereux, *The Formulation of British Defence Policy towards the Middle East, 1948–56* (London, 1990); Ritchie Ovendale, *The English-Speaking Alliance: Britain, the United States, the Dominions and the Cold War 1945–51* (London, 1985), pp. 89–142; Ovendale (ed.), *British Defence Policy since 1945*, pp. 1–130.
6. Ritchie Ovendale, *The Origins of the Arab–Israeli Wars*, (2nd edn, London, 1992), pp. 53–8.
7. Ritchie Ovendale, *Britain, the United States, and the End of the Palestine Mandate, 1942–1948* (Woodbridge, Suffolk, 1989), p. 32. Michael Cohen suggests that Churchill's Zionism was predicated by imperial considerations and that the murder of Lord Moyne 'convinced Churchill that the Zionists were not to be relied upon as colonial clients', see Michael Cohen, *Churchill and the Jews* (London, 1985), p. 329.
8. Ovendale, *Britain, the United States, and the End of the Palestine Mandate*, pp. 64–5, 183.
9. Ibid., pp. 128, 40.
10. Ibid., p. 153.
11. Louis, *The British Empire in the Middle East*, pp. 467, 11.
12. Ovendale, *The Origins of the Arab–Israeli Wars*, pp. 139–40.
13. See Timothy H.A. Owen, 'Britain and the Revision of the Anglo-Egyptian Treaty, 1949-1954' (Ph.D. thesis, University of Wales, Aberystwyth, 1991), pp. 18–20; Louis, *The British Empire in the Middle East*, pp. 238–41; Wm. Roger Louis, 'Churchill and Egypt', in Robert Blake and Wm. Roger Louis (eds), *Churchill* (Oxford, 1993), pp. 473–8.
14. Eisenhower Library, Abilene, Ann Whitman File, Dulles–Herter Series, Box no. 1, File Dulles John F. Prior Inauguration, Dulles to Eisenhower, 14 November 1952; Public Record Office, London, PREM 11/208, fol. 6, M16(C)/51, Churchill to Lord Cherwell, 10 November 1951; fol. 7, Lord Cherwell to Churchill, 8 November 1951.
15. Ritchie Ovendale, *'Appeasement' and the English Speaking World: Britain, the United States, the Dominions, and the Policy of 'Appeasement', 1937–1939* (Cardiff,

1975), pp. 93–116; Victor Rothwell, *Anthony Eden: A Political Biography 1931–57* (Manchester, 1992), pp. 116, 120, 128; Evelyn Shuckburgh, *Descent to Suez Diaries 1951–56* (London, 1986), pp. 168–204; Anthony Eden, *Full Circle* (London, 1960), foreword, p. 99; Victor Bator, *Vietnam: A Diplomatic Tragedy: Origins of U.S. Involvement* (London, 1977), pp. 70, 73, 105, 134; Leonard Mosley, *Dulles: A Biography of Eleanor, Allen, and John Foster Dulles and Their Family Network* (London, 1978), pp. 411–3.

16. Selwyn Lloyd, *Suez 1956: A Personal Account* (London, 1978), p. 4; Keith Kyle, *Suez* (London, 1992), pp. 86–7; Shuckburgh, *Diaries*, p. 312, Diary 15 December 1955.
17. Lloyd, *Suez 1956*, p. 79; Shuckburgh, *Diaries*, p. 210.
18. Public Record Office, London, FO 371/91200, E1057/8, Memorandum by G.W. Furlonge on Middle East policy, 29 October 1951.
19. Anthony Adamthwaite, 'Introduction: The Foreign Office and Policy-making', in John W. Young (ed.), *The Foreign Policy of Churchill's Peacetime Administration 1951–1955* (Leicester, 1988), pp. 1–28 at pp. 8–9; PREM 11/49, fos 21–5, Franks to Foreign Office, Telegram no. 822, Top Secret, 1 August 1952 recd. 3 August 1952; PREM 11/1475, fos. 2–4, Norman Brook to Eden, 14 April 1956; CAB 128/26 pt 2, fol. 540, CC73(53)3, Secret, 30 November 1953; W. Scott Lucas, *Divided We Stand: Britain, the US and the Suez Crisis* (London, 1991), p. 31.
20. *FRUS* 1951(5), pp. 257–64, Draft study by the National Security Council on the position of the United States with respect to the general area of the Eastern Mediterranean and Middle East, Top Secret, 27 December 1951; Lucas, ibid pp. 13–4; Devereux, *British Defence Policy*, pp. 111–2; H.W. Brands, 'The Cairo–Tehran Connection in Anglo-American Rivalry in the Middle East, 1951–1953', *The International History Review*, XI (1989), pp. 434–56 at p. 444; *FRUS* 1952–4(9), pp. 256–62, Memorandum by Hoskins to Byroade, Secret, 25 July 1952.
21. Robert H. Ferrell (ed.), *The Eisenhower Diaries* (New York, 1981), pp. 222–4, Diary 6 January 1953; Eisenhower Library, Abilene, White House Office, Office of the Special Assistant for National Security Affairs, Records 1952–61, Special Assistant Series, Presidential Series, Box no. 1, File Presidential Papers 1953(10), An evaluation of the psychological impact in the United Kingdom of United States Foreign Economic Policies and Programs, Confidential, 28 January 1953; Eisenhower Library, Abilene, White House Office, National Security Council Staff Papers, 1948–61, NSC Series, Policy Paper Subseries, Box no. 5, File NSC155/1-Near East(2), National Security Council Staff Study on United States Objectives and Policies with respect to the Near East, Top Secret, 14 July 1953; *FRUS* 1952–4(9), pp. 334–43, National Intelligence Estimate on conditions and trends in the Middle East affecting American security, Secret, 15 January 1953; pp. 525–32, Statement of policy by the National Security Council on American objectives with respect to the Near East, Top Secret, 23 July 1954.
22. PREM 11/49, fos 180–3, M190/52, Churchill to Alexander, Top Secret, 3 April 1952.
23. *FRUS* 1952–4(9), pp. 171–6, Minutes of meeting at the White House, Top Secret, 8 January 1952; Martin Gilbert, *Winston S. Churchill 'Never Despair' 1945–1965* (London, 1988), pp. 688–9; Ayesha Jalal, 'Towards the Baghdad Pact: South Asia and the Middle East Defence in the Cold War, 1947–1955', *The International*

History Review, XI (1989), pp. 409–33 at pp. 430–1; FO 371/110828, fos 5–8, V1196/3, Minute by Falla on Middle East defence, Secret, June 1954.

24. Peter L. Hahn, 'Containment and Egyptian Nationalism: The Unsuccessful Effort to Establish the Middle East Command, 1950–53', *Diplomatic History*, XI (1987), pp. 23–40 at pp. 32–8; *FRUS* 1952–4(9), pp. 249–51, Acheson to Department of State, Top Secret, 27 June 1952; pp. 251–4, Acheson to Department of State, Secret, 27 June 1954.

25. Louis, *The British Empire in the Middle East*, p. 672.

26. Gilbert, *Winston S. Churchill*, p. 617.

27. Ibid., pp. 617–8.

28. Moyara de Moraes Ruehsen, 'Operation "Ajax" Revisited: Iran, 1953', *Middle Eastern Studies*, XXIX (1993), pp. 467–86 at pp. 468–9; FO 800/812, fol. 8, Per/51/5, O. Harvey to Foreign Office, Telegram no. 457, Secret, 5 November 1951; *FRUS* 1952–4(10), pp. 256–8, Memorandum of Conversation by Acheson, Secret, 4 November 1951; James A. Bill, 'America, Iran, and the politics of intervention, 1951–1953', in James A. Bill and Wm. Roger Louis (eds), *Mussadiq, Iranian Nationalism, and Oil* (London, 1988), pp. 261–95 at p. 279; Dean Acheson, *Present at the Creation* (London, 1970), p. 511; John Colville, *The Fringes of Power. Downing Street Diaries 1939–55* (London, 1985), pp. 764–5; CAB 128/23, fol. 19, CC51(5)6, Secret, 8 November 1951.

29. FO 371/91472, EP1024/10, G19002/18/51, Middleton to Furlonge, Confidential, 19 November 1951; Minute by A.K. Rothnie, 13 December 1951; George McGhee, *Envoy to the Middle World: Adventures in Diplomacy* (New York, 1983), pp. 388–404; PREM 11/725, fol. 24, M89C/51, Churchill to Foreign Office, 24 November 1951; fol. 22, Foreign Office to Washington, Telegram no. 5796, Confidential, 27 November 1951; fos 9–11, PM/51/138, Eden to Churchill; H.W. Brands, 'The Cairo–Tehran Connection in Anglo-American Rivalry in the Middle East, 1951–1953', *The Review of International History*, XI (1989), pp. 434–56 at pp. 440–3; Ritchie Ovendale, *The Longman Companion to the Middle East since 1914* (London, 1992), pp. 66–7; CAB 128/25, CC74(52)6, Secret, 29 July 1952.

30. Brands, ibid., pp. 449–50; FO 800/813, fol. 13, Per/52/11, Foreign Office to Washington, Telegram no. 3403, Secret, 20 August 1952; fol. 17, Per/52/14, Franks to Foreign Office, Telegram no. 1588, Secret, 21 August 1952 recd. 22 August 1952; fol. 24, Per/52/17, Foreign Office to Washington, Telegram no. 3503, Secret, 23 August 1952; fol. 28, Franks to Foreign Office, Telegram no. 1611, Secret, 24 August 1952.

31. CAB 128/25, fol. 213, CC82(52)5, Secret, 30 September 1952.

32. C.M. Woodhouse, *Something Ventured* (London, 1982), pp. 120–2.

33. Ruehsen, pp. 472–5; FO 371/104615, EP1531/243, Minute by P.E. Ramsbotham on future policy with regard to Iranian oil, Secret, 14 April 1953.

34. Bill, p. 286; Wm. Roger Louis, 'Mussadiq and the dilemmas of British imperialism', in Bill and Louis (eds), *Mussadiq, Iranian Nationalism, and Oil*, pp. 252–6; Kermit Roosevelt, *Countercoup: The Struggle for the Control of Iran* (New York, 1979), pp. 87–9, 119; Brian Lapping, *End of Empire* (London, 1985), pp. 216–23.

35. CAB 128/26 pt. 2, fol. 388, CC50(53)4, Secret, 25 August 1953.

36. CAB 128/26 pt. 2, fol. 543, CC74(53)3, Secret, 1 December 1953; CAB 128/27 pt. 1, fos 31–2, CC1(54)2, Secret, 7 January 1954; PREM 11/726, fos 267–8,

Foreign Office to Representatives, Telegram no. 13, Secret, 13 January 1954; fol. 258, Makins to Foreign Office, Telegram no. 163, Secret, 22 January 1954 recd. 23 January 1954; fos 248–52, POM(54)1, Secret, 2 February 1954; fos 245–7, P(M)(54)1st Meeting, Secret, 3 February 1954; fos 192–3, R. Makins to Foreign Office, Telegram no. 448, Confidential, 17 March 1954; Eisenhower Library Abilene, NSC Series 1951–61, Box 5, Discussion at the 184th Meeting of the National Security Council on 11 February 1954, Top Secret, 12 February 1954; NSC Staff Papers, 1948–61, Operations Coordinating Board Central File Series, Box 42, File OCB 091.Iran (3) January–May 1954, Memorandum of meeting of OCB Working Group on NSC 5402(Iran) on 18 March 1954, Top Secret, 22 March 1954; Ovendale, *Origins of the Arab–Israeli Wars*, p. 154.

37. See Ritchie Ovendale, 'Egypt and the Suez Base Agreement', in Young (ed.), *Foreign Policy*, pp. 137–55; Wm. Roger Louis, 'The Tragedy of the Anglo-Egyptian Settlement of 1954' in Wm. Roger Louis and Roger Owen (eds), *Suez 1956. The Crisis and its Consequences* (Oxford, 1989), pp. 43–71; W. Scott Lucas, 'The Path to Suez: Britain and the Struggle for the Middle East, 1953–56', in Anne Deighton (ed.), *Britain and the First Cold War* (London, 1990), pp. 253–72; Louis, 'Churchill and Egypt', in Blake and Louis (eds) *Churchill*, pp. 480–90; Owen, *Britain and the Revision of the Anglo-Egyptian Treaty 1949–1954*, pp. 234–493. Accounts of American policy towards Egypt at this time can be found in Laila Amin Morsy, 'The Role of the United States in the Anglo-Egyptian Agreement of 1954', *Middle Eastern Studies*, XXIX (1993), pp. 526–58; Muhammad Abd el-Wahab Sayed-Ahmed, *Nasser and American Foreign Policy 1952–56* (London, 1989), pp. 13–96; Geoffrey Aronson, *From Sideshow to Centre Stage. U.S. Policy Toward Egypt 1946–1956* (Boulder, Colorado, 1986), pp. 39–76.
38. CAB 128/23, fol. 4, CC1(51)7, Secret, 30 October 1951.
39. Shuckburgh, *Diaries*, p. 29.
40. PREM 11/91, M21/52, Churchill to Eden, 30 January 1952.
41. PREM 11/91, M21/52, Churchill to Eden, 15 February 1952.
42. CAB 128/24, fos 90–1, CC18(52)5, Secret, 18 February 1952; fol. 93, CC19(52)2, Secret, 18 February 1952.
43. PREM 11/91, PM/52/24, Eden to Churchill, 10 March 1952; M198/52, Churchill to Alexander, 5 April 1952; M201/52, Churchill to Eden, 6 April 1952.
44. PREM 11/392, M424/52, Churchill to Eden, 7 August 1952.
45. PREM 11/392, PM52/107, Eden to Churchill, Minute by Churchill, 2 September 1952.
46. PREM 11/392, Churchill to Eden, 6 January 1953.
47. Shuckburgh, *Diaries*, pp. 74–5, Diary 20 January 1953.
48. PREM 11/392, Churchill to Eden, 20 February 1953.
49. PREM 11/486, T38/53, Churchill to Eden, Telegram no. 1077, 7 March 1953; T40/53, Churchill to Eden, Telegram no. 1079, 7 March 1953.
50. PREM 11/486, Churchill to Eden, 4 April 1953.
51. PREM 11/392, Shuckburgh to Colville, 24 March 1953; Pitblado to Shuckburgh, 26 March 1953.
52. PREM 11/485, Churchill and Acting Foreign Secretary to Bedell Smith, 10 May 1953 (draft).
53. Eisenhower Library, Abilene, Ann Whitman File, International Meeting Series, Box no 1, File Bermuda Miscellaneous, Memorandum on relative United States–United

Kingdom roles in the Middle East for Bermuda, Meeting 4–8 December 1953, Top Secret, 27 November 1953; PREM 11/484, PM/53/347, Eden to Churchill, 21 December 1953; T315/53, Foreign Office to Washington, Telegram no. 5366, 22 December 1953.

54. Shuckburgh, *Diaries*, pp. 137–9; Eden, *Full Circle*, pp. 257–9; Lloyd, *Suez 1956*, pp. 14–23.
55. CAB 1228/27 pt. 1, fos 158–60, CC18(54)1, Secret, 15 March 1954.
56. PREM 11/702, Colville to Shuckburgh, 7 April 1954.
57. CAB 128/27 pt. 1, fos. 227–8, CC29(54)2, Secret, 15 April 1954.
58. CAB 127/27 pt. 1, fos. 320–2, CC43(54)1, Secret, 22 June 1954.
59. PREM 11/702, Records of Meetings held at the White House on 26 and 27 June 1954.
60. CAB 128/27 pt. 2, fos, 350–1, CC47(54)2, Secret, 7 July 1954.
61. Lord (C.M.W.) Moran, *Winston Churchill: The Struggle for Survival, 1940–1965* (London, 1968), pp. 612–5.
62. PREM 11/702, C(54)248, Secret, 23 July 1954; CAB 128/27 pt. 2, fol. 473, CC63(54)1, Secret, 5 October 1954; Eden, *Full Circle*, pp. 260–1.

4

Churchill and 'Getting the Americans In': Saudi Arabia, Iraq, Jordan, Israel

The rise of a new nationalism in the Middle East challenged the British position in Egypt and Iran. The Arab world that Britain confronted was not a unified one. Indeed, the First Arab–Israeli War led to upheavals in individual Arab countries, often fomented by a new, young and disillusioned generation which had been nurtured on what was considered the injustice of Zionist dispossession of Arab land with the assistance of Western powers. This emerging Arab nationalism found a common focal point in the hatred of Israel. But it also disliked what it saw as the reactionary influence of the old dynasties. Increasingly, Arabism was not just synonymous with the Islamic religion, the Arabic language and the geographic area of Arabia. The inhabitants of North Africa also stressed their Arab identity. This Arab renaissance which had cultural, political and economic manifestations was not always understood by leaders in the West.

As British influence lessened, London concentrated on establishing friendly relations with amenable Arab states on the basis of equality envisaged in the policy of the postwar Labour governments, and to secure its oil supplies. Just as London experienced difficulties with Washington over the latter's sympathy for nationalism, and its diagnosis that this manifestation could not be controlled, so too it had to contend with American hostility and competition over the British presence in the Gulf at a time when Britain was reducing its forces in the Middle East and hoping for greater American participation in the defence of what was considered a vital area for the West.

At the same time as the Americans moved more towards the concept of a Northern Tier defence structure, of the sort Acheson had considered a few years previously and would involve Turkey, Pakistan and possibly Iran, British policy, initiated by nationalist stirrings in Iraq, began to move in a similar direction, though Britain saw this primarily as a means of replacing the Anglo-Iraqi Treaty with a satisfactory defence arrangement. But Anglo-American relations throughout this period were marred by divisions over policy towards the Gulf, the American view of Britain's relationship with the leaders there as being anachronistic; and the British view of America's dominance in Saudi Arabia being controlled by oil interests that wanted to challenge the British position in the Gulf. Increasingly, apparent aggressive moves by Israel led both Washington and London to look for a solution, possibly imposed, to the Arab–Israeli conflict.

Early in 1952, in preparation for a visit to the Gulf by Sir Roger Makins, an Under-Secretary at the Foreign Office, C.M. Rose of the Eastern section of the Foreign Office, offered an assessment of British responsibilities to the Gulf states and Britain's future policy.

British interests in the Gulf dated from the seventeenth century when the East India Company established trading posts there, primarily for trade with Persia through Hormuz. Early in the nineteenth century British influence became predominant by the signing of agreements with Sheikhs on the Arabian side. As well as the humanitarian interest, Britain wanted to safeguard the trade route and stop arms from reaching Baluchistan and the North West frontier. The treaties changed from agreements over the suppression of piracy and the slave trade to agreements in which the countries gave the British government the responsibility for their relations with other countries. Britain gave specific undertakings of protection to Kuwait in 1914, Qatar in 1935, and Bahrain in 1951. Britain had intervened directly in 1923 to depose the Sheikh of Bahrain after gross maladministration, and in 1950 had sent a Royal Navy ship to settle a tribal dispute on the Trucial Coast.

It was not British policy to educate these states to full independence. The conclusion was that Britain's obligations to these states, together with its economic interest in the production of oil, precluded a premature British withdrawal. Britain 'should not initiate any relinquishment of our present position, and should take no steps which would lead to this end'.

Anglo-American co-operation in the Gulf was seen as having two aspects: oil interests, and security. Oil concessions in all the states were either held by American companies, as in Bahrain, or by companies in which there was American participation. All these companies were under British jurisdiction. The oil companies thought that the main American interest was in Saudi Arabia, and that the State Department would favour ARAMCO rather than the British registered companies in the Gulf. The State Department had cautioned ARAMCO against involvement in the frontier dispute with Saudi Arabia. In 1951 Britain had allowed the appointment of an American consul in Kuwait, the first foreign representative in the Gulf states. There was close and effective Anglo-American co-operation over security in the Gulf, and a small American naval attachment at Bahrain worked closely with the British.

In 1952 the British protected states in the Gulf were Bahrain, Kuwait, Qatar, and the Trucial Sheikhdoms on the Oman coast of Abu Dhabi, Dubai, Sharjah, Ajman, Umm al-Qaiman, Ras-al-Khaima and Kalba.

Bahrain was the only one of these states not on the mainland of Arabia. It had a population of 112,000 and was the seat of the Political Resident in the Persian Gulf and of the British Political Agent. The Ruler of Bahrain was thought to be conscientious and his administration to be probably the best in the Middle East.

He had a British adviser and about ten British officials in his government. Public services were well developed and there was a civil airfield and Royal Air Force and naval stations. It was estimated that the income from oil in 1952 would be about £2.5 million. There was also a refinery which used crude oil imported from Saudi Arabia.

Kuwait with its population of 150,000 had a British Political Agent subordinate to the Political Resident. The administration was being improved by the Ruler. Oil had replaced pearling, boat building and other trading activities and in 1952 it was estimated that the Ruler would have an income of £60 million from oil.

Qatar, population around 18,000, also had a British political Officer subordinate to the Political Agent at Bahrain. Its administration was not satisfactory. Income from oil was over 3.5 million and was increasing. The seven states comprising Trucial Oman had a population of about 80,000.

There was a British Political Officer at Sharjah, subordinate to the Political Agent at Bahrain. A Royal Air Force station was also based at Sharjah, as well as the headquarters of the Trucial Oman Levies, a small Arab force under a British commandant which kept order and stopped trading in slaves. The country was backward. There was no administration in the Western sense of the word, and no oil had been discovered.

Makins reported after his visit in March 1952 that there was no Anglo-American co-operation on strategic issues in the Gulf: Washington had not consulted London about the renewal of its rights at the Dhahran air base in Saudi Arabia. Makins detected a lack of Anglo-American understanding in the Middle East and thought that the Americans were undermining the British position there without advancing their own. General Sir Brian Robertson, who accompanied Makins warned of the military dangers of ignoring the Gulf: 'the prize could go elsewhere'.

These issues were touched upon again in November 1952 by the British ambassador at Jedda, G.C. Pelham, who, in commenting on the decline of British prestige in the Gulf, advocated close co-operation with the Americans whose interests there were almost as great as those of Britain. The Americans were untrammelled with the political complications Britain had under its treaty arrangements, arrangements which the Americans viewed as anachronistic. Pelham doubted whether the Americans could be expected 'to trust their interests to us because of our ancient charm'. Pelham suggested that Britain work out jointly with the Americans the future development of the Gulf area.

B.A.B. Burrows, the Counsellor at the British embassy at Washington, however, thought that it would always be difficult, if not impossible, to get real American support for the British position in the Gulf. The American instinctive reaction against colonialism was too strong, and this was an area in which Britain could not hold out the hope of independence for the states concerned. Moreover, the greatest American interest in Arabia was in Saudi Arabia with ARAMCO and the Dhahran air base, and the greatest threat to Britain's position in the Gulf came from Saudi Arabia. It would be vain to hope that the Americans would ever be willing to prejudice their one success in the Middle East by action in support of the British position, support that would lose them the good grace of the Saudis. The Americans could not understand why Britain thought it worthwhile to have rows with the Saudis over the Trucial States and Muscat, areas where Britain could not even bring about the conditions needed to discover for certain whether oil existed there. The Americans were likely to regard any absorption of these areas by Saudi Arabia as 'a natural and inevitable result of the growth of Saudi strength and nationalism and that it would be harmful to Western interests for them to oppose it'.

In this respect Burrows drew attention to Aden where Britain was taking successful action against the Yemen, and was able to do so because it had a levy force proportionate to its tasks: a Royal Air Force station equipped with aircraft, and a political situation in which it could use these resources effectively. In Buraimi, in contrast, Britain had inhibited itself from using its resources. The situation in Aden later deteriorated. In 1954 the Imam of Yemen intensified the pursuit of his claim to the whole Colony and Protectorate of Aden by supporting the activities of the rebels against the loyal chiefs as part of a sustained campaign to undermine British authority. The Cabinet, in July 1954, was told that friendly tribes expected Britain to take more vigorous measures.[1]

By 1952 there had been little progress in the negotiations between Britain and Saudi Arabia over the frontier dispute, which increasingly focused on Buraimi. The Foreign Office was scornful of the American suggestions. W.P. Cranston minuted that it was surprising how Washington, after its failure to get Ibn Saud to moderate his claims, thought that a gesture like the Sheikh of Qatar placing himself unreservedly in the hands of Ibn Saud would result in any settlement other than one granting the most extravagant of the Saudi claims. Further talks were a waste of time. Britain could either resort to arbitration or exercise a firm assertion of rights over the territory which it considered belonged to its Sheikhs.

There was increasing concern over apparent American interference in the Gulf. Soliloquies by Raymond A. Hare, of the State Department's Near East division, about a federation of Gulf states, and also the need for a meeting of Anglo-American minds on the subject, met with a response that the Americans should not be given the impression they could interfere directly in political planning in the Gulf or participate with Britain in control of affairs there. In any case the Americans were anxious to avoid any strategic commitment in the area. Britain was not aligning itself with Iraq against Saudi Arabia as Ibn Saud claimed. But Britain could not allow any restriction on its freedom to consult Middle East countries because such consultation was construed by Ibn Saud as being directed against Saudi Arabia. Churchill did send a friendly message to Ibn Saud. Washington, however, continued to be disturbed at what its embassy described as the 'coldly correct' British response to American suggestions.

The State Department warned London about their concern over the continued deterioration of Anglo-Saudi relations, and their apprehensions that there could be a conflict in which the Arabs would rally around Ibn Saud in opposition to Britain. According to the State Department, ARAMCO was not encouraging the Saudi claims, and also was not interested in oil in the area, but had no alternative other than to help the Saudis when called upon to do so. Officials from the American embassy in London did seem to acknowledge that Britain had done all it could to effect a reasonable settlement.

R.F.G. Sarell, the acting Counsellor at the Foreign Office, observed with satisfaction that B.A.B. Burrows and D.A. Greenhill in Washington had done much to counter the State Department's tendency to appease the Saudis, and to badger Britain into doing likewise. Sarell further observed that ARAMCO, though, ostensibly a neutral agent, had done much to stiffen the Saudis. The inclination of the Americans to swallow the Saudi line also contributed to British difficulties. And there was a tendency noted among Arabs and certain American individuals to consider the British Empire in the past tense. This led the Arabs to deduce it was time to press their claims against the British. The Americans needed to be educated to the consequences of actions, which to them appeared innocent, of giving way to the Saudis, and to the true nature of Saudi policy.

The Foreign Office pointed to the activities of an organization in Dhahran employed by ARAMCO for collecting evidence in support of Saudi claims. It was ARAMCO documentation that had been used by the Saudis in the frontier negotiations, negotiations which the British considered reflected Saudi intransigence, and a resumption of which would probably just further damage Anglo-Saudi relations. The British were thinking instead of the appointment of a neutral investigator with arbitral powers, but saw no chance of a solution in Ibn Saud's lifetime. The Foreign Office complained that Washington was adopting the attitude of impartial mediator. It felt that there could be no impartial stance in the Middle East: 'Those who are not with us are against us. This is the interpretation of the peoples of the Middle East and, whatever the wishes of the State Department, it is as if it were the fact.' Ibn Saud had moved from being a grateful pensioner of the British to being the recipient of a shower of American-produced wealth. His treatment of the British military mission, and his acceptance of the American military mission, was 'symptomatic of a trend which is read by many Arabs not only in Saudi Arabia, but in the Yemen and no doubt elsewhere as meaning that the British are on the way out and that now is the time to encroach on British preserves'. There were enough Americans who would welcome such a development 'to keep alive the widespread belief that American policy is to hasten and profit from this trend'.[2]

In December 1952, the British ambassador at Jedda pointed to the American paramountcy in Saudi Arabia, and the consequences of this for the British position there. Pelham found his American colleague, Raymond Hare, cautious and uncommunicative when it came to discussing policy. Hare believed that a close partnership with Britain in Saudi Arabia was as much of a hindrance as a help to the United States, and found it difficult to avoid the implications of American paramountcy. The Americans 'are now unmistakably the bigger firm and spare no pains to show it'. They were even extending their assistance to the Hejaz, a province which Britain had liked to think of as being predominantly under British influence.

Pelham observed that the Americans seemed anxious to build their empire on their own, and found Britain an embarrassing partner. The American attitude reminded him of advertisements warning against bad breath. ARAMCO had imported 5,500 Americans into Saudi Arabia. Pelham described that company's officials as dealing with the Saudi Arabian government as if ARAMCO were an autonomous state, only calling on the American ambassador when it suited them. ARAMCO were, in effect, unpaid consultants to the Saudi government, and the most objectionable activity in this regard had been the advice they offered over the frontier dispute.

There remained some evidence of British influence, but it was insignificant beside the 'mighty new figure of Uncle Sam with his bag full of dollars'. Britain's position had formerly had the secure basis of its control of India, the Gulf and the pilgrimage trade, but it rested only on some degree of inherited respect and such power as it could maintain on the periphery of the peninsula. On the other hand, the Americans wanted to provide the Saudis 'with the instruments of Western life ... make them feel grown up, equal in status to westerners and as much like Americans as possible'.

Pelham recommended that Britain needed to co-operate more with the United States. It should even involve the United States in formulating policy in the Gulf, advice which the Foreign Office rejected. The ambassador insisted he had only meant that Britain might have to listen to the United States, as well as expecting the United States to listen to Britain.[3]

On 22 December 1952, Eden outlined to the Cabinet preparations for a show of force to counter Saudi Arabian attempts to extend its influence into the Trucial Sheikhdoms and the Gulf. The Saudis, he said, had been encouraged by the British failure to protect their interests at Abadan. The Foreign Secretary envisaged increasing the Trucial Oman Levies to three or four hundred persons, and also to provide a further cadre of two hundred for the Sultan of Muscat. There would be a cruiser and a frigate in the Gulf from the middle of January 1953, 12 Royal Air Force armoured cars would be sent to Iraq and a squadron of Vampires would also go there for short periods. Churchill wanted to send stronger forces. The Americans were not to be told in advance of these measures.

In the Foreign Office, R.C. Blackham noted that any co-ordination of policy with the Americans had to rest on recognition by Washington of the justice of the British-protected Sheikhs' claims, and of the British right to resist Saudi encroachment in the Sheikhs' territory. On 31 March 1953, Washington was told of some of the British preparations. Reference was made by Sir William Strang in his conversation with the American ambassador at London, Winthrop Aldrich, to the Saudi incursion into the Buraimi oasis in August 1952, to the despatch of a further Saudi party there on 12 March 1953, and of Saudi activities under an officer, Turki, canvassing support for their claim by proper and improper means. Britain was to inform Saudi Arabia that it was to reserve freedom of action in the disputed area, that it was no longer restricted by previous agreements, and that it would move levies into positions in the disputed area.

In later talks with ARAMCO officials about the dispute Joseph Palmer, the First Secretary at the American embassy in London, advised of the concern the Conservative government faced about the loss of British prestige in Iran and Egypt. With talk of 'scuttle' Britain was unlikely to be willing or able to make concessions to the Saudis in the Gulf.

Eden assured the Cabinet on 21 April that efforts to supply Turki and his 80 followers had been frustrated, but they could still get food from the local inhabitants.

On his visit to the Middle East in May 1953 Dulles was told by the Crown Prince of Saudi Arabia, Saud, that the Americans had deserted Saudi Arabia. Saud wanted to know what Washington would do if Britain attacked Saudi Arabia. Dulles spoke of the real efforts Washington had made on Saudi Arabia's behalf, and thought that the acceptance of the principle of arbitration was helpful.[4]

Saudi levies, under Sheikh Obaid took up positions along the lines of communication to the British troops in Buraimi, and on 29 June Lloyd asked the Cabinet for permission to attack, though he resisted the recommendation of the local commander for an air attack. A warning was sent to Jedda. British troops dislodged the Saudi levies.

London proposed to Washington a scheme which entailed both sides withdrawing troops from Buraimi, but Washington declined on the grounds that Ibn Saud, for reasons of prestige would not be prepared to withdraw his troops. Washington preferred a scheme whereby Britain lifted the blockade, the Saudis discontinued their attempts to suborn the local population, and that a commission of three, one British, one Saudi and one neutral went to the area to see that the conditions were carried out. There should also be a public announcement that the two sides had agreed to arbitration. Lloyd could not recommend acceptance while Turki remained stirring up the local population. It would also be damaging to British prestige to abandon the attempts to remove Turki.

Despite the danger of taking issue with the Americans, the Cabinet decided that if Britain gave way its prestige would be seriously weakened throughout the area. Lord Salisbury, the Lord President, advised the Cabinet on 21 July that there was little understanding in Washington of the British interests involved. The American administration, dependent on oil from Saudi Arabia, wanted to placate Ibn Saud, and was ready to deprecate the British action as 'symptomatic of what they regarded as a reactionary attitude towards the problems of the Middle East as a whole'. The Cabinet agreed that Britain should not endanger its own oil concessions by giving in to Saudi claims. Dulles was informed accordingly, and the Americans submitted a modified proposal. The Secretary of State was cross, and warned of the increasingly important position of Saudi Arabia in the pattern of Anglo-American common defence.[5]

It was, however, Eden who was really angry when, on 5 June 1954, he told the Cabinet that with the agreement of the government of Saudi Arabia, ARAMCO had sent a prospecting party over the Saudi Arabian border into territory where the Trucial Sheikhs claimed jurisdiction. There could be substantial quantities of oil there, and it was vital to British interests that the American company should not establish a claim to work it. ARAMCO had no rights in the area and should not have the support of the American government. Eden proposed that the prospecting party be removed, if necessary by force. Churchill was worried that the British forces there were not strong enough. Eden was prepared to entertain modifications to the plan to reduce the risk of personal injury to American citizens. But, on 30 July 1954, an Arbitration agreement was signed between Britain acting on behalf of the Sultan of Abu Dhabi and the Sultan of Muscat and Oman, and Saudi Arabia. The tribunal started sittings in Geneva on 11 September 1955.[6]

At loggerheads with the Americans over policy towards Saudi Arabia and the Gulf and confronted with rising nationalisms in Egypt and Iran, London was forced by Middle Eastern considerations, as well as by its overall reassessment of British defence policy in the light of financial stringency and the development of thermo-nuclear weapons, to revise its alliances and military commitments in the Middle East. Britain wanted to sustain some sort of anti-Soviet tier of defence while at the same time reducing its commitments and protecting its oil interests. What emerged was a line of defence along the Northern Tier which became the Baghdad pact in November 1955.

On 2 March 1953 the Prime Minister of Iraq, Nuri al-Said, in a conversation with the British ambassador at Baghdad, Sir John Troutbeck, and General Sir Brian Robertson (a conversation in which Nuri was somewhat incoherent), indicated that Iraq wanted to modify the Anglo-Iraqi Treaty of 1930, and that he, personally, would prefer Iraq to rely on collective defences based on the Arabic Collective Security Pact, and was likely to ask for modifications of the existing conditions under which Britain held bases in Iraq.

Churchill did not like the implications of this and asked if this were part of a plan to get Britain out of Habbaniya air base. Strang advised the Prime Minister that revisions of the treaty had been possible since October 1952, and in anticipation of a possible Iraqi request the Foreign Office and the Chiefs of Staff were examining how Britain's strategic requirements in Iraq could be secured by some instrument other than the existing treaty. Churchill minuted: 'We are being hunted down everywhere.' Nuri envisaged an increase in Iraqi forces with equipment from Britain, possibly paid for by the United States through off-shore purchase. He wanted British forces withdrawn from Iraqi bases apart from training visits. Troutbeck thought that Iraq was motivated by a determination to face the Communist menace and, as well as the external danger, also confronted internal difficulties as was shown by student demonstrations. Troutbeck also thought that a reason was Iraq's reluctance to get tied up too closely with Turkey. He suspected that Nuri saw this as his last chance of consolidating his country internally and externally, and thought that he was the only man who could do it. Troutbeck suggested tripartite discussions between London, Washington and Baghdad. The Foreign Office doubted whether Iraq was in a position to pay for the envisaged build up of its forces to four divisions and four fighter squadrons over four years. It was necessary to consult the Americans, and to reach an agreed policy with Washington.[7]

On 22 April 1953, the British suggested to the Americans that they should both welcome Iraq's request to strengthen its military forces, but that their assistance would be limited to helping Iraq to build up its strength to defend the Middle East area as a whole. Furthermore, Britain should not be supplanted as the principal source for Iraq's arms. Dulles, after his Middle Eastern tour in May 1953, decided to pursue the Northern Tier strategy as an alternative to MEDO. Washington investigated co-ordinating military assistance to Iraq and Jordan with the British supply programmes. London had reservations about the sort of Northern Tier the Americans were pursuing. In particular, in October 1953, the Chiefs of Staff were concerned about the implications for the British economy of Washington supplying military equipment to a traditionally British sphere of interest like Pakistan. In December, when Nuri warned that he might have to say in parliament that the Anglo-Iraqi Treaty had already been largely liquidated by mutual agreement, Churchill told Eden that this did not look good, and would not be a good sequel to an Egyptian settlement.

On 7 January 1954 the Cabinet considered a suggestion from Washington that the American offer of military aid to Pakistan should be linked with the initiation of military collaboration between Pakistan and Turkey which could eventually be developed into a system of collective defence for the Middle East. Churchill thought the scheme could be to Britain's advantage, particularly if Britain did not reach an agreement with Egypt and disengaged its forces from the Canal Zone, and redeployed its forces in the Middle East in a northward direction. He was, however, concerned about the timing of any announcement of this as he did not want it to aggravate the Soviets before the envisaged Four Power meeting at Berlin. There was concern in the State Department over the extent to which Britain had been consulted about this American policy, particularly in view of the American recognition of Britain's primary responsibility for defence in the area.[8]

Churchill continued to question vigorously the nature of any British military presence in the Middle East. On 12 January 1954 the Foreign Secretary, Anthony Eden, suggested that given the state of the defence negotiations with Egypt, it might be opportune to pursue the suggestion of the Turkish government. This entailed Britain pre-stocking military equipment at Mardi, which was on the frontier between Turkey and Syria, and if Britain could make satisfactory arrangements with Turkey for joint defence of the area, and afterwards include Iraq, Egypt could be of less strategic advantage. Churchill thus demanded to know what forces the Chiefs of Staff would propose to operate from Mardi, how many British troops would be needed there in peacetime, and what aid the Turks would give. Eden favoured the Turkish proposition as it would strengthen Britain's hand with the Iraqis by demonstrating that it was serious about the defence of Iraq.[9]

The Chiefs of Staff, however, wanted to delay military conversations with the Iraqis for as long as possible, as Britain could not disguise the great discrepancy between the forces required to hold the Middle East and the forces Britain could make available for the area in peace. The British embassy at Baghdad warned that there was a risk in the Americans making all the running in promoting the proposed Turkish-Pakistan axis. If Washington persuaded Iraq to join, this could be against British interests in that Iraq, with that sort of support, might feel less dependent on Britain for defence. The Iraqis could even encourage the Americans to take a hand in the Anglo-Iraqi discussions about bases. That could mean the same thankless results as there had been in Iran and Egypt. Britain needed a proposal ready to put forward to the Iraqis.

On 24 February Henry Byroade of the State Department was told that Britain might in time become closely linked with any defence association that could grow from the agreement that Turkey and Pakistan had concluded. But it was unlikely that Britain could accept any obligation for the defence of Iran, and that a future inclusion of Iran might embarrass Britain. Byroade warned that the National Security Council had decided that, eventually, Iran should be encouraged to join a regional defence organization, and that this could mean a difference between British and American policy.[10]

On 26 February 1954, Britain and the United States signed a memorandum of understanding about the provision of military aid to Iraq. Washington would, as far as possible, co-ordinate its military aid to Iraq with the plans already agreed to by London and Baghdad. Baghdad would continue to look primarily to London for arms and training. Off-shore purchases in Britain would be used by the United States to avoid dislocation in the equipment and expansion plans of the Iraqi forces. There would be an American Military Assistance Advisory Group stationed in Iraq which would maintain close liaison and exchange all relevant information with the British military authorities in Iraq. The American survey team went to Baghdad with a clear understanding of these conditions.[11]

The Head of the British Middle East Office, Sir John Sterndale Bennett, advised on 4 March that Britain should cultivate still more closely those individual Arab states which remained relatively stable: pursue military talks with Iraq, increase the subsidy for the Arab Legion in Jordan, and encourage Iraqi interest in the alignment between Turkey and Pakistan. Eden, however, told Churchill that the Foreign Office did not agree with Bennett's diagnosis of greater disunity and instability in the Arab world, and the greatest danger was the possibility of 'a break-out by Israel'. In any case, Baghdad, at that time, did not intend to accede to the Turco-Pakistan agreement.

The Foreign Office recommended to the Cabinet on 31 May 1954 that as no Iraqi government was likely to be willing to negotiate a new formal treaty granting Britain military facilities in Iraq, Britain should invite Baghdad to examine their mutual defence requirements on the basis of returning the bases at Habbaniya and Shaiba to Iraqi ownership. This would be acceptable provided that effective mutual defence arrangements could be made and the Iraqi bases were capable of immediate and effective use by the Royal Air Force in war. It was important that this should be done otherwise, with the American interest in the Northern Tier of Middle Eastern states as evidenced by the Turco-Pakistan pact and the agreement over American military aid to Iraq, unless Britain put its military relations with Iraq on a footing acceptable to both sides, the Iraqis and others might get the idea that Britain was leaving it to the Americans to make the running in that part of the world.

Alexander, the Minister of Defence, endorsed these recommendations. He advised that thermo-nuclear weapons had changed the whole picture of defence in the Middle East, and the rapid advance of Soviet forces did not have to be feared anymore. There was a good chance that the Iraqi frontier could be preserved intact. Alexander thought that the military talks with the Iraqis should plan for a defence arrangement which could link up with NATO defence plans in Turkey.

The Chiefs of Staff, however, wanted more. They wanted Britain to be able to maintain at least one air squadron in Iraq with service personnel at the base for maintaining the operational machinery. The air bases in Iraq were needed for staging British military aircraft in transit to the Far East, Australia and New Zealand. If Britain retained limited forces in Iraq it was less likely to be under pressure to yield important facilities elsewhere, as, for example, in Jordan or Libya. The two bases were a real estate asset, and accommodated more than 4,000 personnel who could require accommodation to be built elsewhere.[12]

An American National Intelligence Estimate, in its examination of the Northern Tier approach, suggested that the creation of this regional defence grouping could facilitate the eventual development of a formal defence organization with some form of direct British and American participation. Dulles hoped that the 'evil influence' of the Arab League could be broken by the movement of Iraq towards the West and Turkey and Pakistan, and explained to Churchill and Eisenhower that American aid to Iraq was being given with that long-term objective in view. Nuri also wanted to split the Arab League and told Selwyn Lloyd and Evelyn Shuckburgh on 15 July that he wanted to make a treaty with Pakistan, and then bring in Syria and the Lebanon, and he hoped that Britain would join.[13]

The Chiefs of Staff liked Nuri's suggestion of an arrangement among the Northern Tier states. Such an arrangement, they felt, would be less offensive to Israel. The association of Britain with one or another Middle Eastern security system might make it easier for the Iraqi parliament to agree to the continued granting of defence facilities to Britain. The disagreement between the Foreign Office and the Chiefs on the need for facilities in Iraq in peacetime had not been resolved. The Chiefs of Staff agreed that the Ministers should not decide the dispute, but instead the talks with Iraq should be on an exploratory basis and

Britain should not decide its position until the military talks were followed by ones at government level.[14]

Nuri outlined his refined ideas to Lloyd on 20 September 1954. He preferred a pact of five powers: Iraq, Turkey, Syria, Iran and Britain. If Iran were not prepared to join, then the objective should be a pact between Iraq, Pakistan and Britain. This was to be an arrangement that resembled NATO and should replace the Anglo-Iraqi Treaty. In the Foreign Office, P.S Falla was anxious that Nuri should not move too fast and alienate Egypt, and prejudice 'the hope of improved Arab-Western relations resulting from the Anglo-Egyptian Agreement'. Shuckburgh, however, observed that in the above case Britain would 'get neither plan'. The British ambassador at Baghdad, Sir John Troutbeck, thought that all Britain could do was to support Nuri, and get the best terms possible.[15] Dulles was of the opinion that Iran should be encouraged to participate in Middle Eastern defence arrangements, and that both Britain and the United States should encourage it to do so.[16]

In December 1954 Troutbeck offered, at the end of his term as ambassador at Baghdad some thoughts on the changing nature of Britain's position in Iraq, and the intrusion of a new American influence. Troutbeck asserted that Iraqis owed their freedom solely to the force of British arms. Since that time they had never stopped trying to restore their sense of self-esteem by attacking their deliverers, 'sometimes physically and incessantly in their press and public speeches'. The Iraqis considered that they were part of a general Oriental upsurge against the West. And although they owed everything they had, their wealth and freedom, to the imperialists, and although they had no shame in pocketing free gifts from the Americans in the shape of economic and military aid, their emotions were 'all on the other side'. Their three main emotions, Arabism, Islam and anti-imperialism met in concentrated fanaticism on the question of Israel.

In his account of Britain's ally, Troutbeck observed that the Republican administration in the United States seemed to have become convinced that the British were outdated in their whole approach to the Middle East, and that it was time fo. the New World to intervene. American business was certainly not prepared to leave what could be a highly profitable field to British enterprise. Troutbeck complained: 'No Englishman living in Iraq can remain unmoved as he sees a horde of highly paid American experts sweeping into a country whose traditional ties are with ourselves and hears them denigrating all that Britain has done here in the past and is attempting to do at the present.' But Britain had to accept, and accept with good grace, an increase in American influence in that part of the world. British prestige still remained high. Troutbeck concluded: 'Even though we cannot hope to restore our former exclusive position in Iraq, there should be a great future for us. I only trust that we shall be able to work it out in harmony with our American allies.'[17]

As well as a reassessment of the relationship with Iraq, Britain, at a time of a realization of the need to reduce its commitments in the Middle East, concentrated on establishing friendly relations with states who appeared to welcome a British connection. This led to the negotiation of a treaty with Libya in 1953, and the examination of the extent to which Israel could play a part in the British defence of the Middle East. The possible connection with Israel was determinedly pursued by Churchill, who described himself as a life-long Zionist and preferred Israel to the Arab states. But, as transpired in 1954, a potential relationship with Israel was seen as complicating the British pledge to go to Jordan's assistance. As Prime Minister, Churchill played a dominant role in the formulation of British policy in this field.

In 1952, Britain hoped to negotiate a treaty with Libya giving it the right to station troops there for a substantial period of time. In March there were difficulties in that local sentiment in Libya was increasingly hostile to the presence of British troops in Libyan towns and in particular in Benghazi. It was suggested that they should be moved away from the populated areas, but Churchill opposed the expenditure necessary to build new quarters at a time 'when the whole future of the British garrison in the Middle East remained uncertain'.[18]

France and the United States also pursued treaties with Libya, but almost a year later, in February 1953, Eden was able to ask the Cabinet for permission to sign the text of a treaty with the Libyan government at a time when Libya did not seen so anxious to conclude similar agreements with Washington and Paris. In July Lloyd warned the Cabinet that the interim treaty with Libya was due to expire at the end of that month, and if Britain wanted to maintain its position in Libya a permanent treaty had to be concluded. Lloyd thought it of great political and strategic importance that Britain should maintain its influence in Libya. A 20-year treaty with Libya was possible if Britain were prepared to make concessions over the removal of troops from existing installations in Tripoli and Benghazi.

In discussion in the Cabinet it was emphasized that the size of the British garrison in Libya should not be determined in advance of decisions regarding Britain's long-term strategy in the Middle East. What was important was to secure the right to station British troops in Libya. Alexander warned wryly that the size of the garrison was likely to be determined by the amount of accommodation available, and that as Libya was unlikely to allow Britain to retain the existing accommodation, and the government would not be willing to find money to build any new, there would probably be a reduction of troops. In any event Britain had to raise the offer of assistance towards the Libyan development plan to £1 million a year for 5 years. Britain concluded the treaty.[19]

Churchill's approach to the Middle East during his final premiership was not only influenced by his conviction that the Americans had to be involved, but by an overriding wish to help Israel which he described as 'the great experiment', 'one of the most hopeful and encouraging adventures of the 20th Century'.[20] Churchill did not have the same regard for the Arab states as his predecessors. His conviction that Israel was likely to be the most reliable ally in the area and his emotional support for Zionism, combined with his friendship with David Ben-

Gurion, at times led Churchill to try to blunt the enthusiasm of his Foreign Secretary and the Chiefs of Staff for the need to protect Jordan against Israel.

Above all, Churchill wanted to prevent a war between Jordan and Israel in which Britain might have to honour the Anglo-Jordanian Treaty of 1948 and go to Jordan's assistance. This was particularly evident in his handling of the situation in the aftermath of the frontier incident at Qibya on the night of 14–15 October 1953 when around 70 villagers, mainly women and children were killed by Israeli soldiers. American newspapers, normally sympathetic to Israel, compared the incident to the Nazi massacre of 185 men of the village of Lidice in Czechoslovakia on 10 June 1942 in reprisal for the assassination of an SS chief.[21]

On 29 October 1953, Eden reported to the British Cabinet that the Jordanian government had invited Britain to send a squadron of an armoured regiment to Ma'an which was around 100 miles to the north-east of Aqaba. As the envisaged squadron would have no reason to go near the Jordan–Israeli frontier, its arrival should not exacerbate the tension between those two countries. Indeed the Foreign Secretary thought that 'it might have a stabilising effect by reassuring the Jordan Government of our fidelity to our obligations to them'.[22] On 17 November, Eden pointed out to the Cabinet that in addition to the despatch of the squadron under consideration – the despatch of which had been delayed pending the Security Council discussions on Qibya – Britain had to consider whether to send additional forces to Jordan at that time or in the event of an attack by Israel. Eden emphasized: 'Any action of ours should be sufficiently firm to deter Israel from an act of aggression and sufficiently forthcoming to prevent Jordan from invoking the terms of the Treaty and possibly precipitating the hostilities with Israel which we wanted to avoid.'

Cabinet discussion suggested that although a major act of aggression would be reported to the Security Council that would not absolve Britain from its treaty obligations to come immediately to the aid of Jordan in the event of war. If Britain tried to escape its obligations by denouncing the treaty Britain would impair its influence with other Arab states. Furthermore, the Anglo-Iraqi treaty was of particular value, and Britain could not overlook its oil interests in the other Arab countries of the Middle East. In strategic terms even the supplementation of the envisaged armoured squadron with an additional battalion and four RAF squadrons would be inadequate in the event of major hostilities between Israel and Jordan. In the event of war reinforcements would have to come from the Canal Zone.

Churchill pronounced the situation 'one of grave potential danger'. But he did not share the view that emphasized Britain's position, particularly with the Arab states, in the Middle East. The Prime Minister expounded: 'It was beyond our strength to carry all the burdens of trouble in the Middle East and he was inclined to think that this particular source of trouble concerned the United Nations more than it concerned the United Kingdom.' It was important to know where the Americans stood. Sending small forces might provoke Israel: 'If we had to intervene at all, it could be better to use overwhelming force which could provide an effective deterrent.'[23] Because of the financial restrictions the Chiefs of Staff were reluctant to do more than send an armoured squadron to Jordan for training with the Arab Legion, and to build this up, as resources allowed, to the strength of a regiment. In view of this it was decided not to specify to Jordan any use of British troops in fulfilment of obligations under the Anglo-Jordanian Treaty. Churchill reiterated that care should be taken to avoid a situation in which British troops were engaged in hostilities between Israel and Jordan.[24] Indeed it was Churchill's government which considered seriously what role Israel could play in Britain's strategy. Israel had made approaches during the last year of the Attlee administration.

On 19 and 21 February 1951, David Ben-Gurion and the British Commander-in-Chief Middle East Land Forces, General Brian Robertson, had spoken cordially to one another. Ben-Gurion wanted Israel to survive. There was a 'great danger to civilisation'. The situation called for the 'closest possible collaboration' between Israel and Britain. By this Ben-Gurion meant that 'in an emergency Israel should act "as if" she were part of the British Commonwealth and should be regarded by Great Britain in exactly the same way'. Morrison replied on 24 April that the development of a relationship between Israel and Britain should be a gradual process, 'taking account of the realities of the existing situation and our respective world interests'. The best way to start could be practical co-operation in the military field, co-operation that would contribute to Israel's security and the safeguarding of Britain's vital interests in the Middle East.[25]

The Israeli general election and Ben-Gurion's difficulties over forming an administration delayed the matter. But on 22 December 1951 Eden wrote to Churchill that, although it was difficult to see how the relationship with Israel could be placed on a Commonwealth footing, there was no reason why Britain could not collaborate closely with that country in defence of the Middle East. The Chiefs of Staff were considering the role Israel could play in the framework of British strategy. Eden suggested that discussions with Israel, which should be started as soon as possible, would not affect plans being developed for an Allied Middle East Command as these could be adjusted should Israel agree to be associated with the command. Churchill welcomed 'this line of advance'.[26]

A British military mission went to Tel Aviv in October 1952, and had exploratory talks with the Israelis. The Chiefs of Staff wanted Israeli co-operation in the defence of the Middle East. This was not only because of Israel's geographic position in the Middle East, but because 'the Israelis were potentially the best military material in the area'. The Chiefs of Staff, however, did emphasize that Arab good will was more important than that of Israel: early in 1953 British strategy in the Middle East assumed the active assistance by Iraqi and Jordanian forces, as well as Egyptian co-operation in running the base in the Canal Zone. The Israelis accepted that they could not participate directly in any Middle East Defence Organization, but the Chiefs of Staff felt that Israel could make a major fighting contribution in the air.

It was felt necessary to co-ordinate a policy towards Israel with the United States. There were two reasons for this: 'first, it is a cardinal point of our policy to secure American participation in Middle East defence; secondly, we must look to the United States for the finances require (sic) to equip Israeli forces and, more particularly, to develop their communication and storage facilities'. Britain needed American agreement 'to examine sympathetically Israel's requests for the arms and equipment necessary to enable her to play her correct rôle', and to assure Israel that it would be given as much information on the progress of British defence planning as other Middle Eastern countries.[27]

Churchill, in placing this policy before the Defence Committee of the Cabinet, used the argument that the fear of stronger Israeli forces 'would constitute a useful deterrent against Egyptian aggressive aspirations'. The Defence Committee, however, felt that nothing could be done without American support as the United States would have to supply Israel with the arms and equipment. It concluded further that Britain's aim should be to strengthen the armed forces of Israel generally without undue emphasis on its contribution in the air: the British aim 'should be to help Israel build up her armed strength, not only for her own defence, but also as a contribution to a settled situation in the Middle East'.[28]

The despatch drafted by Lord Salisbury to be sent to the British ambassador in Washington, outlined the approach to be made to the American government for their approval for this policy. It once again placed emphasis on the need to build up Israel's air force, but an awareness was shown of the difficulties of convincing Washington at a time when it would be reluctant to see the West more closely identified with Israel. In addition it was felt that there was no reason why the policy should become public and reach Arab ears.[29] But, at the request of Salisbury, the Cabinet on 10 August 1953 agreed to delay this despatch in case the Arab states discovered that Britain was contemplating building up Israel's strength. Salisbury argued that this could both prejudice the British negotiations with Egypt, and lose Britain the goodwill of the Arab states.[30]

At the time this new British policy towards Israel was evolving, Churchill made his sympathies for Israel clear. Earlier, in May 1952 Churchill had been very 'sorry' that, because of Britain's financial problems, no financial assistance had been possible to help Israel finance oil purchases.[31] Later in November 1952, Churchill had been horrified by a suggestion from the Iraqi ambassador to Cairo that there could be a solution to the Arab–Israeli dispute which included the cession of the Negev by Israel, though Eilat could be kept as a free port. The Prime Minister noted: 'Surely there can be no question of Israel being asked to give up the Negev, as its development might afford the only means of sustaining their great population of refugee immigrants.' The Foreign Office had reassured Churchill that the Israelis could not be asked to give up the Negev.[32]

The Prime Minister was sympathetic to Israeli concerns over the consequences to its interests of a renegotiated Anglo-Egyptian Treaty. He complained that 'the late Mr Bevin, who had a strain of anti-Semitism in his thought, put the Foreign Office in on the wrong side when Israel was attacked by all the Arab States'. Churchill insisted that Israel was the most powerful fighting force in the Middle East and 'could come in very handy in dealing with Egypt if [Muhammad] Neguib [Egyptian Prime Minister] attacks us'. Britain, in Churchill's view, ought never to have allowed 'the obstruction in the Suez Canal of oil for Haifa'.[33] On 23 April 1953 Churchill declared:

> I do not mind it being known here or in Cairo that I am on the side of Israel and against her ill-treatment by the Egyptians. The idea of selling Israel down the drain in order to persuade the Egyptians to kick us out of the Canal Zone more gently is not one which attracts me. We have probably got to have a showdown with Neguib, and Israel will be an important factor both *Parliamentary* and military. We must not throw away any important card we have in our hand.

British officials in Cairo were instructed accordingly.[34] Churchill assured the Israeli ambassador in London that 'Her Majesty's Government will always be mindful of Israel's interests'.[35]

In May, when Lebanon started to implement the Arab League's economic blockade of Israel, and drafted a decree denying facilities at their ports to ships that had carried oil or other strategic materials to Israel, Churchill was furious. The Prime Minister demanded to know what Britain could do in retaliation, and wondered whether it might be possible to stop aeroplanes from being delivered.[36] Churchill minuted on Selwyn Lloyd, the Minister of State's reply, that the Lebanese had signed a contract for the delivery of three Vampire aircraft, and that interference with the order would only discourage Britain's friends in that country, particularly in defence circles, and that the Lebanese could probably get jets elsewhere: 'Delay shd. be easy'. Lloyd explained that Britain was not in a good position to retaliate as it exported more to Lebanon that it bought from that country. Britain was a 'hostage to fortune in that two of the Iraq Petroleum Company's pipelines from Kirkuk to the Mediterranean terminate at Tripoli and the Lebanese could interfere with the transit of oil through them'. Churchill approved Lloyd's suggestion for 'vigorous representations' rather than retaliation.[37]

Churchill, around the same time, did make representations to Israel over its actions in Jerusalem on 22 April when Israeli snipers fired across the armistice line and killed six Jordanians in retaliation for killings by Arab infiltrators of Israelis.[38] But he insisted in moderating William Strang, the Permanent Under Secretary's draft, which said that Churchill 'could not defend what has occurred', to describing the clashes as 'regrettable' and emphasizing that the representation came from one who had been a Zionist since the Balfour declaration.[39] Following Israeli raids on West bank border villages in May 1953[40] Churchill remonstrated to Ben-Gurion: 'I hope you will be able to assure me that there is no truth in the report or anything like it. Nothing can do more harm to your interests, which I value so highly, than the continuance of petty warfare. I have also communicated with Jordan.'[41]

When, towards the end of January 1954, Egypt decided to intensify its blockade of Israel, Churchill warned the Cabinet that this would lead to increased interference with the passage of ships through the Suez Canal and that the Israeli government intended to raise the matter in the Security Council and had asked for British and American support. The Prime Minister wanted prompt and effective support for Israel. The Prime Minister thought that members of all parties would welcome an assertion of the right of free transit through the Suez Canal. Eden, however, sounded a warning: Egypt has legal grounds for its action as its war with Israel had not been terminated. The Foreign Secretary cautioned that Britain should not take any public position until it knew that it had the support of the other maritime powers.[42]

Despite Churchill's overt support for Israel the Qibya raid in October 1953 had, according to the Israeli ambassador in London, aroused opinion in Britain to the extent that it was possible that London would either intervene or apply sanctions against Israel. Indeed the ambassador quoted Churchill as saying that he had not been so shocked since the murder of Lord Moyne in Cairo in November 1944[43] which had led to the Prime Minister suspending his pro-Zionist Palestinian policy. Against this background, on 24 January 1954, Eden announced to the Cabinet that the airfield at Amman had been completed and that he had agreed to the stationing there of a fighter squadron of the RAF. Israel would be informed a few days in advance. In response to the suggestion from King Hussein of Jordan that Britain station more troops in his country, Eden recommended to the Cabinet that the armoured squadron, already authorized be sent, and other arrangements be investigated.[44]

The Chiefs of Staff developed a plan to aid Jordan in the event of major aggression by Israel: the Israeli air force would be destroyed, a naval blockade established, and Israel would be invaded from the south with a force of one infantry division and one armoured regiment. Britain would have to declare war on Israel within four days of an Israeli invasion of Jordan. Norman Brook advised Churchill that a British invasion of Israel would be unfortunate, and that every diplomatic means should be tried first. But he also explained that Britain had an obligation to aid Jordan, and the Jordanians wanted to know what Britain intended to do. Disclosing the plans to the Jordanians would help Britain secure requirements for airfield facilities there as well as stationing British troops. If the Israelis learnt of these plans they might be deterred from aggression. Churchill was unmoved. He refused the request to disclose the British plans to assist Jordan to a meeting of the Anglo-Jordan Joint Defence Board scheduled for the first week of April 1954: the Prime Minister minuted that he had not approved any of this procedure and that the Cabinet had to consider the whole question.[45]

Churchill wrote this against the background of the attack on 16/17 March by Arab infiltrators on a civilian bus travelling up Scorpions Pass from Eilat to Tel Aviv in which 11 were killed.[46] Moshe Sharett, the new Israeli Prime Minister, informed Churchill that Israel felt the Anglo-Jordanian Treaty gave Britain a powerful influence in Amman: 'We are hard put to it to explain to our public why that influence has so far been inadequate to prevail upon the Jordan Government to abandon its present attitude, and put an end to the armed incursions.'[47] Although Eden doubted whether a reply was necessary, Churchill amended various drafts and wrote: 'We must ourselves be the judge of our obligations to Jordan, but we shall certainly neglect no opportunity to use our influence in the direction of a peaceful settlement of the problems which afflict you and them.'[48] In July 1954, the Jordanian government was assured that if Israel were to launch an unprovoked large-scale attack, amounting to an act of war, Britain would honour its obligations under the Anglo-Jordanian Treaty.[49]

This followed Anglo-American conversations on the Middle East where the emphasis moved towards Cold War politics in the area and the conclusion that a final solution to the Arab–Israeli conflict was unlikely until the Arabs became convinced that the real danger was not Israel but Soviet communism. The American Secretary of State, John Foster Dulles, explained that American aid to the area was being given with a view to the long-term objective of moving Iraq towards the West, and Turkey and Pakistan: no hint of this should be leaked to the Israeli government.[50]

It was Churchill's peacetime administration which oversaw the dramatic change in British defence policy. The move was away from considering the Middle East as one of the three cardinal pillars of British strategy towards the conclusion that it was an area of more limited significance in the age of thermonuclear weapons and at a time when Britain's financial strictures meant a limitation of its world role. Churchill, privately, questioned the strategic significance of the Middle East for Britain, and when he became Prime Minister actively criticized the validity of a defence policy which gave the area priority. Churchill was unable to see why such an emphasis should be placed on protecting the area from a Soviet invasion, an invasion which the Prime Minister felt could not be mounted.

Churchill felt that the Americans should become involved in an area for which Britain had undertaken responsibility in the agreement made between their two countries at the end of 1947. In this respect Churchill's Middle East policy was radically different from that of Attlee's first Labour government which had initially decided that the Middle East was a British preserve, and one from which the Americans should be excluded.[51] Dulles on his visit to the Middle East in 1953 concluded that Britain could no longer meet its responsibility for the defence of the Middle East on behalf of the West. In July, the National Security Council advocated 'greater independence and greater responsibility in the area by the United States vis-à-vis Britain'.[52] Churchill's last government welcomed the beginnings of the transfer of power in the Middle East from Britain to the United States.

Churchill, however, still had imperial leanings in the 1950s. He was reluctant to give up Egypt and abandon a considerable British presence in an area in which Britain had exercised influence for over half a century. His personal predilections influenced his policy. He scorned the Egyptians and described himself as a

Zionist with a high regard for Israel. As Prime Minister, he openly preferred the Israelis to the Egyptians. At times he was critical of Israel, particularly after the Qibya raid in October 1953 which he said had shocked him as much as the murder of Lord Moyne in November 1944 by Zionist terrorists. It was during Churchill's premiership, however, that Britain pursued overtures from Ben-Gurion and considered how to develop a military alliance with Israel. Churchill personally interrupted the decision of the Chiefs of Staff to let the Jordanians know of British plans to invade Israel if Jordan were invaded by that country. He tried to help Israel in whatever way he could. But he was confronted by a British policy which insisted that Britain could not support Israel at the expense of losing Arab goodwill.

During his final premiership Churchill did dominate policy towards Egypt. He would not leave Eden alone. From the outset the approach of the two men diverged radically on this subject. Eden's absences through illness or at conferences enabled Churchill to play a decisive role. When Eden was present, the Prime Minister fought against the policy of 'scuttle' being proposed by his Foreign Secretary. At the outset Eden wanted to involve the Americans. Churchill was prepared to go it alone on Egypt. These two men had a volatile relationship.[53]

Towards the end of Churchill's period of office the image of Britain – through its negotiation of the withdrawal from the Suez Canal base, the weakened position it had in Iran's oil exploitation, the challenge it faced to its traditional base in Iraq and the difficulties with Saudi Arabia and its American ally over territorial disputes in the oil-rich Gulf – suggested, at the very least, a declining role in an area that had been largely a British preserve since the modern Middle East had been created by the Western powers in their own interests in the settlements that followed the end of the First World War. But this declining influence was in accord with Britain's revised defence policy. The growing American involvement in the Middle East was not always viewed with favour by British ambassadors in the area, but, as Troutbeck astutely observed in December 1954, Britain had to accept, and with good grace, an increase of American influence in this part of the world. But, by the end of 1954, the relationship between Washington and London in the Middle East was such that the two powers were able to consider a joint plan to impose a settlement of the Arab–Israeli dispute.

Notes

1. Ritchie Ovendale, *The Longman Companion to the Middle East since 1914*, (London, 1992), pp. 3–21; Public Record Office, London, FO 371/98358, EA1059/1, Memorandum by C.M. Rose on British responsibilities in the Persian Gulf States and the future policy, Confidential, 4 February 1952; FO 371/98332, EA1022/1, Brief by Rose for Makins on Anglo-American co-operation in the Gulf,

9 February 1952; FO 371/98358, EA1059/3, Minute by D.N. Lane on the British protected states in the Gulf, received in registry 3 March 1952; David R. Devereux, *The Formulation of British Defence Policy towards the Middle East, 1948–56* (London, 1990), p. 111; FO 371/98358, A1059/6, 10511/3/52, G.C. Pelham to D.A. Greenhill, Confidential Guard, 26 November 1952; EA1059/8, Burrows to Greenhill, Secret, 13 December 1952; Public Record Office, London, CAB 128/27 pt. 2, fol. 335, CC45(54)2, Secret, 1 July 1954.

2. FO 371/98828, fos 3–7, ES1051/2, Aide memoire from American embassy, 7 April 1952; Minute by W.P. Cranston, 18 April 1952; fos. 26–8, Minute by W.P. Cranston, 29 April 1952; fos 126–8, Summary by W.P. Cranston of recent exchanges on Anglo-American-Saudi Arabian relations, 21 May 1952; fol. 42, ES1051/5, Minute by Sarell, 29 May 1952; fos. 55–8, ES1051/5, A.D.M. Ross to B.A.B. Burrows, Secret, 5 June 1952.

3. FO 371/98828, ES1051/18, G.C. Pelham to Anthony Eden, Confidential Guard, 17 December 1952; FO 371/98358, EA1059/10, G.C. Pelham to D.A. Greenhill, Confidential, 23 December 1952.

4. CAB 128/25, fol. 372, CC107(52)1, Secret, 22 December 1952; fol. 380, CC108(52)2, Secret, 30 December 1952; FO 371/98828, fos 160–1, ES1051/18, Minute by R.C. Blackham, 7 January 1953; *Foreign Relations of the United States* (hereafter cited as '*FRUS*') 1952–4(9), pp. 2527–9, Aldrich to Department of State, Telegram no. 5371, Secret, 31 March 1953; pp. 2535–8, Memorandum of conversation by Palmer, Secret, 16 April 1953; CAB 128/26 pt. 1, fol. 218, CC28(53)2, Secret, 21 April 1953; *FRUS* 1952–4(9), pp. 99–105, Memorandum of conversation, Secret, 18 May 1953; pp. 105–12, Memorandum of conversation, Secret, 19 May 1953.

5. CAB 128/26 pt. 1, fol. 281, CC37(53)4, Secret, 29 January 1953; CAB 128/26 pt. 2, fol. 289, CC38(53)6, Secret, 1 July 1953; fol. 317, CC42(53)3, Secret, 13 July 1953; fos 324–5, CC43(53)4, Secret, 16 July 1953; fos 332–4, CC44(53)5, Secret, 21 July 1953; *FRUS* 1952–4(9), pp. 2559–60, Salisbury to Dulles, Confidential, 27 July 1953; pp. 2561–2, Smith to embassy at London, Secret, 7 August 1953; pp. 2565–6, Dulles to Salisbury, Confidential, 28 August 1953.

6. CAB 128/27 pt. 1, CC39(54)4, Secret, 5 June 1954; for details of the establishment of the tribunal and its members see *FRUS* 1952–4(9), pp. 2615–6, Editorial note; *FRUS* 1955–7(13), pp. 274–5, Editorial note.

7. Public Record Office, London, PREM 11/1408, fos 282–3, Troutbeck to Foreign Office, Secret, 4 March 1953 d r 5 March 1953; fol. 281, M41/53, Churchill to Strang, 7 March 1953; fos 279–80, PM/WS/53/20, Strang to Churchill, Confidential, March 1953; fol. 278, A.M.B. to N.G. Morrison (Ministry of Defence), 13 March 1953; fos 276–7, Troutbeck to Foreign Office, Telegram no. 145, Secret, 24 March 1953 d r 25 March 1953; fos 273–5, Troutbeck to Foreign Office, Telegram no. 146, Secret, 24 March 1953 d r 25 March 1953; fos 261–2, F.J. Leishman (Foreign Office) to A.A.D. Montague-Browne, Secret, 7 April 1953, enclosing Memorandum on Iraq and Middle East defence.

8. *FRUS* 1952–4(9), pp. 361–3, British Embassy to Department of State, Confidential, 22 April 1953; H.W. Brands, 'The Cairo–Tehran Connection in Anglo-American Rivalry in the Middle East, 1951–1953', *The International History Review*, XI (1989), pp. 452–3; *FRUS* 1952–4(9), pp. 2370–1, Editorial note; A. Jalal, ('Towards the Baghdad Pact: South Asia and Middle East Defence in the Cold

War, 1947–1955', *The International History Review*, XI (1989), pp. 430–1; PREM 11/1408, fol. 249, Troutbeck to Foreign Office, Telegram no. 723, Secret, 22 December 1953; fol. 248, M339/53, Churchill to Eden, 23 December 1953; CAB 128/27 pt. 1, fos 31–2, CC1(54)2, Secret, 7 January 1954; *FRUS* 1952–4(9), pp. 450–2, Memorandum to Merchant, Top Secret, 12 January 1954.

9. CAB 128/27 pt. 1, fos 43–4, CC2(54)6, Secret, 12 January 1954; PREM 11/1408, fol. 244, PM/54/4, Eden to Churchill, Secret, 12 January 1954.
10. PREM 11/1408, fos. 241–2, D(54)4, Memorandum by Eden for the Defence Committee of the Cabinet on the Anglo-Iraqi Treaty, Secret, 19 January 1954; FO 371/111002, VQ1054/7/G, R.W.J. Hooper to P.S. Falla, Top Secret, 24 February 1954; PREM 11/726, Makins to Foreign Office, Telegram no. 321, Secret, 24 February 1954.
11. *FRUS* 1952–4(9), pp. 2371–3, Memorandum of Understanding between the Governments of the United States and the United Kingdom, 26 February 1954; p. 2385, Editorial note.
12. PREM 11/941, fos 116–8, Sterndale Bennett to Foreign Office, Secret, 4 March 1954; fol. 111, PM/54/47, Eden to Churchill, Confidential, 15 March 1954; PREM 11/1408, fos. 236–9, C(54)181, Memorandum by Lloyd on future defence arrangements with Iraq, Secret, 31 May 1954; fos 232–3, Alexander to Churchill; fos 227–9, Secretary of Chiefs of Staff Committee to Churchill, 3 June 1954 and annex, Note by Chiefs of Staff on strategic requirements in Iraq.
13. *FRUS* 1952–4(9), pp. 516–20, National Intelligence Estimate on the prospects for a Middle East defence grouping, Secret, 22 June 1954; PREM 11/941, fos 24–5, Record on meeting at White House on 25 June 1954; Evelyn Shuckburgh, *Descent to Suez: Diaries 1951–56* (London, 1986), pp. 224–5.
14. FO 371/111000, VQ1054/36/G, Minute by P.S. Falla on Iraq treaty revision, Secret, 20 August 1954; VQ1054/39/G, Minute by Falla on Anglo-Iraqi defence questions, Secret, 25 September 1954; VQ1054/38/G, Minute by Falla on defence arrangements with Iraq, Secret, 13 September 1954.
15. PREM 11/1408, fol. 211, V1076/36, Eden to Troutbeck, no. 176, Secret, 24 September 1954; FO 317/111003, VQ1054/39/G, Minute by P.S. Falla on Anglo-Iraqi defence questions, Secret, 25 September 1954; Shuckburgh, *Diaries*, Diary, 4 October 1954.
16. *FRUS* 1952–4(9), pp. 559–60, Dulles to American embassy at London, Top Secret, 13 November 1954.
17. PREM 11/1408, VQ1015/83, Troutbeck to Eden, no. 245, Confidential, 9 December 1954 recd. 20 December 1954.
18. CAB 128/24, fol. 143, CC30(52)7, 13 March 1952.
19. CAB 128/26 pt. 1, fol. 130, CC14(53)5, Secret, 24 February 1953; CAB 128/26 pt. 2, fos 303–4, CC40(53)6, Secret, 8 July 1953; fol. 339, CC45(53)5, Secret, 23 July 1953.
20. PREM 11/941, fol. 51, Churchill to Sharett, 23 April 1954. These words were drafted by Churchill see fol. 53, draft by J.R. Colville, 23 April 1954.
21. See Benny Morris, *Israel's Border Wars 1949–1956* (Oxford, 1993), pp. 244–62; Ritchie Ovendale, *The Origins of the Arab–Israeli Wars* (2nd edn, London, 1992), p. 150.
22. CAB 128/26 pt. 2, fol. 479, CC62(53)5, Secret, 29 October 1953.
23. CAB 128/26 pt. 2, fol. 504, CC67(53)5, Secret, 17 November 1953.

24. CAB 128/26 pt. 2, fol. 512, CC68(53)6, Secret, 19 November 1953.
25. Ritchie Ovendale, *The English-Speaking Alliance: Britain, the United States, the Dominions and the Cold War 1945–51* (London, 1985), pp. 132–3; Uri Bialer, *Between East and West: Israel's Foreign Policy Orientation 1948–1956* (Cambridge, 1990), pp. 235–41.
26. PREM 11/489, fos 18–20, PM/51/153, Eden to Churchill, 22 December 1951.
27. PREM 11/489, fos 13–16, NCDB/PM/15, N.C.D. Brownjohn to Churchill, Top Secret, March 1953, enclosing D(53)21, Memorandum by Chiefs of Staff for Cabinet Defence Committee on Israel and Middle East Defence and Discussions with the Americans, Top Secret, 26 March 1953.
28. PREM 11/489, D(53)8th mtg, Top Secret, 7 May 1953.
29. PREM 11/489, fos 4–7, C(53)228, Draft Despatch to the British Ambassador at Washington, 7 August 1953.
30. CAB 128/26 pt. 2, fos 366–7, CC48(53)5, Secret, 10 August 1953.
31. PREM 11/186, fol. 10, Minute by Churchill, 8 May 1952.
32. PREM 11/207, fol. 2, Sir R. Stevenson (Cairo) to Foreign Office, Telegram no. 1697, Confidential, 14 November 1952; fol. 4, M543/52, Churchill to Foreign Office, 17 November 1952; fol. 5, PM(52)137, Strang to Churchill, Confidential, Minute by Churchill, 20 November 1952.
33. PREM 11/465, fol. 18, PM/MS/53/48, Selwyn Lloyd to Churchill, undated; fol 16, M94/53, Churchill to Selwyn Lloyd and Sir William Strang on draft aide memoire to Israel. Churchill failed to understand that Bevin was not anti-Semitic, but opposed Zionism. See Ritchie Ovendale, *Britain, the United States, and the End of the Palestine Mandate*, (Woodbridge, Suffolk, 1989) p. 133.
34. PREM 11/465, fol. 8, M103/53, Churchill to Strang, 23 April 1953; fol. 2, Foreign Office to Cairo, Telegram no. 857, Confidential, 24 April 1954.
35. PREM 11/465, fol. 5, Foreign Office to Tel Aviv, Telegram no. 154, Confidential, 24 April 1953; fol. 4, Foreign Office to Tel Aviv, Telegram no. 155, Confidential, 24 April 1954.
36. PREM 11/490, fol. 4, PM/WS/53/100, Strang to Churchill, Confidential, 1 May 1953; Minute by Churchill, 1 May 1953.
37. PREM 11/490, fol. 2, Lloyd to Churchill, 8 May 1953; Minutes by Churchill, 9 May 1953.
38. See Morris, *Israel's Border Wars*, pp. 220–1.
39. PREM 11/ 941, M110/53, Strang to Churchill, 24 April 1953; fol. 217, Churchill to Ben-Gurion, Urgent and Personal, 25 April 1953.
40. See Morris, *Israel's Border Wars*, pp. 221–2.
41. PREM 11/941, fol. 184, Foreign Office to Tel Aviv, Telegram no. 209, Secret, 22 May 1953 d 23 May 1953.
42. CAB 127/28 pt. 1, fos 58–9, CC4(54)6, Secret, 21 January 1954.
43. Morris, *Israel's Border Wars*, p. 254.
44. CAB 128/27 pt. 1, fol. 58, CC4(54)5, Secret, 21 January 1954.
45. PREM 11/941, fol. 94, Brook to Churchill, 30 March 1954; Minute by Churchill, 30 March 1954.
46. Morris, *Israel's Border Wars*, p. 295.
47. PREM 11/941, fos 68–70, E. Elath to Churchill, Personal and Confidential, 13 April 1954.
48. PREM 11/941, fol. 56, Evelyn Shuckburgh to J.R. Colville, 21 April 1954; fol. 51,

Churchill to Sharett, 23 April 1954.
49. PREM 11/941, Foreign Office to Amman, Telegram no. 527, Secret, 4 July 1954.
50. PREM 11/941, fos 24–5, Record of a meeting at the White House on 25 June 1954 between Churchill, Eisenhower and others.
51. Ovendale, *Britain, the United States, and the End of the Palestine Mandate*, pp. 220–1, 88–91.
52. *FRUS*, 1952–4(9), pp. 394–8, Memorandum of meeting of National Security Council on 9 July 1953.
53. See Robert Rhodes James, *Anthony Eden* (London, 1986), pp. 345, 358.

5

Eden and the 'Flexing of British Muscles': The Baghdad Pact

In his account of his years as Prime Minister, Anthony Eden recalled that British policy in the Middle East had had two main objectives: the protection of British interests in Iraq, and the protection of British interests in the Gulf. The main threat to these interests was posed by Gamal Abdul Nasser, the Egyptian leader, whose ideology was anti-Western and who colluded with the Soviet Union especially over matters like arms supplies.

At this time Allen Dulles, the Head of the Central Intelligence Agency, in a report to the National Security Council on 22 December 1955, observed that the British 'had been lately flexing their muscles' in the Middle East, and as a consequence had created problems for the United States. He singled out British pressure on Iran to join the Baghdad Pact, the quarrel with the Saudi Arabians in the Buraimi area, and the efforts to push Jordan into the Baghdad Pact. Allen Dulles thought that the only explanation for some of these moves was 'the hope of the British to restore something of their lost prestige in the Middle East'.

Eden had earlier, on 4 October 1955, told the Cabinet that British interests in the Middle East were greater than those of the United States because of Britain's dependence on Middle Eastern oil. Britain's experience in the area was also greater than the United States: 'We should not therefore allow ourselves to be restricted overmuch by reluctance to act without full American concurrence and support.' Britain needed to frame its policy in the light of its interests in the area and to obtain as much American support as it was able to. Britain's policy, Eden told the Cabinet, should be based on the need to help its acknowledged friends like Iraq and the Trucial States on whom Britain depended for oil. The Americans could help Britain by aiding the supply of arms.[1]

Under Eden's guidance, first as Foreign Secretary and then as Prime Minister, Britain pursued what in effect had been initially an American vision going back to the early 1950s, and one which Washington has pursued more actively in the second half of 1954, that of the Northern Tier of defence against the Soviet Union. Britain accepted the concept as a means of maintaining a military relationship with Iraq to replace the Anglo-Iraqi Treaty of 1930. But as the

Northern Tier concept became British policy, Washington while endorsing the move, suddenly became aloof and declined to become part of the arrangement. It transpired that Washington felt that if it joined an alliance of Arab states and Turkey, and possibly Iran, Israel would expect a defence guarantee from the United States, and given the power of the Zionist lobby this might be difficult to resist particularly in election years. There was also a calculation as to whether the Soviet Union might be provoked if the Americans became involved. Britain wanted the Americans to join. This was a part of an attempt to get the Americans more committed to the defence of the Middle East. These developments did take place at a time when there was a great deal of agreement between Washington and London in their joint diagnosis of the problems of the Middle East, and the need for a solution, if necessary imposed from outside, to the Arab–Israeli dispute.

This new British policy for the Middle East was developed against the background of a further reduction in defence expenditure outlined in the Defence White Paper of February 1955. The paper still envisaged a role for conventional land and naval forces, as it was felt that troops on the ground would be needed to hold a line to the east in Europe in the vital initial stages of the war to give time for the effect of the strategic air offensive to be felt. The reliance on strategic airpower and thermo-nuclear weapons, though not exclusive, was great. And this reliance was seen as enabling Britain to strengthen the basis of its economy and maintain a balance between the demands of defence and other claims. The external economic aid Britain had relied on was being reduced. Following the general election at the end of May 1955, in which the British electorate returned the Conservative administration to office, Eden decided on further economies in the defence programme. Selwyn Lloyd, the Minister of Defence, advised in July that unless existing programmes were revised defence expenditure would rise over the following four years from £1,527 million in 1955 to £1,929 million in 1959, and that the economy of the country would not be able to stand that. The defence estimates for 1956–57 were cut to £1,535 million.[2]

At the beginning of 1955, the shifting enthusiasms of Washington and London for the Northern Tier concept were evident. On 11 January, Evan Wilson of the American embassy in London warned Evelyn Shuckburgh, the Assistant Under-Secretary of State at the Foreign Office, regarding the State Department's concern that Britain's thinking about Iraq joining the Turco-Pakistan Pact was not as positive as it had been the previous autumn. Washington did not believe that there would be a worsening of relations between Egypt and Iraq, or between Egypt and the West if Iraq joined the Northern Tier. Shuckburgh gave the assurance that London was being more cautious than Washington, and did not want to put pressure on Iraq. It was encouraging every move that Iraq might make. Britain was even providing the Turks with arguments to use with Nuri. Shuckburgh did concede, however, that following the treaty with Egypt and the move of the Nasser government towards the West, the British attitude had shifted. London felt that no Middle East defence arrangement was likely to have much value unless it enjoyed Egyptian support and participation. If the American pursuit of the Northern Tier succeeded it could be a great success, but Shuckburgh thought it risky, and stressed that Britain had to avoid being blamed for its failure.[3]

The agreement between Turkey and Pakistan of 2 April 1954 was the first stage in the creation of the Northern Tier. Nuri al-Said, who became Prime Minister of Iraq for the twelfth time on 4 August 1954, was at first cautious about his country joining any security arrangement outside the Arab world. But Nuri was tempted by hints from the Turkish Prime Minister, Adnan Menderes, that there might be increased American military assistance for Iraq if it concluded an agreement with Turkey. Menderes apparently had no authorization to make this suggestion. Indeed both the British and American embassies in Baghdad were taken by surprise in January 1955 when there were rumours of a bilateral Turkish-Iraqi pact, and remained sceptical until the agreement was signed on 24 February 1955.

When asked to comment on this proposed pact, John Foster Dulles, the American Secretary of State, told a press conference on 18 January 1955 that Washington regarded such a move as a constructive development, one towards building up the Northern Tier of which Turkey and Pakistan were already pioneers. Dulles, however, went on to refer to Iraq and Iran which lay in the gap between Turkey and Pakistan, and whose participation would greatly improve the defence of the area.[4] The British learnt from the State Department that Dulles' preliminary reaction was that he favoured eventual American association with the pact, provided such association was along the lines of the American association with the Manila Pact: the United States would only be involved if there were aggression from outside the area.

The State Department view, as explained to Shuckburgh on 27 January 1955, was that as Washington did not have the same responsibility in the Middle East as London, the Americans thought of the associations they tried to foster, such as the Northern Tier, as being aimed in the first instance at fighting the Cold War. But there was acknowledgement of the importance of British supply lines, and the need for any major equipment to be supplied to Iraq to be British.

Shuckburgh pointed to British requirements in Iraq as being pre-stocking facilities, the use of aerodromes for air squadrons on a rotation basis alongside overflying rights and the maintenance of technicians. He spoke of joint training with indigenous forces as a means of enjoying facilities. Shuckburgh explained that London thought that it would be a mistake for the Shah of Iran to move too rapidly towards treaty association with the West: London considered the Shah exposed and that he had overestimated the strength of his own position. The Americans took the opposite view: there was the danger that the Iranians might lean towards the Soviets; American army instructor personnel were leaving shortly for Iran. There was agreement on the need for periodic Anglo-American talks on the defence of the Middle East between the State Department and the

Pentagon on one side, and the British embassy at Washington and the British Joint Services Mission on the other. Britain saw the proposed Turco-Iraqi Pact as a way for Nuri to terminate the Anglo-Iraqi Treaty of 1930, and at the same time have a multilateral instrument to take its place with which Britain was associated. Nuri wanted to secure sanction from the Iraqi parliament for further accession, and at an appropriate moment Britain would join. Britain saw this as a means of maintaining its basic defence requirements.

Washington and London hoped for Egyptian help in securing a settlement of the Arab–Israeli dispute. Indeed there was the thought that the more Nasser helped over Israel the more he could be rewarded by military and economic assistance from the West. Shuckburgh pointed to the need to deflect Nasser's ambitions away from British and French territories in Africa. This issue also concerned the French. R. Massigli, the Secretary General at the Quai d'Orsay, a former ambassador at London and a noted Anglophile, denied that France's concern over the proposed treaty had at its base a French abhorrence at seeing any increase of British influence in the Middle East. Paris was worried about the possible break-up of the Arab League, and feared that Nuri wanted to absorb Syria into Iraq under a single monarchy, the 'Fertile Crescent'. Massigli denied that France had real interests in Syria, but insisted that from the psychological point of view the absorption of Syria into what was still considered a British controlled state, Iraq, could be disastrous, particularly for French parliamentary opinion.[5]

Cairo did not like the envisaged Turco-Iraqi Pact. It feared that Baghdad might challenge its claims for leadership of the Arab world. At the meeting of Arab Prime Ministers in Cairo, the Egyptians tried to tempt the Iraqis to delay with the offer of arms without conditions. The Iraqis thought that the Egyptians were telling lies. But the Egyptians were getting some tanks and aircraft from Britain and had been offered arms from the United States. Cairo even hinted to Washington that the United States could gain credit in the Middle East by achieving a postponement of the Turco-Iraqi Pact, and so allowing Egypt time to develop an alternative arrangement for the defence of the region.[6]

There were difficulties over the conclusion of the Turco-Iraqi Pact. Nuri had a phobia about Turkey. Britain felt it unwise to get tough with Jordan and to talk to the French about Syria, fearing that there might be an adverse Arab reaction to the pact, and did not want to be seen to be lobbying the Arabs against the Egyptians at a time when Eden was scheduled to visit Nasser. The Egyptians had suspicions, particularly about Eden's proposed stop in Baghdad on the way back from Bangkok. The Egyptian ambassador at London also asked about the new British look at the defence of the Middle East. Ivone Kirkpatrick, the Permanent Under-Secretary of State at the Foreign Office, explained that the development of thermo-nuclear weapons had led to a revision of Britain's concept of Middle East defence, and that Britain was attaching greater importance to organizing a coherent system of defence in Iraq. The Egyptian Foreign Minister, Mahmud Fawzi, warned that a pact between Turkey and Iraq would make an attack by the

Soviet Union on Iraq more likely. Fawzi reported that many Arab countries viewed this as the first step taken by the Western powers to disintegrate the Arab League through making piecemeal arrangements with the different Arab states. In the event Nuri suggested that London and Washington might like to be original signatories to the Turco-Iraqi Pact. Dulles reasoned that this might lead to the impression being given of a pact imposed from outside the region.[7]

When Nasser came to dinner at the British embassy in Cairo on 21 February 1955, Eden reported that they had a two-hour discussion afterwards in a most friendly atmosphere. Although not negative on the question of a settlement with Israel, Nasser remained obdurate on the subject of the Turco-Iraqi Pact. He did agree with a strategic appreciation given by Field-Marshal Sir John Harding, and said that his interest and sympathy were with the West. But the Turco-Iraqi Pact, with its 'bad timing and its unfortunate content' had set back collaboration between the Arab states and the West. Eden suggested to Nasser that he should not treat the pact as a crime, to which the Egyptian leader retorted: 'no but it is one'. Eden hinted that Nasser should talk to Nuri and Menderes, and sort out the differences. The Foreign Secretary was impressed by Nasser, and reported that he 'seemed forthright and friendly although not open to conviction on the Turco-Iraqi business'. Eden attributed this partly to jealousy, partly to Nasser's frustrated desire to lead the Arab world. Shortly after this conversation the Foreign Secretary recorded that it had been conducted on the basis that Egypt should expect the Turco-Iraqi pact to be concluded shortly, and that its government should reconcile itself to that. But the Egyptians did not succumb to the British persuasion, and Eden concluded that there was nothing to be gained from delaying the matter on Egypt's account.[8]

Britain wanted the Americans to join the pact. But Washington, in March, advanced yet another argument as to why this would not happen immediately: if the United States was not a signatory it would be easier for the French to stay outside. The response, given by the Counsellor and Head of Chancery at the British embassy at Paris, J.G.S. Beith, was to quote Shuckburgh that Britain attached great importance to the eventual American accession, and that French feelings were a minor consideration in comparison with the importance of having the Americans in.[9]

Prior to its accession to the Turco-Iraqi Pact, Britain had preliminary talks with Iraq at the end of February and the beginning of March about the terms of a new defence agreement to replace the Anglo-Iraqi Treaty of 1930 that would follow on accession. The British strategic assessment was that with modern weapons the whole Middle East including the Gulf needed to be defended on the frontiers of Iraq. Iraq accepted this view. Britain realized that it could now only do this in co-operation with local forces, and that it could no longer expect to keep armed forces in the Middle East under the old system of unilateral treaty rights.

It was Article 1 of the Turco-Iraqi Pact of 24 February 1955 which provided for the co-operation of the parties for their security and defence, and for special agreements between them to give effect to this, and thus gave the umbrella under which Britain should negotiate a new defence agreement with Iraq. Under the proposed new arrangements Britain's obligations towards Turkey and Iraq would be less than existing ones.

Eden acknowledged that there were difficulties over the air bases at Habbaniya and Shaiba, but thought that the essential British requirements were met. Iraq would need modern weapons. Its forces needed the same weapons as the British if the lines of communication and supply were to be maintained. But Britain had to prepare to counter American attempts to supplant it, in spite of the understanding between Britain and the United States that the Iraqi forces should continue to look primarily to Britain for equipment and training. The difficulty was that the American supplies could be free while the British ones would have to be paid for.

There was no immediate prospect of any other state acceding to the pact in the immediate future. Washington would not. Egypt and Saudi Arabia were organizing an opposition camp. The Syrian government, in Eden's words, had fallen a victim to 'Egyptian cajolery, bribery and threats'. Egyptian pressure would stop Jordan and Lebanon from acceding for some time. Pakistan could join in time and Iran was also favourably disposed. France might want to, but such a move would not be welcomed by Iraq, and maybe even Turkey.

From Baghdad the ambassador, Sir Michael Wright, warned that the domestic political situation was favourable to an agreement, and this could not be reasonably expected to recur: 'If we allow the pot to come off the boil we may never be able to bring it back again'. He warned that Nuri could throw in his hand. Sir Ralph Stevenson in Cairo, however, pointed to the Iraqi-Egyptian conflict and advised that there would be little advantage to the West if Iraqi realism and co-operation were matched by neutralism and irresponsibility in Egypt and the other Arab states. Stevenson thought that Egypt's nuisance value could be neutralized by the accession of Iran. In the Foreign Office, G.C. Arthur agreed with Stevenson that Britain should play down its emphasis on the pact, but could not allow it to die for want of attention. Arthur also endorsed the need to work for the accession of Iran and possibly also Pakistan, and to stop Nasser from concluding a rival pact with Syria and Saudi Arabia. Shuckburgh, in replying to Stevenson, hoped that Egypt would cool and some means could be found of hitching it to the new system. The Egyptians asked the British whether the pact was to be extended to Jordan, Syria and Lebanon.

Washington was concerned that there was no non-aggression clause in the pact: that could provide the Israelis with propaganda material, and also the Indians when Pakistan acceded. This worried the Americans as they were supporting the pact by supplying arms to some of its members, and the problem could become acute before the question of American accession. Indeed the Operations Coordinating Board of the National Security Council reported on 21 March 1954 that Washington had given 'behind-the-scenes encouragement' to the Turco-Iraqi agreement and the Northern Tier concept. But although

Washington had acted to a great extent in concert with London, and had capitalized on and supported the relatively strong British position in Jordan and Iraq, it had also acted independently of Britain and other countries by taking the lead in the scheme for the development of the 'Unified Plan for the Jordan Valley'. This scheme distributed the waters of the Jordan and Yarmuk rivers equitably between Lebanon, Syria, Jordan and Israel. Eric Johnston, the Special Representative of the President, was negotiating this plan. On 4 April the Anglo-Iraqi agreement was signed and on 5 April, following a debate in the House of Commons, Britain acceded to the Turco-Iraqi Pact, and it became known as the Baghdad Pact.[10]

There were ceremonies at Habbaniya and Shaiba, on the fortieth anniversary of the outbreak of the Rashid Ali revolt, marking the transfer of control of the bases to the Iraqis. Wright spoke of Britain coming to Iraq's immediate assistance if its freedom were in danger. The speech in reply referred to Iraq's twin aims of self-defence and co-operation with its neighbours. The Royal Air Force ensigns were lowered and replaced by Iraqi flags.

After a visit to the Middle East, Field-Marshal Sir Gerald Templar, who became the Chief of the Imperial General Staff in September 1955, told Shuckburgh on 13 June that Nuri was the only 'man' in the area. Nuri, himself, disappointed at the timid attitude of the Americans with their fears of Israeli reactions if any of its Arab neighbours joined the pact, wanted Jordan to take a more positive attitude. He was enthusiastic over the hint Anthony Nutting, the Minister of State for Foreign Affairs, had given to King Hussein of Jordan in June 1955 that if Jordan wanted treaty revision the most convenient way of obtaining it would be to join the Turco-Iraqi Pact and make a special arrangement with the British government in the same way as Iraq had done. In many ways Nuri was the key: Wright urged that it was necessary to consolidate the agreement with Iraq while Nuri was in power. In early August, Britain let the Iranians know that it wanted Iran to sign the pact as well.[11]

Alongside these British moves, a State Department and Pentagon working group advised in June 1955 on the development of a Middle East defence arrangement in which Anglo-American co-operation would be essential, and that of Turkey, Jordan, Iran and Iraq required. Eventually Lebanon, Syria and Egypt would also be needed, and the help of Saudi Arabia would be desirable. The co-operation of Pakistan was important to complete the Northern Tier, but that of Israel would not be essential. A regional defence organization would be necessary. To move towards this, Washington should induce Iran to join the Turco-Iraqi Pact by offering to support Iranian military programmes. Potentially, over a five-year period, Washington could expect to spend between $1.5 to $2 billion on the defence of the area. The United States, within a year, would need to adhere to a Middle East defence organization, probably after that Pakistan and Iran.[12]

Anglo-American policy towards what became known as the Baghdad Pact was, in part, conditioned by what followed from a suggestion that Eden made to

Sir Roger Makins on 4 November 1954 that Arab–Israeli relations offered a challenge to American and British statesmanship and skill. Using the analogy of the Trieste dispute where a joint Anglo-American team between 1953 and 1954 managed to bring Italy and Yugoslavia together,[13] Eden suggested applying a similar technique to Israel and the Arab states. Shuckburgh was in the Middle East, and Eden asked that Dulles send one of the State Department experts to join forces with him when he returned in December to work out the ingredients of a solution. Eden wanted to avoid having the French closely associated with this. Shuckburgh put some ideas to Dulles in Paris on 16 December 1954. The Secretary of State did not want to involve the French, and dilated on the influence of the Zionists in the United States where subscriptions to Israel were exempt from tax. But Dulles thought there were 12 months in which it might be possible to do something, before the next election loomed. Eden also admitted to the power of the Zionist lobby in the House of Commons.

The Anglo-American plan that evolved was known as 'Alpha'. Shuckburgh discussed proposals with State Department officials in Washington in January. There were differences between the two sides over the amount of territory Israel should be required to cede. But it was thought that the best approach was for Britain and the United States to work out the terms of a reasonable settlement, and then through separate discussions with the parties concerned, and maybe even through direct talks between them, to get them to agree to it.

Initial proposals included some territorial concessions by Israel, and the readmission of the Arab refugees who wanted to return up to a fixed number, say 75,000. Should the Gaza Strip be ceded to Israel that number could be increased to 150,000. The Arab states would lift their boycott of Israel and permanent frontiers would be established. Britain, the United States, and possibly Turkey and France would guarantee the frontiers. Jerusalem would be demilitarized.

When Eden referred to the Arab–Israeli dispute after the dinner in Cairo on 21 February, Nasser was not entirely negative, though the Egyptian leader did emphasize that no solution was to be found in partial settlements. Dulles thought that special consideration should be shown to Nasser in preparation for Alpha. But Eden argued that Nasser could not be helped at the cost of weakening support for the Turco-Iraqi Pact.

It was, Eden insisted, the declared British objective to make the pact the foundation for an effective defence system for the Middle East. To achieve this the accession of Syria, Lebanon and Jordan would eventually be necessary. Britain could not afford 'to risk giving the impression in the Middle East that we are weathervanes and that our policy has changed'.

Eden was scathing about the State Department: they needed to be persuaded that the United States could not expect to command respect in the Middle East unless it pursued a consistent policy based on its convictions. The enthusiastic American support of the Turco-Iraqi Pact was 'too recent in men's minds to enable them to execute a *volte-face* with safety or dignity'. George Allen, the

Assistant Secretary of State, agreed. Dulles endorsed his recommendation that Washington should try to work out a compromise arrangement with London involving the latter's adherence to the Turco-Iraqi Pact. Allen argued that Nasser should not be given the impression that Washington was underwriting his attainment of undisputed leadership over the other Arab states. Nasser's influence in the Arab world would be a natural by-product of American aid, but Washington would not want Nasser to be in a position 'to demand our unswerving support in the vagaries of intra-Arab politics'.[14]

By April the agreed Anglo-American plan to settle the Arab–Israeli dispute included the establishment of a sovereign Arab right of way across the Negev, which would not impair the Israeli sovereign right of way to Eilat on the Red Sea. Israel would cede two small triangles of territory, one to Egypt on the Egyptian–Israeli frontier, and one to Jordan a few miles north of Eilat. There were indications that the Israelis were not prepared to make concessions, and by June Britain thought that Dulles would be unwise to publish the plan. Given Britain's balance of payments difficulties, the Chancellor of the Exchequer, R.A. Butler, thought that Britain would not be justified in providing Israel with the financial assistance the plan involved. Dulles, however, envisaged making a general statement consistent with 'Alpha', but without referring specifically to it after the Israeli elections.

Macmillan explained to the Cabinet on 14 July 1955 that Dulles wanted to make an announcement around 18 August to prevent the Palestine question becoming an issue in the election campaign. Macmillan thought it might be better for Dulles to make the statement then as, if he did it later under pressure from the election campaign, he might make proposals even more favourable to Israel. Even so there was the danger of trouble in the Middle East after Dulles' envisaged announcement, and it could also endanger the progress over the Northern Tier. Britain needed something in return: an indication of American willingness to join the Turco-Iraqi Pact should there be a settlement of the Arab-Israeli dispute; an undertaking by the Americans to supply Centurion tanks to Iraq by off-shore purchase in Britain; to give Britain physical support if there were fighting after the announcement. The Cabinet thought, in any case, that as the plan had been worked out jointly between Britain and the United States, it would be difficult for Britain to dissociate itself from it. These points were made to Dulles. The Secretary of State said that, in any case, he had assured Mr Eric Johnson that he would not make the statement until after Johnson's visit to the area in connection with the division of the waters of the Jordan River.

On 19 August Eden was reported to be in a 'flap' at the news that Dulles intended to make a statement in general terms on 25 or 26 August. Dulles was worried that events could outdate the 'Alpha' project, and that the proposal should be made at a time when Washington seemed to be the friend of both sides. Johnson had also withdrawn his request for delay as his water project was encountering Arab opposition.[15]

The British were worried about Arab reaction. Macmillan asked that Dulles be even less specific. He thought the Arabs might have the impression that Washington believed only a few minor adjustments to the frontier were necessary, and that they were being expected to enter into direct negotiations with Israel on that basis.

Dulles' speech of 26 August given to the Council on Foreign Relations in New York referred generally to the need for a comprehensive settlement, the plight of 900,000 refugees, fears over Israeli expansion and Arab aggression. There was little that was tangible. Israel appeared sympathetic, but would not give up territory. Nasser complained that there was nothing specific in the proposals. The Johnson mission foundered. Dulles' fears about events overtaking 'Alpha' were fulfilled: on 22 August Israeli patrols crossed the Egyptian border, Nasser retaliated with fedayeen raids into Israel, and on 31 August 36 Egyptians were killed in an Israeli raid on Egyptian positions at Khan Yunis.

In September the Egyptians maintained that there would have to be a transfer of defensible territory to establish the continuity of the Arab world: a corridor type arrangement would not be sufficient. In any case there was no significant body of opinion in the Arab world seeking an immediate settlement. Nasser's own reaction was negative: the other Arab states would attack Egypt politically if it took steps towards a settlement with Israel. After the announcement that Egypt would be receiving arms from Czechoslovakia, Dulles following a talk with Shuckburgh, advised that a settlement of the Arab–Israeli conflict remained a primary Anglo-American goal in the Middle East.[16]

During these months, Israel moved steadily towards an activist policy and the acceptance of the belief that it would have to fight another war against the Arabs. On 17 February 1955, David Ben-Gurion returned as Minister of Defence. He brought with him a philosophy that the only way to secure Israel was to force the Arabs, probably by military measures, to accept peace with Israel. Great Power and United Nations' intervention were to be avoided, and the Arabs should be made to sue for peace on Israel's terms. In doing so Israel might add to its territory. For Ben-Gurion, the Gaza Strip was seemingly an obvious target: it was populated not by Egyptians, but by Palestinian refugees.

On 28 February two Israeli platoons of paratroopers stormed an Egyptian encampment at Gaza and killed 38 people. The Israelis lost eight men. The United Nations Mixed Armistice Commission and the Security Council condemned Israel for a 'prearranged and planned attack ordered by Israeli authorities'. Ben-Gurion's policy of direct confrontation was underway. Israel returned to its policy of activism knowing that it had at least the support of France. Many French officers and members of the ministries of the Interior and Defence disliked both Britain and the Arabs. Not only had the Israeli army earned their sympathy with its defeat of the Arabs, and in effect earlier of Britain, but Israel's victories over the Arabs were seen as having delayed the rebellions in North Africa. In January 1955 Paris overrode British objections, and agreed to sell Mystère aircraft to Israel. There was only a mild reaction in France to the Gaza raid.[17]

Israel claimed that the Turco-Iraqi Pact was likely to increase its sense of isolation. This was the case made by the Israeli ambassador at London, Elihu Eilat, in a conversation with Eden on 10 February 1955. Eilat said that Israel wanted a bilateral agreement with Britain over defence, and also asked for at least a dozen Centurion tanks. A week later Eilat complained that the Americans had been more forthcoming about Israel's desire to be associated with the West. Eden had minuted on 29 November 1954 that the Israelis were trying to trap Britain everywhere they could into some further commitment, but only saw such commitment as part of an Arab–Israeli settlement. But E.M. Rose did note that Britain might have to arrive at some more definite arrangement with Israel to help it overcome its feeling of isolation as that feeling could lead Israel to attack the Arabs. Britain would have to associate the Americans, and possibly the French, with any such agreement so that it did not become the only guarantor of Israel's frontiers.

Churchill, at this time favoured a suggestion he had heard from James de Rothschild that the Israelis should join the British Commonwealth. He thought that would be a wonderful thing at a time when 'so many people want to leave us; it might be the turning of the tide'. Churchill thought that the Jews should have Jerusalem; according to him, it was they who had made it famous.[18]

The British ambassador at Tel Aviv, J.W. Nicholls, did advise on 8 March that Britain should examine how Israel could be associated directly with Western defence plans, and that the British should take the Israelis into their confidence over the wider strategic problems in the Middle East. Nicholls felt it necessary to feed the Israeli passion for being appreciated and understood, and to satisfy 'the gnawing sense of insecurity which, however imaginary – and it is of course by no means entirely so – unfortunately poisons all Israel's policies'.

He elaborated on what he saw as the British dilemma. Possibly a British defence of the Arabs against Israel would be impractical: Zionist opinion in the United States and 'liberal' opinion would not accept the possibility of British troops and bombers being used to fight the Israelis. As surgery was excluded, Nicholls thought that Britain had to face the prospect of 'administering a long and troublesome course of treatment to this very diseased part of the world'. The centre of infection was Israel, and Nicholls thought that the Israelis had to be treated as a sick people whose illness was psychological. The ambassador's diagnosis was that almost every individual Israeli bore some psychological trace of the past 2,500 years of Jewish history: 'unsureness, over-confidence, emotional instability, fierce intolerance, superiority complex, inferiority complex, guilt complex', and moreover there was a deep conviction that the world was in Israel's debt. He doubted whether it was reasonable to expect a nation made up of individuals so psychologically unstable to mount a mature foreign policy – 'though their superior intelligence tempts one to expect it of them'. Nicholls warned that if Britain could not find some way of treating Israel's psychological condition, it 'was more likely to embark on an apparently suicidal policy in a state of national exultation, based on a compound of mystical conviction that somehow Jehovah would intervene to save his people and shrewd calculation that the United States Jewry might turn out to be his chosen instrument'.

He warned that Britain might have to reckon with the possibility that the Israelis might decide to risk a military conflict with the Arabs, even in the face of Britain's commitments to Jordan, and before the balance of power shifted decisively against them. Shuckburgh agreed with Nicholls's diagnosis, but thought that his suggested treatment would only be possible as part of a general settlement in the Middle East. The State Department was also concerned that Israel might want to annex all or part of the Gaza Strip and so shorten its land frontier with Egypt. It suggested that London and Washington might explore the possibility of using economic sanctions or even military measures to deal with such an eventuality.

At this time the Zionist lobby was organizing pressure in Britain to secure a treaty to guarantee Israel's existing conquests, and the Labour Party took up the Zionist cause in the run-up to the general election in May 1955. Eilat kept blaming Britain, and after a visit to Israel complained that his government thought Britain was behaving in a discriminatory fashion against Israel by making bilateral treaties with Arab states. The Israelis were not prepared to start talks with the Arabs on the basis of any programme which involved changing the territorial status quo, or the acceptance of Arab refugees into Israel. Presumably as a consequence of the return of a Conservative administration, and the defeat of Labour with its pro-Zionist stance, Israel was abandoning its attempts to secure a treaty of guarantee from Britain, though it hoped that Washington would be more forthcoming. Shuckburgh warned Eilat that he should not rely on any difference between the attitudes of Washington and London. Shortly afterwards, Macmillan told the Cabinet that there were indications that Israel was thinking of an incursion into Egyptian territory near Gaza, and he was accordingly delaying the supply of military equipment to the Middle East.[19]

Britain was increasingly concerned over the internal developments in Israel. On 20 June, Shuckburgh even suggested that the ban on the release of six Centurion tanks for Israel, imposed after the Gaza raid of 28 February, should be lifted, as that could help the gradualist Israeli Prime Minister, Moshe Sharett, to stand up to the extremists: 'unless he can show results in the near future, power will pass to the wild men'. But the Chiefs of Staff effectively wanted to abandon the Tripartite Declaration, and stop supplying Israel with 'sharp' weapons like tanks and fighter aircraft. This did not apply to 'blunt' weapons. It was, the Minister of Defence, Selwyn Lloyd, informed the Cabinet Defence Committee on 6 July, considering Britain's treaty obligations, undesirable from the purely strategic point of view to continue to build up the armed strength of Israel to maintain a balance of forces between Israel and the Arab states collectively. It was appropriate, however, that Iraq which had accepted regional responsibility in the Middle East, and Jordan to which Britain owed special obligations, should have preferential treatment. This should be explained to the Americans as also coinciding with their strategic interests. Israel accepted the transfer of two destroyers from Britain in July, but asked for eight more Meteor fighter aircraft, six Meteor night fighters, and the release of six Centurion tanks already promised.[20]

After Egypt acquired Soviet arms through Czechoslovakia, Israel asked Britain at the end of November 1955 for a large consignment of weapons. This time Eilat was told by Kirkpatrick that the opening of the new front of the Cold War in the Middle East had placed Israel in a situation of mortal peril. If the Arab states became estranged from the West, Soviet tanks, arms and volunteers could appear in the Middle East, and before too long Israel would face 40 million Arabs under Soviet command, and there would be nothing Britain could do to save it from annihilation.

Once again the issue of Israel becoming a member of the British Commonwealth was raised, this time by Israel M. Sieff, the Joint Managing Director of Marks and Spencer Ltd., though Sieff did acknowledge that the idea was hopeless and Israel would prefer to keep a strong British connection, 'for instance a naval base or something of the kind'. This could be under NATO arrangements, or as an outpost of Cyprus. Another possibility was a British air base in the Negev. R.M. Hadow of the Foreign Office had earlier pointed out that membership of the Commonwealth could be a convenient solution for Israel as the Commonwealth would be able 'to pull her chestnuts out of the fire for her'. Sieff told Macmillan that the Israelis wanted to keep their ties with the West, and did not want to be sunk into an oriental world. When, in December 1955, the French wanted to give priority to supplying 12 Mystère aircraft to Israel, as part of an off-shore purchase at the expense of the United States which would mean a delay in the completion of a NATO programme, Britain opposed this.[21]

While there was extensive consultation between Washington and London on political issues in the Middle East, the Americans were hesitant about conducting military talks. Eden broached the matter of military talks on 23 February 1955 when he met Dulles in Bangkok. Talks did take place between the British, the Americans and the Turks in London early in 1955, and in April the Joint Chiefs of Staff insisted that informal bilateral talks with the British might be possible, but formal talks should be avoided as these could offend the Turks. The State Department regarded bilateral Anglo-American defence talks on the Middle East essential.[22]

Britain was increasingly concerned about American military aid to the Middle East which could mean that American equipment would be used instead of British. Britain hoped that Pakistan would eventually play a part beside British forces and would be maintained on British supply lines, something which could not be done if the Pakistanis had American equipment. The British were also worried about indications that the Americans were modifying their attitude over the supply of equipment to Iraq which Washington and London had agreed should be British.

These were issues which Nuri raised with Shuckburgh in London on 22 April

1955. Shuckburgh told the Iraqi Prime Minister that it had been agreed between Washington and London that in the Middle East major weapons should be based on British patterns. Nuri asked about the overall command structure in the Middle East, and Shuckburgh had to explain that such military matters would remain uncertain until it was clear how the Baghdad Pact developed. Nuri thought that the Shah of Iran was keen to join, but this was dependent on his receiving American aid.[23]

There was scepticism in Washington about the British motives for wanting conversations on the defence of the Middle East. Herbert Hoover, the Under Secretary of State, said that previous conversations had shown two British objectives: first, Britain wanted command responsibility in the area in the event of difficulties; and, secondly, the British expected the United States 'to foot the bill required to place the area in some posture of defence'. Hoover told the National Security Council on 5 May 1955 that in future conversations with the British on the Middle East the Americans would confine themselves to discussion on a political level, and avoid further discussion on the military level. On 16 June, however, the Joint Chiefs of Staff recommended that the United States, while continuing to place reliance upon Turkey and Pakistan to further its plans in the Middle East, should co-operate closely with Britain in moving towards the establishment of a Middle East defence arrangement. The National Intelligence Estimate of 21 June, co-ordinated by the Central Intelligence Agency, pointed out that the defence of the Middle East for sometime to come would depend almost entirely on the willingness and ability of Britain and the United States to commit the necessary ground, naval, and air forces. In the final analysis, however, the course of Middle East defence would depend in large measure on the United States, which was generally regarded as the prime mover. Although the outlook for a British and American orientated Middle East defence grouping had improved, moves in this direction had created instability and the Turco-Iraqi Pact had in the view of Egypt, Saudi Arabia, France and Israel, posed challenges to their prestige and interests. Despite its initial reservations Britain had accepted the Northern Tier approach as the best means of defending the Middle East.

The report did emphasize that although Britain accepted the established fact of American participation in Middle East affairs, it remained 'deeply concerned with protecting as much as possible of its own special interests and influence in the area'. It was stressed that Britain adhered to the Turco-Iraqi Pact because it provided a framework for a new base agreement with Iraq: 'British views on developing the pact, as well as British policy toward associating other states in area defence arrangements, will continue to reflect the UK's over-all political and economic interests in the area as well as military concern over the Soviet threat.' But Britain would want American aid and commitments in consolidating defence arrangements in the Middle East.[24]

Between 23 and 24 June American and British representatives did discuss, at the request of the British, the defence of the Middle East in Washington. Hoover mentioned that the United States had been giving some thought to increasing counter-subversion activities in the area, and that this would include the training of internal security forces. This, Hoover thought, could be a cheaper way of buying security in the Middle East than building up the military forces. British capabilities might be greater than those of the United States in this connection in some Middle East states. Sir Roger Makins, the British ambassador, said that London wanted both American and British support for indigenous initiatives for common defence in the area. Britain wanted Washington to adhere to the Turco-Iraqi Pact, and hoped for an indication of this during the talks. But Hoover refused to offer any views on this matter. Makins said that the French had been intriguing in Syria against the Turco-Iraqi Pact, but their behaviour had improved.

Although the main responsibility for the defence of the Middle East had in the past fallen to Britain, Makins insisted that Britain did not want an exclusive position in this field and that it was a central point of British policy to enlist American support. Britain would welcome an increased American interest in Middle East defence. Britain was the only Western power with binding defence commitments in the area, and combat personnel on the ground. At that time Britain had one and one-half divisions plus two brigades and odd bits and pieces of ground forces. But, with the reduction in defence expenditure, over the following year these would be phased down to around one division. Britain also maintained air and naval forces in the Middle East. In a detailed consideration of arms supplies, Makins asked that Iraq be informed of the Anglo-American Memorandum of Understanding of February 1954 that Iraq would be supplied mainly with British equipment. This was of immediate concern because of the need to supply Centurion tanks to Iraq. Hoover claimed not to know of the memorandum, and mentioned with regard to the Centurion tanks that Washington had assured Israel that there would be no heavy build-up in Iraq.[25]

A meeting of officials from the Departments of State and Defence on 30 June did agree that Washington might establish a liaison with a military planning organization to be set up under the Baghdad Pact (the Turco-Iraqi Pact), and that the United States should continue its policy of off-shore procurement of certain items in Britain for delivery to Iraq and Pakistan. Britain had complained that it was not being given information about the American military aid to Pakistan, and should be asked what information it needed. Although there was agreement that Middle East defence arrangements should be based on the Baghdad Pact, any Anglo-American consideration of the command structure in the Middle East should be left in abeyance.

The Department of State took the position that Washington could not increase its military aid to the Middle East, apart from Iran, a case in which it was hoped that a moderate increase would encourage adherence to the Baghdad Pact. It noted, in a report to Eisenhower on 11 July 1955, that Pakistan had decided to adhere to the Baghdad Pact, but that Iranian accession would be dependent on American military aid. State Department advice was that the Baghdad Pact should not extend to other Arab countries until there had been a lessening in Arab–Israeli tensions. Furthermore, Washington should not formally associate itself with the pact as such a move could adversely affect its influence in bringing about a reduction in Arab–Israeli tensions. Washington intended to continue the existing policies on off-shore procurement in Britain for Iraq and Pakistan. Eisenhower's reaction was that every effort should be made to make the British 'dig further into their own resources to help in the defense of the area'. Washington should also make a concerted effort to 'woo' Nasser.[26]

There were further conversations between British and American officials on Middle East defence in Washington on 11 August. Makins mentioned that he had been worried that Washington 'had not been as keen regarding Middle East defense as previously', and felt that he was encouraged by the American position. The Americans pointed to Syria and Egypt as the 'most worrisome spots' in the region, and felt that Nasser in particular was susceptible to Soviet blandishments of trade and arms. They also pointed to the position in Saudi Arabia where there was a conflict between Western ideas and the generally backward state of development. But it was in Kuwait where the Americans thought the real danger lay and were concerned that Communist-inspired propaganda could jeopardize the stability of that state. Both Britain and the United States had an important stake in Kuwait oil. Kuwait had been exclusively a British responsibility. Washington did not want to undermine British influence and prestige in Kuwait. But it wanted an opportunity to work with London to correct situations that threatened common Anglo-American interests there.

Makins pointed to the new agreement that Britain had concluded with South Africa over the Simonstown base, and explained that South Africa did not at that time really see itself as committed to the defence of the Middle East. It might eventually come around to the British position that the defence of Africa lay primarily in the Middle East, but Pretoria's interests were primarily in the area south of the Sahara. There would be little point in asking Pretoria to participate in a Middle East defence pact as had been done in the early 1950s.

At the end of the meeting George V. Allen of the State Department explained that Washington thought of the Baghdad Pact more along the lines of a defence organization than London. Makins said that Britain viewed it as a regional organization, 'but special arrangements were needed to put teeth into it'. Dulles, on 19 August, informed Eden that he did not think it feasible for the United States to join the Baghdad Pact until there was a relaxation of tension between the Arab states and Israel.[27]

Unable to secure American adherence to the Baghdad Pact, Britain did have some success in persuading Eisenhower to fund Centurion tanks for Iraq. But Eisenhower maintained his view that the British should be forced to take on as much of the burden of Middle East defence as they could, and at Geneva on 17 July Eisenhower told Eden that it was impossible for Washington to put up the money to enable the British to manufacture and give away Centurion tanks to Iraq. If Britain would provide a substantial part of the costs, it might be possible for Washington to participate.

A meeting, chaired by Hoover on 27 July, of representatives from the

Department of Defence and the Central Intelligence Agency, concluded that Eisenhower should not accede to Eden's request for Centurion tanks for Iraq. Such a gesture could adversely affect the Arab–Israeli problem and there were likely to be difficulties in Congress from those supporters of Israel who had been reassured that there would be no heavy equipment for Iraq. The precedent could encourage other Arab states to ask for similar equipment. In any case Iraq had indicated to Washington a preference for American equipment, and had complained that the Centurion tanks Britain had supplied previously were obsolete. Furthermore, Turkish, Iranian and Pakistani forces were being supplied with American equipment, and the logistical problems would not be simplified by providing Iraq with British equipment.

The British Cabinet was told on 28 July 1955 that Eisenhower, at Geneva, had undertaken to do his best to arrange that if 10 of the 80 tanks required by Iraq were supplied by Britain on easy terms, the supply of the remaining 70 would be supplied by the United States on off-shore terms. Dulles was unhappy at the thought that Britain might take all the credit, but this was offset by the realization that if Washington took this there would be a corresponding debit from Israel and its supporters in the United States.

When the Secretary of State placed the dilemma before the President on 11 August, Eisenhower reaffirmed the stand which he had often taken before: the United States 'should encourage the British to take the lead in the Middle East and not seek to compete with them in that respect'. Eisenhower thought it better to let the British deal directly with the Iraqis over the tanks. It was decided that the British ambassador at Baghdad should tell Nuri in confidence that Britain and the United States had agreed that Iraqi forces should be equipped with British tanks, and that initially Iraq would receive 12 Centurions. The use of American funds in this was to be played down.

Eden told the Cabinet on 5 September that he wanted a speedy delivery of the tanks to Iraq. When the British ambassador at Baghdad outlined a scheme in November 1955 under which Iraq would in effect receive British installations there as a gift instead of paying for them, despite the opposition of the Chancellor of the Exchequer, it was argued that such a move might be a good idea. The agreement with the Americans was that combatant equipment for the Iraqi army should come from British sources, and non-combatant equipment from American sources. But there was 'a tendency on the part of the United States authorities to undermine this agreement'. The ambassador's proposals could help to resist this tendency.[28]

At the time of the formation of the Baghdad Pact and the American reluctance to adhere to it, since the President insisted that it continued to be American policy to encourage Britain to take the lead in the Middle East, the British position in the area was increasingly challenged both by local nationalisms, as in Aden, and the country over which the Americans had paramount power, Saudi Arabia, which was aligned with American oil interests and supported by Kim Roosevelt and the Central Intelligence Agency.

In the middle of 1955, Rabizi rebels attacked a combined convoy of Aden Protectorate Levies and Government Guards, and inflicted heavy casualties on the way to Robat Fort in the west of the Aden Protectorate. On 23 June the Cabinet was told that the king of the Yemen was helping dissident elements in the Western Protectorate. More money was needed to strengthen the administration of the states in the area and to form three additional squadrons of the Aden Protectorate Levies. Eden said that the successful challenge of a handful of rebels armed with rifles of the combined security forces of Aden called for a review of the scale and organization of those forces. An immediate punitive expedition was arranged, and the Commanders-in-Chief of the Army and Air Force in the Middle East were instructed to go to Aden to revise the long-term measures for security.[29]

Aden was a British matter. The difficulties with Saudi Arabia over the Buraimi oasis involved Washington. To please the United States Britain, late in 1954, had agreed to go to arbitration by an international tribunal made up of one Briton, one Saudi and three 'neutral' representatives. The tribunal was to decide on a common frontier between Saudi Arabia and Abu Dhabi within a line claimed by Saudi Arabia in 1949, and one claimed by Abu Dhabi in 1952, and to determine the sovereignty over an area in a circle the centre of which would be the village of Buraimi. The British suspected that ARAMCO was collaborating with the State Department and Central Intelligence Agency representatives, and was helping the Saudis. The new king of Saudi Arabia, Saud, and his brother, Prince Feisal, were both paid by the Central Intelligence Agency. It has been alleged that in return for this assistance they offered to give oil concessions in the Buraimi area to ARAMCO if the Americans could bring the oasis under Saudi control. Furthermore, it is claimed that Kim Roosevelt was assigned the task of arranging the annexation and that he sent Saudi troops, transported in ARAMCO trucks into Buraimi. After days of feasting Saudi citizenship was offered to the inhabitants and an air-conditioned Cadillac to the Local sheikh, Prince Zaid, in return for his acknowledgement of Saudi sovereignty. Zaid apparently told the British, who it seems were also distributing largesse to potential witnesses. At Geneva there was a sense that the Central Intelligence Agency was trying to bribe the arbitrators. It was Eden's view that Buraimi had not in modern history formed part of Saudi territory, and that Britain was only helping the Sultan of Muscat and the Sheikh of Abu Dhabi to reoccupy their own territory, though it could be disputed which one of these rulers had suzerainty over the territory.[30]

The arbitration tribunal started in Geneva on 11 September 1955. Hearings finished on 15 September, and the tribunal withdrew to consider its decision. On 17 September the British member, Sir Reader Bullard, resigned. The Foreign Office on 4 October explained this in terms of having evidence that Saudi Arabia had violated the arbitration agreement, attempted a *coup d'etat* in Abu Dhabi, directed a campaign of bribery against the ruling family of that state, and that Sheikh Yusuf Yasin, the Saudi member of the tribunal, had conducted the proceedings 'on behalf of' the Saudi government. The Saudi ambassador at

London complained that the British public accusations of Saudi bribery were more like an Egyptian broadcast than a British government statement. Ironically, that same day, 7 October 1955, the British ambassador to Syria, Sir John Gardener, told Shuckburgh that he could bring about the merger of Syria with Iraq at any time if given enough money.

The Foreign Office view was that Britain had to get control of Buraimi. Military plans were made involving both troops from Muscat and Sheikh Zaid's armed retainers. Macmillan thought it wiser not to consult Washington or the members of the old Commonwealth about the proposed military action. Shuckburgh recommended to the Defence Committee that although it might look politically more reasonable when declaring the frontier line with Saudi Arabia to allow the Saudis a small strip of coast, this view was not taken by the Chiefs of Staff and, in any case, the Ruler of Abu Dhabi had laid claim to this piece of coast. The Saudis should not be given a corridor to the sea. Early in the morning of 26 October 1955 the Buraimi oasis was reoccupied as well as the main part of the disputed Abu Dhabi territory.[31]

That same day, 26 October, Macmillan explained to Dulles in Paris that the State Department had been warned by Shuckburgh a month previously that Britain would probably be compelled to abandon arbitration and seek a clearer way of settling the matter. Macmillan had decided not to give Dulles advance notice of the attack as he would clearly not want to assume any responsibility for it. Macmillan said that the arbitration had proved a mockery: the Saudis had just used it as an opportunity to suborn the inhabitants of the disputed areas, and when Britain had complained to the tribunal about this, had extended their corrupt methods to the tribunal itself. Britain knew that one member of the tribunal, the Pakistani, Dr Mahmud Hasan, had taken Saudi money. Shuckburgh recorded that Dulles did not like the news of the reoccupation of Buraimi, and thought it would react against ARAMCO, but the Secretary of State 'was not unpleasant about it'.

John Foster Dulles had another version of the events via his brother Allen, the head of the Central Intelligence Agency, who passed on the version from Terry Duce of ARAMCO, a man Allen described as an able reporter, though he did acknowledge that this particular report could be prejudiced by Duce's business connections. Duce warned of the danger to American interests of the events in Buraimi. According to Duce the British charges of Saudi bribery were 'fantastic' and just as the tribunal was ready to adopt the Saudi proposals for the establishment of neutral supervision in the Buraimi area, Bullard had resigned. Duce gave a categorical assurance that ARAMCO had played no role in the Buraimi 'goings on'. The Saudis notified the Americans on 28 October of their view that the British move into Buraimi would destroy the Saudi efforts to resist communism and aid from the Soviet Union. The Saudis questioned the 'friendship' between Britain and the United States, and referred to the British 'arrogant indifference, conceit and distortion of facts'. Hoover reassured the Saudis that Washington had received no advance intimation of the British action, and he had personally expressed his 'astonishment and concern at this precipitate move' to the British embassy. Allen Dulles told his brother that the British appeared to have sabotaged arbitration and resorted to force when arbitration seemed to be going against them. The most desirable solution would be the prompt reconstitution of the arbitration tribunal.[32]

The Saudis drew Eisenhower's attention to the possibility of raising the Buraimi issue in the Security Council. As D.M.H. Riches, the Head of the Eastern Department of the Foreign Office, observed this placed the Americans in a delicate position. The American company, ARAMCO, and the American air base at Dhahran were 'hostages in Saudi hands'. Furthermore, the Americans were inclined to look on the British position in the Gulf as a manifestation of colonialism. And the Americans were 'perhaps a little shocked at our action in Buraimi and a little hurt that we did not tell them about it beforehand'. But the Americans knew that the British accusations against the Saudis were true. Besides the common Anglo-American interests in the Middle East this evidence meant that Britain should have a strong claim on American support if the matter came before the Security Council. That would face the Americans with a painful choice: they could either refuse to support Britain; or they could give the Saudis a pretext to taking damaging action against ARAMCO and Dhahran. Washington should restrain the Saudis from raising the matter in the Security Council.

In response to a hint from Macmillan on 25 November 1955, following a meeting of the Baghdad Pact, that the position in the Middle East was so serious it was all too big for Britain and the United States to act separately and Britain would be prepared to discuss Buraimi as frankly as anything else, Dulles returned to the idea of a resumption of arbitration with an effective neutral supervisory commission, which was the preferred Saudi option. Dulles reiterated this on 13 December, mentioning that the Saudis would be prepared to replace Yasin. He thought there were advantages in avoiding United Nations action.

The British were not sympathetic. Riches noted that Washington had persistently ignored the British case about the impossibility of proceeding with arbitration given the Saudi methods of bribery. Britain wanted 'to try and jerk them out of this attitude (which is to some extent at least dictated by Aramco lawyers)' by showing them the seized documents which proved the British case. Riches thought it very difficult to believe that Britain would ever agree to arbitration again on this matter.[33]

At this time Britain took further action in the area, supporting the Sultan of Muscat against the Imam of Oman. This could be justified in terms of Britain's treaty obligations to the Sultan and as it did not affect American oil interests consideration was given by the Cabinet on 24 November as to whether Washington should be informed in advance. The British liked the Sultan of Muscat. On 6 July B.A.B. Burrows and Shuckburgh had been told by him in the Dorchester Hotel in London that he would be able to clean up the Imam of Oman by a brief show of force as soon as his troops were ready. Shuckburgh had found him 'a charming friendly little man with apparently complete confidence in us and in himself, and a contempt for the Saudis and their bribery which was very encouraging'.

On 12 December 1955 the Foreign Office informed the American embassy at London in confidence that the Sultan of Muscat had initiated an offensive against the Imam of Oman. Dulles complained that had he been informed earlier, he would have urged Britain to restrain the Sultan. Saudi Arabia might now consider asking the Security Council to consider Buraimi and Oman.[34]

These American responses threw Foreign Office officials into a rage. The Permanent Under-Secretary, Kirkpatrick, was observed 'breathing fire' and he summoned Walworth Barbour, the new Minister-Counsellor at the American embassy in London. Against the background that Nizwa in Oman had fallen without any resistance, and that the Imam had fled to a mountain village, Kirkpatrick, in his own words, 'made a fairly savage attack on the American Minister ... emphasising that Americans were playing the Russian game and violating justice'. Kirkpatrick professed bewilderment over American policy: Saudi Arabia seemed to be at best a neutral state and at worst to be pursuing a Soviet policy by the purchase of arms, through its antagonism to the Northern Tier, and its general anti-Western activity. The Americans were supporting the Saudis in their drive to absorb the small pro-Western states of South-East Arabia. On Buraimi Barbour did admit that the Saudis had broken the arbitration agreement. Kirkpatrick expounded that no new tribunal acceptable to the Saudis would be immune from bribery. As Washington knew of the Saudi malpractices it was astonishing that it had never upbraided them for the breach of a treaty. There was no evidence that even if Britain agreed to arbitration Washington would object to further encroachments by the Saudis. Furthermore, it was only the Saudi occupation of Buraimi that had led to the Imam of Oman claiming independence. Kirkpatrick asserted that if Washington did not believe that the Sultan of Muscat should take any action he saw fit to restore his authority in what he regarded as his own territory, then the Americans were 'inevitably supporting the establishment of Oman as a Saudi puppet preparatory to its inclusion in Saudi Arabia'. Barbour protested that Washington regarded the Saudi government as staunchly anti-Soviet.

Kirkpatrick, in his report to Makins, was scornful of Dulles: at Paris Dulles appeared to think that Muscat was part of the Aden Protectorate; there was his 'strange, dangerous and novel doctrine that because he deprecated the use of force by the Soviet Union', he had to 'deprecate the use of force to resist encroachments or even subversion from outside'. Kirkpatrick thought that the State Department had not faced up to the task of countering the Soviet invasion of the Middle East and of the need to make a coherent plan.

The same day, in Washington, Dulles spoke to Macmillan about his anxieties over Saudi Arabia. Macmillan agreed that it was necessary to reach an agreed policy with the Americans. British policy on Saudi Arabia, he acknowledged, had to fit in with the general Anglo-American Middle East policy. Macmillan thought that the situation in the Middle East was comparable to the situation which faced the West in Europe in 1948 after the Soviet take-over in Czechoslovakia, and before the consolidation of NATO. The Foreign Secretary observed that the retraction of British power in the Middle East had created a vacuum. In this situation any Anglo-American policy in the Middle East had to make the most of British and American assets in the whole area. He thought that the British position in the Gulf was a valuable asset in dealing with the Arab world. That relationship depended not so much on power as on confidence. If the confidence of the British protected rulers were shaken they could not be blamed for turning to the nearest protector, whether communist or neutralist. That, Macmillan explained, was why Britain had taken action in Buraimi. If Britain allowed Saudi Arabia to infiltrate the Trucial Sheikhdoms and Muscat, the whole British position in the Gulf would be undermined. And the situation in the Gulf related to the Baghdad Pact. Unless the pact were strengthened it would disintegrate. No source of power or influence in the whole Middle Eastern area should be neglected.

Dulles argued that the American position in Saudi Arabia was one of the assets in the area which London and Washington enjoyed. The two leaders agreed that there should be a joint study, and that Shuckburgh should go to Washington early in 1956. By then Selwyn Lloyd had replaced Macmillan as Foreign Secretary. Eden made his new appointment on 21 December. Eden regarded Macmillan as 'woolly', and complained that he followed Dulles around like an admiring poodle, and that was bad for Dulles and even worse for British interests in the Middle East. Macmillan wrote to Dulles at the time of the shift that just as Britain's connection with the United States was the most important aspect of its foreign relations, so his personal connection with Dulles was at all times in the front of his thinking. Macmillan thought that their work together had been useful and good.[35]

On 20 December 1955, Makins gave Hoover copies of some of the documents the British had captured in Buraimi. Hoover warned him that if an agreement could not be reached soon on arbitration, the Saudis would take the matter to the Security Council, the Soviet Union would support them, and the best that Washington could do would be to abstain. The British were not impressed: if the Saudis went before the Security Council they would have an unhappy experience as the British would make public the documents placing the Saudi action in Buraimi in an unflattering light. Washington doubted the effectiveness of this moral deterrent. The ambassador at Paris, Sir Gladwyn Jebb, observed to Kirkpatrick that the real reason for Britain's difficulties in the Middle East was American dollars flowing through the Saudi leaders. The Americans had to be brought around to the British way of thinking. Britain might have to bargain, and agree to not to press some objective dear to its heart in some other part of the world, in return for Washington's consent 'to put the screw on the Saudis'.[36]

Eden recalled that during the Suez crisis he learnt that the Americans had considered British action in reoccupying Buraimi and in helping the Sultan of Muscat as an act of aggression. It took place at the time of the realization that the Soviet Union had opened a new front in the Cold War. Nasser, threatened both by the Baghdad Pact and the Gaza raid of 28 February needed money and arms to build his new Egypt. He tried for arms from the West. Britain stalled: it was backing another part of the Arab world. The Americans hesitated as well. In April 1955, en route to the Bandung conference Nasser spoke to Chou En-lai, Communist China's delegate, about the aggression of Israel. Chou agreed to place Nasser's difficulties over arms supplies to the Soviets. Dulles was furious: the Chinese were threatening Quemoy and Matsu. The Soviets made the necessary overtures in Cairo between April and July, and then, on 20 July 1955, explained to Nasser that as talks with the Americans were progressing well at the Geneva summit, the arms would have to come through Czechoslovakia.

The Central Intelligence Agency uncovered what had happened and its head, Allen Dulles, urged his brother to get Henry A. Byroade, then ambassador at Cairo, to put pressure on Nasser. John Foster had lost faith in Byroade's attempts to keep Nasser in the Western camp, and flew Kim Roosevelt there instead. When Nasser learnt this, he publicly announced Egypt's arms deal with Czechoslovakia before Roosevelt even arrived. In September Eisenhower had a heart attack while on holiday in Colorado, and Dulles, under the guidance of Vice-President Richard Nixon, took charge.[37]

Macmillan warned Dulles on 26 September, in New York, that this constituted an aggressive entrance by the Soviets into a new area. Shuckburgh told the Americans on 3 October that the Foreign Office did not want United Nations action as that would give the Soviet Union the chance to pose as supporters of the Arabs. Macmillan suggested encouraging Iran to join the Baghdad Pact. Dulles told him that Britain and the United States should stand together: 'there should be great caution on your Government's part in starting a course of action which might lead to consequences which the United States could not share'.

The Foreign Secretary warned the Cabinet on 18 October that both the Egyptians and the Saudis were trying to undermine British influence in the Middle East, and it was also evident that the Soviets were working to spread their influence there. British oil companies owned investments valued at £600 million in the Middle East. The economy of Britain was dependent on the oil produced in this area, and the dependence would increase. Adequate steps needed to be taken to protect this asset of vital importance which had grown up in the region within 50 years. He asked the Cabinet to endorse a report, drawn up by Robert Belgrave, that British expenditure in the Middle East should be on a scale more closely related to British interests there.

Macmillan later explained that the Soviets had embarked on a deliberate policy of opening up another front in the Cold War. Britain needed to adopt a policy of moderation between extremes in its dealings with Egypt and should try to persuade the Americans to do the same. Eden argued that the allocation of the

Aswan High Dam project to the European consortium would be of immense value in restoring the prestige of the West, and particularly of the older European powers in the Arab world generally. The Prime Minister thought that the main objective of British policy should be to protect its vital oil interests in the Middle East.[38]

Macmillan wanted to include Iran in the Baghdad Pact, and have the Americans reduce their economic aid to Egypt, and transfer it to Iraq instead. Eden felt that Britain should not be restricted by a reluctance to act without full American concurrence and support. On 5 October he was indiscreet in telling the King and Crown Prince Abduililla of Iraq about 'Alpha'.

Makins said to Dulles on 6 October that Britain wanted to ship immediately the ten off-shore procurement tanks to Iraq. Dulles, however, wanted to respond favourably to a request from the Saudis for tanks. He also did not want Iran to join the Baghdad Pact until Soviet intentions were clear. The most effective action Washington could take would be to accede to the Baghdad Pact; this was the view that Eden put to Dulles in Paris on 26 October.

Dulles, however, was concerned about the situation in Syria, which he felt was the nearest of all the Arab states to becoming a Soviet puppet. He did suggest to Macmillan on 28 October that it would be a fine thing if Jordan joined the Baghdad Pact; Dulles regarded Jordan as a British affair. Jordan could even settle its frontier with Israel.[39] The State Department warned that Washington believed it had the right to expect British co-operation in taking measures to stop the Saudis turning from the West. Britain should consider the boundary policies on the Arabian peninsula in the light of maintaining good relations with all the Arab states. Dulles remained reserved about the Baghdad Pact. On 9 November, at Geneva, he told Macmillan that he had acquiesced to Iran's adherence because the alternative would have been to hold up a tendency towards co-operation with the West. Middle Eastern countries were unstable, and did not present a good foundation on which to build anything like NATO.[40]

Britain and the United States reached an agreed position at Geneva on 10 November. This was based largely on a Foreign Office document which recognized the need for a consistent long-term policy for the Middle East. The diagnosis was that it was the Arab–Israeli conflict which had weakened Western influence in the Middle East and opened the door to the Soviet Union. Egypt should not be written off and driven into the arms of the Soviet Union. A guiding principle should be that the West should not be seen to be moving in to supply Israel with arms on a large scale to offset Soviet supplies to the Middle East. The Northern Tier could constitute a focus of Western influence. This document was not shown to the French. It is perhaps illuminating to note that on 2 November 1955 Eisenhower inquired whether the Baghdad Pact was the same as the Northern Tier Pact.

An American National Intelligence Estimate of 15 November suggested that Egypt wanted to retain Washington's friendship and support, but would oppose certain policies which it thought might favour Israel, or involved support of the

Northern Tier defence scheme.[41] Dulles summarized his views to the National Security Council on 21 November. He warned of the catastrophe the loss of Middle East oil would pose for the West. Egypt was also the gateway to Africa, and if Europe lost Africa little would be left of Europe in a short time. There could be no significant cleavage between British and American policy in the Middle East. Dulles felt that Britain was trying to swing support towards the Arabs, and to regain the lost British position with the Arab states. Israel could not, however, be ignored. The Northern Tier had originally been Dulles' own concept. He reminded the National Security Council of this, and remarked on Britain's initial scepticism of the idea and its now strong support which was more than was wise. The British were 'putting all their money on Iraq', and the whole situation needed careful reappraisal as the British were tending to run away with it: 'While we could not let the British make our policy for us in this area, or follow the British line blindly, we should certainly cooperate with the British.' Dulles subsequently told Macmillan on 5 December that any immediate move to expand the Baghdad Pact would deny the West Nasser's co-operation; 'we should wait a little before trying to bring in Jordan and Lebanon'. American adherence to the pact would probably have to be coupled with a security guarantee to Israel.[42]

This message from Dulles annoyed the British. He seemed to keep changing his mind. Earlier he had wanted Jordan to join the Baghdad Pact. Against the background of an apparent American ambivalence or at best, prevarication, and a refusal to acknowledge the importance of the British position in the Gulf and the justice of Britain's case against Saudi Arabia, Eden decided to strike out on his own.

As he had told the Cabinet earlier a success for the European consortium in the bidding for the building of the Aswan High Dam, Nasser's scheme for moving Egypt into the modern age as the harnessing of the waters of the Nile would provide the necessary energy, would be a way for the old Powers to re-establish their influence in the Middle East. On 3 November the Cabinet learnt that the financial risks in financing the Aswan High Dam had been substantially underestimated. American financial support, either through the International Bank or directly from the American government, or both, was needed. The Cabinet still felt that the contract had to be obtained for the European consortium and Eden agreed that this was of the greatest national importance. But the Prime Minister conceded that another attempt would have to be made to get financial support from America. Nasser had let Washington know that he would prefer to finance the dam with American money, and so maintain his neutral posture. The American response was slow: Eisenhower was being protected from difficult matters; George Humphrey, the Secretary of the Treasury, saw the scheme as a British plot and Humphrey did not like Britain. Hoover was one of Humphrey's closest friends and Dulles placed him in charge of negotiations. Hoover saw it as a greedy ploy mounted by British manufacturers and construction companies. Discussions took place in

Washington between Eugene R. Black, the President of the World Bank, the Egyptian Finance Minister, Abdel Kaissouni, and Makins between 21 November and 16 December. The United States would provide $56 million, and Britain $14 million, for the first stage of the construction, and consider later grants up to $200 million. Contingent on the Anglo-American grants, the World Bank would lend $200 million.[43]

The American Zionists disliked the scheme as did the 'cotton' senators who felt their industry in the south would be damaged. Early in December Dulles secured Eisenhower's approval for a scheme that would lessen their domestic risks. An American emissary, Robert B. Anderson, would try to persuade Nasser that with a strengthened domestic position the President could negotiate a peace with Israel, in effect an attempt to revive the 'Alpha' project. But shuttle diplomacy between Cairo and Tel Aviv was fruitless: Nasser felt he could not speak for other Arab states; Ben-Gurion did not think the Aswan dam good for Israel. Dulles perhaps hoped that American financing would mean control of the Egyptian economy and thus no more arms from Czechoslovakia. But the Secretary of State became disillusioned with the domestic opposition, probably partly engineered by the anti-British alliance of Hoover and Humphrey.[44]

Eden also decided to revive 'Alpha'. Shuckburgh noted that the Prime Minister wanted 'to take a hand'. Eisenhower was ill, as was the West German leader, Konrad Adenaeur. Dulles and Macmillan were talking to the Soviet Prime Minister, V.M. Molotov in Geneva. Shuckburgh gave the impression that Eden thought there was 'only one great man left in the world capable of giving a lead and that is himself'. Eden would have preferred to go to Cyprus and summon the Israelis and Egyptians to meet him there. But the disturbed situation on the island ruled that out. The Prime Minister decided instead on a stirring declaration in his Mansion House speech at the Guildhall in London on 9 November.

Harold Caccia and Shuckburgh explained to Eden that to have any effect on the Egyptians, Eden would have to say something that the Israelis would detest. Shuckburgh was accordingly instructed to draft a passage mentioning the November 1947 United Nations resolutions as a factor to be taken account of in any settlement. Dulles was told in advance, but at the last moment and the Secretary of State complained to the National Security Council that Eden had tried to drag him in but he had 'bucked at full endorsement'.

In his speech Eden said that if an arrangement could be reached between Israel and its Arab neighbours about the boundaries, Britain and the United States, and perhaps other powers, would be prepared to give a formal guarantee to both sides. Although Eden mentioned other United Nations resolutions, it was the reference to the 1947 one that was noted. Israel had extended its boundaries during the First Arab–Israeli War in 1948–49, and its occupation of the Negev desert prevented any land link between Egypt and Jordan. Nasser found the speech constructive. David Ben-Gurion, who, following the general elections on 2 November, was Prime Minister of Israel as well as Minister of Defence, complained to the American ambassador at Tel Aviv that it was an attempt by Eden's government to eliminate Israel.[45]

Eden was also annoyed by Dulles's message of 5 December opposing any expansion of the Baghdad Pact. Dulles, at one stage, had pushed the idea himself. The Americans had known two weeks before that Britain had decided to try to induce Jordan to join the Baghdad Pact. In preparation for this, in November Britain decided to give ten Vampire jets to Jordan. Jordan had no fighter aircraft whereas Israel had sixty-four. It was thought time to give preferential treatment to those Arab states which supported the West. Britain prepared a substantial gift of military equipment for Jordan, and prepared the text of an agreement to replace the Anglo-Jordanian Treaty. Macmillan thought that the Chief of the Imperial General Staff, Sir Gerald Templar, should fly to Amman to discuss the proposals. Templar, accompanied by Michael Rose of the Levant Department of the Foreign Office, was in Jordan from 6 to 18 December. Dulles' message urging Britain to wait a little before trying to secure Jordanian accession to the Baghdad Pact arrived after Templar had left.

The Jordanian government fell over the issue of adherence to the Baghdad Pact. Palestinian Cabinet members argued that might divert attention from the Israeli problem. Hussein asked a proponent of the Pact to form a new government, but after demonstrations in Jordanian cities and towns on 18 December, he resigned. Hussein dissolved parliament, a caretaker government was formed, and elections were set for four months hence.[46]

The first months of Eden's premiership saw a shift in British policy in the Middle East towards emphasis on a more direct British role, needed it was felt to preserve oil interests, to the extent that Britain was prepared to pursue a policy in the area without the close concurrence or agreement of the United States. The basis of that policy was the Northern Tier concept, as it took form in the Baghdad Pact (initially called the Turco–Iraqi Pact). This had been originally an American concept. In the beginning Britain pursued it as a means of renegotiating the Anglo-Iraqi Treaty of 1930. Britain continually stated that it wanted the Americans to adhere to the pact. But there were reasons for Washington's reluctance to do so. These lay partly in the domestic situation in the United States and the power of the Zionist lobby at election time, partly out of a concern not to provoke the Soviet Union. And Eisenhower kept reiterating that it was his policy to allow Britain to take the lead in the Middle East, and to leave it with principal responsibility for the area's defence. This was when some State Department assessments suggested that Britain was no longer in a position to assume that responsibility on behalf of the West, and that the United States would have to prepare to take over. Eisenhower, however, insisted that Britain should be made to pay as much as possible for the defence of the Middle East at a time when Britain was drastically reducing its defence expenditure to sustain the domestic economy, and when British forces in the Middle East were scheduled to be run down in accordance with the new strategy based partly on thermo-nuclear weapons. The Middle East was no longer one of the three pillars of British strategy.

Britain had interests in the area, and saw its oil supplies there as vital. This meant an emphasis on the British position in Iraq and the Gulf. British policy remained based on links with the pashas and not the peasants. This was a period when Britain decided to work with its friends in the area. That policy brought it into conflict with the friends of the United States, and in particular, Saudi Arabia, a country over which Washington was seen as exercising paramountcy. Washington seemed unable to understand the importance for Western interests of the Gulf states. It appeared to think that they could be sacrificed to Saudi Arabia, if that would keep Saudi Arabia on the side of the West. Washington and London diverged in their assessment of the Soviet influence in Saudi Arabia.

By the end of 1955 Britain, in the view of some American officials, was flexing its muscles in the area, trying to establish its former influence in the Arab states, and where possible trying to get the Americans to pay for this. London was increasingly infuriated over what it saw as an ambivalent American policy, difficult to discern and continually changing, and one which appeared in part to be dictated by American oil interests. It was hoped that there would be a meeting of minds in Washington in January 1956.

Notes

1. Anthony Eden, *Full Circle* (London, 1960), p. 352; *Foreign Relations of the United States* (hereafter cited as '*FRUS*'), 1955–7(12), p. 88, Editorial Note of Whitman File, NSC Records, 22 December 1955, Eisenhower Library; Public Record Office, London, CAB 128/29, fos 364–5, CM34(55)8, Secret, 4 October 1955.
2. Public Record Office, London, FO 371/125262, ZP5/20/G, Minute by Mallet on Defence White Paper, 2 February 1955; Eden, pp. 370–1.
3. FO 371/121282, V1079/1/G, Annex A, Minute by C.A.E. Shuckburgh, Secret, 11 January 1955.
4. Hermann Frederick Eilts, 'Reflections on the Suez Crisis: Security in the Middle East', in Wm. Roger Louis and Roger Owen (eds), *Suez 1956: The Crisis and Its Consequences* (Oxford, 1989), pp. 347–61 at pp. 350–1; Waldemar J. Gallman, *Iraq under General Nuri: My Recollections of Nuri al-Said, 1954–1958* (Baltimore, 1964), p. 46.
5. FO 371/115469, V1023/3/G, Makins to Foreign Office, no. 63, Top Secret, 28 January 1955 d 29 January 1955; V1073/270, 1195/175/55, British embassy Cairo to Africa Department, Confidential, 15 February 1955; FO 371/115492, V1023/295, Gladwyn Jebb to Kirkpatrick, Secret and Personal, 19 February 1955.
6. FO 371/115492, V1073/297, 1194/225/55, R.A. Beaumont to T.E. Evans, Confidential, 10 February 1955; 1195/201/55, T.E. Evans to R.A. Beaumont, Secret, 21 February 1955; V1073/293, Minute by J.E. Powell-Jones, Confidential, 17 February 1955.
7. FO 371/115492, V1073/258, Minute by E.M. Rose on Turco–Iraqi agreement,

14 February 1955; V1073/264, Minute by Kirkpatrick, 15 February 1955; V1073/263, R. Stevenson to Foreign Office, Telegram no. 250, Confidential, 16 February 1955; *FRUS* 1955–7(12), pp. 19–20, Circular telegram from Department of State to certain diplomatic missions, 15 February 1955.

8. FO 371/115492, V1073/289, Stevenson to Foreign Office, Telegram no. 269, Secret, 21 February 1955; Robert Rhodes James, *Anthony Eden* (London, 1986), pp. 397–9; FO 800/776, fol. 7, Eg/55/4, A. Stark to Adam Gordon, Secret, 24 February 1955; *FRUS* 1955–7(14), pp. 71–2, Dulles to Department of State, 24 February 1955.

9. FO 371/115504, V1073/638, J.G.S. Beith to E.M. Rose, Confidential, 3 March 1955.

10. Public Record Office, London, PREM 11/1408, fos 148–52, C(55)70, Memorandum by Eden on Middle East defence, Secret, 14 March 1955; fol. 178, M. Wright to Foreign Office, Telegram no. 221, Secret, 5 March 1955; fos. 170–2, M. Wright to Foreign Office, Telegram no. 239, Confidential, 8 March 1955; FO 371/115504, V1073/637, Stevenson to Shuckburgh, Secret, 28 March 1955; Minute by G.C. Arthur, 12 April 1955; V1073/637, Shuckburgh to Stevenson, Secret, 28 April 1955; V1073/635, Minute by Shuckburgh, 31 March 1955; V1073/630, Makins to Foreign Office, Telegram no. 185, 29 March 1955; Eisenhower Library, Abilene, National Security Council Staff Papers 1948–61, OCB Central File Series, Box no. 77, File OCB 091.4 Near East (10) May 1954–March 1955, Detailed Development of major actions relating to NSC 5428 (Near East) from 1 July 1954 to 28 February 1955, Top Secret, 21 March 1955; Eden, *Full Circle*, pp. 222–3.

11. Gallman, pp. 61–2; Evelyn Shuckburgh, *Descent to Suez Diaries 1951–56* (London, 1986), pp. 260–1, Diary, 13 June 1955; FO 371/115762, VQ1052/20, Rose to Wright, no. 147, Secret, 1 July 1955; PREM 11/1408, VQ1224/27, Wright to Macmillan, no. 159, Confidential, 19 July 1955; FO 371/114818, EP1051/20, Minute by Lord Reading of conversation with the Iranian Foreign Minister (Entezam), 3 August 1955; EP1051/18, Minute by Reading of conversation with Entezam, 5 August 1955.

12. *FRUS* 1955–7(12), pp. 63–70, Memorandum from the State-Defence working group to Hoover and Anderson, 6 June 1955.

13. See Eden, *Full Circle*, pp. 175–88.

14. FO 371/111095, UR1079/1/G, Foreign Office to Washington, Telegram no. 5512, Secret, 4 November 1954; Shuckburgh, *Diaries*, pp. 242–3, Diary 16 December 1954; *FRUS* 1955–7(14), pp. 24–8, Memorandum of a conversation in the Department of State, 27 January 1955; pp. 34–42, memorandum from Russell to Hoover, 2 February 1955; pp. 98–107, Points of agreement in London discussions of Arab–Israeli settlement, 10 March 1955; FO 371/121282, V1079/1/G, Annex F, Foreign Office to Washington, Telegram no. 1349, 31 March 1955; *FRUS* 1955–7(12), pp. 48–9, Allen to Dulles, 1 April 1955 (some of text not declassified).

15. PREM 11/945, CP(55)35, Memorandum by Macmillan, Top Secret, 11 June 1955; PREM 11/1464, fol. 286, PM/55/62, Macmillan to Eden, 10 June 1955; CAB 128/29, fos 136–7, CM15(55)5, Secret, 16 June 1955; *FRUS* 1955–7(14), pp. 248–9, Department of State to Embassy in Egypt, 20 June 1955; CAB 128/29, fos 210–11, CM23(55)9, Secret, 14 July 1955; *FRUS* 1955–7(14), pp. 295-8,

Memorandum of conversation, 14 July 1955; Harold Macmillan, *Tides of Fortune 1945–1955* (London, 1969), p. 633, Diary 19 August 1955; *FRUS* 1955–7(14), pp. 366–8, Dulles to Macmillan, 19 August 1955; pp. 368–9, Dulles to Eisenhower, 19 August 1955.

16. *FRUS* 1955–7(14), pp. 370–1, Macmillan to Dulles, Undated; W. Scott Lucas, *Divided We Stand: Britain, the US and the Suez Crisis* (London, 1991), pp. 50–1; *FRUS* 1955–7(14), pp. 468–9, Embassy in Egypt to Department of State, 14 September 1955; pp. 493–5, Minutes of meeting of British and American representatives at Foreign Office, 21 September 1955; pp. 504–5, Embassy in Britain to Department of State, 22 September 1955.

17. Ritchie Ovendale, *The Origins of the Arab–Israeli Wars*, (2nd edn, London, 1992), pp. 151–2.

18. FO 317/115825, fos 12–3, VR1051/4, Eden to J.W. Nicholls, no. 26, Confidential, 10 February 1955; fol. 39, Minute by Shuckburgh, 18 February 1955; fos 29–30, VR1051/4A, Minute by E.M. Rose on Israel's suggestion for an arrangement with Britain, Secret, 18 February 1955; Shuckburgh, *Diaries*, p. 251, Diary 18 February 1955.

19. FO 371/115825, fos 50–3, VR1051/8/G, 1041/6/55, J.W. Nicholls to Shuckburgh, Secret, 8 March 1955; fos 57–8, VR1051/8G, Shuckburgh to Nicholls, Secret, 25 March 1955; PREM 11/945, fol. 254, Makins to Foreign Office, Telegram no. 795, Secret, 7 April 1955 recd. 8 April 1955; Shuckburgh, *Diaries*, p. 255, Diary 13 April 1955; PREM 11/1464, fos 290–1, Foreign Office to Tel Aviv, Telegram no. 324, Confidential, 4 June 1955; CAB 128/29, fol. 128, CM14(55)7, Secret, 14 June 1955.

20. PREM 11/1464, fos 278–9, Shuckburgh to Sir Nevil Brownjohn, Confidential, 20 June 1955; fos 208–10, DC(55)13, Memorandum by Lloyd on supply of arms to Middle East countries, Secret, 6 July 1955; fos 254–5, DC(55)22, Record of conversation between Shuckburgh and Peres on 6 July 1955, Secret, 11 July 1955.

21. PREM 11/1464, fol. 144, PM/IK/55/169, Kirkpatrick to Eden, 23 November 1955; FO 371/115826, fos 120–1, VR1051/26, Minute by R.M. Hadow, 6 December 1955; fos. 124–6, VR1051/27, Macmillan to Shuckburgh, 8 December 1956; PREM 11/1464, Paris to Foreign Office, Telegram no 430, Secret, 15 December 1955.

22. *FRUS* 1955–7(12), pp. 21–2, Telegram from delegation at the SEATO council to the Department of State, 24 February 1955; pp. 51–3, Murphy to Dulles, 22 April 1955.

23. FO 371/125271, ZP16/3/G, W.H. Hanna to Sir Anthony Rumbold, 14 February 1955; V1023/4/G, Foreign Office to Washington, Undated; FO 371/115761, VQ1052/9, Shuckburgh to Wright, Confidential, 27 April 1955.

24. *FRUS* 1955–7(12), pp. 54–5, Memorandum of Discussion at the 247th Meeting of the National Security Council, Washington, 5 May 1955, Whitman Files, Eisenhower Library; pp. 70–4, Memorandum from the Joint Chiefs of Staff to Wilson, 16 June 1955; pp. 77–97, NIE 30–55, Middle East defence problems and prospects, 21 June 1955.

25. *FRUS* 1955–7(12), pp. 103–11, Memorandum of conversation, Department of State, 23 June 1955; pp. 112–22, Memorandum of a conversation, Department of State, Washington, 24 June 1955.

26. *FRUS* 1955–7(12), pp. 127–9, Memorandum of conversation, Department of

State, Washington, 30 June 1955; pp. 129–32, Department of State Position Paper, 11 July 1955; pp. 132–3, Hoover to Dulles, 11 July 1955.
27. *FRUS* 1955–7(12), pp. 135–151, Memorandum of a conversation, Department of State, Washington, 11 August 1955; for the South African position see G.R. Berridge, *South Africa, the Colonial Powers and 'Africa Defence' the Rise and Fall of the White Entente, 1948–60* (London, 1992), pp. 110–32; *FRUS* 1955–7(12), p. 152, Dulles to Makins, 19 August 1955.
28. *FRUS* 1955–7(14), pp. 301–2, Editorial note, Eisenhower Diaries, Whitman File, Eisenhower Library; pp. 323–5, Memorandum of a conversation, Washington, 27 July 1955; Eisenhower Library, Abilene, White House Office, Office of the Staff Secretary, Records 1952–61, Subject Series Department of Defence Subseries, Box no. 6, File Military Planning 1954–5, Memorandum by Dillon Anderson on Centurion Tanks for Iraq, Top Secret, 26 July 1955; CAB 128/29, fol. 270, CM27(55)2, Secret, 28 July 1955; *FRUS* 1955–7(14), pp. 345–6, Wilkins to Russell, 10 August 1955; pp. 346–7, Editorial Note, Dulles Papers, Meetings with the President, Eisenhower Library; *FRUS* 1955–7(12), p. 971, Telegram from department of Sate to embassy in Iraq, 21 August 1955: CAB 128/29, fos 311–2, CM30(55)9, Secret, 5 September 1955; PREM 11/1408, fol. 70, DC(55)15th Meeting, Minute 4, Top Secret, 18 November 1955.
29. CAB 128/29, fol. 141, CM16(55)4, Secret, 21 June 1955; fos 148–9, CM17(55)3, Secret, 23 June 1955; fol. 158, CM18(55)4, Secret, 28 June 1955.
30. Leonard Mosley, *Dulles: A Biography of Eleanor, Allen, and John Foster Dulles and Their Family Network* (London, 1978), pp. 348–9; Lucas, *Divided We Stand*, pp. 71–2; Eden, *Full Circle*, pp. 334–5.
31. *FRUS* 1955–7(13), pp. 274–5, Editorial note; Shuckburgh, p. 289, Diary, 7 October 1955; FO 371/114624, EA1081/378, Bahrain to Foreign Office, Telegram no. 730, Secret, 13 October 1955; EA1081/378, Minute by Shuckburgh on further comments on the Buraimi question for use in the Defence Committee, Secret, 19 October 1955; Macmillan, Tides of Fortune, p. 641; Shuckburgh, *Diaries*, pp. 292–3, Diary 26 October 1955.
32. FO 371/114624, A1081/379, Minute for Macmillan, 26 October 1955; Shuckburgh, *ibid.*, pp. 292–3, Diary 26 October 1955; *FRUS* 1955–7(13), pp. 281–2, Allen Dulles to John Foster Dulles, Undated, Dulles Papers, White House memoranda, Eisenhower Library; pp. 282–3, Editorial note; Eisenhower Library, Abilene, John Foster Dulles Papers, 1951–59, White House Memoranda Series, Box no. 8, File conversations with Allen W. Dulles (2), Allen W. Dulles to John F. Dulles, Personal and Private, Undated.
33. FO 371/114624, A1081/376(A), Minute by D.M.H. Riches, 31 October 1955; *FRUS* 1955–7, p. 293, Editorial note; pp. 301–2, Telegram from Department of State to embassy in Britain, 13 December 1955: FO 371/114631, EA1081/558, Minute by D.M.H. Riches, 9 December 1955.
34. CAB 128/29, fol. 488, CM43(55)4, Secret, 24 November 1955; Shuckburgh, *Diaries*, p. 265, Diary 6 July 1955; *FRUS* 1955–7(13), pp. 222–3, Telegram from the Department of State to embassy in Britain, 13 December 1956.
35. FO 371/114559, E1021/6, Kirkpatrick to Shuckburgh, 15 December 1955; Kirkpatrick to Makins, Secret and Personal, 17 December 1955; E1021/2, Record of conversation on the Middle East, Top Secret, 15 December 1955; Lucas, *Divided We Stand*, pp. 80–1.

36. *FRUS* 1955–7(13), pp. 303–4, Hoover to Dulles, 20 December 1955; pp. 307–8, Telegram from the embassy in Britain to Department of State, 29 December 1955; FO 371/120525, E1021/1, Sir Gladwyn Jebb to Kirkpatrick, Secret, 28 December 1955.
37. Eden, *Full Circle*, p. 334; Ovendale, *The Origins of the Arab–Israeli Wars*, pp. 158–9.
38. *FRUS* 1955–7(14), pp. 516–19, Memorandum of conversation, New York, 26 September 1955; pp. 531–49, Memorandum of conversation, Department of State, Washington, 3 October 1955; p. 550, Memorandum of conversation between Dulles and Macmillan, 3 October 1955; CAB 128/29, fos 378–9, CM35(55)6, Secret, 18 October 1955; PREM 11/1464, fos. 186–7, CM36(55)1, Secret, 20 October 1955.
39. Macmillan, *Tides of Fortune*, p. 639, Dairy 4 October 1955: CAB 128/29, fos. 364–5, CM34(55)8, Secret, 4 October 1955; Shuckburgh, *Diaries*, p. 288, Diary 5 October 1955; *FRUS* 1955–7(14), pp. 558–62, Memorandum of conversation, Department of State, 6 October 1955; FO 371/115469, V1023/14/G, Jebb to Foreign Office, Telegram no. 419, Secret, 26 October 1955; *FRUS* 1955–7(14), Memorandum of conversation, British embassy, Paris, 26 October 1955; FO 371/114624, V1023/16, Macmillan (Geneva) to Foreign Office, Top Secret, 28 October 1955.
40. *FRUS* 1955–7, pp. 713–6, Telegram from the Department of State to the Consulate General at Geneva, 5 November 1955; pp. 720–3, Memorandum of conversation, Geneva, 9 November 1955; FO 371/115469, V1023/25G, Record of meeting between Macmillan and Dulles at Geneva on 9 November 1955, Secret.
41. FO 317/121271, V1075/39/G, Annex B, Memorandum on the Middle East, Top Secret, 9 November 1955; FO 371/115469, V1023/23/G, Shuckburgh to Kirkpatrick, 10 November 1955; Eisenhower Library, Abilene, Anne Whitman Diary Series, Box no. 7, File ACW Diary November 1955 (7), Eisenhower's conversation with Governor Adams, 2 November 1955; *FRUS* 1955–7(14), NIE 36.1–55, National Intelligence Estimate of the outlook for Egyptian stability and foreign policy, 15 November 1955.
42. *FRUS* 1955–7(12), pp. 200–3, Memorandum of Discussion of National Security Council, 21 November 1955, Whitman File, NSC Records, Eisenhower Library; p. 207, note.
43. CAB 128/29, fos 423–4, CM39(55)5, Secret, 3 November 1955; *FRUS* 1955–7(14), pp. 777–80, Memorandum of Conversation, Department of State, Washington, 16 November 1955; pp. 818–9, Memorandum by Hoover, 2 December 1955; pp. 849–51, Memorandum of Conversation, Department of State, Washington, 12 December 1955; Ovendale, *The Origins of the Arab–Israeli Wars*, pp. 159–60.
44. *FRUS* 1955–7(14), p. 725, Editorial note; Ovendale, *The Origins of the Arab–Israeli Wars*, p. 160.
45. Shuckburgh, *Diaries*, pp. 296-7, Dairy 4 November 1955; Eden, *Full Circle*, p. 330; Lucas, *Divided We Stand*, p. 73; *FRUS* 1955–7, pp. 200–3, Memorandum of discussion at the meeting of the National Security Council on 21 November 1955, Whitman File, NSC Records, Eisenhower Library.
46. PREM 11/1464, fos 147–8, G.E.M. to Eden, 19 November 1955; FO 371/115469, V1023/28/G, Minute by Shuckburgh, Secret, 6 December 1955; *FRUS* 1955–7(12), pp. 211–2, Editorial note; Eden, *Full Circle*, pp. 343–4.

6

Eden and the 'Flexing of British Muscles': The Suez Crisis

The origins of the Suez crisis of 1956 lie partly in a mythology, current in the West in the 1950s, of Neville Chamberlain's policy for the appeasement of Europe, and in the perhaps dangerous and inaccurate idea that history can repeat itself – that historical analogy can be used to determine political policy. Eden, as he recorded in his memoirs, viewed the events of the 1950s through the spectacles of the 1930s. His historical analogies were reinforced by the views of his Permanent Under-Secretary of State, Ivone Kirkpatrick, who had been First Secretary in the British embassy at Berlin between 1933 and 1938 and disliked the 'appeasement' policy of his ambassador, Sir Nevile Henderson, and the Munich settlement. Nasser's nationalization of the Suez Canal not only threatened Britain's national economy dependent on supplies of oil from the Middle East, but the Egyptian leader was also viewed by the British Prime Minister as another Mussolini. This time Eden felt that the 'dictator' should not be appeased, and should be stopped before he went any further.[1]

Suez was not 'the lion's last roar'. Britain was already retreating from empire. Suez did not force Britain to turn to Europe: Harold Macmillan as Prime Minister only decided on that after South Africa's exclusion from the Commonwealth in 1961. Above all, Suez was not an unfortunate break in the Anglo-American 'special relationship'. Britain had been demoted to the status of just one among a number of allies as soon as Eisenhower came into office. Rather Suez lead to a revival of the special relationship on old terms. Eisenhower later regretted Suez as his major foreign policy mistake. In May 1982 Henry Kissinger, American Secretary of State between 1973 and 1977, publicly regretted the American action over Suez, action in which Eisenhower was seen to have humiliated Britain and France, and argued that it forced the United States to take over Britain and France's burdens in the Middle East.[2]

As Eden had explained to the Cabinet on 4 October 1955, because British interests were greater than those of the United States in the Middle East, Britain had to frame its policy in the light of its own interests in the area and get the

Americans to support it to the extent that Britain could induce them to do so. A preliminary to an attempt to do this at Anglo-American meetings in Washington in January 1956, was a conference of British ambassadors in the Middle East held between 4 and 5 January 1956. That gathering decided on the need to support the Baghdad Pact 'staunchly', though not to press other Arab countries to join the Pact. Because of the importance of oil for the British economy, Britain needed to retain its friendly relations with Iraq and the Gulf states. Although an understanding with Egypt was desirable, this could not be allowed at the cost of weakening support of the Baghdad Pact. The ambassadors deplored the effect of Saudi bribery and corruption in the Middle East and saw it as being liable to strengthen Communism in the area. Britain would take all measures to support the Rulers in the Gulf against Saudi encroachment.

Sir Pierson Dixon, the Permanent Representative at the United Nations, hoped to encourage Anglo-American co-operation in the United Nations by illuminating Cabot Lodge, the American representative, and through him the State Department. He proposed to do this via a paper. The paper which the Foreign Office amended slightly tried to emphasize the American interests in the Middle East as a whole, and not just Saudi Arabia. It looked back to the relatively stable situation in the area between the two world wars, once possible because of the special position enjoyed by Britain with its armed forces in Egypt, Iraq and India, its status as the mandatory power in Transjordan and Palestine, and its special relationship with the Gulf states. Having played a large part in the Arab revolt against the Ottoman Empire, Britain was also able to act as a guide to the young Arab states. That situation had been changed by the creation of the State of Israel, and the growth of Arab nationalism.

The paper observed that there was no longer any single influence in the area of sufficient power to bring stability to the Middle East. But it argued that 'close Anglo-American co-operation' could fill this role. Britain could bring substantial advantages to this partnership by its treaty engagements with Iraq and Jordan, its agreement with Egypt, its special arrangement with the Gulf states and Muscat, the British military bases in Cyprus and forces in the Middle East, and the large British oil interests.

Britain hoped for American co-operation in achieving a stabilizing influence in the Middle East. In particular it wanted Washington to leave London free to fulfil its obligations in the Aden Protectorate, the Gulf states where American oil companies' interests were as large as their British counterparts, Muscat and Oman, and to protect these territories from the encroachments and intrigues of Yemen and Saudi Arabia. Britain expected American support if this wholly defensive policy were attacked in the United Nations. Furthermore, Britain wanted Washington to do its best to secure a change of the system in Saudi Arabia. Saudi oil revenues were used irresponsibly: in other Middle Eastern countries for subversive purposes which directly benefited the Communists; a lot disappeared in 'graft'; a small clique spent a great deal on itself. Unlike Iraq and the Gulf, there were no long-term development projects underway in Saudi

Arabia and this could only expose the inhabitants of Saudi Arabia to the appeal of Communism.

Britain desired American assistance to strengthen the Baghdad Pact, preferably by the United States joining the pact, but, failing that, by American economic assistance and arms supplies. Iraq had to be able to show the other Arab states that co-operation with the West paid. What was also needed was a joint Anglo-American policy towards Egypt, one which recognized 'the restless ambitions' of the new regime, but which would help to keep Egypt quiet. Soviet influence in the Middle East should be countered by economic aid. Britain wished to continue the close co-operation with the United States over Israel, and wanted to work for a final settlement on compromise lines. Washington should also discourage the Greeks from stirring up fresh trouble in Cyprus, the site of Britain's Middle East base and headquarters.[3]

Dulles, on 4 January 1956, was advised of American interests in the area by George V. Allen, the Assistant Secretary of State for Near Eastern Affairs. The Arabian Peninsula and the Gulf contained America's largest foreign investment and a large community of American citizens. The American air base at Dhahran was subject to renegotiation that spring. American responsibilities for the economic viability and defence of Western Europe depended on the resources in this area. Its stability and the paramount position of the West there were threatened by the boundary disputes involving Saudi Arabia, the Yemen and Britain. Saudi Arabia was also co-operating with anti-Western and 'leftist elements' to oppose the inclusion of Jordan, Syria, and Lebanon into Western sponsored security arrangements. Communist and extreme nationalist movements had appeared in the area, and it was vital that Washington co-ordinate its position with London to control this. There were also tensions in the labour force of the oil producing areas of Bahrain and Qatar. Allen Dulles, the head of the Central Intelligence Agency, told the National Security Council on 21 January, that the British, having just 'suffered their most humiliating diplomatic defeat in modern history as a result of developments in Jordan' were rethinking their policy in the Middle East, and were emphasizing more the need for securing peace between Egypt and Israel.[4]

The Foreign Office prepared briefs for Shuckburgh to use in Washington. One viewed the Baghdad Pact as a concern which engaged the prestige of the West, and of Britain in particular. It could provide a focus for Arab political energies. If left to their own devices, the Arabs would destroy themselves and perhaps fall under Soviet influence. Using the words of the British ambassador at Baghdad, Britain was fighting for the soul of the Arab world. The Iraqis had committed themselves to Britain. They had to show that association paid. They needed large quantities of free arms, and apart from Jordan, gifts of arms to other Arab countries should be avoided. An Arab Economic Organization could be established, perhaps under joint Egyptian and Iraqi auspices, to reconcile Nasser and allow him some scope for Egyptian leadership. Defence in war had become a secondary consideration, though organized defence systems had political value. The Soviet military threat had been replaced by a political and economic one.

If Britain were to retain its position in the world it had to win the struggle for the Middle East. Britain had to hold its place in the Gulf at all costs; Saudi Arabia would become reconciled to that.

Egypt was the centre of the Arab world, and attempts to isolate it would probably not succeed. In the eyes of Arab youth, Nasser had the makings of a hero. Nuri, whatever the admiration for his statesmanship might be, belonged to a time that was past. Iraq could be the Arab country of the future, but the present was with Egypt. As Nasser had taken against the Baghdad Pact, Britain had to reconcile him to it and not rush others into membership. Should Britain not be able to do business with Nasser, it would try to unseat the Egyptian leader before despairing of Egypt. Although the Americans should be left to make the running with Israel, public opinion in Britain used only to hearing the Zionist case, and the Labour Party, should be prepared for a solution dependent on Britain's stake in the Middle East.

On Buraimi, the British remained unyielding. Washington was enjoying all the advantages of the special British position in the Gulf, and refusing to say a word in support of it. The United States had to realize that if it connived at 'the undermining of one corner of the edifice of British influence, the whole [edifice] will be in danger of collapsing'. American pressure to retreat was always on Britain, and never, seemingly, on the Saudis. The implication of Hoover's view, that unless the situation in South-East Arabia was cleared up, the Americans would have zero influence with the Saudis, was that the British should abandon their friends and clear out. It was thought that would be a shameful abdication on Britain's part, and furthermore the history of 'appeasement' did not suggest that the American influence would rise much above zero even if Britain did go. Britain did have influence above zero in South-East Arabia and would be able to retain it without asking the Americans to abandon ARAMCO or Dhahran. Reference was made to the 'lamentable démarche' the Americans had made over the Nizwa operation in Oman. American pressure on Britain to restrain the Sultan of Muscat was 'an example in the purest form of U.S. policy: it is to take no action that can possibly offend an enemy, but not to worry about the interests of friends'. The concluding sentence of this acerbic brief was deleted: 'Our policy in Arabia and elsewhere in the Middle East is now based on supporting our friends and not worrying too much about the interests of our enemies.'[5]

In talks in the State Department on 13 January, Shuckburgh started with the observation that the real objective of the West in the Middle East was to secure the right to extract and use the oil of the region. George V. Allen of the Near Eastern Bureau was not sure whether he could accept that proposition. There was an obvious divergence between London and Washington. Shuckburgh thought that if Arab opposition were encountered, a policy of withdrawal was not automatically indicated. Withdrawal created vacuums. There were obvious differences over Saudi Arabia: Britain thought that Saudi oil revenues were not used for constructive development. Geoffrey Arthur of the Foreign Office expressed the view that outside influence was important for Arab unity; only Western participation could produce that unity. That afternoon, against the background of the news of further riots in Jordan, Shuckburgh insisted that the British did not think of Jordan as a colony: they were there to prevent a vacuum. Allen wondered whether it would help to tell Nasser that Britain and the United States did not object to Jordan joining the pact that had been made between Egypt, Syria and Saudi Arabia. Shuckburgh reported that the views the State Department expressed were neither 'clear not confident'. But the department did show a disposition to favour a long-term policy of encouraging Arab unity under Egyptian leadership. The State Department had admitted that Saudi bribery was a major danger for the West, and that Saudi activity had the effect of helping the Communists.[6]

Eden warned Eisenhower directly that if the Saudis were allowed to go on spending and behaving the way they were there would be 'nothing left for anybody but the Bear': Saudi money was subsidizing Communist newspapers in Syria, Lebanon and Jordan; Saudi Arabia, nominally together with Egypt and Syria who had no money, had offered to replace the British subsidy to Jordan. The Soviets had also offered Jordan everything it wanted provided that Jordan denounced its treaty with Britain. The friends of the West in Jordan and Iraq had to be backed or the whole of the Middle East would fall into Communist hands. In Washington, on 16 January, Allen told Shuckburgh that while the British described the Saudi activities in terms of evil, the Americans attributed many of the Saudi actions to Arab nationalism. Rather than seeing the Saudis motivated by Marxist idealism, the State Department thought the Saudis were motivated by irritation against the United States for preserving Israel and their fear of British domination of the Gulf. Allen reported to Hoover that the British could not understand their position in the Gulf had elements of imperialism. He had told the British they had to realize that the nineteenth century was no more. Washington was not persuaded by the British case over Buraimi, and thought that Eden, in his forthcoming talks with Eisenhower, would need to be persuaded that Britain would have to ameliorate the situation so that Saudi Arabia did not take the matter to the Security Council. Shuckburgh replied on 18 January: it was unfortunate that where Britain tried to work with a government in the Middle East it was labelled domination. But if others did the same it was not labelled domination. The Americans did not seem to understand the importance for the West of the British position in Jordan. The American and British officials agreed that both countries should avoid isolating Egypt and help with the building of the Aswan High Dam.

Views on the Saudi threat, however, were not reconciled. Britain insisted, and the Americans had initially agreed, that captured documents showed the Saudis knew they were breaking the arbitration agreement. Britain reiterated, in relation to the Saudi problem, that its position on the Gulf was acceptable and beneficial to the inhabitants, useful to the United States, and vital for Britain. British industry and the balance of payments depended on continued access to Middle East oil, 33 per cent of which lay under the Gulf states. Britain could not allow that oil to fall under the control of 'an irresponsible and unstable' state like Saudi Arabia. Britain's position in the Gulf was not one of occupation or of 'colonialism'; it was based on the confidence of the rulers and inhabitants in Britain's ability to protect them. Britain was 'not prepared to abandon these friendly Arab States or advise them to resume a process which we know must lead to their destruction'. Ian Samuel of the Foreign Office requested that ARAMCO be asked to stop its advances to the Saudi government.

Dulles warned Eugene Holman of the Standard Oil Company of New Jersey that Eden, during his forthcoming visit, was likely to emphasize the British feeling that American oil companies were helping the Saudis to finance a war against British interests in the Middle East. Francis Russell told Shuckburgh how Dulles was more receptive than Hoover to the British views on Buraimi. Hoover looked at the matter from the point of view of ARAMCO and American oil interests, and Dulles had pointed out to Hoover that Britain, too, was an American interest. At Allen's suggestion Lloyd sent Dulles a letter about Buraimi. The Foreign Secretary said that Britain could not afford to lose. Arbitration was unacceptable, and he asked for Dulles' support in defeating any resolution in the United Nations.[7]

The discussions on the Baghdad Pact in Washington were 'irregular and formless'. In the Foreign Office, Lord John Hope observed that the Americans probably had not taken the trouble to analyse the Soviet reaction to the pact. The Americans should have realized what 'a stumbling blow to Communist penetration' the Baghdad Pact was. R.M. Hadow commented that although the Americans had sent official observers to the Baghdad Pact Council meeting in November 1955, and to the January 1956 meeting of the Economic Committee, they were not supporting the pact with any enthusiasm.[8] The British ambassador at Washington warned that some of these American views were those of specialists and might not be generally held. There was scepticism over the implication of a policy that could encourage neutralism, particularly where British interests were involved. Anthony Nutting minuted that: 'we must also back up our chums'.[9]

Sailing to the United States on board the *Queen Elizabeth*, Eden flared up when the American ambassador at London, Winthrop Aldrich, reiterated Hoover's case over Buraimi, and complained that the United States always wanted Britain to abandon its interests and give away its rights. Aldrich reassured the Prime Minister that Washington did not want to expand the Saudi kingdom at British expense. In preparation for the meeting with Eisenhower, the Foreign Office thought Eden might like to consider the warning from the British ambassador at Baghdad, Sir Michael Wright, that possible American ideas of helping neutralist countries could lead to bewilderment in Iraq if corresponding aid were not made available to the Northern Tier. The conclusion could be drawn in the Middle East that it was a neutralist rather than a pro-Western policy which brought benefits.[10]

On 30 January Eden, Dulles, and their officials met at the White House. On 8 February Eisenhower confided to his diary that he had never before taken part in official international talks with such a noticeable spirit of friendship. The British kept asking for American support. Lloyd felt that the Shah of Iran had gone against the tradition of Iranian neutrality in supporting the Baghdad Pact. He had no concrete benefits, and hearing of Western offers to build the Aswan High Dam wondered whether he had made a mistake. Dulles said that the United States had not urged Iran to join; the Shah had joined on the basis of Iranian judgement. Eden hoped he could let Nuri know that he would have tanks paid for by the Americans. Dulles thought that Syria was behaving like a Soviet satellite and that if the decision were taken to move against Nasser, Syria could also be included. Lloyd pointed to the problem of Saudi intrigue and bribery in Jordan. After Eisenhower had joined the group the issue of Buraimi was tackled. Eisenhower thought that surely the British would not maintain that every mile in every border line in the vast area would be a matter of British prestige. To this Eden responded that the British had had to give up many things in the world. The impression was that if the British were pressed hard enough, they would 'be off'. If the British yielded in South-East Arabia they would soon be completely out of the Middle East.

Eisenhower then wondered about the importance of Buraimi itself, apart from its significance for British prestige and as a crossroads. Lloyd explained that it would be valuable to the Saudis as a vantage point from which the tribes in the whole region could be corrupted. There were difficulties in allowing the Saudis through to the sea at Qatar: there could be oil there. The British did not share the American view that if the Buraimi dispute were settled the Saudis would behave in an acceptable way. The Americans were inclined to see the king of Saudi Arabia as the key to the situation. Shuckburgh thought that on this Dulles and Eisenhower were closer to Britain than Hoover. They accepted that Britain could not go to arbitration, and wanted some negotiation 'to save King Saud's face'. Hoover also explained that ARAMCO was not making advance payments to the Saudis. The Saudis were receiving money though the banks in anticipation of payments by ARAMCO, and Hoover saw no way of stopping these credits. At the same time, in London, Nutting told Walworth Barbour that it was time the British and American positions on Buraimi were brought into line.[11]

From the British perspective, the talks in Washington suggested modifications in the American approach to the Middle East. On the divisive issue of Buraimi, Allen told the Saudi ambassador at Washington, Abdullah al-Khayyal, on 2 February, that the British might be prepared for direct discussions with the Saudis. The ambassador recommended to King Saud that he delay submitting the Buraimi issue to the Security Council. When Shuckburgh told Allen, on 3 February, that the Saudis had approached the British about direct talks, Allen, while welcoming the start of such talks, insisted that Washington could not tell the Saudis that it would support the British case in the Security Council.

Eden reported to the Cabinet on 9 February the reaffirmation of Britain and the United States to carry out the terms of the Tripartite Declaration. A few months previously, Britain had doubted whether the Declaration had much meaning. Eden spoke of the need for Eisenhower to secure the approval of Congress before engaging American forces, but said that nonetheless American warships were proceeding unobtrusively to take up positions in the Eastern Mediterranean and the Red Sea, and that British naval forces were conforming with that movement. On the matter of arms, Lloyd observed that he was surprised to find the American government so ready to take a firm line over Israel in election year. It wanted to send as little as possible to Israel.[12]

In the Washington talks, Britain had insisted to the Americans that Jordan was not a colony. The American attitude to the British position in Jordan continued to show the same uncertainty and ambivalence as had been evidenced in 1955. In January 1956, the new Jordanian government indicated a policy of keeping Jordan out of the Baghdad Pact. British troops flew to Cyprus, and provisions were made to fly other troops from Iraq to Jordan. Lloyd notified Amman in February that, in the event of war between Israel and Egypt or Syria, if an Arab state fought against Israel, there were limits to what Britain could do. On 28 February 1956 the Cabinet discussed a Jordanian request for the assurance of British military assistance in the event of an attack by Israel on Syria. The Anglo-Jordanian Treaty would not apply if Israel attacked an Arab country other than Jordan. But it was agreed that the Tripartite Declaration would apply, and as there were indications that the Americans would honour their obligations under the Tripartite Declaration, Britain could commit itself to sending reinforcements to Jordan. Indeed Makins reported from Washington on 3 March, following a conversation with Hoover, that the Americans were groping for a policy in the Middle East and needed British help and advice. They were bracing themselves in preparation for accepting additional responsibilities there.[13]

Lloyd was with Nasser in Cairo when King Hussein dismissed Sir John Glubb (Glubb Pasha), the head of the Arab Legion, on 1 March. Nasser congratulated Lloyd on Britain's removing Glubb to improve relations with Egypt. Eden initially thought that Nasser was behind Glubb's dismissal, but Glubb probably persuaded the Prime Minister otherwise. The Ambassador at Amman, advised that Hussein's act was directed against Glubb personally because of the awe in which he was held in Jordan, and it would be a mistake to assume that the basis for mutual confidence and friendship between Britain and Jordan had been destroyed. The view was confirmed by Sir Alec Kirkbride who had been British Minister until 1951 and was in Jordan at the time of the dismissal. Eden told Shuckburgh on 3 March to consider reoccupation of the Suez base as a move to counteract the blow to British prestige implicit in Glubb's dismissal. On 4 March, the Prime Minister wrote to Eisenhower urging American accession to the Baghdad Pact, and support for Nuri, particularly in respect of the Centurion tanks. It was not safe to wait on Nasser any longer. A policy of appeasement would bring nothing. There seemed to be a sinister coincidence of Egyptian and Soviet interest in sinking the Baghdad Pact, and that could mean further moves against Nuri. Britain and the United States had to do everything to support Nuri 'as our one reliable asset in this gloomy situation'.[14]

Exchanges between Washington and London were not satisfactory. Dulles proposed to Lloyd that there should be a bargain struck with Nasser: in return for no more Arab members of the Baghdad Pact, he would call off his propaganda and help to promote a Palestine settlement. Eden was dismayed: appeasement of Nasser had to stop; the Baghdad Pact friends should be aided and comforted. Dulles could not oblige: he was being attacked viciously by the Zionists. American membership of the Baghdad Pact would thus have to be coupled with a guarantee for Israel. A political crisis over Washington's relations with Israel could rob Eisenhower of victory in the forthcoming presidential elections. But Hoover did agree to ask Congress for funds to supply Centurions to Iraq, but he wanted this kept quiet until the actual request was made.[15]

Eden reminded the Cabinet, on 6 March, that Britain's policy in the Middle East had to be founded on the need to protect its oil interests in Iraq and the Gulf. The main threat to those interests was the growing influence of Egypt. On 8 March, Dulles told Lloyd that the Americans were going to take a lot more interest in the Middle East and enter into things more in future. How they were to do that had not been thought out. Shuckburgh recorded 8 March 1956 as being the day when Washington and London gave up hope of Nasser, and began to look around for a way to destroy him. He wrote on 10 March to Kirkpatrick, lamenting that with the collapse of 'Alpha' Britain was left without a Middle East policy. It was a situation of grave national emergency. Supporting the Tripartite Declaration could lead to an obligation to defend Israel against the Soviet Union and the Arabs. London had to have a common policy with Washington. If Britain had despaired of Nasser and wanted to overthrow him, American co-operation would be needed.

Lloyd told the Cabinet, on 15 March, that it was clear Britain could not establish a basis for friendly relations with Egypt. There had to be Anglo-American agreement on a general alignment of policy towards Egypt. This included support for Libya to prevent the extension of Egyptian and Communist influence there, and an attempt to establish a government in Syria more friendly to the West. Action, such as the withholding of military supplies, the withdrawal of financial support for the Aswan Dam, the reduction of American aid and the freezing of sterling balances could also be aimed directly at Cairo. Eden spoke of Israel's need for interceptor aircraft and wondered whether the Americans could help. Kirkpatrick, however, reported that Allen was not convinced that Nasser was on the path to perdition.[16]

At this time, Britain faced disturbances in Bahrain. The resentment focused partly on Sir Charles Belgrave, who had been adviser to the Ruler for 30 years, and was mounted by a middle-class body, called the High Executive Committee, which had been agitating for a more liberal form of government. Eden did not appreciate being reminded by Norman Brook, the Secretary of the Cabinet, of the principles he had outlined in February 1953 as Foreign Secretary: Britain could not maintain its position in the Middle East by employing the methods of the nineteenth century; Britain had to have a policy designed to harness nationalist movements rather than struggle against them. Eden felt that this did not apply to Bahrain.

On 13 March, the Cabinet also authorized the Governor of Aden to start discussion with the local Rulers on the future constitutional development in the Protectorate. The Colonial Policy Committee favoured moves towards a Federation or Federations. Lloyd had reservations about raising the issue as it could offend the rulers of Yemen and Saudi Arabia, and lead to them increasing their efforts to stir up trouble when Britain had troubles elsewhere in the Middle East. This took place at a time when Shuckburgh advised Eden that the maintenance of Britain's position in the Gulf would depend on its success or failure in countering the Egyptian drive for revolutionary leadership of the Arab world. To do this Britain needed to maintain physical strength in the area, but Shuckburgh emphasized that the commitment of British forces to quell local disorders should be avoided.[17]

As British policy became resolute, American policy developed. The Chiefs of Staff warned Eisenhower on 15 March that there were indications the British were 'shying away from joint planning', probably because they felt that they could not find themselves in a position of fighting the Arabs. Eisenhower advised how the time was coming when Washington would 'have to serve some notice on certain of the Middle Eastern countries'. He thought that King Saud of Saudi Arabia could be the leader of the Arab world, and a rival to Nasser. The President did not know Saud, and did not know if he could be built up into the position he visualized for him. Over two years later, on 15 June 1958, Eisenhower regretted this policy and acknowledged that it had been a mistake. The president recorded how Washington had tried to build up King Saud, but it had started too late, and that Saud was probably too weak an individual. Eisenhower acknowledged that the man the British had wanted to support, Crown Prince Feisal of Iraq, would have been better. On 28 March the President endorsed an American approach to the Middle East, in line with the revised British policy, of reinforcing ties with friendly countries, modifying the policies of Egypt and Syria, and increasing American support for the Baghdad Pact. This policy became known as 'Omega'. Air Marshal Sir William Dickson, the Chairman of the British Chiefs of Staff, was scheduled to visit Washington, and the British expected to have their plans for contingencies in the Middle East ready by 21 April. Admiral Radford, at a Pentagon meeting of members of the State Department and the Joint Chiefs of Staff on 30 March 1956, observed that the best help the British could provide Washington would be to give in on bitter issues like Buraimi. On 1 April, Dulles implied the gist of this new American policy to Makins: Washington believed that it might be possible to win Saud away from Nasser. Saud could give important anti-Communist leadership in the Arab world. But the winning away of the Saudis from Egypt depended on Britain reaching an accommodation with the Saudis over Buraimi.[18]

Dickson, in Washington between 3 and 5 April, saw Eisenhower, John Foster Dulles, Allen Dulles, and the Joint Chiefs of Staff. He outlined a British policy based on the conclusion that to allow Nasser to continue building an Arab Empire around himself was a major threat to the interests of the West and of benefit to the Soviet Union. London and Washington should have an agreement on a policy to defeat Nasser's plan. Dickson referred to the need to create a split between the Egyptians, and the Saudis and Syrians. Eisenhower spoke as if American and British interests were identical. Dulles suggested an examination of the effect of closing the Suez Canal. It was evident that Admiral Radford was not flinching at the consideration of plans of a scope necessary to handle the wider implications of dealing with Egyptian aggression. Eisenhower told Dickson in private that he thought that Nasser was heavily committed to the Soviets. Dickson reported that the Americans thought the British were on the retreat in the Middle East, they were rattled, and consequently their judgement was warped.[19]

To a recommendation from the Joint Chiefs of Staff that the United States join the Baghdad Pact, Dulles, on 9 April, explained to Radford that he had raised the issue with Senators, and it was evident that the Senate would not agree. Dulles also thought that the pact formed to resist Soviet aggression, had become a forum for Arab politics and intrigue, and a body through which Britain hoped to preserve its position in Iraq and support Nuri against Nasser and Saud.[20]

Frontier incidents between Egyptian and Israeli troops near Gaza led to a statement by Eisenhower that the United States would observe its formal commitments within constitutional means to oppose any aggression in this area, and would support any nation subject to this aggression. Lloyd told the Cabinet on 10 April that he thought this statement ambiguous. It could mean that Washington was emphasizing more United Nations action than action under the Tripartite Declaration. Britain would, however, associate itself with this statement. There was some concern that little progress had been made in the formulation of actual military plans in the joint Anglo-American planning.

The Chiefs of Staff, on 17 April, considered a series of reports by the Joint Planning Staff on combined Anglo-American action that could be taken under the Tripartite Declaration. These were to form the basis of combined planning with the American Joint Chiefs of Staff. They suggested that every effort should be made to get the Americans to agree to some form of a Joint Command Organization for naval and air operations in particular. The Chiefs of Staff further thought that as it would take some time before the final Anglo-American plan were produced, there could be a covert release of some indication of Anglo-American military intentions towards both Egypt and Israel if war broke out, as a sort of deterrence.[21]

Dulles was worried about the visit of Nikita Khrushchev and Nikolai Bulganin to Britain in April. There, on 27 April, Khrushchev spoke about the Soviet Union preferring an arms embargo in the Middle East and offered Soviet participation in this if it were organized by the United Nations. Nasser thought this threatened his arms supply from the Soviet Union and hastily recognized Communist China. Dulles was furious. Eden initiated meetings between the Foreign Office and the State Department to consider a coup against Nasser. British external intelligence, MI6, and the Central Intelligence Agency investigated the matter, but Dulles prevaricated. Dulles and Eden, however, were in agreement about the overall objective of Anglo-American policy from this point and throughout the Suez crisis: the removal of Nasser.[22]

Lloyd and Dulles lunched together in the British embassy at Paris on 3 May during a NATO meeting. They agreed to allow the High Aswan Dam project to 'languish'.

Dulles could not find an immediate answer to Lloyd's enquiry as to how the American plan of detaching Saud from Nasser was progressing. On Buraimi Britain hoped for protracted negotiations with Saudi Arabia which would keep the matter 'on ice'. The forthcoming negotiations with the Saudis on Dhahran, Dulles warned, might mean the need to sell the Saudis arms. Lloyd 'jokingly' asked whether the purpose of the arms would be to attack Buraimi. Dulles informed Eisenhower after this meeting that the British and the Americans were coming closer together on the Middle East, but that the British were still sensitive about what they saw as an American policy of weaning the Saudis away from Egypt at the expense of selling out the British at Buraimi.

After lunching with State Department officials on 4 May, however, Shuckburgh complained that they did not see the British point of view on Saudi Arabia and 'I beat my head against a wall'. On 23 June, Lloyd asked Dulles for a common Anglo-American intelligence assessment on the American policy over the British concession of Buraimi to Saudi Arabia, and the subsequent likely detachment of Saud from Egypt. Dulles replied, on 10 July, that there was not 'the leisure to complete any formal exchange of intelligence prior to proceeding toward a solution of the Buraimi matter, which in our view remains the Gordian knot'. On 26 July 1956 Lloyd reiterated to the Cabinet that Britain could not contemplate the creation at Buraimi of either a neutral zone, or a zone under Saudi sovereignty. The most Britain could do was to offer to explore the possibility of giving Saudi Arabia access to the sea at Qatar. Lloyd informed Dulles on 28 July that the results of the talks with the Saudis had been meagre. The Foreign Secretary, however, later informed Dulles, on 5 September, that although Britain could not give away Buraimi, he did not think that made an improvement of relations with the Saudis impossible.

On 18 May, Dulles told appropriate American diplomatic missions that British chiefs of mission in the Middle East had been instructed to stress, in their dealings with third parties, the general agreement between American and British policy in the area. American officials should emphasize the similarity of Anglo-American interests in developing reciprocally beneficial relations with the countries of the area. Third parties should not be allowed to play London and Washington off against each other.[23]

At a time when Eden instituted a reassessment of British defence policy in the light of economic necessity, the Libyans tried the tactic of securing more money from Britain by threatening to go to the Soviet Union and Egypt. Britain would not be able to satisfy these demands unless Washington increased the level of its assistance. The moment had come for Britain to consider how much it was prepared to pay for the continuation of this treaty.

Accordingly, Lloyd told the Cabinet on 28 June that he had agreed to provide a small increase in the financial aid for Libya. But financial support for Libya was becoming an increasing burden, and an urgent reappraisal needed to be made of the value of Britain's connection with Libya under the prevailing conditions. The United States, which had transferred its principal base in North Africa to Libya from Morocco, could reasonably expect to bear a greater share of the expenditure involved in supporting Libya.[24]

This envisaged policy towards Libya was in line with the review instituted by Eden, on 4 June 1956, to take account of the changes in the methods, if not the objectives, of the Soviet Union. The review was to include Britain's economic and financial circumstances, and would cover changes in domestic and overseas policy, and adjustments in Britain's defence programme. The Policy Review Committee of the Cabinet, in a note to Eden of 15 June, approved as a basis for military and political planning two objectives: avoiding global war; and the protection of Britain's vital interests overseas, particularly access to oil. These objectives would fail unless Britain maintained North American involvement in Europe, and a large measure of identity between its interests and those of the United States and Canada and developed closer co-operation with those countries. Britain also had to maintain the cohesion of the Commonwealth. It had to be remembered that the main threat to Britain's position and influence in the world was now political and economic rather than military. Effort had to be transferred from military preparations to the maintenance and improvement of Britain's economic position. The period of foreign aid was finishing. Britain had to find means of increasing by £400 million a year the credit side of its balance of payments. In its defence programmes Britain was doing too much to guard against the least likely risk, that of major war. Britain was spending too much on forces of types which were no longer of primary importance.[25]

On 27 June 1956, Norman Brook, the Secretary of the Cabinet, sent A.D. Dodds-Parker, the Joint Parliamentary Under-Secretary of State for Foreign Affairs, an extract from a report submitted to the Policy Review Committee by Officials of the Foreign Office, the Treasury, and the Ministry of Defence, on the future of the United Kingdom in World Affairs. It was for consideration by the inter-departmental committee which Dodds-Parker was to chair on the study of non-military measures to be taken in the Middle East. The section of the report on Britain's future that dealt with the Middle East saw the uninterrupted flow of oil as being vital, but regarded this as an increasingly political rather than a military problem. There was no question of Britain reducing the very limited force it had in the Gulf. Britain, also, could not jeopardize the stability of Iraq and Iran by not supporting the Baghdad Pact. But there were commitments in the Middle East that could be reviewed: the headquarters and forces in Cyprus; British forces and air bases in Jordan, and the Arab Legion; the right to use the air bases in Iraq; the civilian-operated base in Egypt; British forces in Libya; Aden and the Protectorate; and the Gulf. Britain's military expenditure in the area, from the balance of payments point of view, amounted to about £25 million. In addition there was £15 million spent on grants to Jordan and Libya, and the British contribution to Palestinian relief. And about £5 million went on other government services such as a loan to Jordan, grants to Aden and the Middle East information services. The scope for reduction of military expenditure was not, however, comparable to that in Europe. There were adverse factors such as the probable increase in the military strength of trouble-makers like Egypt and Saudi Arabia. The potential air barrier between Britain and the Middle East was likely to increase the limit of Britain's flexibility in the use of forces.

Consequently, a policy was recommended that Britain should not allow the Baghdad Pact to be treated just as a military association. Britain should develop plans with the Americans to build up the political, economic and social side of the Pact, and to show its members that membership paid. Military assistance could be channelled through the Pact, 'but the Middle East States should be encouraged to look to the United States for the provision of any equipment and to the United States and ourselves for training facilities'. Britain should try to ensure that its military contribution was not in the form of stationing large conventional forces in the Middle East: 'We should examine whether, at the expense of taking some risks, for example with the implementation of our undertakings under the Tripartite Declaration, we cannot plan a substantial run-down over the next few years of our forces in Libya, Jordan and Cyprus, starting with the first.' Britain, the report said, would need facilities in these places. Britain also had to be in a position, if necessary, to exercise military power if its interests were threatened. But it should not prove necessary for Britain in the long run to station permanent forces in the Middle East on anything like the present scale. There needed to be an examination of how soon the Canal Zone base could be liquidated.

Britain had to realize that the Middle East was the most critical theatre politically, and required a corresponding priority of attention. Britain needed to develop non-military methods of maintaining and extending its influence, including technical assistance and information services, and to improve its intelligence services. In the dependent territories, Britain had to do all it could to promote education on the right lines, and to improve the police, local security forces and counter-subversion.[26]

Dodds-Parker sent his committee's report to Lloyd on 19 July. Apart from referring to the need to enlist American economic participation in Libya, only four lines concerned the United States. They emphasized the necessity for continuing to work for the greatest possible American support for British policies, and in particular to obtain American aid, and that of the International

Bank wherever possible in countering Soviet economic penetration. The report stressed that Britain needed, in view of the political irritant of foreign forces, to keep any British forces in the Middle East to the minimum requirement for strategic purposes, and to divert them away from the centre of political activity.

That committee concluded that military expenditure in the Middle East on a balance of payments basis would amount to £56.7 million in 1956–57. There was the other expenditure of £31.25 million in other directions supporting local military forces, and the subventions paid to Jordan, Libya and towards the Palestinian refugees. This was considerable when compared with £9 million in the Far East, and £18 million for all Colonial Welfare and Development. It was about half the total expenditure of Britain on non-military items overseas. There was a serious lack of balance in this expenditure. Jordan offered no commensurate return. Expenditure on Baghdad Pact countries was small, and so was that in the Trucial States which was short of what the Political Resident considered to be the minimum necessary to maintain Britain's position there. The committee recommended that Britain, while retaining its essential bases in Jordan, should reduce its commitments there. The expenditure of around £600,000 on broadcasting, information and development was recommended.[27]

In the Foreign Office, A.R. Walmsley thought that the points about the harmonization of Anglo-American policy needed to be expanded. S. Falle prepared a special brief on this which emphasized Britain's aim to do everything possible to align American policy with British in the Middle East. Further, it was to convince the Americans that a defeat for Britain in a country in the Middle East was a defeat for the West, as British influence would not be replaced by American. Official American opinion was coming to realize this, but there was the complication of unofficial advice, often more influential, which regarded the British as old-fashioned imperialists and embarrassing allies. There was also a difference over the tactics to be used in the Middle East. Britain's position was weakened by the tendency of the Americans to take a middle position in disputes between Britain and Middle Eastern states, rather than supporting Britain.

There was satisfactory co-operation between British and American oil interests in Kuwait with the 50 per cent share of British Petroleum and the 50 per cent share of Gulf Oil, and also with the Iranian consortium which had a 40 per cent American participating interest. The American interest, 23.75 per cent in the Iraq Petroleum Company, was more passive. ARAMCO was the difficulty. The British ambassador at Jedda had described this 100 per cent American company as the most undesirable influence to which King Saud was subjected. ARAMCO considered their quiet life upset by British imperialism which annoyed the King who then took his annoyance out on the nearest Westerner. All would be well provided Britain gave way to the King. ARAMCO posed the greatest obstacle to Anglo-American harmony in the Middle East. Otherwise Washington and London saw 'eye to eye on Egypt in general'. There was continuous close co-operation on Palestine. London had suggested to Washington a joint Anglo-American review of the Libyan development plan, and Britain was exploring the possibility of the Americans taking over eventual responsibility for the Libyan Air Force. The Americans accepted Britain's special position in the Gulf, and they even seemed to be pulling their weight in the Economic Committee of the Baghdad Pact. On 24 July Harold Macmillan, the Chancellor of the Exchequer, explained that he was due to propose the appointment of a Ministerial Committee to weigh the competing claims on our limited resources for economic aid to countries overseas. Even so, he agreed that mention could be made in the House of Commons of developing the economic side of the Baghdad Pact in the form of further technical assistance.[28]

At the time Eden initiated his review of British policy, Nasser nationalized the Suez Canal. It seems that neither the Foreign Office, nor the State Department anticipated Nasser's actions. Nasser, envisaging the possibility of a Soviet loan, decided to force the issue. Suddenly he agreed to accept the conditions that had been imposed. The last British troops withdrew from the Canal Zone on 13 June: London concluded that it could not renege on the agreements of 1954.

Against this background Nasser sent his ambassador, Ahmed Hussein, to Washington. Dulles was having trouble with Congress. He summoned his staff and they decided that it was not worth fighting every clause of the loan through that body. There was some opposition to a sudden cancellation, but that was what was agreed.

On 7 June Eisenhower had been stricken with an attack of ileitis and had undergone major surgery; for a while the President lost control of his faculties. He was still recovering in Gettysburg when Dulles informed him on 13 July of the new developments. Having decided to run again as President, Eisenhower resented having to take any political risks domestically for Nasser. But it seems that Eisenhower left the handling of policy to Dulles. On 16 July Dulles informed Eisenhower that the Senate Appropriations Committee was insisting on approving the use of American funds for the construction of the Aswan Dam. Dulles later wrote to Eisenhower on 15 September 1956, in reply to the President's query as to whether the American withdrawal from the Aswan Dam project had been abrupt, that the Egyptians knew the reason for the withdrawal, and that the actual reason was that mounting Congressional opposition would have made it impossible to finance the dam anyway. Britain was informed but not consulted about Dulles' decision: the British tactic was to 'play this long'. The press releases were prepared before Dulles, accompanied by Hoover and Allen, saw Hussein on 19 July 1956. Hussein gave Dulles the opportunity for a staged show of temper when he patted his pocket in agitation at the drift of Dulles' statement and said that he had there a Soviet promise of finance. Probably Hussein did not want Soviet finance: the ambassador was pro-American and wanted American aid. But Dulles apparently retorted that anyone who built the dam would earn the hatred of the Egyptian people because the burden would be crushing: the United States was leaving that pleasure to the Soviet Union. Dulles seemed to doubt whether the Soviets would offer the money anyway.

The British Cabinet decided, on 20 July, that it also had to withdraw from the dam project. Sir Harold Caccia told the Egyptian ambassador that the decision had been an economic one: Egypt was indulging in other expenditures which would prevent it from giving priority to the Aswan dam. Britain still wanted good relations with Egypt. On 26 July, Nasser, speaking in Alexandria, referred to his revolution restoring Egypt's sense of dignity. The West's terms for the Aswan Dam loan were 'imperialism without soldiers': with Eugene Black, the President of the World Bank concerned with the financing arrangements for the Aswan Dam, Nasser had felt he was sitting in front of Ferdinand de Lesseps, the French engineer to whom the ruler of Egypt had granted a concession in 1854 to build the Suez Canal. That was the signal for the seizure of the company's premises.

Eden heard the news at a dinner at Number 10 given for Feisal and Nuri al-Said, Nasser's rivals in the Middle East. Nuri, on 3 August, said that when Arab opinion realized that Britain meant business, there would be a good effect. Britain rejected recourse to the Security Council: the issue would just be delayed there. There was concern as to how far the United States would support economic sanctions against Nasser and, if necessary military action. Lloyd told Andrew Foster, the American chargé d'affaires, that he inclined to the view that the only solution would be for a Western consortium to take over and operate the canal, establishing itself by military force if necessary.

Initially, London wanted to act together with Washington and Paris, but most of the British leaders failed to appreciate the significance of American elections. In 1949, the Permanent Under-Secretary's committee at the Foreign Office, headed by William Strang, had pointed to the dangers of this factor for Anglo-American relations. Bevin had had bitter experience of it. Eisenhower wanted to be re-elected President: this time on the platform of peace. It was his main preoccupation. He could not afford to have the principal allies of the United States fighting what the American public would probably regard as an imperial war. His administration had, after all, avoided allying itself with Britain and France in the Middle East, and had tried to pursue a policy of even-handedness towards the Arabs and Israelis at the cost of Zionist discontent in the United States. Eisenhower wished to project the image of the United States as an anti-colonial power. Dulles understood this. But the Secretary of State during his previous year had wielded considerable control of policy towards the Middle East during Eisenhower's illnesses. Nasser had offended Dulles, and John Foster agreed with Eden that the President of Egypt had to go. The only way of reconciling Eisenhower's election preoccupation with their objective was to delay any military action until after the presidential elections. As a lawyer, Dulles was also conscious of the possible consequences of Nasser's nationalization for the American-operated Panama Canal.

On 27 July, Eden told the House of Commons of the serious situation Nasser's action had created. Immediately afterwards the Cabinet met together with some of the Chiefs of Staff. It was told that the canal was vital to Western Europe: two-thirds of the oil supplies for that area passed though it. The Cabinet decided unanimously that if economic and political pressure failed, then Britain should be prepared to use force. The threat might be enough. But as all British interests in the Middle East were threatened, Britain should be prepared to act on its own. This would be a last resort. The Chiefs of Staff were ordered to make the necessary military preparations. Eden informed Eisenhower that same day that firm action was necessary otherwise Anglo-American influence in the Middle East would be destroyed. Economic pressures on their own were unlikely to be successful, and Britain was, in the last resort, prepared to use force. But the Prime Minister thought that the first step should be for France, the United States and Britain to align their policies, and put maximum pressure on Cairo.

Eisenhower knew the British position both from Andrew Foster and Eden. Dulles was in South America, so the President consulted with Hoover and they decided to send Robert Murphy, the Deputy Under-Secretary, to the proposed meeting in London. On 30 July, Murphy met Christian Pineau, the French Foreign Minister, in London and learnt about American naivety. Macmillan, with Eden's acquiescence, impressed on Murphy that Britain and France were prepared to participate in a military operation. Lloyd told the Under-Secretary that Nasser would be unimpressed by economic and political pressures unless there were military preparations in the background. Significantly, Murphy advised that American public opinion was not prepared for the use of force: the possibility of military intervention should be kept in the background. Murphy saw Lloyd and Pineau on 31 July; that day Paris accepted British command of forces that might be used. Dulles, just back from Peru, met Eisenhower to discuss reports from Murphy that Britain had decided to 'break Nasser': it would take six weeks to mount the operation. The President immediately despatched his Secretary of State with a message for Eden asking for a conference of maritime nations before corrective measures were taken: that would have 'a great educational effect around the world'. Initial military successes might be easy, but the eventual price would be too high. If American forces were to be used, it would be necessary to show that every way of resolving the matter peacefully had been tried. Should such efforts fail, then world opinion would understand that 'we simply could not accept a situation that would in the long run prove disastrous to the prosperity and living standards of every nation whose economy depends directly or indirectly upon East-West shipping'.

In London, Dulles saw Lloyd and Pineau on 1 August. The Secretary of State reiterated Eisenhower's policy: what was needed was a conference of the users of the canal. Washington did not exclude the use of force, but it needed to be backed by world opinion. Lloyd explained that Britain might have to use force in the end. Dulles conceded that Nasser would have to be made to 'disgorge'. But Dulles was obviously playing for time: he thought it would take three weeks to prepare for the envisaged conference, but 16 August was the compromise date agreed. Dulles was cheered by a crowd in Downing Street and was pleased. He also saw Macmillan and was told that the question for Britain was one of survival.

The Secretary of State met Eden privately the next day. In view of their clash at Geneva in 1954, the two men appeared to have had a friendly talk. Dulles was particularly flattered by the Prime Minister's suggestion that he would go down in history as one of the great foreign ministers. It appears he gave Eden the assurance that he understood the Anglo-French position, and that Britain could count on the moral support and sympathy of the United States. Eden apparently offered the details of the Anglo-French military preparations, but Dulles interrupted to say that it would probably be better if Washington did not know. Presumably Dulles had possible domestic complications in mind; and the Central Intelligence Agency's activities were such that it would find out anyway; friendly exchanges between American and British military officials would also keep American officials apprised. After this warm talk both London and Washington were relieved and pleased. Later, the Egypt Committee was informed by Lloyd on 27 August that he had discussed the request from the American military attaché for information about the movements of British troops, and that Dulles had indicated that Washington would prefer that such information should not be passed to their military authorities. Lloyd informed Makins that Dulles had told both he and Eden on at least two occasions that it would be an embarrassment for Washington if it were given this military information. But, if the State Department were complaining, it was possible that Dulles had not told Eisenhower or the State Department of this.

Eisenhower became increasingly involved in his election campaign. He wanted to delay the use of force until after its successful conclusion, and was probably disturbed by Eden's letter to him of 5 August. The Prime Minister did not think Nasser a Hitler, but the parallel with Mussolini was close. Thus Nasser's removal, and the installation of a regime less hostile to the West, was important. If the forthcoming conference ensured that Nasser disgorged his spoils, he would be unlikely to maintain his internal position. Eden concluded that London was determined that Nasser should not get away with it, because if he did the British people's existence would be at Nasser's mercy. On 10 August, in response to the argument of the Israeli ambassador at London, Elihu Elath, that the Israelis were in entire agreement with Britain, and had long pointed out the dangers of allowing Nasser, 'this mad dictator to grow in power', Eden noted that Israel should be allowed a trickle of useful arms – Britain might need Israel's help one day.[29]

Britain and France prepared for the possible use of force. At the meeting of the maritime nations in London between 16 and 23 August, Dulles, in line with Eisenhower's thinking, suggested an international Suez Canal Board, and it was agreed that Sir Robert Menzies, the Australian Prime Minister, would take the suggestion to Nasser. Macmillan wrote to Eden on 24 August about what might follow the use of force and the fall of Nasser. Macmillan envisaged putting to a conference the potential capacity of the Middle East provided that harmony and co-operation could be restored and a firm basis created for increased European and American investment. Britain should have a plan for territorial rearrangements: Jordan might disappear; Syria and perhaps Lebanon might be merged in

Iraq; a final solution of 'the Israel problem would be essential' and the refugees would have to be dealt with. He observed that 'we should try to appear not as reactionary powers returning to old days of "colonisation" but as a progressive force trying to bring about a permanent and constructive settlement': 'We must not be like Louis 18th returning in 1815 to a dull restoration, but rather like Napoleon breaking through the Alps towards the unification of Italy.' That same day Macmillan again told Dulles that Britain and France were determined that if diplomatic pressure did not work, they would have to use force.

On 27 August Eden wrote to Eisenhower about the Russian Bear using Nasser with the object of dislodging the West from the Middle East and getting a foothold in Africa. Soon the Soviet Union would have a wider field for subversion as the colonies achieved self-government. Nasser 'must not be allowed to get away with it this time'. The firmer the front Britain and the United States showed together, the greater the chance that Nasser would give way without the need for resort to force. If Nasser's reply were negative, Eden suggested to Dulles on 28 August, the matter should be referred to the Security Council. Macmillan also advised the Cabinet that if Nasser succeeded Britain's position in the Middle East would be undermined, its oil supplies placed in jeopardy, and the stability of its national economy gravely threatened.[30]

In Washington, on 5 September, a special National Intelligence Estimate on the probable repercussions of British and French military action against Egypt, pointed to the deep resentment over such action that would mean 'that fundamental nationalist and anti-Western feelings would be magnified for years to come'. Eisenhower wrote to Eden on 2 September reiterating that American public opinion flatly rejected the use of force: the President doubted he could get congressional support for the lesser support measures Britain might want. Peaceful measures had to be exhausted first.

On Duck Island Dulles devised another delaying tactic, which later became known as the Suez Canal Users' Association: the users should manage the canal themselves and prevent Nasser from making a profit. Lloyd received the plan just before leaving for Paris: he told Pineau that he was worried that Dulles intended to delay matters and so make a military operation impossible.

Kirkpatrick drafted Eden's response. That pointed to a difference in Eisenhower and Eden's assessment of Nasser's plans and intentions. Eden, in stating his view, referred to Hitler in the 1930s establishing his position by a series of carefully planned movements. Eden reflected the establishment historical opinion of the time with his analysis of Hitler's plan. Hitler, he said, began with the occupation of the Rhineland, and followed this with a succession of acts against Austria, Czechoslovakia, Poland and the West. His actions were tolerated and excused by the majority of the population of Western Europe. Eden argued that the Soviet Union had attempted similar tactics in recent years. He referred to the Berlin blockade. The Prime Minister then went on to argue that the seizure of the Suez Canal was the opening gambit 'in a planned campaign designed by Nasser to expel all Western influence and interest from

Arab countries'. The oil resources would be controlled by a united Arabia led by Egypt, and be under Soviet influence. Eden referred to Iraqi warnings about this. He did not feel that it would be right, even if that were the American sentiment, to wait until Nasser had unveiled his intentions: that had been the argument which had prevailed and which both Washington and London had rejected in 1948.

Eden's reply had Cabinet endorsement. Eisenhower stressed the need for delay in another letter to Eden on 8 September: American public opinion was not yet ready for the use of force; though there should be no capitulation to Nasser, slower and less dramatic measures should be explored. But the President implied that force might in the end be necessary if Nasser resorted to violence. Then it would be Nasser and 'not we' who were violating the United Nations charter. This policy tied in closely with Eisenhower's election campaign on the platform of peace.

Macmillan favoured the Users' Association, and London decided Dulles was acting in good faith. But the government's precarious position in the House was undermined when Dulles, during a debate on the 12–13 September, said that the United States did not intend to shoot its way through the canal. Britain took the affair to the United Nations, and revised the military plans with France to allow for more time.[31]

Between 20 September and 1 October Macmillan was in the United States. He saw Eisenhower on 24 September, and found the President very keen to win his election. Eisenhower was sure that Nasser had to go. The question was how to achieve this. Macmillan made it clear that Britain could not play it long without aid on a large scale. Macmillan also saw Dulles, and told the Secretary of State that he devoutly hoped there was no question of the President's re-election. Dulles hoped that Britain would do nothing drastic that would diminish the Republican chances. Macmillan recalled how helpful the Americans had been with Eden's general election in that they had arranged an appropriate summit conference to enable Eden to project an image of being a world statesman. Dulles said that he felt there was a basis for some reciprocity, and Macmillan replied 'he quite agreed'. When he returned, the Chancellor assured Eden that Eisenhower was determined to stand up to Nasser. Dulles had given no indication that he did not recognize Britain's right to use force. Macmillan acknowledged later that he should have attached greater weight to the date of the presidential election. The Chancellor arrived back in Britain to Dulles' statement that he did not know of any teeth in the Users' Association.

Under criticism from sections of his party for not taking more resolute action and from others who opposed force, threatened by the French that the weather would preclude military action after the end of October, and believing that Pineau did not want a settlement at all, and faced with an opposition determined to undermine national unity, Eden's health deteriorated. The Prime Minister collapsed on 5 October, and had to resort to Benzedrine. Before that, on 1 October, he had reiterated his 'appeasement' thesis to Eisenhower: there was no doubt that Nasser was effectively in Soviet hands, 'just as Mussolini was in Hitler's'. Eden drew the parallel of showing weakness to placate Nasser with that of showing weakness to Mussolini. The result would be the same in that the two would be brought together: Cairo would join Moscow just as Rome had joined Berlin.[32]

In New York, Lloyd was encouraged by the attitude of the Egyptian Minister for Foreign Affairs, Dr M. Fawzi, who went some way to agreeing on the principles governing the operation of the Suez Canal, but was vague on the important aspect of application. Lloyd warned the Security Council, on 12 October, against exaggerated optimism. That day Eisenhower undermined Britain's position with a statement about these developments: 'it looks like here is a very great crisis that is behind us'. Even Dulles appeared shocked, and murmured to Lloyd that the Foreign Secretary should not pay too much attention to what people said in the middle of an election campaign. That evening the Secretary of State suggested to Lloyd that the Users' Association should give 90 per cent of the dues to Nasser. Lloyd did not consider this a way of securing reasonable counter-proposals from Egypt.

On 13 October the Foreign Secretary warned Eden that Egypt might feel the critical phase was over: Eisenhower's naive statement had shown the danger of excessive optimism. On 14 October Albert Gazier and Maurice Challe, two French emissaries, met Eden and Anthony Nutting at Chequers. Eden agreed to ask Nuri to suspend Iraqi movements into Jordan. When reminded by Gazier that Egypt had claimed that it was not bound by the Tripartite Declaration, Eden concluded that Britain was under an obligation to stop Israel from attacking Egypt. After this, Challe outlined a plan for Britain and France to gain physical control of the Suez Canal. Israel should be invited to attack Egypt across Sinai. Once Israel had seized all, or most of the area, Britain and France would then order Egypt and Israel to withdraw from the canal and allow an Anglo-French force to occupy it to safeguard it from damage. Eden's response was non-committal.

On 16 October Eden and Lloyd saw Guy Mollet, the French Prime Minister, and Pineau in Paris. Lloyd's experiences with Pineau in New York had left him with the impression that it would be extremely difficult to reach an agreement with the French. The French gave no indications of the state of their planning with Israel. Eden explained that the Americans had made it clear to him during his visit to Washington earlier in the year that they would need congressional authorization before they could participate in any action under the Tripartite Declaration. If Israel were to act before the end of the American election campaign it was most unlikely that Congress would be re-summoned, and if it were that it would give the necessary authority.

On 18 October the British Cabinet assembled; before it met, Lloyd saw R.A. Butler and mentioned Anglo-French intervention to separate Israel and Egypt in the canal area. The Cabinet agreed that Britain and France should intervene to protect the canal if Israel attacked Egypt. Israel would be warned through the

French about British treaty obligations to Jordan. Because of Israeli objections Iraqi troops would not be moved to Jordan. An Israeli delegation, including Ben-Gurion, Moshe Dayan and Shimon Peres flew to Paris on 21 October, the day a government opposed to the West was elected in Jordan.

At Chequers a group of Cabinet ministers including Butler and Macmillan decided that it was important for Britain to be represented at the Franco-Israeli meeting scheduled the next day. Lloyd and one of his private secretaries, Donald Logan, were despatched incognito. At this meeting at Sèvres on 22 October Lloyd tried to make it clear that an agreement between Israel, France and Britain to attack Egypt was impossible: it could result in the slaughter of British subjects in Arab countries. There was some discussion as to whether it would be possible for Britain and France to intervene within 36 hours of the start of the Israeli campaign, but nothing was agreed.

On 23 October Lloyd saw his senior colleagues and then the Cabinet. Mention was made of the secret conversations held in Paris with representatives of the Israeli government. Lloyd was doubtful about the prospects of a negotiated settlement, and what was possible would not diminish Nasser's prestige. The Cabinet adjourned to enable Eden and Lloyd to see Pineau who was flying to London. Lloyd wrote to Pineau afterwards making it clear that Britain had not asked Israel to take action: London had only stated its reactions in the event of certain things happening. When the question of discussions with the Americans was raised it was agreed that they would not serve any useful purpose because of the pre-occupation with the American election campaign, and 'the generally unsatisfactory nature of our exchanges with Mr. Dulles about U.S. action of any character'. Lloyd had to answer questions in the House. He and Eden agreed that Patrick Dean, a deputy Under-Secretary at the Foreign Office, accompanied by Logan, should go instead to the further meeting with the French and Israelis at Sèvres.

At Sèvres, on 24 October, while discussions were in progress, a document was typed on plain paper in an adjoining room outlining the contingency plan and anticipated action in given circumstances. This outlined a 'large-scale' Israeli attack on Egyptian forces on 29 October with the aim of reaching the Canal Zone the following day; an Anglo-French ultimatum followed by an attack on Egypt early on 31 October; Israeli occupation of the west shore of the Gulf of Aqaba and the islands in the Straits of Tiran; provided Israel did not attack Jordan, Britain would not go to its ally's aid; all parties were enjoined to the strictest secrecy. Dean and Logan did not expect anything to go on paper. They discussed the matter and decided that Dean should sign the document merely as a record of the discussions.[33]

Dayan immediately ordered his chief of operations to mobilize Israeli units in secrecy, and to give the impression that this was aimed against Jordan. The contingency plan was referred to the full British Cabinet on 25 October. Lloyd supported Eden: unless prompt action were taken to check Nasser's ambitions Britain's position would be undermined throughout the Middle East. The

Cabinet considered whether such action would offend the United States. Disapproving noises were anticipated, but it was thought that, in view of American behaviour, Washington would have no reason to complain. The Cabinet decided without dissent to accept the plan. Eden wrote to Mollet affirming that in the situation envisaged in the talks at Sèvres between 22 and 24 October, Britain would take the planned action. Mollet saw fit to send Ben-Gurion a copy of this. Paris concealed from London the extent of prior Franco-Israeli planning. In effect the contingency plan typed at Sèvres on 24 October was in origin French, and modified by Dayan to overcome objections made by Ben-Gurion. The British Cabinet miscalculated on the importance of the timing of the presidential election. Macmillan failed to emphasize Dulles' warnings on this.

Dayan's forces, on 29 October, mounted an attack 30 miles (50 km) from the Suez Canal. Israel maintained its independent action: it merely used the dispute over the Suez Canal to secure the Straits of Tiran. The United States requested a meeting of the Security Council. When Cabot Lodge, the American representative at the United Nations, informed his British counterpart, Pierson Dixon, of this Dixon virtually snarled that the Americans were being silly and moralistic. The British would not go along with any move against Israel.

On 28 October Eisenhower spoke to Dulles on the telephone and the president was given information about the Anglo-French build-up of forces around Cyprus. Eisenhower could not believe that Britain would be dragged into this. Dulles explained that he had spoken to both the British ambassador and the French chargé and that they both professed to know nothing about the build-up. Dulles considered their ignorance as being a sign of a guilty conscience.

Eisenhower, on 29 October, told John Coulson, in charge of the British embassy in Washington between ambassadors, that he wanted to work in harmony with Britain. The President seemed worried that Britain could be misled by the French into not taking a firm stand against the evident Israeli aggression. On 30 October Eisenhower wrote to Eden, not only as head of the British government, but as his long-time friend who, together with him, had believed in and worked for real Anglo-American understanding, about this interview with Dixon. Eisenhower wanted to know what was happening, particularly between Paris and London. Washington had discovered that the French had provided Israel with a considerable amount of equipment, including aeroplanes, in excess of the amounts of which the Americans had been informed. This constituted a violation of the Tripartite Agreement. Washington consequently watched the affairs of the Eastern Mediterranean and had concluded that the Israelis were contemplating something more than defence. Indeed, though Eisenhower did not give the details, American intelligence had, by 28 October, concluded that a favourable opportunity had been provided 'for a major attack'. There were also indications of Anglo-French involvement in any possible Israeli attack on Egypt. Intelligence had reached the conclusion on 29 October that 'the British and French are prepared to and probably will intervene with force in the Middle East as opportunity occurs in connection with the Israeli-Egyptian action'. The President complained that these actions had left a very sad state of confusion over any possibility of unified understanding and action. Egypt could ask the Soviet Union for help. This consideration had led Washington to conclude that the West had to ask for a United Nations examination and possible intervention. Eisenhower warned that London and Washington could shortly find themselves 'not only at odds concerning what we should do, but confronted with a *de facto* situation that would make all our present troubles look puny indeed'.

On 30 October, Lloyd suggested an appeal to Washington to support the action the French and British were proposing to bring an end to hostilities between Egypt and Israel. There was general agreement. It was thought it was unlikely that Washington would respond to such an appeal, but the utmost should be done to reduce the offence to American public opinion which was liable to be brought about by the notes to Egypt and Israel. Britain's reserves of gold and dollars were falling at a dangerously rapid rate. In view of the extent to which Britain might have to rely on American economic assistance, London could not afford to alienate Washington more than was absolutely necessary.

Israel's campaign plans, withheld from London and Paris, made a nonsense of the Anglo-French ultimatum when it was issued: Israel could hardly withdraw 10 miles (16 km) from the canal when it was still 30 miles (50 km) away. By 3 November, when the United Nations was demanding a cease-fire, Israel had occupied nearly all of Sinai except Sharm el-Shiekh. Israel's lack of interest in the Anglo-French operation could be attributed to the British delay in bombing the Egyptian airfields owing to the American evacuation in progress.[34]

The Israeli invasion of Egypt foiled a coup in Syria, apparently planned by the Central Intelligence Agency. It would seem that Britain had also been involved in plans to change a regime which both London and Washington had viewed increasingly as a Soviet puppet.[35]

Dulles was angry over the Anglo-French ultimatum. On 18 October he had complained to his brother, Allen, that he did not have any clear picture of what the British and French were up to. The Americans were deliberately being kept in the dark. Allen told him that he knew what was going on in Syria, and knew what was happening in Egypt fairly well. The afternoon of the Anglo-French ultimatum the Secretary of State met State Department officials and his brother, the head of the Central Intelligence Agency, and Kim Roosevelt. Dulles was angry over the Anglo-French ultimatum. At a time when the Soviet Union was taking repressive action against Hungary he denounced Britain and France in the United Nations. The uniting for peace resolution was used to overcome the veto. Dulles, however, did know from General Alfred M. Gruenther, the Supreme Allied Commander, Europe, that Lloyd had given the impression on 25 October that he was unhappy about Dulles' attitude over Suez, and felt that Dulles had changed his mind in a major way over the American position, and this change was to the disadvantage of the three major powers involved. Dulles then, on 3 November, entered hospital for what was thought to be kidney stones, was operated on for appendicitis, and was diagnosed as suffering from a perforated intestine.

On 2 November Lloyd warned the Cabinet about the strength of feeling the Anglo-French action in Egypt had aroused in the United States. The Foreign Secretary advised that if no concession to these feelings were made, it was possible that oil sanctions would be imposed against Britain. Britain could then be compelled to occupy Kuwait and Qatar, the only suppliers of oil which were not members of the United Nations. Britain would alienate, perhaps irretrievably, all the Arab states. Syria had already broken relations with Britain. It was possible that Iraq, Jordan and Libya would follow Syria's example. That could mean the fall of Nuri and the overthrow of the King. Britain 'could not hope to avoid serious difficulties with the Arab States for more than a very short time longer, certainly not for as long as it would take us to complete an opposed occupation of Egypt'. Dulles was effectively out of the way for the rest of the immediate crisis. In the middle of November he protested from his hospital bed to Eisenhower and Lloyd about Britain not going though with the venture and dispensing with Nasser. The Secretary of State later attributed his stand in the United Nations to his illness. After all, throughout the Suez crisis, Britain and the United States had the same objective: to dispose of Nasser. The only difference was in the timing.[36]

But that timing was crucial for Eisenhower. Few doubted that he would be re-elected, but Eisenhower felt that the least Eden owed him for arranging the summit conference in 1955 to help his general election was to hold off the Suez operation until after the presidential election. Shortly after the Anglo-French invasion Eisenhower confessed to Air Chief Marshal William Elliott that he had known how Britain intended to strike at Nasser, but had thought it would be after the elections. London adhered to Dulles' wishes that no official information be passed about the military operation; both Eisenhower and Dulles were worried that Adlai Stevenson could use that against them in the election campaign if he found out. But Washington knew through unofficial contacts. By 2 November, Eisenhower was aware of the Sèvres discussions; Dulles knew of the impending Israeli attack by 28 October.[37]

Before the election results came through in which the Republicans, Eisenhower's party, lost both Houses of Congress – though Eisenhower himself was returned as president – Eisenhower seemed open to Eden's reasoning. The President's Secretary, Mrs Ann Whitman, recorded that on 30 October at the time of the Israeli invasion of Sinai, Eisenhower, while drafting a message to Eden, was in 'remarkably good humor', and that the President that day spent all his free moments reading his own book on the Second World War, *Crusade in Europe*. Eisenhower, however, did write to Alfred M. Gruenther on 2 November about Eden's reaction in the Victorian manner, and the pointlessness of entering into a fight to which there could be no satisfactory outcome, and one in which the rest of the world viewed Britain as the bully, and even the British population as a whole was not able to back. The following day Eisenhower confided to his friend, Lew W. Douglas, that he thought the British had been stupid, and the leaders had allowed their hatred of Nasser to warp their judgement and were trying to deflate the Egyptian leader in the wrong way. The president wrote how it was clear that France and Israel had concocted the crisis, but the evidence of Britain's involvement in the hoax was less persuasive. Although Eisenhower felt Britain must have known something of what had been going on, the president was not prepared to use the British government as a whipping boy. On 5 November, the Prime Minister explained to the President that he had always felt the Middle East was an issue on which, in the last resort, Britain would have to fight. He appreciated that Dulles thought Britain should have played it longer. But Eden remained convinced that if the affair had been allowed to drift, everything would have gone from bad to worse: 'Nasser would have become a kind of Moslem Mussolini and our friends in Iraq, Jordan, Saudi Arabia and even Iran would gradually have been brought down.' Nasser's efforts would have then spread westwards and Libya and all North Africa would have been brought under his control. The French and British 'police action' had to be carried through: this was 'our opportunity to secure an effective and final settlement of the problems of the Middle East'. If Britain and France withdrew, the Middle East would go up in flames. They had to hold their positions until responsibility could be handed over to the United Nations: 'we shall have taken the first step towards re-establishing authority in this area for our generation'. Eden assured Eisenhower that he believed as firmly as ever 'that the future of all of us depends on the closest Anglo-American co-operation'. The temporary breach in this had been a sorrow for Eden. But Britain had acted with a genuine sense of responsibility not only to itself but to all the world.

On 6 November London accepted a cease-fire. Eisenhower told Eden over the telephone that he did not care a damn how the election went. Eden wrote to Eisenhower the following day about the lack of understanding between Britain and the United States on the Middle East since the end of the Second World War. London and Washington needed to work towards common objectives there. Should the Soviet Union seize the opportunity of intervening by giving substantial support to Nasser, there could be major war. Eden had been going to Washington to see Eisenhower. The Republican losses in Congress changed that. Eisenhower would have to consult with the new Congressional leaders.[38]

Before the cease-fire, Eisenhower concerted action with the anti-British Humphrey and Hoover. Intelligence information was not passed to Britain, with the exception of the American assessment that the Soviet nuclear threat was a bluff. Eisenhower and Humphrey co-ordinated economic sanctions against Britain: the American Federal Reserve sold quantities of sterling; they held up emergency oil supplies to Europe; and in Macmillan's view almost illegally blocked Britain's drawing rights on the International Monetary Fund. No documentation on this has been found in the Department of State files. It has been argued that Macmillan's allegations of heavy selling of sterling in New York are unfounded, and that the figures he gave to the Cabinet about the drop in the reserves were also untrue. There is evidence, however, that Eisenhower did block Britain's drawing rights on the International Monetary Fund. That act forced Britain to stop a successful military operation before it had secured both ends of the canal. The parity of sterling was considered important.[39]

In the Foreign Office, on 7 November, R.M. Hadow considered the prevailing factors in the Middle East on which Britain would have to construct its future policy. Britain needed the oil, and if it could not maintain physical possession of oil producing and oil transit states, it had to retain the friendship of those states. It needed the friendship of certain Arab states more than that of Israel. Israel was hated by all Arabs. The French had lost all influence in the Middle East, and after the Israelis were the most unpopular foreigners. Anglo-American co-operation in the Middle East was vital. It was the championship of the Arab cause against Israel which was the main attraction of the Soviets for the Arabs. There was an underlying struggle between Iraq and Egypt for leadership of the Arab world. Stacked against Britain was the damage to its position created by the appearance of acting in Israeli interests and in co-operation with the French. Furthermore, Britain had not destroyed Nasser's prestige, and had weakened the position of pro-Western elements like Nuri and President Camille Chamoun in Lebanon. The structure of the Baghdad Pact had been weakened, and the future of Britain's oil supplies made more uncertain. In favour was the realization that the Baghdad Pact had not yet dissolved. The Americans had acquired considerable goodwill in the Middle East, and the Soviet intrusion would not be welcomed by the ruling classes in the Arab world. The military weakening of Egypt also left Iraq in a position of strength in relation to the other Arab states. Many of these points were embodied in the paper by S. Falle on future Middle East policy.

Hadow went on to suggest that although British prestige and influence in the Middle East might have received a crippling blow, Britain might still be able to safeguard its main interest, oil production and the pipelines, by working through the Baghdad Pact. But the Americans would have to play a major role. Iraq would need to be built up as a rock to which the Arab states, apart from Egypt, would have to cling because of their fear of Israel. Britain should use the threat of the spread of Communism to make the Americans play a leading role in the Baghdad Pact. Also there should be a federation, if not union, of Syria and Jordan with Iraq. Falle's paper hoped that oil production arrangements in Iraq, Iran, Kuwait and Qatar could be developed from the existing basis without an immediate revolutionary change. It did point out that Iraqi and Kuwaiti claims for ownership of their own oil industries were likely to increase in strength. The arrangement in Iran could be a guide to the future. Britain would not be a welcome guest in the Arab world for some time to come. Indeed whether Britain had an entry at all would depend on what could be done in the following few days to hold the situation in Iraq and Iran.[40]

On 7 November, the Cabinet discussed the recommendation of a United

Nations force in the Middle East excluding contingents from the Great Powers. Discussion in the Cabinet pointed to the need to resume close relations with Washington and to get it to acknowledge the existence in the Middle East of 'the dangerous situation' which the Americans had 'consistently refused to recognize since the end of the war'. The Cabinet wanted Eden to persuade Washington that a decision on the functions and composition of the international force in the Suez Canal area should be deferred until Washington and London had reached a clearer understanding on their common objectives in the Middle East.

Eisenhower, talking to Dulles in hospital that same day, took a similar stance: there was no point in indulging in recriminations with the British; rather the Americans should consider jointly with the British what should be done in the face of the Soviet threat. Washington had no military study of its own based on what it could do if the Soviets entered the Middle East. It also had no co-ordinated intelligence estimate with the British. But Dulles insisted that it was important to get the British and French out of Egypt as soon as possible.

The Cabinet, on 8 November, agreed to staff conversations with the Commander-designate of the international force over the transfer of responsibility from the Anglo-French contingent. It was hoped that Washington would support this proposal in the United Nations and that this would mark the beginnings of a common Anglo-American policy in the United Nations and the Middle East.

Sir William Dickson, Chairman of the Chiefs of Staff committee, reiterated these arguments in his discussion with General Alfred M. Gruenther, his American equivalent, at SHAPE headquarters in Paris on 9 November: there was the danger that Britain's friends in Iraq would topple, the Soviet Union would gain a firm grip of the Middle East and the oil, together with potential bases which would menace the NATO position. Everything depended on Washington being willing and able to act quickly. On 13 November, a meeting in Beirut of all nine independent Arab states demanded the withdrawal of the invading troops from Egypt. Nuri proposed Britain's expulsion from the Baghdad Pact. Pakistan seconded the motion. Turkish mediation moderated this to a vote of censure. At a dinner in New York on 13 November, Lloyd complained to Lodge that Washington had led the hunt against Britain and France: Britain had needed to act or it would have been shut out of the Middle East.[41]

Washington remained cool to the British blandishments. Dulles sustained his reservations about the United States joining the Baghdad Pact. He thought that under the pact Britain was using Iraq to advance its interests in the Middle East. An American commitment to the Northern Tier concept would be better served by Iran joining the South East Asia Treaty Organisation (SEATO). The American military hierarchy was cool, reluctant to discuss political issues in the Middle East with the British, and appeared ignorant of the previous extensive Anglo-American discussions on the area. They were also mystified by the British solidarity with the French, 'about whose failings' Britain had seen eye to eye with the Americans.

R.G. Casey, the Australian Foreign Minister, reported on the 'almost physical cleavage' at the United Nations between London and Washington. Hoover told Casey that this cleavage went a great deal deeper than was thought, and had started a long time ago before Suez with the Buraimi incident.

Acting on Lloyd's instructions Dixon saw Lodge in the United Nations on 21 November. Dixon complained that the Americans were making no attempt to consult the British; there would be indignation in Britain if this were known. In reply Lodge referred to the long-standing difference of opinion between Washington and London about the effect of force on the Arab world: London seemed to believe that force impressed the Arabs; Washington thought that the use of force merely united the Arabs against the West. Dixon warned of the danger of the hardening of the British attitude: Britain could not accept a position in which it would be publicly humiliated, 'or suffer a loss of prestige which would bring about, as surely as anything could, the collapse of our supporters in the Middle East, which in turn would open the flood-gates to Soviet penetration'.

The new British ambassador at Washington, Harold Caccia, asked Hoover that same day whether Washington wanted London to take independent decisions in concert with Washington. Hoover explained to Caccia that the Americans had thought that Britain wanted to avoid frank discussion, particularly on Middle Eastern affairs. Britain had taken action which affected American interests without any prior warning as at Buraimi, over Jordan and then Suez. Washington had experienced a blackout from London since the middle of October. In retaliation, Caccia blamed the crisis on the Americans cancelling the Aswan Dam loan without consulting Britain. The ambassador reported that the American administration had worked themselves 'into a state where moral indignation and legalism' were dominating their powers of reasoning. Lloyd offered a similar diagnosis: the Americans were impervious to the consequences of failing to grasp the opportunity Britain had created in the Middle East, or the risks of allowing a Soviet success. The Americans were 'temporarily beyond the bounds of reason'. Caccia agreed: Britain was beyond the point of talking to friends; it was now negotiating a business deal. The administration's estimate of the value of British judgement in the Middle East had been shaken.[42]

Eisenhower's thoughts on the Middle East did not coincide with those of London. He told a conference of State Department, Central Intelligence Agency, and military officials on 21 November that he thought Washington should work towards building up King Saud as a major figure in the Middle East, and the British should be induced to get out of Buraimi. Eisenhower wanted to use Buraimi 'as an ace in the hole' to restore the oil markets in Europe. Once the withdrawal from Suez was underway, Washington should aid Western Europe financially. Eisenhower thought that if Britain persuaded the United States to join the Baghdad Pact, and that would be how it would appear to the Arabs, the United States would lose its influence with the Arabs, and the British would be able to take an intransigent stand. If, however, the British abandoned Buraimi, the Americans and Saudis could then declare their support for the Baghdad Pact. Humphrey thought that there should be no talks with the British leaders until the Americans had spoken to Saud. The next day Allen Dulles reported that Britain's position in Iraq was precarious. Some Iraqis might look more to Washington for leadership, but should Nuri's government fall anti-Western elements could come to the fore. Churchill also wrote to Eisenhower about the vacuum in the Middle East and the danger that the Soviet Union would 'ride the storm'.

There was a disagreement between Eisenhower and Hoover on 25 November over the approach to Britain. Hoover thought it might be necessary to inform Britain that it seemed it was finished in the Middle East, and ask if London wanted Washington to take over its commitments. Eisenhower, however, still believed in an Anglo-American partnership and thought Britain should be given every chance to work itself back into a position of influence and respect in the Middle East.[43]

The British also wanted to re-establish satisfactory political relations. London was encouraged when Washington announced that it would view with the utmost gravity any threat to the territorial integrity of political independence of the Middle Eastern members of the Baghdad Pact. Washington would maintain oil supplies to Europe. These were viewed as indications of a gradual move by official opinion in Washington towards re-establishing friendly relations with London.[44]

The American administration considered a proposal for a new Middle East grouping which would merge the Baghdad Pact into a larger body. Britain also began to review Middle East policy. It was suggested to the Cabinet on 7 December 1956 that the military value of agreements such as the Anglo-Jordanian Treaty had been shown to be less than Britain had hoped, and could be expected to decline still further in the future. Britain's whole Middle East policy needed to be re-examined urgently. It might emerge from such a review that it would be preferable to rely on financial subventions to the Arab countries rather than on the maintenance of bases in their territories.[45]

Towards the end of 1956 relations between Washington and London were such that the two administrations hardly seemed to be speaking to one another. It seemed to the Americans that yet again, as had happened over the use of force to drive the Saudis out of the Buraimi oasis, and the despatch of the Templar mission to Jordan, London had acted without informing Washington, this time about the invasion of the Suez Canal. London viewed the American policy as prevaricating, dictated by oil interests over Saudi Arabia and showing scant regard for British interests in the Gulf on which the British economy was to a certain extent dependent, and, as had happened during the period at the end of the British mandate in Palestine, dictated by American domestic elections.

It was particularly over the timing of the operation in relation to Eisenhower's presidential and the congressional elections where the British miscalculated. And here it was not so much Eden who was responsible but Harold Macmillan.

Macmillan had visited the United States, and heard that Eisenhower expected the same consideration from Eden in relation to his election as Eden had received from the President over his general election in 1955. It has been argued too that Macmillan misled the Cabinet over the state of sterling, and it was that advice which forced the British withdrawal from the Suez Canal.

Perhaps Macmillan saw his chance to become Prime Minister. He had resented Eden as the younger man and the heir apparent to Churchill, and when Eden had become Prime Minister probably saw his ambition for the premiership thwarted. The relationship between Eden and Macmillan was not easy. Macmillan resented Eden's interference when he was Foreign Secretary, but only agreed to move to the Exchequer on the understanding that he remained as the number two in government, that position traditionally having been reserved for the Foreign Secretary. It was Macmillan who was chosen by Queen Elizabeth II as her Prime Minister. His relationship with Eisenhower during the Second World War and his American connections – his mother was American – were a consideration. Macmillan was seen as the man best able to restore the relationship with the United States.

By early December, British and American officials both saw the need to re-establish the close relationship between London and Washington. During the years of the first Eisenhower presidency that relationship had not been 'special': Eisenhower from the outset had insisted that Britain was only one among a number of allies. His close advisers Hoover and Humphrey disliked the British, and often viewed them as colonialists who wanted the Americans to pay for the safeguarding of British interests in the Middle East while still leaving the British in command.

Eden, as Prime Minister, exerted a distinctly British policy in the Middle East. Churchill had wanted to involve the Americans in the area and to get Washington to assume more of the responsibility of defending the area in the interests of the West. Eden felt that with the British dependence on Middle East oil, and the experience it had of the area, meant London had to be prepared to mount a policy in the Middle East, if necessary, without the full agreement and support of Washington. Both Washington and London concluded that Moscow had opened up another front in the Cold War by agreeing to supply the Egyptians with arms. Where they differed was in their diagnosis of how to deal with the Arabs over this. Britain felt that its Arab allies might react favourably to firmness. Washington thought shows of force would drive the Arabs to Moscow.

Britain, as a means of securing a favourable renegotiation of the Anglo-Iraqi Treaty of 1930 initiated the Northern Tier concept that had initially been an American brain-child as early as 1950. The Americans, and particularly Dulles, had seen the Northern Tier primarily as a means of defence against the Soviet Union. Dulles felt that the British version, the Turco-Iraqi Pact which became known as the Baghdad Pact, was mainly about inter-Arab politics, and had little to do with defence against the Soviet Union. After the Suez crisis, however, there was increasingly a common Anglo-American diagnosis of the danger of the

Soviet Union moving into the vacuum in the Middle East, a vacuum that had been referred to for some time as Britain increasingly withdrew from the area.

During Eden's premiership the main objective of British policy in the Middle East was to ensure the flow of oil in Iraq and the Gulf. This brought London into head-on clashes with Washington. Washington, and Eisenhower as president, could not grasp the importance of the Gulf for Britain. Eisenhower chose King Saud as his man in the Middle East. He confessed that he knew little about Saud. But ARAMCO and American oil interests dictated that Saud should be humoured. Eisenhower could not understand why Britain was not prepared to allow Saud to take over Buraimi, and effectively Muscat and Oman as well. To Eisenhower this seemed a small sacrifice to pacify Saud. Of course it was a sacrifice that Britain would have to make. But Britain refused to co-operate. Eisenhower was aided in his assessment of British motives by Hoover. Britain chose Nuri. Iraq saw Egypt as its rival for the leadership of the Arab world. Britain saw Nasser challenging its position not only in the Middle East, but in Africa and in the Muslim world. Nasser had to go. With this the Americans agreed. The Anglo-American difference hinged on the timing of this.

Notes

1. Public Record Office, London, CAB 128/30 pt. 2, fos 525–8, CM62(56)2, Confidential Annex, 28 August 1956; Ritchie Ovendale, *The Origins of the Arab–Israeli Wars*, (2nd edn, London, 1992), pp. 182–3; John Colville, *The Fringes of Power; Downing Street Diaries, 1939–53* (London, 1985), pp. 753–4.
2. Ovendale, *The Origins of the Arab–Israeli Wars*, pp. 182–3; Jonathan Aitken, *Nixon: A Life* (London, 1993), p. 244; Henry Kissinger, 'Suez weakened Europe', *The Listener* (20 May 1982), pp. 9–11.
3. CAB 128/29, fos 364–5, CM34(55)8, Secret, 4 October 1955; Public Record Office, London, FO 371/121233, V1054/13, Minute by Chapman Andrews, 30 December 1955; FO 371/121234, V1054/41, Commonwealth Relations Office to High Commissioners, Telegram no. 15, 23 January 1956; FO 115/4548, 1041/1/56, A.M.W. Platt for Pierson Dixon to Shuckburgh, Secret, 6 January 1956; FO 371/121270, V1075/11, Anglo-American co-operation in the Middle East, Secret, 7 January 1956; V1041/6, Anglo-American co-operation in the Middle East, Secret, undated.
4. Foreign Relations of the United States (hereafter cited as '*FRUS*') 1955–7(13), pp. 309–10, Memorandum from Allen to Dulles, 4 January 1956; p. 19, Editorial note of NSC meeting, 12 January 1956, Whitman File, NSC Records, Eisenhower Library.
5. FO 371/121271, V1075/40, Minute by G.G. Arthur, 7 January 1956; V1075/39, Memorandum by G.G. Arthur on British and American interests and objectives in the Middle East in the light of current Soviet Strategy, Top Secret, 7 January 1956; Annex A, Some notes by Geoffrey G. Arthur on Middle Eastern policy in the light of the Soviet threat, Top Secret, 7 January 1956; FO 371/120525, E1021/2, Minute by Ian Samuel, American views on Buraimi and Oman, Secret, 10 January 1956.

6. *FRUS* 1955–7(12), pp. 216–28, Memorandum of conversation, Department of State, Washington, 13 January 1956 (section on Saudi Arabia deleted); pp. 228–34, Memorandum of conversation, Department of State, Washington, 13 January 1956; FO 371/121270, V1075/16, Makins to Foreign Office, Telegram no. 33, Secret, 14 January 1956 d 16 January 1956.
7. *FRUS* 1955–7(13), pp. 313–4, Eden to Eisenhower, 16 January 1956; pp. 314–7, Allen to Hoover, 17 January 1956; *FRUS* 1955–7(12), pp. 234–9, Memorandum of conversation, Department of State, Washington, 18 January 1956; FO 371/121270, V1075/5/G, Memorandum by Shuckburgh on the interests of Britain and the United States in the Middle East, Top Secret, 19 January 1956; *FRUS* 1955–7(13), pp. 317–21, Memorandum of Conversation, Department of State, Washington, 19 January 1956; pp. 321–2, Editorial note, Memorandum of conversation by Dulles, 19 January 1956, Dulles Papers, Eisenhower Library; Evelyn Shuckburgh, *Descent to Suez: Diaries 1951–56* (London, 1986), p. 323, Diary, 20 January 1956; *FRUS* 1955–7(13), pp. 322–4, Lloyd to Dulles, 23 January 1956.
8. FO 371/121270, V1075/22, G.G. Arthur to E.M. Rose, Secret, 20 January 1956; V1075/21, Minute by Lord John Hope, 18 January 1955; V1075/18, Memorandum by R.M. Hadow on changes in United States attitude to the Baghdad Pact, Secret, 24 January 1956.
9. FO 371/121270, V1075/3, Minutes by W.D. Allen, 21 January 1956; H.A.F. Hohler, 23 January 1956; Anthony Nutting, 25 January 1956.
10. *FRUS* 1955–7(13), p. 324, Editorial note; FO 371/121270, V1075/2/G, Shuckburgh to Lloyd, 27 January 1956; M. Wright to Foreign Office, Telegram no. 82, Secret, 18 January 1956.
11. Eisenhower Library, Abilene, Ann Whitman File, DDE Diary Series, Box no. 9, File Diary copies of DDE personal (1955–6) (2), Diary, 8 February 1956; *FRUS* 1955–7(12), pp. 240–2, Memorandum of conversation, White House, 30 January 1956; *FRUS* 1955–7(13), pp. 567–8, Memorandum of conversation, White House, 30 January 1956; pp. 20–1, Memorandum of conversation, White House, 30 January 1956; pp. 329–34, Memorandum of Conversation, White House, 30 January 1956; pp. 334–7, Memorandum of conversation, White House, 31 January 1956; Shuckburgh, *Diaries*, Diary, 30 January 1956; Public Record Office, London, PREM 11/1334, fol. 40, Record of Meeting at White House on 31 January 1956; FO 371/121270, V1075/31, Minute by Nutting, 1 February 1956; Eisenhower Library, Abilene, Ann Whitman File, International Series, Box no. 22, File Eden visit 30 January–1 February 1956 (3), Middle Eastern Matters, Secret, Undated.
12. *FRUS* 1955–7(13), pp. 338–9, Memorandum of conversation, Department of State, Washington, 2 February 1956; pp. 340–1, Memorandum of conversation, Department of State, 3 February 1956; CAB 128/30, fos 112–4, CM10(56)1, Secret, 9 February 1956.
13. CAB 128/30, fol. 54, CM33(56)3, Secret, 11 January 1956; FO 800/731, PM/56/42, Lloyd to Eden, Top Secret, February 1956; CAB 128/30, fos. 164–5, CM17(56)3, Secret, 28 February 1956; FO 371/121271, V1075/55, Makins to Foreign Office, Telegram no. 582, Secret, 3 March 1956 d r 4 March 1956.
14. Ovendale, *The Origins of the Arab–Israeli Wars*, p. 160; CAB 128/30, fos 173–5, CM18(56)2, Secret, 5 March 1956; fos. 197–8, CM21(56)2, Secret, 9 March 1956; Shuckburgh, *Diaries*, p. 341, Diary 3 March 1956, pp. 342–3, Diary 4

March 1956; *FRUS* 1955–7(12), p. 249, Eden to Eisenhower, 4 March 1956; FO 371/121271, V1075/57, Foreign Office to Karachi, Secret, 5 March 1956.

15. FO 371/121271, V1075/59, High Commissioner in Pakistan to Commonwealth Relations Office, Telegram no. 17, Secret, 6 March 1956; Foreign Office to Karachi, Telegram no. 595, Secret, 6 March 1956; V1075/61, High Commissioner in Pakistan to Commonwealth Relations Office, Telegram no. 29, Top Secret, 7 March 1956: *FRUS*, 1955–7(12), pp. 992–3, Telegram from Department of State to embassy in Britain, 6 March 1956.

16. CAB 128/30, fol. 178, CM19(56)1, Secret, 6 March 1956; FO 371/121271, V1075/64, Wright to Foreign Office, Telegram no. 292, Secret, 9 March 1956; Shuckburgh, *Diaries*, Diary 8 March 1956; FO 371/121235, V1054/70/G, Shuckburgh to Kirkpatrick, 10 March 1956; CAB 128/30, fos 225–7, CM24(56)5, Secret, 15 March 1956; FO 371/118869, JE 1071/3/G, Kirkpatrick to Makins, Top Secret, 19 March 1956.

17. CAB 128/30, fol. 216, CM23(56)1, Secret, 15 March 1956; fos 266–7, CM29(56)4, Secret, 17 April 1956; PREM 11/1457, fos 2–5, Norman Brook to Eden, 14 April 1956; F.A. B. to Brook, 15 April 1956; CAB 128/30, fol. 212, CM22(56)13, Secret, 13 March 1956; FO 371/120571, EA1055/1/G, Minute by Shuckburgh, Secret, 14 March 1956; see Glen Balfour-Paul, *The End of Empire in the Middle East. Britain's Relinquishment of Power in her last three Arab dependencies* (Cambridge, 1991), pp. 49–95.

18. *FRUS* 1955–7(12), pp. 258–9, Memorandum of conference with Eisenhower, White House, 15 March 1956, Whitman File, Eisenhower Library; p. 264, Editorial note; pp. 264–5, Editorial note; Eisenhower Library, Abilene, Ann Whitman File, Ann Whitman Diary Series, Box no. 8, File April 1956 Diary ACW (2), Diary, 10 April 1956; File June 1958 Diary ACW (2), Diary 15 June 1958; Lucas, *Divided We Stand*, pp. 110–13; Robert H. Ferrell (ed.), *The Eisenhower Diaries* (New York, 1981), pp. 323–4, Diary 28 March 1956; *FRUS* 1955–7(13), pp. 351–2, Editorial note.

19. FO 371/121273, V1075/111/G, Report by Dickson on visit to Washington 3–5 April 1956, 10 April 1956; FO 371/121272, V1075/89/G, Minute by P. Dean on account given by Dickson to Lloyd of his visit to America, Secret, 6 April 1956.

20. *FRUS* 1955–7(12), pp. 275–6, Memorandum of conversation, Department of State, 9 April 1956.

21. CAB 128/30, fos 255–6, CM27(56)1, Secret, 10 April 1956; Shuckburgh, *Diaries*, p. 352, Diary 10 April 1956; FO 371/121273, V1075/108/G, Extract from COS(56)42, Top Secret, 17 April 1956; FO 371/121272, V1075/100/G, Annex to COS(56)150, Top Secret, 17 April 1956.

22. Ovendale, *The Origins of the Arab–Israeli Wars*, pp. 160–1.

23. FO 371/121273, V1075/117/G, Memorandum on discussions with Dulles on 3 May 1956, Secret; *FRUS* 1955–7(13), pp. 365–6, Editorial note; Shuckburgh, *Diaries*, Diary 4 May 1956; *FRUS* 1955–7(12), pp. 366–8, Memorandum of conversation, Paris, 4 May 1956; *FRUS* 1955–7(13), pp. 377–8, Lloyd to Dulles, 23 June 1956; pp. 388–9, Dulles to Lloyd, 10 July 1956; CAB 128/30 pt. 2, fol. 465, CM53(56)6, 26 July 1956; *FRUS* 1955–7(13), pp. 392–3, Lloyd to Dulles, undated; p. 397, note 3; *FRUS* 1955–7(12), pp. 298–9, Instruction from Department of State to certain diplomatic missions, 18 May 1956.

24. CAB 128/30, fol. 395, CM45(56)8, Secret, 21 June 1956; CAB 128/30 pt. 2, fol. 405, CM47(56)7, Secret, 28 June 1956.

25. Ritchie Ovendale (ed.), *British Defence Policy since 1945: Documents in Contemporary History* (Manchester, 1994), pp. 110–11.
26. FO 371/120812, UEE10062/4/G, Norman Brook to Dodds-Parker, 27 June 1956; Annex, Extract from 'The Future of the United Kingdom in World Affairs', Top Secret.
27. FO 371/120812, UEE10062/9/G, A.D. Dodds-Parker to Lloyd, Secret, 19 July 1956; Annex, Report by the Committee on Middle East Policy, Secret.
28. FO 371/120812, UEE/10062/1/G, ZP9/14/G, A.R. Walmsley to P. Dean, Top Secret, 19 July 1956; Draft brief by S. Falle on harmonisation of Anglo-American policy in the Middle East, Secret, 24 July 1956; CAB 128/30 pt. 2, fol. 454, CM52(56)2, Secret, 24 July 1956.
29. Eisenhower Library, Abilene, Ann Whitman File, Dulles-Herter Series, Box no. 7, File John Foster Dulles July 1956, Dulles to Eisenhower, 16 July 1956; Ann Whitman Diary Series, Box no. 8, File September 1956 Diary ACW, Diary 17 September 1956; Ovendale, *The Origins of the Arab–Israeli Wars*, pp. 161–72; CAB 134/1217, EC(56)12, Top Secret, 8 August 1956; CAB 128/30 pt. 2, fos 469–72, CM54(56), Confidential Annex, 27 July 1956; fos 481–3, CM56(56), Confidential Annex, 1 August 1956; fos 525–8, CM62(56)2, Confidential Annex, 2 August 1956; Leonard Mosley, *Dulles: A Biography of Eleanor, Allen, and John Foster Dulles and Their Family Network* (London, 1978), pp. 409–11; PREM 11/1176, EC(56)22nd Meeting, Secret, 27 August 1956; Foreign Office to Washington, Secret, 1 September 1956; FO 800/726, Foreign Office to Washington, Telegram no. 3568, Secret, 5 August 1956; PREM 11/3431, JE14211/368G, Lloyd to Westlake, no. 133, Secret, 8 August 1956; Eden to Lloyd, 10 August 1956.
30. FO 371/121237, V1054/125/G, Macmillan to Eden, Top Secret, 24 August 1956; FO 800/726, Foreign Office to Washington, Telegram no. 3913, Top Secret, 27 August 1956; Foreign Office to Washington, Telegram no. 3931, Top Secret, 28 August 1956; CAB 128/30 pt. 2, CM62(56)2, Confidential Annex, 28 August 1956; Howard J. Dooley, 'Great Britain's "Last Battle" in the Middle East: Notes on Cabinet Planning during the Suez Crisis of 1956', *The International History Review*, XI (1989), pp. 486–517; Anthony Gorst and W. Scott Lucas, 'Suez 1956: Strategy and the Diplomatic Process', *Journal of Strategic Studies* XI (1988), pp. 391–436.
31. *FRUS* 1955–7(16), pp. 382–91, Special National Intelligence Estimate, 5 September 1956; FO 800/726, Foreign Office to Washington, Telegram no. 4061, Emergency, 6 September 1956; Keith Kyle, *Suez* (London, 1992), p. 224; CAB 128/30 pt. 2, fol. 531, CM63(56), Confidential Annex, 6 September 1956; FO 800/726, Makins to Foreign Office, Telegram no. 1939, Secret, 8 September 1956 d r 9 September 1956; Ovendale, *Origins of the Arab–Israeli Wars*, pp. 172–3.
32. Eisenhower Library, Abilene, John Foster Dulles Papers, 1951–9, General Correspondence and Memoranda Series, Box no. 1, File Memoranda of Conversations – General L through M (2), Memorandum of Conversation with Macmillan, Personal and Private, shown to Hoover but no further distribution, Personal and Private, 25 September 1956; Ovendale, *The Origins of the Arab–Israeli Wars*, p. 173; FO 800/726, Foreign Office to Washington, Telegram no. 4540, Top Secret, 1 October 1956.

33. FO 800/725, Memorandum by Lloyd, Top Secret, 15 October 1956; Memorandum by Lloyd, Top Secret, 24 October 1956; CAB 128/30 pt. 2, fos 599–600, CM71(56)4, Confidential Annex, 18 October 1956; FO 800/725, Second memorandum by Lloyd, Top Secret, 24 October 1956; Ovendale, *The Origins of the Arab–Israeli Wars*, pp. 173–9.
34. Eisenhower Library, Abilene, Ann Whitman File, DDE Diary Series, Box no. 18, File Phone Calls Sunday 28 October 1956, from Dulles; PREM 11/1454, Coulson to Lloyd, Telegram no. 2200, Top Secret, 29 October 1956 recd. 30 October 1956; PREM 11/1177, T486/56, Eisenhower to Eden, Top Secret, 30 October 1956; *FRUS* 1955–7(17), pp. 590–5, Armstrong to Acting Secretary of State, 3 May 1957 and enclosure, draft letter from Allen Dulles to John Foster Dulles, 2 May 1957; CAB 128/30 pt. 2, fol. 633, CM75(56)1, Secret, 30 October 1956; Ovendale, *The Origins of the Arab–Israeli Wars*, p. 180; *FRUS* 1955–7(16), pp. 840–2, Editorial note; Zeid Raad, 'A nightmare avoided: Jordan and Suez 1956', *Israel Affairs*, I (1994), pp. 288–308; Stuart A. Cohen, 'A still stranger aspect of Suez: British operational plans to attack Israel, 1955–1956', *The International History Review*, X (1988), pp. 261–81.
35. Lucas, *Divided We Stand*, pp. 276–7; David W. Lesch, *Syria and the United States Eisenhower's Cold War in the Middle East* (Boulder, Colorado, 1992), pp. 96–7; Patrick Seale, *The Struggle for Syria: A Study of Post-War Arab Politics 1945–1958* (London, 1987), pp. 246–82; Wilbur Crane Eveland, *Ropes of Sand: America's Failure in the Middle East* (London, 1980), pp. 172–239.
36. Eisenhower Library, Abilene, John Foster Dulles Papers, 1951–9, General Correspondence and Memoranda Series, Box no. 2, File Strictly Confidential E–H(2)Gruenther to Dulles, 29 October 1956; Ann Whitman File, Ann Whitman Diary Series, Box no. 8, File November 1956 Diary ACW(2), Diary 3 November 1956; *FRUS* 1955–7(16), pp. 745–6, Editorial note; CAB 128/30 pt. 2, fol. 641A, CM77(56), Confidential Annex, 2 November 1956; Geoffrey Warner, 'Review article the United States and the Suez crisis', *International Affairs*, 67 (1991), pp. 303–17.
37. FO 115/4545, VR1091/960G, Record of conversation between Lloyd and Elliot at Washington on 18 November 1956; Ovendale, *The Origins of the Arab–Israeli Wars*, p. 181; for a critique of Allen Dulles's later claims before the Senate that he had offered forewarnings see Richard J. Aldrich, 'Intelligence, Anglo-American Relations and the Suez Crisis, 1956', *Intelligence and National Security*, IX (July 1994), pp. 544–54 at p. 550; Peter L. Hahn, *The United States, Great Britain and Egypt, 1945–1956* (Chapel Hill, 1991).
38. Eisenhower Library, Abilene, Ann Whitman File, Ann Whitman Diary Series, Box no. 8, File October 1956 Diary ACW(2), Diary 30 October 1956; DDE Diary Series, Box no. 20, File November 1956 Miscellaneous (4), Eisenhower to Gruenther, Personal, 2 November 1956; Eisenhower to Lew W. Douglas, Personal, 3 November 1956; FO 800/726, Foreign Office to Washington, Telegram no. 5181, Secret, 5 November 1956; *FRUS* 1955–7(16), pp. 1025–7, Telephone conversation between Eisenhower and Eden, 6 November 1956, Whitman File, Eisenhower Library; FO 371/121274, V1075/13/G, Eden to Eisenhower, Telegram no. 5254, Top Secret, 7 November 1956; Eisenhower Library Abilene, Ann Whitman File, Ann Whitman Diary Series, Box no. 8, File November 1956 Diary ACW(2), Diary 6–8 November 1956.

39. *FRUS* 1955–7(16), pp. 1012–3, Editorial note; Ovendale, *The Origins of the Arab–Israeli Wars*, pp. 182, 186; Diane B. Kunz, *The Economic Diplomacy of the Suez Crisis* (Chapel Hill, 1991); Lewis Johnman, 'Defending the Pound: the economics of the Suez crisis, 1956', in Anthony Gorst, Lewis Johnman and W. Scott Lucas (eds), *Post-war Britain, 1945–64: Themes and Perspectives* (London, 1989), pp. 172–81.
40. FO 371/121237, V1054/13/(A), Minute by R.M. Hadow on the Middle East, Secret, 7 November 1956; Minute by R.M. Hadow on future Middle East policy, 7 November 1956; Memorandum on future Middle East policy, Secret, undated.
41. CAB 128/30 pt. 2, fos 652–3, CM81(56), Secret, 7 November 1956; *FRUS* 1955–7(16), pp. 1049–53, Memorandum of conversation, 7 November 1956; CAB 128/30 pt. 2, fos 656–7, CM(82)56, Secret, 8 November 1956; FO 371/121274, V1075/132/G, Dickson to Foreign Office, 10 November 1956; Victor Rothwell, *Anthony Eden: A Political Biography 1931–57* (Manchester, 1992), p. 240; *FRUS* 1955–7(16), pp. 1123–5, Telegram from mission at United Nations to Department of State, 14 November 1956.
42. *FRUS* 1955–7(12), pp. 330–1, Memorandum by Dulles, 16 November 1956; FO 115/4545, Admiral Sir Michael Denny to Caccia, MMD/75/56, Secret Guard, 16 November 1956; FO 115/4550, 1042/69/56, Australian embassy Washington to External Affairs Canberra, Secret, 20 November 1956; FO 371/121274, V1075/35/G, P. Dixon to Foreign Office, Telegram no. 1331, 21 November 1956; *FRUS* 1955–7(12), pp. 340–2, Memorandum of conference with Eisenhower, 21 November 1956; FO 371/121274, V1075/137/G, H. Caccia to Foreign Office, Telegram no. 2330, 21 November 1956 d r 22 November 1956; V1075/138, Washington to Foreign Office, Telegram no. 2334, Secret, 23 November 1956; *FRUS* 1955–7(16), p. 1181, Department of State to Embassy in Britain, 23 November 1956; FO 115/4550, 1042/73/56G, New York to Washington, Top Secret, 27 November 1956; 1042/74/56G, Washington to Foreign Office, Telegram no. 2359, Top Secret, 28 November 1956; FO 115/4545, 1040/21/56(G), Caccia to P. Reilly, Personal and Confidential Guard, 29 November 1956.
43. *FRUS* 1955–7(12), pp. 340–2, Memorandum of conference with Eisenhower, 21 November 1956, Whitman File, Eisenhower Library; Colville, *Downing Street Diaries*, pp. 718–9, Churchill to Eisenhower, 22 November 1956; Lucas, *Divided We Stand*, p. 315 quoting Whitman files, DDE Diaries, Box 19, November 1956, Goodpaster memorandum, 26 November 1956, Eisenhower Library.
44. CAB 128/30 pt. 2, fol. 693, CM89(56)2, Secret, 27 November 1956; fol. 707, CM93(56), Secret, 30 November 1956.
45. *FRUS* 1955–7(12), pp. 376–82, Memorandum from Rountree to Dulles, 5 December 1956; CAB 128/30 pt. 2, fos 728–9, CM97(56)2, Secret, 7 December 1956.

7

The American Involvement: The Eisenhower Doctrine

At a time when British and American officials on the higher levels had difficulty in talking to one another in a civil fashion, in the aftermath of the Suez crisis, London and Washington reassessed Middle Eastern policy. On London's part there was perhaps a little more emphasis on the Churchill administration's aim of 'getting the Americans in', and a little less on 'the flexing of British muscles' evidenced by the Eden government. The Americans finally realized, against the background of the Soviet threat, that they would have to assume an increasing responsibility for the defence of the Middle East, and the winning of the 'hearts and minds' in the area in Cold War terms. The State Department, particularly after the visit to the Middle East of the Secretary of State, John Foster Dulles, had warned Eisenhower that Britain could no longer play the role assigned to it for the defence of the Middle East in Western strategy, and that the United States would have to prepare to take over. The Eisenhower Doctrine for the Middle East was a reflection of this. In British defence policy and global strategy, the Middle East was no longer of cardinal importance. Eden had initiated further assessments of Britain's reduced role in world affairs before the nationalization of the Suez Canal. Britain's defence and foreign policy had to take account of economic realities. The government of Harold Macmillan implemented the cost effectiveness principal of empire, assessed what value associated and dependent countries were to Britain, and who would move in if Britain moved out. The 'wind of change' associated with Africa, was evident elsewhere.[1] In the Middle East the British interest shifted increasingly to securing the oil supplies from Kuwait in particular, and the Gulf in more general terms. This effectively constituted a transfer of power.

On 8 December 1956 the British ambassador at Tehran, Sir Roger Stevens, expounded on Britain's position in the Gulf in relation to Iran. Stevens ruminated: with the liquidation of the Indian empire the reason for Britain's position in the Gulf ceased to exist and British positions there 'became stations on a road leading nowhere'; 'this process has now been completed from the other side by the loss of our traditional footholds in Egypt, Palestine, Jordan and

Iraq; the Persian Gulf road now starts nowhere either, and has become a sort of double-ended cul-de sac'. Vitality was needed from a new source, and Stevens thought that could only be the Baghdad Pact. He summarized British assets in the Gulf as oil, the naval base and sea communications. Set against this was the liabilities of treaties with the Sheikhs, and the threat to sterling if the Ruler of Kuwait moved his reserves from sterling to dollars. There was also the nineteenth century conception of prestige. The Iranians, however, viewed the British presence in the gulf as a relic of an imperial and colonial past. Britain seemed to be supporting weak and feudal rulers against a rising tide of popular discontent. The Iranians wanted windfalls for themselves and wanted to assert the 'Persian' position in the 'Persian' Gulf. This was the reason for Tehran's claim to Bahrain, and for the seizure of small islands belonging to Kuwait.

Stevens pointed to Washington's views and ambitions: the American navy appeared to be building up for itself a predominant position in the Gulf and was challenging what influence Britain had left with the Iranian navy. The Gulf was increasingly important in American thinking about the protection of oil supplies and lines of communication for defence purposes. He suspected that sections of the American administration viewed the British outposts in the Gulf with a jaundiced eye: partly because they had a colonial air, partly because they could be thought to be crumbling.

The ambassador at Tehran doubted whether, with regard to oil, the maintenance of the British position in Kuwait and Qatar was essential to the maintenance of Britain's commercial interests. He suggested that Britain had to find a constructive way out of this dead-end, 'even at the loss of a little prestige, rather than wait to be overwhelmed by events and thrust onto the inevitably disastrous defensive'. Federation could be a possible solution. Alternatively Britain could try to reinforce its whole military, naval and air position in the Sheikhdoms as a British contribution to underpinning the Baghdad Pact. If Washington joined the Pact, it could be necessary to make the operation an Anglo-American one. That could solve the problem of Anglo-American rivalry in the Gulf. Stevens warned: 'We must either go forward or we shall be forced to quit. And forward, as you see from here, means forward into a stronger, wider and more vital conception of the Baghdad Pact.'

From Beirut, Sir George Middleton observed, when commenting on Stevens' view that the Americans were not making a conscious effort to supplant Britain in the Middle East, that while the official policy of the State Department was not unfriendly towards the maintenance of British interests, American big business corporations, particularly the oil companies, were fiercely competitive, and the main resistance to their expansion came from established British connections. Lacking the same resources, Britain could not compete.

Middleton continued: 'This may be inevitable and we must face the fact that our declining influence is all the more obvious because of our inability to contribute in any important degree towards the needs of the countries of the Middle East for capital investment.' Britain, the ambassador at Beirut observed, had become very much the junior partner in the Western alliance, and in the Middle East this was particularly evident. This new position could have lessened suspicions of British imperialism, but it was not as a result of American benevolence, and Middleton thought that Britain could not afford to be complacent. Britain had to concentrate its efforts both in the political and commercial spheres. The tacit support of the Americans would help, but Middleton doubted whether this could be achieved, and Britain had to be prepared to continue facing American 'competition which in the Middle Eastern minds is indistinguishable from opposition'.[2]

On 7 December 1956, the British Cabinet asked the Foreign Secretary, in consultation with the Minister of Defence, to review future British policy in the Middle East and the redeployment of forces there. It was possible that it would be preferable to offer financial subventions to Arab countries rather than to maintain bases there. The military value of agreements like the Anglo-Jordanian Treaty had been shown to be less that Britain had hoped for, and could be expected to decline further. But the Cabinet agreed to make the next monthly payment of £800,000 to Jordan, in case it turned to the Soviet Union.

Lloyd explained this to Dulles in Paris on 10 December. Apart from keeping the Soviets out, the expenditure of £13 million a year on Jordan was a waste: Lloyd doubted whether there was much future for Jordan, except perhaps as a satellite of Syria, and thus indirectly of the Soviet Union. Dulles explained that he was not worried about the possibility of countries becoming Soviet satellites, provided that they were not in geographical contact with the Soviet bloc. Dulles told Lloyd that he thought the ground was prepared for a resumption of close relations between Britain and the United States. The American Secretary of State insisted that it was not American policy to placate Nasser or to woo the Arabs. It was Dulles' view that Saudi Arabia, in time, could be built up as a counter to Nasser. If Washington joined the Baghdad Pact it would annoy the Saudis. Such a move would also create problems with Israel, and was unlikely to be passed in Senate. Dulles explained that consideration was being given to a Congressional resolution which would authorize Eisenhower to take strong action in the Middle East. These thoughts, however, were intimate, and had only been shared with three of four members of the State Department, and Lloyd was asked to confine the information to as few of his colleagues as possible.[3]

The British view, however, was that the Americans should join the Baghdad Pact: if the Americans believed that British influence in the Middle East had declined they should be all the more ready to take their place at the side of those countries which understood the Communist menace in the Middle East and were fighting against it. The British thought that the prevailing vacuum in the Middle East was dangerous. From Washington, Caccia warned that the American administration was undertaking a reappraisal: Britain should inject its thinking at a formative stage. The ambassador did not think that Dulles' comments about the American feeling of having been deceived should be taken too seriously.[4]

At this time London did not pursue suggestions from Nuri that it might be possible to draw Nasser to co-operate with Arab countries who were anti-Communist and with the West. Eden scorned this idea, and thought that any attempt by Nuri and the Americans to help Nasser would only build up trouble for the future. The ambassador at Baghdad saw this move by Nuri merely as an attempt to out-manoeuvre Nasser in terms of Arab unity against Communism.[5]

Lloyd endorsed a Foreign Office paper dated 26 December 1956 on future military policy in the Middle East in which it was argued that it was not realistic to plan in terms of local wars in the Middle East without the United States being Britain's active ally, or at least a benevolent neutral. The Soviets and hostile Arabs could try to use the United States to get Britain out of the Middle East, but they would do so in the hope that the Americans would not after all effectively replace Britain. Britain had to ensure that Washington did not fall for this trick, and also encourage the Americans 'to accept responsibilities in the Middle East and to seek irrevocably to commit them to the major role in the defence of common positions which we have hitherto sustained'. London had to work loyally with Washington, and Washington had to recognize London's special interests in particular areas. On this basis it could be possible to create a partnership whereby Western influence throughout the region could be maintained.

The matter of timing was vital. Withdrawal of British influence in circumstances which made it difficult for the Americans to take Britain's place was the major danger. There was little chance of the Americans moving in unless they were convinced that Britain really was going to get out. It was necessary to face the Americans with an unpleasant announcement such as notice of Britain's intention to give up its commitments in Jordan. Furthermore, Britain had to drastically curtail its military expenditure in the Middle East, and abandon any facilities which made only a marginal contribution such as Jordan, or which could not be used because of adverse political factors such as those in Libya.

The paper suggested that the continued stationing of British land forces in the non-Arab territory of Cyprus and, to a lesser extent, in Bahrain and Sharjah, exercised an intangible but very real influence on surrounding countries, and it was politically necessary to maintain this. Britain hoped to maintain the present facilities in Iraq, but not in the Canal Zone base in Egypt. A neutral Egypt was the most that could be hoped for. The size of forces to be stationed in or kept available for the Gulf would depend on how far it was possible, or desirable, to associate the Americans in the defence of Western interests there. It was more important that British forces in the Middle East should be well trained and equipped, and easily transportable, than large.[6]

The evolving British policy in the Middle East started to be implemented early in January 1958 when Jordan indicated its desire to terminate the Anglo-Jordanian Treaty of 1948. Lloyd told the Cabinet, on 3 January 1957, that this treaty was no longer of any significant strategic value to Britain as a support for its interests in the Middle East. Nuri wanted Britain to defer a decision on this. Lloyd advised that Washington would react adversely to any attempt to consult it formally, or to involve it in a joint policy towards Jordan. But it would be premature to sever the British connection with Jordan without any assurance of the extent to which the United States would be prepared to take over British responsibilities. The Cabinet agreed to wait on consultation with the Americans, and a consideration of this in the context of Britain's Middle East policy as a whole. On 4 January, the Joint Planning Staff concluded that British and American strategic aims in the Middle East as a whole, and in Libya in particular, were sufficiently close to ensure that any military interest which Britain might want to retain in Libya could be safeguarded under the American aegis. If Washington were prepared to shoulder more of the burden, this should be welcomed by Britain.[7]

Alongside this British reassessment, the Americans refined the envisaged Congressional resolution which Dulles had described to Lloyd in Paris on 10 December. Initially drafted by Herman Phleger, the Chief Legal Officer in the State Department, it incorporated suggestions made by Dulles, outlined by Eisenhower on 1 January 1957, and was to the leaders from both parties and houses in Congress. The President delivered it on 5 January to a joint session on Capitol Hill. The reasoning behind what became known as the Eisenhower Doctrine for the Middle East was a vacuum in the Middle East which had to be filled by the United States before it was filled by the Soviet Union. The President outlined a programme to strengthen economically the nations of the Middle East, and asked for flexibility to use funds, and for provision to use the armed forces of the United States. Caccia pointed out that there was nothing in the doctrine that was addressed to Britain or Washington's other Western allies. This was American unilateral action. Shortly afterwards, Dulles was reported to have said he would not like to be a American soldier in the Middle East with a Briton on one side and a Frenchman on the other. This 'slip' apparently embarrassed both Dulles and the State Department, and the British decided not to press the matter.[8]

On 8 January, Lloyd outlined to the Cabinet a plan for closer military and political association between Britain and Western Europe. The Marquess of Salisbury, however, doubted whether such a policy was consistent with the maintenance of the Anglo-American alliance which he regarded as the best hope of securing the free world from Soviet aggression. It would, he thought, and the Cabinet agreed, be especially unfortunate if an approach towards a closer military association with Europe were based on proposals for the common development of nuclear weapons.[9]

Norman Brook, the Secretary of the Cabinet, suggested to Eden on 14 December 1956 that post-Suez long-term policy in the Middle East should be looked at by a Cabinet Committee smaller than the existing committee of officials, and consisting of the Foreign Secretary, the Chancellor of the Exchequer, the Commonwealth Secretary, the Colonial Secretary and the Minister of Defence. This was agreed to on 7 January 1957. The existing Official Committee on the Middle East was reconstituted to keep under review the political and economic problems in the area and to report to the Middle East Committee.[10]

Harold Macmillan was chosen as Prime Minister by Queen Elizabeth II, acting on advice. Perhaps he was seen as the man best able to heal the breach with the United States. Eden had to go, and the reason given was his health. In his message to Eden about this, Eisenhower omitted any mention of 'regret', and merely referred to past associations. Macmillan told the Cabinet on 9 January 1957 that when the history of the Suez crisis was written, it would be recognized that Eden had been inspired by motives of the highest patriotism. When he addressed his first Cabinet as Prime Minister, Macmillan, while agreeing that Britain's treaty with Libya no longer had a military value commensurate with the commitment to subsidize Libya to the sum of £12 million a year, emphasized 'it was important that in present circumstances we should not create the impression of withdrawing entirely from the Middle East'.[11]

The policy that evolved early in 1957 from the Cabinet Committees on the Middle East was based on the premise that to safeguard its vital interest in communications through the Middle East, for both strategic and trade purposes, Britain did not have to dominate the Middle East itself. It had long been British policy to deny the domination of the Middle East to any hostile or potentially hostile power, viewed at that time as the Soviet bloc. Britain had to maintain its position in the Gulf and Aden, one which safeguarded the sea routes for oil supplies from the Gulf to the Suez Canal and around South Africa. Britain's best hope of securing its aims lay in co-operation with the United States. With the Eisenhower Doctrine for the Middle East Washington was showing an increased interest in the area, but it was thought likely that the United States would pursue its policy there with less reference to Britain than had been made in the past. While Britain hoped that the Americans would take over its long-term commitments in Jordan and Libya, there was some reluctance to abdicate in favour of the Americans in Iraq where it was felt that Britain still had a special position, and the Iraq Petroleum Company wanted assistance for that country to be retained in British or Anglo-French hands. The Cabinet Committee did acknowledge that in the Gulf British influence was founded on the desire there of the Rulers for independence from Saudi Arabia and Iraq, one which might not be shared by the emergent middle classes who were already impregnated with Nasser's propaganda.[12]

The Joint Planning Staff, at the end of January 1957, when considering Britain's long-term defence policy, a policy evolved to relate to the economic resources of the country and one as later outlined in the Defence White Paper of April 1957 which relied on nuclear deterrence, similarly concluded that the main British interests in the Middle East lay in the Gulf Area, and in East and Central Africa.[13] In February, the Joint Planning Staff emphasized the importance of the Baghdad Pact in promoting stability in the oil producing regions of Iraq and Iran; with the conclusion that Britain's strategy in the Cold War in the Middle

East was dependent on what policy the Americans adopted, Britain had, in any event, to safeguard oil supplies and the routes for the transportation of oil. Britain had maintained its position in the Gulf, and the main external threats to that area were seen as Egyptian propaganda and Saudi Arabian bribery and subversion. In the prevailing circumstances the Royal Navy could not assume sole responsibility for the protection of the Arabian peninsula.[14] In this connection Britain assumed that, following observations by the American Secretary of State, John Foster Dulles, Washington would not underwrite the British position in the Gulf.[15] There was also Foreign Office concern that Britain should not 'use the Gulf for the purposes of the Baghdad Pact' as the Rulers were anxious not to be dragged into the Pact.[16]

Macmillan was able to report to the Cabinet on 29 January that Eisenhower was prepared to resume friendly relations with Britain, and had suggested a meeting either in Washington or Bermuda. Macmillan chose to meet under the Union Flag at Bermuda: there was to be no image of British supplication to Washington. The Eisenhower Doctrine encountered difficulties in Congress. These hinged on the Israeli position. On 14 November 1956 the Knesset had agreed to withdraw from the territories captured in the Sinai campaign, provided there was a satisfactory arrangement with the United Nations Emergency Force (UNEF). Abba Eban, the Israeli ambassador at Washington, was working with Robert Murphy, the Under-Secretary of State, assisted by the party leaders in the Senate, Lyndon B. Johnson and William K. Knowland, and Rabbi Abba Hillel Silver who synchronized the Zionist pressure groups. The Senate started debating the Congressional resolution on the Middle East (the Eisenhower Doctrine) on 18 February. This took place against the possibility of a vote by the United Nations General Assembly in favour of applying economic sanctions against Israel over its refusal to withdraw from territories it had occupied during the Suez–Sinai War. Senators of both parties made it clear to the American administration that they would delay a decision on the Eisenhower Doctrine until this sanctions issue was out of the way. Eisenhower took a stand in support of the Gulf of Aqaba being an international waterway on 7 March. This favoured Israel. The Eisenhower Doctrine became law on 9 March 1957. The Americans secured the freedom of passage through the Straits of Tiran: on 24 April 1957 an American ship, the *Kernhills*, docked in Eilat carrying a cargo of crude oil. An Egyptian administration, but not an Egyptian army, returned to the Gaza Strip.[17]

When Macmillan and Eisenhower met at Bermuda on 21 March, Macmillan was 'frank' about Middle Eastern questions, and warned of the danger of a 'real rift' between London and Washington if Nasser succeeded in imposing his proposed long-term arrangements over the operation of the Suez Canal. Eisenhower spoke of his delight in sitting down with his former comrade-in-arms, and agreed with Macmillan that Anglo-American solidarity was the core of the Western alliance: if the English-speaking peoples could not live and work together there was little hope. The American President thought that nationalism was a stronger spirit than communism. Eisenhower confided to his diary that this was the most successful international meeting he had attended since the end of the Second World War. Macmillan concluded that Eisenhower 'appeared to be genuinely anxious fully to restore the traditional relationship between the two countries'. Indeed Eisenhower's briefing paper for the conference had pointed to the traditional concept of the Anglo-American alliance, and had emphasized that British and American policies were in agreement regarding areas of vital interest to Britain, particularly in the Middle East.[18]

When the British and American leaders discussed the Middle East at Bermuda, Lloyd emphasized that one of Britain's main aims had to be to consolidate its position in the Gulf, and above all in Kuwait which had enormous oil reserves. Lloyd argued that the position there was not unpromising as Egyptian penetration had made little headway, and the governments in the area were reasonably steady. But the possibility of a *coup d'etat* in the area engendered by Nasser could not be ignored. Kuwaiti oil would solve Nasser's financial problems. There was no British garrison there, and British influence was dependent on advisers in government departments. Britain would have to take 'prompt action' to maintain stability. Dulles thought it important that Britain should have more power in Kuwait, and this would be essential if things went wrong in Saudi Arabia and Iraq. Eisenhower agreed, and insisted that the preservation of the Kuwait oil reserves should be 'a first objective': Britain should look at all aspects of its policy in the area from the point of view of holding Kuwait and its oil. Lloyd observed that 'forces would not be required for this purpose': Britain's position 'depended more on our relations with the Ruler and on his absolute belief in our word'.[19] Macmillan was relieved by Dulles' assurances that the United States did not want to take over from Britain in the Middle East and welcomed Eisenhower's proposal that there should be joint Anglo-American studies of the problems there.[20]

The first of these were held in Washington in the middle of April 1957, and considered the supply of oil to the Free World.[21] These talks took place against the background of a crisis in Jordan. On 13 March 1957 Jordan had abrogated the 1948 treaty with Britain. The British subsidy was to be replaced by support from Saudi Arabia, Egypt and Syria. On 10 April Suleiman Nabulsi resigned as Prime Minister after differences with King Hussein over closer connections with the Soviet Union. Hussein replaced Nabulsi with the conservative Ibrahim Hashim. The British Cabinet, on 11 April, concluded that if there were general war in the Middle East following the collapse of the Kingdom of Jordan, there could be a serious threat to British interests in the Middle East. If the territorial integrity of Jordan could not be preserved, it was in the British interest for Iraq to strengthen and extend its influence. But it was possible that the Americans would support the claims of Saudi Arabia. Washington and London needed to concert action. Hussein, however, maintained his position. On 15 April, Lloyd told the Cabinet that Britain should encourage Hussein to look to Saudi Arabia for political support, and to Iraq for military assistance. Britain was reluctant to intervene with military force.

The Cabinet was disturbed by indications that the Americans did not think the Eisenhower Doctrine could be applied as it was designed for use against external aggression. Eisenhower, however, responded to a message from President Camille Chamoun of Lebanon on 24 April asking for swift action to save Jordan. Eisenhower told Dulles that the young King Hussein was 'certainly showing spunk' and that he admired him for it. The American President took action under the Eisenhower Doctrine: he referred to the independence and integrity of Jordan as being vital; moved units of the United States Sixth Fleet into the eastern Mediterranean; and, on 29 April, announced an economic aid grant of $10 million to Jordan. The situation stabilized; on 1 May the Sixth Fleet was recalled to the western Mediterranean. On 6 May the Americans requested the British continue their aid to Jordan, and support Hussein and those elements in Jordan who identified their interests with those of the Free World. The RAF base at Mafrak was transferred to the Jordanians in a ceremony on 31 May 1957.[22]

The difficulties for the revived Anglo-American special relationship established at Bermuda (which in effect marked the move towards the British reliance on American weaponry and a return to an Anglo-American management of world affairs rather than the idea of Britain being treated just as one among a number of allies), which Macmillan had warned of in relation to Egypt's management of the Suez Canal, passed. Eisenhower referred again to the matter on 28 April, and asked for patience. As it became clear that Nasser could run the Suez Canal as well as the Suez Canal Company had, and as Nasser's propaganda against Britain subsided for a while, antagonism on the matter in Britain also subsided.[23]

Following the meeting at Bermuda, the Official Middle East Committee of the Cabinet countered suggestions that continued support for the feudal rulers in the Gulf was a short-sighted policy, in that they were likely to be replaced by more broadly based regimes, with the case that Britain had no prospect of establishing a reliable connection with the forces opposed to the Rulers. British interests lay in maintaining the position of the Rulers rather than in the 'achievement of more liberal regimes'. Furthermore, the situation in the Gulf had important implications not only for the British economy, but for that of Europe as a whole.[24]

Between 12 and 14 June 1957 there were further joint Anglo-American talks on the Middle East in London, and agreed conclusions were reached about the measures needed to ensure continued access to the petroleum resources of the Middle East. Iraq, Iran, Kuwait, and Saudi Arabia were singled out as comprising 'the vital section of the area'. Important assets in this regard included the British position in Kuwait and the Gulf in general, as well as the Baghdad Pact, the Eisenhower Doctrine, and American relations with Saudi Arabia. Note was taken of an American view that Britain should respond more freely to 'constructive pressures for reform' in the Gulf states, but Humphrey Trevelyan, who had just served as ambassador in Cairo, was quick to point out that Loy Henderson, the deputy Under Secretary of State, had not wanted to pursue this theme as his experience in the Middle East had led him to think it 'entirely mistaken and highly dangerous'.[25] This view was reinforced by the British ambassador at Ankara with his observation that the Americans needed to be convinced the British position in the Gulf was important for the Western world in general and was not just an 'out-dated relic' of British imperialism.[26] Indeed the case the British put to the Americans emphasized that Kuwait with its oil merited special attention and that pressures from indigenous nationalist sentiment, stimulated by Egyptian propaganda, teachers and technicians and other educated non-Kuwaiti Arabs had been growing in the Sheikhdom. Preservation of the al-Sabah family depended 'in large measure on the relationship between the ruling family and the United Kingdom', and this was an important part of the wider system of the relationship between Britain and the Gulf rulers. Britain insisted that it could do nothing more to ease the situation over Buraimi.[27]

As ideas of British moves towards Europe lessened, Macmillan endorsed the view that it was far more important to achieve a meeting of minds with the Americans on Middle East questions than with the French.[28] The Americans indicated to the British that they would like to talk about the general defence problems of the Middle East such as support for the Baghdad Pact, the future of Cyprus in defence plans, British intentions in Kenya, and the problem of military overflying rights. But Britain did not discuss its interim directions for Global War in the Middle East with the Americans. These were primarily based on the protection of Cyprus as an air base to support the southern flank of NATO and the Baghdad Pact, the security of the Aden protectorate and colony, and the British protected territories in the Gulf. Land forces not required for these tasks were to be kept in readiness for rapid movement in such limited operations in the eastern Mediterranean or the Gulf 'as would benefit British interests or indirectly assist the main defence of the area'.[29]

But London did inform Washington of its intervention to support the Sultan of Muscat, when, in the middle of July 1957 tribesmen took over the mountains near Nizwa in Oman. Britain considered once again that the establishment of a separate state under the Imam of Oman in Central Oman would be used by Egypt, Syria and Saudi Arabia as a centre for intrigue against British interests in the area. Macmillan told Eisenhower that Nasser was encouraging the trouble and that the Saudis were involved. Lloyd told the Americans it was a minor matter on the military side: 'sending 50 men or so and shooting up a fort or two'. Eisenhower assumed that it was the latest incident in the old Buraimi affair, and refuted the rumours current in London that the troubles had been brought about by the efforts of American oil companies to damage British oil possessions in the region.[30]

American intelligence found no evidence of official Saudi support for the Imam of Oman. Dulles feared a small Suez. He warned Eisenhower on 3 August that the Arab world could be drawn in opposition to Britain, Nasser would have a new chance to assert Arab leadership, and Washington would be caught between its desire to maintain an influence with some of the Arab countries, particularly Saudi Arabia, and the desire to maintain good ties with Britain.

Washington decided to abstain over the inscription of the Oman problem on the agenda of the Security Council. Caccia warned of the danger of such a move for public opinion in Britain, and for Anglo-American relations. In the end Washington did abstain, but the vote in the Security Council was five to four against, and the Oman question was not placed on the agenda.[31]

But the Oman situation turned out to be more serious than had been supposed, and the question of air action was raised in October. The Cabinet Defence Committee, however, thought that bombing was unacceptable on political grounds. Macmillan used his son-in-law, Julian Amery, who employed the Special Air Service in actions in Oman over the following two years to pacify the rebels. As part of the settlement in September 1958 the Sultan of Muscat ceded Gwadar, his small possession off the coast of Baluchistan, to the government of Pakistan.[32]

Over the issue of apparent Communist infiltration into Syria, Macmillan had to struggle to restrain the Americans. For him the problem seemed to be not to discourage the Americans, while at the same time avoiding stimulating them from taking fatal steps. Lloyd went to Washington and had extensive talks with Dulles. Eisenhower inclined towards an interpretation of the Eisenhower Doctrine which could cover subversion from within or without. Moves were made to support countries around Syria. On 9 September, the United States publicized a substantial delivery of arms to Jordan. The Soviet Union claimed that Turkey was concentrating troops against Syria. London and Washington coordinated contingency plans on a military and political basis. After hearing an account by Lloyd of the Foreign Secretary's talks with Dulles, Macmillan noted on 26 September 1957 that it was 'a great comfort to be working so closely and with such complete confidence with the Americans'.

On 8 October a minor border incident led to a protest from Syria to Ankara, and a complaint to the United Nations. The Soviet Union supported a referral of the 'Turkish threat' to the General Assembly in the middle of October. Saud offered to mediate. Dulles warned that if the Soviet Union attacked Turkey, the United States would not restrict itself to a 'purely defensive operation'. Then on 29 October Nikita Khrushchev, the new Soviet leader, at a party given by the Turkish ambassador in Moscow said that there was no threat in the Middle East and that the whole affair had been a misunderstanding. The Syrians withdrew their complaint from the United Nations.[33]

When the Soviet Union launched Sputnik, its space satellite, the United States was shaken. Macmillan was immediately invited to Washington, and in talks there between 23 and 25 October, as Lloyd reported to the Cabinet on 28 October 'as a result of the personal friendship between the Prime Minister and President Eisenhower, we had now succeeded in regaining the special relationship with the United States we had formerly enjoyed'. The relationship between Washington and London was to be one of 'inter-dependence'. Washington agreed to adopt the principle of pooling resources in the development and production of new weapons. Congress was to be asked to amend the Atomic Energy Act to allow greater co-operation with Britain and other friendly countries. This was in effect the end of the McMahon act of 1946 which restricted such an exchange of information, and which had forced Britain to develop its own bomb. Washington and London would concert a common policy against Soviet encroachment. The Middle East was discussed, and in particular the support for the friendly governments of Lebanon, Jordan and Iraq. Lloyd thought that Jordan and Iraq should be told what military help they could expect, and how quickly it could arrive.[34]

By November 1957 the joint planning with the Americans had brought forward proposals from Washington for the protection of Middle Eastern oil. Sir William Stratton, the Vice Chief of the Imperial General Staff, on 14 November warned the Chiefs of Staff that the size of the force which Britain could provide constituted a major limitation, and that it might be worth considering planning to use joint Anglo-American forces in these circumstances. But R.W.J. Hooper, who headed the Permanent Under-Secretary's Department at the Foreign Office, advised that there would be political difficulties if Americans were included in any forces destined for protection measures in the Gulf Sheikhdoms.[35] At this time the Foreign Office, in response to the troubled situation in Muscat and Oman, outlined a British policy which viewed the British position in the Gulf and Southern Arabia as 'a single whole whose parts were mutually self-supporting'. This constituted a domino theory: 'Our withdrawal from any one of the territories for whose protection we were now responsible would thus fundamentally weaken the whole of the present system and if it did not destroy it would at least hasten its final collapse.'[36]

On 24 January 1958, Eisenhower approved a new long-range American policy towards the Middle East which had been drawn up by the National Security Council. This document acknowledged that since the British–French–Israeli invasion of Egypt in November 1958, the United States had been the undisputed leader of the Free World's interests in the Middle East, and that Britain and France had recognized this in all areas except the Gulf and Aden. Washington could not avoid identification with powers who still had 'colonial' interests in the area. Britain remained convinced that its continued predominance in the Gulf was essential to guarantee the flow of oil necessary to maintain Britain's internal economy as well as its international position. Saudi Arabia, however, envisaged the reduction or elimination of British influence in the Gulf, and the reduction of British-protected rulers to Saudi vassals.

It was Washington's policy to 'provide Free World leadership and to assume, on behalf of the Free World, the major responsibility toward the area; acting with or in consultation with other Free World countries, particularly the United Kingdom, to the greatest extent practicable, but reserving the right to act alone'. The United States should keep Britain informed and work with London through both overt and covert channels on area problems 'to the extent compatible with U.S. area objectives'. It should try to achieve peaceful and equitable solutions to questions in which Britain was interested, such as: Buraimi and Saudi Arabia; the

Yemen–Aden Protectorate frontier; the Gulf Sheikhdoms, islands and seabed; and also support a British role in Iraq so long as it is constructive and effective, 'but exercise U.S. responsibility as the situation demands'. Washington was to try to seek open co-operation in military assistance matters between the United States, Britain and Iraq.[37]

The British policy towards Kuwait and the Gulf was challenged early in 1958. On 1 February, Egypt and Syria announced the union of the two states which became known as the United Arab Republic. In response, on 14 February, King Feisal of Iraq and King Hussein of Jordan proclaimed the union of their two countries in an Arab Federation.

Nuri al-Said, the senior Iraqi statesman, told Macmillan in London that he wanted Britain to persuade the Ruler of Kuwait to join this new Iraq–Jordan union.[38] This posed a dilemma for the Foreign Office: recommending this idea could destroy the confidence of the Ruler of Kuwait in the British government 'on which our main interests in Kuwait rest – i.e. the availability of Kuwait oil on existing terms and for sterling and the investment of the Ruler's surplus revenue in the United Kingdom'. But support for Iraq and Jordan was seen as being so important for Britain's position in the Middle East that the Foreign Office felt Iraq had to be helped to produce the most favourable conditions for an approach to the Ruler.[39]

At a meeting with Iraqi leaders, including Feisal and Nuri, early in March, Nuri told Lloyd that Britain should declare Kuwait independent so that it could join the new union as a free and independent member; Britain could negotiate a defence treaty giving Kuwait the same protection 'but there was all the difference between protection given to an independent state and protection given to a protected state'. Iraq would offer Britain guarantees about oil revenue and investment in London. It was also alleged that Kuwait was being used as a base for the invasion of Iraq. Lloyd responded that this confronted Britain with the most serious decision Britain would have to take in the Middle East over the past few years, apart from the evacuation of the Canal base. Lloyd warned of possible consequences for Iraq: the majority of Kuwaitis might want to join Egypt rather than Iraq. The Foreign Secretary doubted whether the removal of Britain from yet another place in the world was much of a remedy. Britain had left too many places already. If it ceased to protect Kuwait the other Sheikhdoms in the Gulf would not 'know where they were', and Bahrain's special position in the Gulf could be ended. Lloyd was told that there was little point in Iraq talking to the Ruler about anything: he was a weak man incapable of taking any decision and the time had come for Britain to tell him what to do.[40] The Foreign Office advised Macmillan that there was little chance Kuwait would want to join the Arab Union: Britain should let the Ruler know where it felt his interest lay.[41] Even if King Saud of Saudi Arabia joined the union, it was thought that the Ruler would still be reluctant to take such an 'unpopular step'. And if the Ruler were persuaded by Britain, there were likely to be serious disturbances particularly in the oil fields where Sheikh Jabir Al-Ahmad controlled security and who would be hostile to such a move. If Britain intervened, some Kuwaitis could appeal to Egypt. Nuri's suggestion of frontier concessions by Kuwait, such as the cession of territory to Iraq for the development of Umm Qasr, were unlikely to be achieved by British persuasion. The Ruler, conscious of the risk of not making compensating investment in the United Arab Republic, might hesitate to extend economic aid to the Arab Union.[42]

The best alternative seemed to encourage the Americans to take seriously the question of aid for the new Arab Union. But the Foreign Office was aware of 'a certain dilatoriness' in American Middle East policy, and was worried that Dulles was thinking 'in rather an airy way about long-term problems' and not addressing the urgent questions.[43] When the Americans did take moves towards aiding Iraq, Britain became agitated as this aid implied that American F-86 aircraft would be made available instead of British manufactured Hawker Hunters.[44]

During his visit to Baghdad in the middle of May, the Ruler of Kuwait complained to the British ambassador there, Sir Michael Wright, that Britain had spoken with the Iraqis about Kuwait without exploring the ground with him first. The Ruler would not join the Union. He also dismissed ideas of joining the United Arab Republic. Wright suggested that Kuwait could benefit if both Iraq and Britain were prepared to defend the Sheikhdom; he argued for Kuwait having some sort of association with Iraq, and also mentioned the possibility of a development bank in which Britain, Iraq and Kuwait might participate. The Ruler, while indicating that he was prepared to strengthen the association with Iraq, 'enlarged at length, and with emphasis, on the trust he felt towards Britain and Kuwait's determination to remain faithful to her relationship with us'.[45] When A.S. Halford, the Political Agent at Kuwait, was asked by the Ruler for guidance about what might be included in an agreement with Iraq, Halford pointed to such matters as the mutual recognition of frontiers with provisions for demarcation (the Ruler agreed to this specifying that frontiers had to include seabed frontiers) and also commercial and economic matters including investments (the Ruler dissented over investments saying that merchants should be free to trade where they wanted).[46]

Baghdad lost patience. On 6 June it suggested a solution to London. Referring to the international position of Kuwait before the First World War, Baghdad argued that 'Kuwait was territory subject to the sovereignty of the Ottoman Government under international law and was a district belonging to the Vilayat of Basra'. It further claimed that Britain had implicitly admitted this sovereignty in the Anglo-Turkish agreement of 29 July 1913, the sixth Article of which 'guaranteed the Ruler of Kuwait's right to exercise his administrative powers as an Ottoman Qaimham belonging to the Vilayat of Basra'. During the period of the British mandate over Iraq the international position of Kuwait remained 'obscure'. Before Iraq joined the League of Nations in 1932 Baghdad had raised with London the question of the Iraq-Kuwait frontier and the islands situated in the territorial waters which had belonged to the Vilayat of Basra in the

Ottoman era. Britain responded with the 1913 agreement with the Ottoman government which included articles about protecting the Ruler of Kuwait, and the fixing of Kuwait's boundaries on existing lines. Baghdad asserted, however, that this agreement had never been ratified. The matter had been raised again, without result, at the time of the formation of the Baghdad Pact in 1955.

Iraq complained that Kuwait did not seem interested in stopping smuggling along the route of the disputed waters; Iraq had trouble in establishing security in the southern areas bordering on Kuwait; Kuwait's refusal to allow Iraq its legitimate outlet in the Gulf had harmed Iraq's economic interests; Kuwait was a base for Egyptian propaganda hostile to Iraq. Baghdad felt that matters of the accession of Kuwait to the Arab Union could no longer be left to the Ruler. If London felt that the accession were not practicable at that time, the Arab Union would find 'itself compelled to announce that all the islands situated in the territorial waters are included in the boundaries of the Arab Union and that the line of the land frontier between the Arab Union and Kuwait begins from the junction of Wadi al-Adja and Wadi al-Batin and runs east in a straight line to Jehara on the Gulf of Kuwait'. The Arab Union recognized the existing oil concessions and financial arrangements 'except as required by the Arab Union to meet its essential financial needs'.[47]

Commenting on this ultimatum Wright observed that the map of the Middle East was being redrawn, and that frontiers and groupings of populations that had been decided by the West without full freedom of choice for those involved, were now being called into question. Nasser and the Communists could redraw that map. Iraq and Jordan were fighting for principles of Arab unity and the maintenance of active friendship with the West. If they succeeded, Lebanon and Kuwait could be saved, and Syria retrieved from Communist influence. Wright felt that if Kuwait were in imminent risk of 'going the way of Syria', 'Iraq might well walk into Kuwait to prevent this happening however hard we might try to prevent her'. The ambassador argued that every Iraqi believed that Kuwait 'ought naturally and historically to be a part of Iraq'. He warned that so long as the uncertainty persisted as to whether aid for Iraq would be forthcoming either from London, Washington, or the Iraq Petroleum Company, the stronger the pressure would be over Kuwait. Nuri was 'taking his usual extreme line' to try to force Britain's hand.[48]

Indeed, on the next day, Nuri threatened to resign as Prime Minister over the budget deficit: the burden of Jordan's increased military budget would fall on Iraq; without Kuwait the Union was going to fail.[49] When Macmillan raised the matter with Eisenhower and Dulles in Washington, the Americans took a poor view over Nuri's behaviour, but agreed to the formation of a United States/United Kingdom sub-committee to prepare a study of how to keep the Arab Union afloat economically for the financial year.[50] Macmillan was anxious that Britain should not let Nuri resign if it could prevent it, but this could not be done at the 'cost of forcing Kuwait into union with Iraq'.[51] A financial package to which the Americans would contribute around $25 million and Britain $4 million was hastily drawn up. The Americans agreed that the Ruler of Kuwait could not be pushed.[52] Macmillan thought the $4 million 'a comparatively small price considering the size of our stake in the Union and the Gulf'.[53] Nuri, on 13 June, in the presence of King Hussein of Jordan, seemed to agree that the Arab Union's immediate budgetary difficulties had to be handled separately from the longer term problem of Kuwait. Nuri, however, at one stage said that if Kuwait could not be brought to join the Arab Union by the end of 1958, Iraq would have no alternative but to claim territorial waters off Kuwait which would give it the resources necessary to balance the budget.[54]

This British dilemma over Iraq and Kuwait was solved by the coup in Baghdad which overthrew Feisal and Nuri. Macmillan learnt of this on the morning of 14 July 1958. This led to the request of the Lebanese President, Camille Chamoun, for London and Washington to honour their undertaking to intervene in Lebanon, and the subsequent Anglo-American invasion of Jordan and Lebanon. With this crisis British and American officials developed their 'joint thinking' about the Gulf and other areas in the Middle East: Kuwait was an area which could and would be held, the oil-fields if necessary with force; a military operation to unseat the rebel regime in Iraq was, however, out of the question. In any case Macmillan suggested that there should not be too great a hurry over Iraq, as the revolutionaries might turn out to be more Iraqi nationalist than Nasserite.[55]

Against this background, a Cabinet committee on 22 July instructed the Foreign Office to prepare a paper on the Middle East which reflected the view that military occupation of Lebanon, Jordan or the Gulf territories, though it might help a short-term settlement, was no solution in the long term; Britain had either to come to terms with the growth of Arab nationalism or, for example, turn the Gulf states 'into territories dominated by ourselves through armed compulsion'. But Arab nationalism was not indivisible, and coming to terms with its growth did not mean the establishment of a friendly relationship with Nasser. Indeed there was much to be said in favour of establishing good relations with the new Iraqi government and building it up as a counterpart to the power of the United Arab Republic. The committee thought that maintaining the independence of Jordan indefinitely was questionable.[56]

On 28 July 1958 at the meeting of the Council of the Baghdad Pact, the American government undertook to co-operate with members of the Pact for their security and defence, and to enter promptly into special agreements designed to give effect to this co-operation. Lloyd told the British Cabinet the next day that this undertaking, which had been incorporated in the public declaration signed by all the countries represented at the meeting, in reality made the United States a full member of the Baghdad Pact.[57]

At the time of the crises in Lebanon, Jordan, and Iraq in July 1958, the United States had, in effect, acknowledged that it had assumed the leadership of the 'Free World' in the Middle East. It was its actions during the Anglo-American invasion of Jordan and Lebanon that showed the extent to which it had taken Britain's place in the Middle East, and filled the vacuum left by the British decline in the area, evidenced in the aftermath of the Second World War, particularly with the end of the Palestine mandate.

Notes

1. Ritchie Ovendale, 'Macmillan and the wind of change in Africa, 1957–60', *The Historical Journal*, **38**(1995), pp. 455–77.
2. Public Record Office, London, FO 371/120571, EA1055/17, 10512/1/56, Stevens to Lloyd, no. 140, Secret, 8 December 1956; FO 371/121238, V1054/162, 10712/76/56, George Middleton to A.D.M. Ross, Personal and Confidential Guard, 20 December 1956.
3. Public Record Office, London, CAB 128/30 pt. 2, fos 728–9, CM97(56)2, Secret, 7 December 1956; FO 371/129327, p. 5, VJ1051/262G, Record of conversation between Lloyd and Dulles in Paris on 10 December 1956; p. 4, Record of conversation between Lloyd and Dulles in Paris on 10 December 1956; *Foreign Relations of the United States* (hereafter cited as '*FRUS*') 1955–7(1), pp. 399–401, Memorandum of conversation in Paris on 10 December 1956.
4. FO 371/121274, V1075/147, Ministerial meetings on United States accession to the Baghdad Pact, 11–14 December 1956; FO 115/4545, 1040/33/56G, Washington to Foreign Office, Telegram no. 2529, Secret, 22 December 1956; 1040/35/56G, Washington to Foreign Office, Telegram no. 2537, Secret, 24 December 1956.
5. Public Record Office, London, PREM 11/1793, Wright to Foreign Office, Telegram no. 1655, Secret, 24 December 1956; M245/56, Eden to Commander Noble, 26 December 1956; Wright to Foreign Office, Telegram no. 9, Secret, 2 January 1957.
6. FO 371/121370, V1197/22/G, Paper on Middle East defence, 26 December 1956; Elie Podeh, 'The struggle over Arab hegemony after the Suez crisis', *Middle Eastern Studies*, XXIX (1993), pp. 91–110.
7. CAB 128/30 pt. 2, fos 777–8, CM1(57), Confidential Annex, 3 January 1957; DEFE 4/94, JP(57)1 Final, Annex, Joint Planning Staff on Anglo-American interests in Libya and assumption of responsibility by the United States, Top Secret Guard, 4 January 1957.
8. *FRUS* 1955–7(12), pp. 410–2, Memorandum from Murphy to Dulles, 15 December 1956; Dwight D. Eisenhower, *The White House Years: Waging Peace 1956–1961* (London, 1966), pp. 178–81; Eisenhower Library, Abilene, Ann Whitman File, DDE Diary Series, Box no. 20, File December 1956 Diary-Staff Memoranda, Memorandum of Conference with Eisenhower, Top Secret, 20 December 1956; FO 371/127739, V10345/2, Caccia to Foreign Office, Telegram no. 30, Secret, 5 January 1957 d r 6 January 1957; FO 371/127753, V1073/1, J.E. Coulson to H. Beeley, Secret Guard, 19 January 1957.
9. CAB 128/30 pt. 2, fos 787–91, CM3(57), Secret, 8 January 1957.
10. PREM 11/1732, Brook to Eden, 14 December 1956; ME(57)1, Secret, 7 January 1957.
11. FO 371/126682, AU1051/15, 1040/4/56, Minute by A. Windham, 16 January

1957; CAB 128/30 pt. 2, fol. 793, CM4(57), Secret, 9 January 1957; CAB 128/31 pt. 1, fol. 24, CC1(57)2, Secret, January 1957.
12. CAB 134/2339, OME(57)7(Final), Secret, 6 February 1957; CAB 134/2338, OME(57)3rd Meeting, Secret, 1 February 1957; OME(57)1st Meeting, Secret, 18 January 1957; OME(57)2nd Meeting, Secret, 31 January 1957; for the situation in Iraq see Wm. Roger Louis, 'The British and the origins of the Iraqi revolution', in Robert A. Fernea and Wm. Roger Louis (eds), *The Iraqi Revolution of 1958: The Old Social Classes Revisited* (London, 1991), pp. 31–61.
13. DEFE 4/94, fos 194–205 at fol. 199, JP(57)8 Final, Top Secret, 24 January 1957; see Ritchie Ovendale (ed.), *British Defence Policy Since 1945: Documents in Contemporary History* (Manchester, 1994), pp. 111–5.
14. DEFE 4/95, fos 163–87 at fos 176–8, JP(57)15(Final), Report by the Joint Planning Staff 'Review of the World Situation', Top Secret, 21 February 1957; fos 200–5 at fol. 205, Responsibilities of the Royal Navy for the Arabian Peninsula, Top Secret, 28 February 1957.
15. FO 371/126843, E10345/1, Minute by A.R. Watson, 7 March 1957.
16. FO 371/126683, ZP5/41/G, Minute by A.R. Walmsley, 17 March 1957.
17. CAB 128/31 pt. 1, fol. 49, CC4(52)8, Secret, 29 January 1957; FO 371/127741, V10345/84, Caccia to Foreign Office, Telegram no. 119, 2 March 1957; Eisenhower, *White House Years*, pp. 186–94; Ritchie Ovendale, *The Origins of the Arab–Israeli Wars*, (2nd edn, London, 1992), pp. 180–1.
18. *FRUS* 1955–7(17), pp. 452–8, Memorandum of a conversation at Bermuda, 21 March 1957; pp. 461–2, Eisenhower Diaries, 21 March 1957, Secret, Whitman Files, Eisenhower Library; CAB 128/30 pt. 1, fol. 171, CC22(57)3, Secret, 22 March 1957; Eisenhower Library, Abilene, Ann Whitman File, International Series, Box no. 3, File Bermuda Conference 20–4 March 1957(1), Summary Briefing Paper, Secret.
19. PREM 11/1838, BC(P)2nd Meeting, Top Secret, 21 March 1957.
20. FO 371/127755, V1075/14, BCC(57)2nd Meeting, Meeting with Canadians on long-term questions and the Middle East, Secret, 26 March 1957.
21. See *FRUS* 1955–7(12), pp. 496–515.
22. CAB 128/30 pt. 1, fol. 231, CC33(57), Secret, 11 April 1957; fos 236–7, CC34(57)2, Secret, 15 April 1957; fol. 244, CC35(57), Secret, 17 April 1957; Eisenhower, *White House Years*, pp. 194–5; Eisenhower Library, Abilene, Ann Whitman File, DDE Diary Series, Box no. 23, File April 1957 Phone Calls, 25 April 1957; *FRUS* 1955–7(13), p. 126, Telegram from Department of State to embassy in Britain, 6 May 1957; CAB 128/31 pt. 2, fol. 301, CC43(57), Secret, 29 May 1957.
23. *FRUS* 1955–7(17), pp. 574–5, Eisenhower to Macmillan, 28 April 1957; Eisenhower, *White House Years*, pp. 191–3.
24. CAB 134/2338, OME(57)17th Meeting, Minute 4, Secret, 3 May 1957.
25. FO 371/127756, V1075/34, Anglo-American talks on Middle East 12–4 June 1957 Agreed Papers, Measures to ensure continued access to Middle East Petroleum Resources; Trevelyan to Caccia, Secret, 18 June 1957.
26. FO 371/127757, V1075/43, J. Bowker to P. Gore-Booth, 19 June 1957.
27. FO 371/127757, V1075/41, Review of Middle East Problems bearing upon the supply of oil to the Free World, Secret, 10 May 1957; *FRUS* 1955–7(12), pp. 548–53, Memorandum from Henderson to Dulles, 20 June 1957.

28. PREM 11/1946, fos 3–5, Letter to Macmillan, 11 July 1957; Minute by Macmillan.
29. FO 371/127757, V1075/39, Minute by J.H.A. Watson, 3 July 1957; DEFE 4/98, fos 137–93, COS(57)57th Meeting, Top Secret, 11 July 1957.
30. CAB 131/18, D(57)4th Meeting, Cabinet Defence Committee, Top Secret, 18 July 1957; CAB 128/35, fol. 383, CC54(57)5, Secret, 18 July 1957; *FRUS 1955–7*(13), pp. 226–7, Macmillan to Eisenhower, 19 July 1957; pp. 228–30, Embassy in Britain to Department of State, 23 July 1957: pp. 230–1, Department of State to embassy in Britain, 24 July 1957.
31. *FRUS 1955–7*(13), pp. 234–5, Memorandum from the Special Assistant for Intelligence (Cumming) to the Acting Secretary of State, 1 August 1957; p. 236, Editorial note, Dulles Papers, Meetings with the President, Eisenhower Library; pp. 237–8, Department of State to Mission at the United Nations, 14 August 1957; pp. 238–40, Memorandum of conversation between Murphy and Caccia, 15 August 1957; pp. 246–7, Editorial Note; Eisenhower Library, Abilene, Christian A. Herter Papers, 1957–61, Miscellaneous Memoranda 1955, Box no. 10, File Presidential Telephone Calls 1957, 14 August 1957.
32. DEFE 4/98, fol. 51, COS(57)83rd Meeting, Top Secret, 24 October 1957; CAB 131/18, D(57)8th Meeting, Cabinet Defence Committee, Top Secret, 30 October 1957; Harold Macmillan, *Riding the Storm 1956–1959* (London, 1971), pp. 270–7; Alistair Horne, *Macmillan 1957–1986* (London, 1989), p. 43.
33. David W. Lesch, *Syria and the United States: Eisenhower's Cold War in the Middle East* (Boulder, 1972), pp. 158–65; Macmillan, *Riding the Storm*, pp. 277–86; Horne, *Macmillan*, pp. 43–5; Eisenhower, *White House Years*, pp. 196–204.
34. CAB 128/31 pt. 2, fos 525–6, CC76(57)2, Secret, 28 October 1957; Eisenhower Library, Abilene, White House Office Central Files, Subject Series Confidential Files, Box no. 74, File Department of State October 1957 Briefing book for Macmillan Visit (1), Position paper on US–UK Policy Differences with respect to Arabian Peninsula, Secret; Box no. 75, File Briefing Book for Macmillan Visit (3), Appraisal of the political and military development of the Baghdad Pact; Ann Whitman File, International Series, Box no. 23, File Macmillan 23–5 October 1957 (4), Memorandum of Conversation on Middle East, Top Secret, 25 October 1957.
35. DEFE 4/101, fol. 192, COS(57)87th Meeting, Top Secret, 14 November 1957.
36. CAB 134/2338, OME(57)32nd Meeting, Minute 1, Confidential Annex, 9 December 1957.
37. *FRUS*, 1958–60(12), pp. 17–32, National Security Council Report, 24 January 1958.
38. Macmillan, *Riding the Storm*, pp. 502–3.
39. PREM 11/2403, Foreign Office to Baghdad, Telegram no. 492, Secret, 22 February 1958.
40. PREM 11/2403, T55/58, United Kingdom High Commissioner in Pakistan to Foreign Office (Lloyd to Macmillan), Telegram no. 89M, Secret, 8 March 1958 r 7 March 1958.
41. PREM 11/2403, Foreign Office to P. de Zulueta, Top Secret, 22 March 1958.
42. PREM 11/2403, Kuwait and the Arab Union, Secret, 14 March 1958.
43. PREM 11/2403, F. Hoyer Millar to Macmillan, Top Secret, 8 April 1958.
44. PREM 11/2403, Foreign Office to Washington, Telegram no. 2288, Secret, 26 April 1958.

45. PREM 11/2403, Baghdad to Foreign Office, Telegram no. 798, Confidential, 14 May 1958.
46. PREM 11/2403, Halford to Foreign Office, Telegram no. 237, Confidential, 27 May 1958.
47. PREM 11/2403, Baghdad to Foreign Office, Telegram no. 977, Secret, 6 June 1958 recd. 7 June 1958.
48. PREM 11/2403, Baghdad to Foreign Office, Telegram no. 989, Secret, 8 June 1958.
49. PREM 11/2403, Baghdad to Foreign Office, Telegram no. 994, Secret, 9 June 1958.
50. PREM 11/2403, Washington to Foreign Office, Telegram no. 1452, Secret, 9 June 1958 d r 10 June 1958.
51. PREM 11/2403, Washington to Foreign Office, Telegram no. 1452, Secret, 10 June 1958.
52. PREM 11/2403, Washington to Foreign Office, Telegram no. 1461, Secret, 10 June 1958; Washington to Foreign Office, Telegram no. 1462, Secret, 10 June 1958.
53. PREM 11/2403, Washington to Foreign Office, Telegram no. 1479, Secret, 10 June 1958.
54. PREM 11/2403, Amman (Johnston) to Foreign Office, Telegram no. 658, Confidential, 13 June 1958 d r 14 June 1958.
55. Ritchie Ovendale, 'Great Britain and the Anglo-American Invasion of Jordan and Lebanon in 1958', *The International History Review*, XVI (1994), pp. 284–303.
56. CAB 130/153, GEN 658/1st Meeting, Top Secret, 22 July 1958.
57. CAB 128/32 pt. 1, fol. 385, CC65(58)3, Secret, 29 July 1958.

8

The Anglo-American Invasion of Jordan and Lebanon

At the Bermuda meeting with Macmillan in March 1957, Eisenhower proposed a joint planning operation between Britain and the United States be undertaken to work out a common Middle Eastern policy between the two countries.[1] 'Useful' Anglo-American talks followed.[2]

An area of concern for this 'Working Group' was Lebanon, a country increasingly split between Muslims and Christians, and pro-Western and pan-Arab sections. Lebanon adjoins Syria on the north and east, Israel in the south, and faces the Mediterranean to the west; between 1937 and 1955, its population grew from 925,000 to 1,466,000. Ruled as a French mandate for 20 years, Lebanon was proclaimed independent on 26 November 1941, effective independence from France being secured by 1945. The new state inherited the 'confessional' system, established in the National Pact of 1943 and based on a census of 1932 which showed a ratio of Christians to Muslims of 6:5, and provided for a Maronite Christian President, a Sunni Muslim Prime Minister, and a Shiite speaker.

Against a background of increasing urbanization, the economy, based on private industries and subject to little government control, flourished. By the mid-1950s, however, discontent erupted amongst the Shiites who had migrated from the rural communities to the cities, especially Beirut. Increasingly, they, along with the Sunnis and Druze, challenged the Christian Maronite ascendancy as represented by Camille Chamoun, who had become president in 1952. Chamoun had accepted the Eisenhower Doctrine for the Middle East and was identified as pro-Western and anti-Nasser; the Sunni Muslims and their allies wanted Lebanon to follow Nasser and a pan-Arab policy.

In June 1957, Chamoun staged parliamentary elections, which the opposition claimed had been manipulated so as to ensure a Chamber that would renew Chamoun's presidential term due to expire the following year.[3] The Anglo-American 'Working Group' proposed, in October 1957, that the British and American representatives at Beirut should give Chamoun certain assurances, and ask whether he could envisage a situation arising in which an appeal might be made to Britain and the United States to intervene militarily in Lebanon. The British ambassador, Sir George Middleton, did not like this suggestion. He and his American colleague thought that the long-term results of an intervention would be bad. Instead they proposed discussing with Chamoun the need to strengthen internal security and to achieve maximum popular support. Any request for military backing could be made contingent on these steps being carried out. Although intervention was not mentioned in the interview between Middleton and Chamoun, the 'Working Group' produced an agreed paper on 'Measures to forestall or counter an anti-Western *coup d'etat* in Jordan or the Lebanon', and the military outlined the Anglo-American forces immediately available for an intervention in Lebanon or Jordan.[4]

Sir Dermot Boyle, the Marshal of the Royal Air Force, told the Chiefs of Staff Committee on 5 March 1958 that the briefs by the Joint Planning Committee should be used only as a capability study, and he was worried about unrealistic plans being evolved in Washington by the 'Working Group'. These planning activities were not even known to some members of the Defence Committee.[5] The briefs covered aspects such as: the provision of air and logistic support for Iraq and Saudi Arabia in the event of a coup in Jordan; further assistance for Jordan including the provision of ground forces; and the provision of assistance by American and British forces to the Lebanese government in the event of a coup. It was the view of the Joint Planning Committee that something had to be done, however small, with the greatest urgency, to assist Jordan, Iraq or Lebanon to counter any attempted *coup d'etat*.[6]

In April 1958, the American Joint Chiefs of Staff hinted that they thought it unnecessary to make further plans on this. The internal situation in Lebanon then deteriorated seriously: strikes and disorders spread from Tripoli to other parts of the country; the Iraq Petroleum Company's pipeline was cut; and following a clash between Lebanese troops and armed intruders, the borders with Syria were closed. The British Cabinet was told that the disturbances were being deliberately fomented by the newly formed United Arab Republic and arms were being covertly introduced into Lebanon from Syria and Egypt. In these circumstances the Chief of the Imperial General Staff, Sir William Dickson, wanted the Americans to resume planning.[7]

The Foreign Office had complained in April of 'a certain dilatoriness' in American Middle East policy. The ambassador at Washington, Sir Harold Caccia, agreed that the Americans had been 'rather slack', and his conversations with Dulles left the Foreign Office with the impression that the Secretary of State was thinking in 'rather an airy way about long-term problems'.[8] Caccia also pointed to the special relationship which had been built up since the Bermuda conference in March 1957 between Macmillan and the Foreign Secretary, Selwyn Lloyd, on the one side and the President and the Secretary of State on the other. If Britain wanted to do anything in the Anglo-American context the Americans might not like, London should talk to Washington first, and as a last resort appeal directly to Eisenhower and Dulles.[9] Before the crisis in Lebanon in May

1958, the Americans on the 'Working Group' had been unwilling to commit themselves to detail, and apart from an indication of the British and American forces, which together might be available for operations in Jordan and the Lebanon, there was no plan of any practical value.[10]

On 13 May, Lloyd told the Cabinet that Chamoun had inquired whether Britain, the United States and France would give military assistance within 24 hours if asked to do so by the Lebanese government to preserve the independence of the country. The Foreign Secretary warned that Lebanon might be forced to accede to the United Arab Republic, and the Cabinet agreed that if Lebanon fell, Iraq and Jordan would probably follow. It was felt the French should be dissuaded as their participation could prejudice the attitude of the Arab states to Western intervention.[11] The Chiefs of Staff were told that the Cabinet felt Britain should be associated with any action, though it was understood the Americans would play the major military role. The Admiral of the Fleet, Lord Mountbatten, pointed to the difficult position of an American commander who held NATO appointments being employed in operations not supported by all the NATO countries, but it was recommended that the British forces should be placed under the American commander in the area.[12]

The Americans also indicated how they were prepared to support Chamoun, and the next day the Chairman of the Chiefs of Staff explained to a meeting of ministers that logistic difficulties meant the American Sixth Fleet could not reach Lebanon for six days. As yet, its commander, Admiral James L. Holloway, Jr, had no instructions. The ministers felt the Americans should send in at least a token force, and even if the British contribution had at first to be the greater, it should be kept as small as possible, and certainly not as much as half the total effort.[13] Once Holloway received his instructions the British and American staffs drew up possible contingency plans involving either the army and air force based in West Germany, or the Sixth Fleet, or both. The proposed British army and air force commandos were in Cyprus and it was suggested that American planners should go there to sort out technical details. Co-operation with Holloway was described as 'excellent'.[14] Macmillan told the Cabinet that the close collaboration with the Americans was 'a clear indication that co-operation between them and ourselves had been re-established'.[15]

The Lebanese government seemed to regain control, but Lloyd warned there might still be civil war if Chamoun insisted on seeking another term of office.[16] Towards the end of June Sir Roger Bower, the Commander-in-Chief Middle East Land Forces, explained to the Chiefs of Staff that conditions had changed: there might be opposition from the Muslim elements of the army; the Christians might not help as they were scared of reprisals; with the assistance of the United Arab Republic the number of armed insurgents was estimated to have risen from 11,000 on 2 June to 14,500; and Tripoli was no longer under government control. The Anglo-American operation needed to be revised to include landings at Tripoli. Holloway, present at the meeting, explained that his information was how the situation was steadying, and a spokesman from the Foreign Office pointed to the possibility of a United Nations force.[17] The Secretary General, Dag Hammarskjöld, was reluctant. The Cabinet felt the United Nations should be forced to take more positive action.[18]

At the beginning of July ministers agreed that a situation originally envisaged in terms of foreign subversion had developed into a civil war. It was important that Lebanon remain an independent state. Continued pressure from the United Nations, combined with the threat of intervention from the Western powers, could force an acceptable solution on the opposing factions. The Cabinet felt that Britain, in concert with the United States, should try to ensure Chamoun was succeeded by an individual likely to maintain Lebanon in general alignment with the West.[19] Sir Pierson Dixon, the British delegate at the United Nations, argued against the idea of trying to obtain Security Council approval, or the two-thirds majority in the General Assembly, prior to an Anglo-American invasion of Lebanon.[20] In Washington, senior members of the Near East Bureau objected to the proposals for additional landings at Tripoli and Sidon: the extra forces would make ultimate disengagement more difficult; a three-pronged landing would look more 'imperialistic'; a landing in Beirut could encourage the Lebanese security forces to assert themselves outside Beirut.[21]

Early in the morning of 14 July Macmillan learnt there had been a *coup d'etat* in Iraq. The initial information was confused. Lloyd told the Cabinet that King Hussein of Jordan, who had just successfully quelled a similar revolt, had declared himself head of the Arab Union of Jordan and Iraq. Within the next 24 hours Chamoun would ask Britain and the United States to honour their undertaking to intervene in the Lebanon. The Americans had indicated they were willing, and would report their action retrospectively to the Security Council. They were prepared to act alone, and suggested that the British contingent envisaged for the operation could be kept in reserve for use elsewhere in the Middle East, if necessary.[22]

In Washington it was Eisenhower who opposed British participation: the American forces would be adequate; the British troops could be kept in reserve for places where congressional disapproval might hinder the despatch of American forces. Dulles told a conference of military and State Department personnel that it was preferable for the United States to go into Lebanon, and for Britain to go into Iraq and Kuwait. Eisenhower insisted that the United States act: the alternative was to get out of the Middle East entirely. Hussein's action had made it easier for Britain to intervene. Towards the end of the meeting, Dulles observed that many would say the United States was simply doing what it had stopped the British and French from doing at the time of Suez. There were differences, but these would be hard to put across.[23]

Sir William Dickson, the Chairman of the Chiefs of Staff, before knowing the American reaction, had advised his colleagues that the initiative should be left to the United States. Indeed the Foreign Office representative, Sir William Hayter, suggested that as Lebanon was of importance principally as a bulwark for Iraq, if Iraq had gone over to Nasser there would be little point in taking military action to support Chamoun.[24] The Cabinet Defence Committee, exercised over the possibility of British troops being required to maintain stability in Jordan, concluded that from the military point of view any operation in Lebanon should be left to the Americans, apart, possibly, from a small token British contribution. British forces could then take the initiative elsewhere in the Middle East, though, except for the Gulf where British interests were paramount, it was desirable that any such actions should be part of a joint Anglo-American plan.[25]

Discussion in the Cabinet focused on the danger of disorder in Jordan if nothing were done in Lebanon, and the subsequent isolation of Israel, Turkey and the Gulf. It could then be too late for the West to retrieve its position in the Arab world by intervention. Members also saw advantages in accepting the American offer to intervene in Lebanon alone: there would be less danger to the British oil interests at Tripoli; the French could be more easily dissuaded from participating; there would be more time to get support from other members of the Commonwealth. There was the risk that if the United States restored order in Lebanon, it could leave Britain on its own in Jordan and Iraq. A token British contingent should be offered for Lebanon, and if this were refused, the Americans should be made to understand that the whole enterprise of establishing political stability in the Middle East was a joint task which they shared with Britain.[26]

Dulles reassured the British chargé in Washington that the suggestion did not reflect a preference for the Lebanese operation to be a purely American affair, but was essentially a matter of military assessment. In view of Britain's special relations with Iraq and Kuwait, British troops might be more appropriately employed there. If British troops did participate in Lebanon the Secretary of State hoped that London would keep adequate troops in reserve to use elsewhere. Washington would help Britain with supplies of oil if the Middle East pipelines were cut.[27] Eisenhower elaborated when he spoke to Macmillan over an open telephone line: the Americans had decided to implement the joint plan; the British contingent of about 3,700 was towards the rear of the procession; in view of the situation in Iraq, Britain might want to keep those troops in reserve and modify the plan unilaterally. The Prime Minister insisted that the Lebanese operation should be seen as part of a joint attempt by Britain and the United States to restore order to the Middle East. Eisenhower realized that they were opening Pandora's box and did not know what would be at the end of it, but insisted that beyond Lebanon he needed to ask for authority to act. The Prime Minister referred to the 'little chap' in Jordan who needed help: Macmillan did not 'want to be left sitting in this tuppeny ha'penny place. It is worth nothing, but nothing'.[28]

Hussein, on 14 July, initially requested American military intervention, should it prove necessary, to preserve the integrity of Jordan. The king told T.K. Wright, the American chargé in Amman, that, as yet, a similar request had not been made to Britain as he particularly wanted to make sure of American support. Hussein spoke of assembling loyal units of the Jordan Arab Army and marching into Iraq to restore order.[29] The Cabinet Defence Committee considered the logistic difficulties of flying troops into Jordan. Previous Jordanian objections to aircraft flying in from Israel might fade, and the best method of obtaining permission from the Israeli government for overflying its territory should be considered.[30] The ambassador at Amman, Charles H. Johnston, had been away for some time, but was returning immediately. On 15 July he told the Chiefs of Staff that if requested to do so Britain should assist Hussein. Johnston doubted whether Israel would take aggressive action.[31]

On the night of 14 July the Cabinet was informed that Hussein had asked Britain and the United States to provide him with assistance should he judge it necessary. The Cabinet favoured such intervention sooner rather than later, while the airfields were in government control. The balance of advantage lay in accepting the American offer to be released from contributing to the Lebanese operation, provided that Washington understood this did not absolve it from actively co-operating with Britain to restore the situation in Iraq and Jordan. London would look to Washington for moral and material assistance, and needed a firm undertaking of support to sustain Hussein.[32] Macmillan wrote to Eisenhower personally on the issues: Britain could handle the Gulf itself but hoped that both countries would be prepared to protect Jordan with the hope of restoring the situation in Iraq; the 'wider issues' had to be faced together. The Prime Minister wanted immediate action in Jordan. Britain could use the forces that had been earmarked for Lebanon and he wanted to know what the Americans could make available.[33] Dulles' immediate reaction to these messages was that there was no plan for giving military assistance to Jordan, and, in any case, he wondered whether Anglo-American military intervention might not alienate Hussein's remaining support. As Macmillan agreed with Eisenhower that British troops intended for Lebanon should be kept in reserve, that should be the decision provided that it were militarily feasible.[34]

The American landings in Lebanon on 15 July had, as Ian D. Scott the British chargé in Beirut observed, some 'curious sidelights'. Chamoun had not dared to tell the military commander, General Fuad Chehab whose loyalty was possibly doubtful, of the imminent arrival of the United States marines. Chamoun asked the American ambassador, Robert M. McClintock, to enlighten Chehab. The ambassador did this an hour and a half before the marines were due to land. The general thought the decision highly regrettable, and said that it made his own position much more difficult as he had guaranteed the ability of the army to provide necessary protection for the country. The American landings would seriously undermine his prestige, and prejudice his future usefulness.

McClintock was persuaded, and instructed the American military attaché to go by launch to the flag ship of the Naval Force and try to prevent the landings. Colonel Stines was ten minutes too late: the first parties were already ashore. McClintock had just returned to his embassy when Chamoun telephoned to say that a military coup was expected within the next half hour, and asked for marines to be sent to the palace within ten minutes. This was not possible: the first men were only then stepping ashore several miles away. But McClintock did telephone Chehab who admitted that a coup might be about to happen. At the request of the American ambassador, the Lebanese general unhesitatingly countermanded it.[35] There was not the slightest opposition to the first wave of American landings, and the British chargé reported that the only reaction in Beirut had been '*feu-de-joie* on the part of the Christian armed gangs in various parts of the town and a rush to the landing beaches by coca-cola and chewing-gum purveyors'. The movement of troops provided the 'happiest occasion Beirut has had for two and a half months. Crowds flocked out to watch and enjoy the spectacle'. All was quiet in Tripoli where Macmillan had warned Eisenhower that oil installations might be sabotaged.[36] The cruiser, *Sheffield*, and two destroyers, however, stayed out of sight but ready to enter Tripoli to evacuate British nationals.[37]

The Cabinet, after being informed how the landings in Lebanon were taking place without British support, and that Eisenhower would ask an emergency meeting of the Security Council to establish a United Nations force there, found the American reaction to the British proposal for immediate action in Jordan disappointing. Members were worried that the American force in Lebanon could be withdrawn after a temporary occupation, and Britain could be left alone to deal with the situation in Jordan and Iraq. They felt Britain should not give a definite commitment to Jordan until it became clear later that day whether the Americans had resolved the legal and political difficulties which appeared, for the moment, to be inhibiting them from joining Britain in giving Hussein the assurance he had asked for.[38] In the meantime the French indicated they would not become involved, and probably would only send in troops to Beirut to protect their embassy and save it from the fate of the British one in Baghdad.[39]

The British embassy at Tel Aviv was instructed to approach the Israeli Prime Minister, David Ben-Gurion, for permission for Britain to overfly Israeli territory: it was, after all, in Israel's interest that Nasser's progress be halted.[40] The Jordan Arab Army envisaged that with the presence of British land forces and the Royal Air Force, Jordanian land forces could be released to enter Iraq and rally tribes and loyal elements of the Iraqi army. This would need Western air cover. Another thought focused on how to bring down the regime in Syria.[41]

London waited on Washington: it hinted that the situation in Iraq might be retrievable; Western forces in Lebanon and Jordan could help to restore the West's position in the Arab world; and there was the danger that the Israelis might feel it necessary to do something violent on their own and re-open the Arab–Israeli conflict.[42] The American administration was preoccupied. When Dulles did see the British chargé, Lord Hood, the Secretary of State complained he was not sure what the purpose of intervention in Jordan would be: was it hoped that it would re-establish the situation in Iraq or rouse the tribes in Syria? Dulles thought Iraq the central problem, and the British were the experts on that. In any case, after the American intervention in Lebanon, Hussein seemed to be in control. The Department of State concluded that the motives of Jordan and Britain were too unclear to allow any conclusion by the United States. There was, furthermore, not only these questions of motives, but of the adequacy of British resources to mount and sustain the despatch of military forces to Iraq without military, or at least, logistical as well as financial assistance from Washington.[43]

Britain began to consider acting on its own. Macmillan met Duncan Sandys, the Minister of Defence, and the Chiefs of Staff. It was decided that the object of a landing in Amman would be to secure the airfield and support the king and the government of Jordan. Operations would have to be confined to the Amman area because of lack of logistic support. Provided a reply from Eisenhower met the main political objective that any British action in Jordan should be part of a joint Anglo-American plan for the whole Middle East, Hussein should be urged to ask for military assistance at once.[44] Macmillan telephoned Hood and asked what was the possible American reaction to a holding operation in Jordan. The chargé thought it would not be 'hostile', though he admitted that Dulles had considerable doubts. He reassured the Prime Minister that the American authorities were friendly and understood his frankness. Macmillan hoped they realized the burden this placed on Britain with the pressure on the pound and the possibility of the oil pipelines being cut: Britain had much more at stake in the area than the United States.[45]

On 16 July, Dulles explained that the Americans would not be able to respond to the Jordanian request themselves. He did not know whether there were American troops available. It would be politically impossible for his government to order such an action anyway, as congressional leaders had been told by Eisenhower only two days previously that there were no plans for sending American forces anywhere but the Lebanon. All that Washington could do was stage a demonstration flight over the Lebanon, Israel and Jordan. This would take place the following day and might deter the United Arab Republic from launching any operation against Jordan.[46]

That same day Macmillan told the Cabinet that the Chiefs of Staff had completed plans for moving two battalion groups of the Parachute Brigade to Amman, and for reinforcing them, if necessary, with the First Guards Brigade. The Prime Minister said that Britain's legal right to deploy troops in Jordan in the prevailing circumstances could not be questioned. He had been advised that Jordan's request should be based, in the first place, on the need for assistance in preserving law and order, and, in the second, on the imminence of a threat to Jordan's independence and integrity. The Cabinet liked the proposal that Lloyd and Dulles should meet, and suggested London and Washington should quickly agree a favourable reply to Hussein's request for assistance from the two governments.

As yet Tel Aviv had not given permission to overfly Israeli territory,[47] but the Cabinet was told that the Israeli government was unlikely to offer serious objections. The Israeli ambassador, Eliahu Elath, told F.R. Hoyer Millar, the Permanent Under-Secretary, that he was 'reasonably confident' his government would agree to Britain's request for overflying rights. The ambassador thought Jordan occupied the key position in the Middle East and the sooner assistance was given the better.[48] The military agreed that intervention of the sort envisaged was feasible, but the Cabinet was told how it was desirable that Washington should provide material support from the outset, particularly large troop-carrying aircraft, and, if possible, heavier armaments and equipment. Macmillan said the Foreign Secretary and the Chief of the Defence Staff would go immediately to Washington with the objective of securing an undertaking from the Americans to give, as well as politically endorse, the maximum of material support in providing military assistance for Hussein, and would also collaborate on planning a joint policy to retrieve the situation in the Middle East.[49]

Later that day the Cabinet was told that Amman had made a formal request for the immediate despatch of British and American forces: Jordan was faced by an imminent attempt by the United Arab Republic to create internal disorder and to overthrow the regime; Jordanian territorial integrity was threatened by the movement of Syrian forces; Amman believed that an insurrection fomented by the United Arab Republic would begin the following day and hoped that some British troops would arrive in the early part of that day.[50] Hussein had indicated that he would agree to Anglo-American forces overflying Israel to get to Jordan.[51]

Macmillan telephoned Dulles from the House of Commons. If time allowed for the formulation of a joint Anglo-American plan Dulles, on his own authority, promised logistic support. There would be public moral support, but congressional authorization would be needed for military action. The Secretary of State also offered a demonstration flight by American aircraft over Jordan. But Dulles did hope that events might allow London to defer action until he had talked to Lloyd.

Arguments in the Cabinet in favour of intervention focused on the need for immediate action to prevent Jordan falling under the influence of the United Arab Republic, which could jeopardize Britain's position in the Gulf. The action would be reported to the United Nations and Britain would be in at least as good a position as the United States over the Lebanon. Logistic support could be expected from the Americans as the situation developed. There were advantages in the intervention being worked out by Lloyd in Washington in an agreed Anglo-American plan, but it was unlikely that Washington would be able to commit itself any further within the next few days, and so there was little to gain from delay.

The case against intervention pointed to the reality that only limited objectives could be secured as the forces were ill equipped for any heavy fighting. The operation might spread disaffection in the Jordanian army. The Cabinet favoured sending British troops, but Macmillan wanted to talk to Dulles again. The Secretary of State reiterated his previous assurances and caveats. The Prime Minister then told the Cabinet that the intervention would be a 'quixotic undertaking': 'It would, however, be an honourable one and the political risks in this country were nicely balanced.' A 24-hour deferment would not make a decision any easier. The Cabinet agreed that a British military force should be despatched forthwith to Amman.[52]

Israel sanctioned the proposed demonstration of American aircraft over its territory and Jordan. But there was no reply from Tel Aviv to London's request for permission to overfly Israel. The British operation from Cyprus started. The explanation offered by the Foreign Office to the ambassador at Tel Aviv was that when it was learnt there would be some delay before the Israeli government could reply to the British appeal it was decided to postpone the operation for some hours. Early in the morning on 17 July the Israeli ambassador at London was told of this by telephone. It was further explained that although orders for postponement had been given, London thought it too late to stop the first aircraft which was on its way. It was hoped that that plane would be allowed to cross Israel without undue difficulty. In fact it was also too late to stop the next five aircraft, although the Foreign Office claimed that was not known at the time. The Israeli ambassador contacted Tel Aviv. Macmillan sent a personal plea to Ben-Gurion, emphasizing the British decision had the full support of the American government. On British initiative Washington gave the government of Israel the assurance that it fully supported the British intervention in Jordan.

The first British aircraft disregarded Israeli orders to turn back and arrived to a friendly reception in Jordan. It was followed by others and the British force there totalled four hundred. But the operation had to be suspended. Macmillan was prepared to tell parliament the reason that afternoon. Then the message came from Ben-Gurion complaining that the sovereignty of his country had been violated. He explained that the Israeli reply to the British request had been delayed as they wanted assurances of American approval and responsibility. These had been forthcoming, and Ben-Gurion consequently consented to the requested passage of 1,500 troops. After this the movement of British troops into Jordan was completed.[53]

Macmillan sent a message to Eisenhower saying that his great consolation was that 'we are together in these two operations in Lebanon and Jordan'.[54] When Lloyd saw the President, the Foreign Secretary emphasized the psychological advantages of American troops being alongside British. Eisenhower foresaw difficulties with congress, but said that 'if it comes to real fighting then of course we will deal with it together'. He promised Britain full logistic support, not only for the economy of Jordan but to sustain the British military effort. The Foreign Secretary had the impression that both 'Foster and the President regard the Lebanon and Jordan as combined Anglo/American operations'.[55]

Over the next few days Lloyd, Dulles and other American officials developed their 'joint thinking' about the Gulf and other areas in the Middle East: Kuwait was an area which could and would be held, the oil-fields if necessary with force; a military operation to unseat the rebel regime in Iraq was out of the question.[56] Macmillan suggested there should not be too great a hurry over Iraq: the revolutionaries could turn out to be more Iraqi nationalist than Nasserite.[57] On

18 July the American President wrote to the British Prime Minister that their two countries' 'thinking on common problems is identical'. The operations in Jordan and Lebanon were satisfactorily co-ordinated, and the President felt it most important that the Gulf remained within the Western orbit.[58]

Eisenhower honoured his undertaking to provide logistical support for the operation in Jordan. The American authorities paid Shell and BP for the initial supplies of oil scheduled to reach Aqaba on 22–23 July.[59] Washington also made possible the alternative supply line when the Israeli government objected to the continued overflying of its territory. On 18 July Sir F. Rundall, the ambassador at Tel Aviv, warned that the Israelis were suffering from bruised sovereignty and it was important to handle them with care and take nothing for granted.[60] That evening Ben-Gurion proposed to the ambassador a working partnership with Britain of the sort that already existed with France. The Israeli Prime Minister referred to his earlier proposals along these lines in February 1951 when he had suggested that 'in an emergency Israel should act "as if" she were part of the British Commonwealth and should be regarded by Great Britain in exactly the same way'.[61] Ben-Gurion emphasized to Rundall that he wanted not only an alliance but 'a close working relationship'. Britain's 'stand-off' policy had to change: it was humiliating that Britain should ask to overfly Israel at short notice; Israel should be able to get arms and tanks from Britain. The Anglo-Israeli partnership needed to be worked out at the highest level in its military, political and intelligence aspects.[62]

On 21 July Macmillan told the Cabinet Defence Committee that Israel had requested that the overflying of its territory should cease forthwith. There was no immediate alternative, but the committee recommended Washington should provide logistic support for the alternative route from Cyprus via the Suez Canal to the Gulf of Aqaba.[63] Not even the full Cabinet was told of Ben-Gurion's demand; on advice, Lloyd explained Israeli objections to British transport overflying their territory as probably being a reflection of division of opinion in the coalition government.[64] Ben-Gurion reiterated his request for a partnership to Randolph Churchill,[65] and the ambassador at London stressed the growing concern of the Israeli people over the implications of the flights, and said that Israel needed a guarantee for its borders.[66]

This Israeli intransigence coincided with what London viewed as a worsening situation in Jordan: a coup could face Britain with the alternatives of a humiliating withdrawal or participating in a civil war. Macmillan asked Eisenhower for the 'political reinforcement' of American troops alongside British on the ground. As British troops in Jordan only had supplies for 12 days, and the Israelis were objecting to the British overflights, Macmillan also wanted the Americans to take on the air lift and to carry the essential supplies in American aircraft to which the Israelis would have less political objections. The Prime Minister explained the Israeli attitude in terms of Ben-Gurion's political difficulties with his colleagues and the opposition, rather than revealing the Israeli Prime Minister's ploy to secure a partnership with Britain.[67]

Lloyd emphasized to Dulles the need to hold on in Lebanon and Jordan until there was a settlement in both places.[68] The British defence staffs started to plan for an alternative supply route through Aqaba, first using the Suez Canal and then Aden.[69] Eisenhower, conscious of the likely reaction of public opinion and congress to his taking any further steps, suggested that British forces had already stabilized the situation in Jordan. He did, however, agree to supplies being flown from Cyprus to Amman in American Globemasters, and Dulles approached the Israeli embassy about this. But the Americans thought this could only be a temporary solution[70] and their planners worked with British colleagues on the Aqaba route. This was at a time when a British Cabinet committee looking at future planning for the Middle East doubted whether a military occupation of the Lebanon, Jordan or the Gulf would provide any solution in the long-term, though it was thought it could establish a favourable climate for a short-time settlement.[71]

Britain wanted the United States to transport aviation fuel, employ one American LST (Landing Ship Tank) on the Cyprus–Aqaba run, and, until the Aqaba line of communication was working, the United States Air Force should provide the maximum possible contribution to the air lift.[72] Macmillan passed the British requirements to Dulles when the Secretary of State was in London on 27 July. On that occasion Lloyd stressed the need for Jordan and Lebanon to be dealt with simultaneously, as Britain would be left in a difficult position if the Americans withdrew from Lebanon while British forces were left in Jordan.[73] An informal working committee was established with the British embassy in Washington to co-ordinate the American logistical assistance for the British operation in Jordan. With considerable difficulty Dulles managed to get clearance for overflights from Israel for 'a few days', but these were scheduled to end after 6 August and the American military felt that they could not undertake a general commitment on this because of the Israeli clearance problem.[74]

After a meeting with Lloyd, Sandys, and military and Foreign Office officials on 1 August, Macmillan concluded it was necessary to send a further battalion to Jordan to secure the new lines of communication to Aqaba and also to strengthen the British position in Amman. Israel, under pressure from Moscow but probably trying to secure a Western guarantee, insisted that the air lift over its territory should cease, and the extra battalion of Cameronians went in through Aqaba.[75]

American State Department officials were gloomy about Jordan and doubted whether it could be held.[76] The American chargé in Amman, Wright, could not see how either the United States or the United Nations could underwrite a monarchy which depended simply on Bedouin bayonets.[77] But Dulles reassured Lloyd that he did not think it desirable or inevitable that Hussein should collapse: Jordan was an artificial creation and dependent on extensive subsidies; the reason for its existence was the dangerous situation which would exist if it did not.

The Foreign Secretary used this opportunity to push the request Hussein had made for help in equipping and raising two new Bedouin brigades.[78] Hussein threatened that he could not continue unless he had the assurance of military and financial support for the following two years. The Americans thought that there was a considerable element of 'the screw' in this.[79] When pressed on the matter of a British contribution Macmillan minuted: 'It will be cheap if it helps to get our troops out.'[80] The Americans agreed to give 'a very large sum' – around $50,000,000 – to support Jordan until the following April; Britain contributed £1,000,000 and the cost of the moorings at Aqaba.[81] In effect Washington had honoured the promises Eisenhower had made to Macmillan in the middle of July.

The British and American withdrawals from Lebanon and Jordan were made possible by the United Nations. Towards the end of July, the Soviet Union suggested that a special session of the Security Council attended by the heads of government should consider the situation in the Middle East. They then proposed a special session of the General Assembly.[82] Partly through the skill of Selwyn Lloyd an Arab resolution was unanimously adopted on 21 August. This asked the Secretary General to make practical arrangements for upholding the principles of the Charter in relation to Lebanon and Jordan, and to bear in mind the assurances that the Arab countries should respect each other's systems of government, and all United Nations members' obligations not to interfere in each other's internal affairs.[83]

Macmillan had been worried that an American withdrawal from Lebanon could leave Britain 'on a hook' in Jordan.[84] This did not happen. The Americans were able to start withdrawing from the Lebanon: Chehab had been elected President, but had been forced to appoint the leader of the opposition party and a friend of Chamoun as Prime Minister. The final departure of American troops on 25 October was hardly noticed. The situation in Jordan stabilized, and after reading the report of the Secretary General and the assurances given by the Arab countries that they would abide by the resolution of 21 August, the Cabinet agreed that British troops could start departing on 20 October. The last troops left on 2 November.[85]

At the end of 1958 the Cabinet's Official Middle East Committee presented discussion papers on future British policy in the Middle East. These regarded the primary threat to British interests in the Middle East: that of Arab nationalism. Soviet, or communist, influence or control of Middle East countries was viewed as a secondary threat. The Middle East Committee concluded that it seemed probable how the use of force against Arab nationalism in the Middle East, which involved bloodletting on any significant scale, could not serve British interests. There was an opposing view that Britain, with the support of the United States if anything more serious than a police action were contemplated, should always be prepared to use military force to protect its interest. That view maintained that the Anglo-American action in Lebanon and Jordan in July 1958 was proof of the effectiveness of such action. With this in mind, the Joint Planning Staff of the Chiefs of Staff Committee recommended that London should be prepared to consider with Washington the conditions under which force could be used in the Middle East to prevent a country from coming under complete Soviet domination.[86]

The Anglo-American invasion of Jordan and Lebanon achieved what it set out to accomplish. Sir George Middleton, the British ambassador at Beirut, however, predicted in his valedictory despatch that the American landings had only confirmed the basically 'confessional' nature of the conflict: 'Lebanon must now by its nature bow to the prevailing wind and henceforward this will blow from Arab lands and not from the West.' He thought that his successor could well witness 'on an infinitely smaller scale, something like the last days of Constantinople'.[87] Chamoun, himself, said that the American intervention had 'not made the slightest difference'.[88] But Eisenhower wrote to Macmillan about his satisfaction in 'the successful accomplishment of undertakings of wide and historic significance'.[89] Macmillan replied that throughout the operations he 'was personally greatly fortified by the knowledge that we and the United States were moving in complete harmony of purpose'.[90] In the wider context the Anglo-American invasion of Jordan and Lebanon in 1958, marked the assumption by the United States, of Britain's traditional role in the Middle East. In the early 1950s Britain had assumed the responsibility for the Middle East in allied defence policy and global strategy. Even then it did not have the resources with which to fulfil the role. Dulles and State Department officials realized this. Straitened financial circumstances led to Macmillan supervising a major retreat by Britain from world responsibilities. In the age of the hydrogen bomb, the Middle East was no longer of the same strategic significance to Britain as it had been in the immediate post-1945 period. The question was who could assume Britain's place at a time when its interests in the area were confined principally to the Gulf and Aden? Britain wanted the United States to take over. This change was eased by Eisenhower's revival of the special relationship which he had discarded when assuming office. This renewed relationship was outstandingly managed at the top by Eisenhower, Macmillan, Dulles and Lloyd. In effect the 1958 crisis marked the transition to the United States effectively playing the dominant role in the area, even to the extent of assuming financial liability for Jordan, but with the full co-operation of Britain. It was 'America in Britain's place'. But this was what Britain wanted.

Notes

1. Public Record Office, London, FO 371/127756, V1075/15, OME(57)14th Meeting, Secret, 29 March 1957.
2. FO 371/127757, V1075/37, Minute by W. Hayter, 17 June 1957.
3. See Helena Cobban, *The Making of Modern Lebanon* (London, 1985), pp. 87–94.
4. FO 371/134156, VL1073/2/G, Minute by E.M. Rose, Top Secret, 9 May 1958; Public Record Office, London, CAB 128/32 pt. 1, fol. 252, CC42(58)1,

Confidential Annex, 13 May 1958.
5. Public Record Office, London, DEFE 4/105, COS(58)21st Meeting, Confidential Annex Specially Restricted Circulation, 5 March 1958; COS(58)25th Meeting, Confidential Annex Specially Restricted Circulation, 18 March 1958.
6. DEFE 6/49, JP(58)16(Final), Specially Restricted Circulation, 21 February 1958.
7. FO 371/134156, VL1073/2/G, Minute by E.M. Rose, Top Secret, 9 May 1958; CAB 128/32 pt. 1, fol. 252, CC42(58)1, Confidential Annex, 13 May 1958.
8. Public Record Office, London, PREM 11/2403, F.R. Hoyer Millar to Macmillan, 8 April 1958.
9. FO 371/132330, AU1051/3/G, D.S. Laskey to F.A. Bishop, Top Secret, 3 April 1958.
10. CAB 130/147, GEN649/16, Brief on British and American Planning in the Middle East, Top Secret, 4 June 1958.
11. CAB 128/32 pt. 1, fos 252–3, CC42(58)1, Confidential Annex, 13 May 1958.
12. DEFE 4/107, COS(58)40th Meeting, Confidential Annex, 13 May 1958.
13. PREM 11/2386, Meeting of Ministers, Top Secret, 14 May 1958.
14. PREM 11/2386, WFD 41, Sandys to British Joint Services Mission Washington, Top Secret Emergency, 14 May 1958; WFD 42, Sandys to British Joint Services Mission Washington, Top Secret Emergency, 14 May 1958; DEFE 4/107, COS(58)43rd Meeting, Confidential Annex, 16 May 1958; COS(58)44th Meeting, Confidential Annex, 16 May 1958.
15. CAB 128/32 pt. 1, fol. 263, CC43(58)6, Confidential Annex, 15 May 1958.
16. CAB 128/32 pt. 1, CC44(58)2, Confidential Annex, 21 May 1958.
17. DEFE 4/108, COS(58)52, Confidential Annex, 20 June 1958.
18. CAB 138/32 pt. 2, fol. 296, CC49(58)1, Confidential Annex, 24 June 1958.
19. CAB 138/32 pt. 2, fol. 312, CC51(58)3, Secret, 1 July 1958.
20. FO 371/134156, VL1073/6/G, Dixon to Hayter, Top Secret, 1 July 1958.
21. FO 371/134156, VL1073/7/G, M.S. Weir (Washington) to E.M. Rose, Top Secret and Personal, 3 July 1958.
22. CAB 128/32 pt. 2, fol. 325, CC55(58), Confidential Annex, 14 July 1958.
23. Dwight D. Eisenhower, *Waging Peace* (London, 1966), pp. 269–73; *Foreign Relations of the United States* (hereafter cited as '*FRUS*') 1958–60(11), pp. 211–15, Memorandum of conference with Eisenhower, 14 July 1958.
24. DEFE 4/109, COS(58)59th Meeting, Confidential Annex, 14 July 1958.
25. CAB 130/151, D(58)12th Meeting, Top Secret, 14 July 1958.
26. CAB 128/32 pt. 2, fos. 325–6, CC55(58), Confidential Annex, 14 July 1958.
27. FO 371/134158, VL1092/1/G, Hood to Foreign Office, Telegram no. 1891, Emergency Top Secret, 14 July 1958; Eisenhower Library, Abilene, White House Office, Office of the Staff Secretary, 1952–61, Subject Series State Department Subseries, Box no. 3, File State Department May–August 1958 (4), Dulles to Eisenhower, Top Secret, 15 July 1958.
28. FO 371/134159, VL1092/17/G, Record of Telephone Conversation between Eisenhower and Macmillan at 10.30 p.m. on 14 July 1958, Top Secret.
29. PREM 11/2380, Mason to Foreign Office, Telegram no. 813, Top Secret, 14 July 1958.
30. CAB 130/151, D(58)12th Meeting, Top Secret, 14 July 1958.
31. DEFE 4/109, COS(58)60th Meeting, Confidential Annex, 15 July 1958.
32. CAB 128/32 pt. 2, fol. 330, CC56(58), Confidential Annex, 14 July 1958.

33. PREM 11/2380, T280/58, Foreign Office to Washington (Macmillan to Eisenhower), Telegram no. 4477, Emergency Top Secret, 15 July 1958; T281/58, Foreign Office to Washington (Macmillan to Eisenhower), Telegram no. 4478, 15 July 1958.
34. PREM 11/2380, Hood to Foreign Office, Telegram no. 1904, Emergency Top Secret, 14 July 1958 d 15 July 1958.
35. FO 371/134159, VL1092/37, Scott to Rose, Guard Secret, 17 July 1958; 134158, VL1092/6, Scott to Foreign Office, Telegram no. 1011, Immediate, 15 July 1958.
36. FO 371/134158, VL1092/4(B), Scott to Foreign Office, Telegram no. 1011, Immediate, 15 July 1958; *FRUS* 1958–60(11), p. 253, Telegram from McClintock to Department of State, 16 July 1958.
37. FO 371/134158, VL1092/4(B), Foreign Office to Beirut, Telegram no. 1814, Secret, 15 July 1958.
38. CAB 128/32 pt. 2, fol. 333, CC57(58), Confidential Annex, 15 July 1958.
39. FO 371/134158, VL1092/9/G, Jebb to Foreign Office, Telegram no. 345, Secret Emergency, 15 July 1958.
40. PREM 11/2380, Foreign Office to Tel Aviv, Telegram no. 332, Emergency Top Secret, 15 July 1958.
41. PREM 11/2380, Mason to Foreign Office, Telegram no. 831, Emergency Top Secret, 15 July 1958.
42. PREM 11/2380, Foreign Office to Washington, Telegram no. 4506, Emergency Top Secret, 15 July 1958.
43. PREM 11/2380, Hood to Foreign Office, Telegram no. 1916, Top Secret, 15 July 1958; *FRUS* 1958–60(11), pp. 303–4, Memorandum for the record of a meeting, Department of State, 15 July 1958.
44. PREM 11/2380, J.M. Wilson to Macmillan attaching a note on Military Assistance for Jordan, Top Secret, 16 July 1958.
45. PREM 11/2380, Record of a Telephone Conversation between Macmillan and Hood at approximately midnight, 15/6 July 1958.
46. PREM 11/2380, Hood to Foreign Office, Telegram no. 1930, Emergency Top Secret, 16 July 1958.
47. CAB 128/32 pt. 2, fos. 337–8, CC58(58)1, Confidential Annex, 16 July 1958.
48. PREM 11/2380, Foreign Office to Tel Aviv, Telegram no. 348, Top Secret, 16 July 1958 d 17 July 1958.
49. CAB 128/32 pt. 2, fos. 337–8, CC58(58)1, Confidential Annex, 16 July 1958.
50. CAB 128/32 pt. 2, fol. 342, CC59(58), Confidential Annex, 16 July 1958.
51. PREM 11/2380, Mason to Foreign Office, Telegram no. 844, Top Secret, 16 July 1958.
52. CAB 128/32 pt. 2, fos 342–5, CC59(58), Confidential Annex, 16 July 1958; PREM 11/2380, Record of a Telephone Conversation between Macmillan and Dulles at approximately 1 a.m. on 17 July 1958.
53. CAB 128/32 pt. 2, fol. 348, CC60(58), Confidential Annex, 17 July 1958; PREM 11/2377, Foreign Office to Tel Aviv, Telegram no. 366, Top Secret, 18 July 1958; T288/58, Foreign Office to Tel Aviv, Telegram no. 356, Emergency Top Secret, 17 July 1958; T289/58, Salt to Foreign Office, Telegram no. 327, Emergency Top Secret, 17 July 1958; Macmillan's diary in Alistair Horne, *Macmillan 1957–1986* (London, 1989), p. 96.

54. PREM 11/2380, T293/58, Foreign Office to Washington (Macmillan to Eisenhower), Telegram no. 4723, Secret, 17 July 1948.
55. PREM 11/2380, T298/58, Hood to Foreign Office (Lloyd to Macmillan), Telegram no. 1943, Top Secret, 17 July 1958 d 18 July 1958.
56. PREM 11/2380, Hood to Foreign Office, Telegram no. 1944, Top Secret, 17 July 1958 d 18 July 1958; Hood to Foreign Office (Lloyd to Macmillan), Telegram no. 1946, Secret, 17 July 1958 d 18 July 1958.
57. PREM 11/2380, T308/58, Foreign Office to Washington (Macmillan to Lloyd), Telegram no. 4794, Top Secret, 18 July 1958.
58. PREM 11/2380, T316/58, Walworth Barbour to Macmillan (Eisenhower to Macmillan 18 July 1958), Secret, 19 July 1958.
59. PREM 11/2380, Minister of Power to F.A. Bishop, 18 July 1958.
60. PREM 11/2377, Rundall to Foreign Office, Telegram no. 343, Secret, 18 July 1958.
61. Ritchie Ovendale, *The English-Speaking Alliance: Britain, the United States, the Dominions and the Cold War 1945–1951* (London, 1985), p. 132.
62. PREM 11/2377, Rundall to Foreign Office, Telegram no. 352, Emergency Top Secret, 19 July 1958.
63. CAB 131/20, D(58)38, Top Secret, 21 July 1958.
64. PREM 11/2377, Bishop to Macmillan, Undated; CAB 128/32 pt. 2, fol. 374, CC64(58)3, Confidential Annex, 24 July 1958.
65. PREM 11/2376, P. de Zulueta to Macmillan, 25 July 1958.
66. PREM 11/2377, Extract from Record of Conversation between Elath and Macmillan on 6 August 1958.
67. PREM 11/2380, Foreign Office to Washington, Telegram no. 5030, Emergency Top Secret, 22 July 1958; T342/58, Foreign Office to Washington (Macmillan to Eisenhower), Telegram no. 5031, Emergency Top Secret, 22 July 1958; Rundall to Foreign Office, Telegram no. 399, Top Secret, 24 July 1958.
68. PREM 11/2380, Foreign Office to Washington (Lloyd to Dulles), Telegram no. 5032, Emergency Top Secret, 22 July 1958.
69. PREM 11/2380, Bishop to Dennis S. Laskey, Secret, 23 July 1958; M258/58, Macmillan to Sandys, Top Secret, 23 July 1958.
70. PREM 11/2380, Hood to Foreign Office, Telegram no. 2034, Top Secret, 23 July 1958; T348/58, American Embassy London to Macmillan (Eisenhower to Macmillan 23 July 1958), 24 July 1958.
71. CAB 130/153, GEN 658/1st Meeting, Policy in the Middle East, Top Secret, 22 July 1958.
72. PREM 11/2380, Pao/P(58)17, Principal Administration Officers' Committee to Sandys, Top Secret, 26 July 1958.
73. PREM 11/2380, V1078/18G, Record of Meeting between British and American officials, 27 July 1957; T356/58, Macmillan to Dulles, Secret, 27 July 1958; T357/58, Dulles to Macmillan, 28 July 1958.
74. PREM 11/2380, T366A/58, American Embassy London to Macmillan (Dulles to Macmillan) 1 August 1958, Top Secret, 3 August 1958.
75. PREM 11/2380, Note by P. de Zulueta, Secret, 1 August 1958; Foreign Office to Amman, Telegram no. 2535, Top Secret, 4 August 1958.
76. PREM 11/2381, Hood to Foreign Office, Telegram no. 2140, Secret, 4 August 1958; de Zulueta to Macmillan, 5 August 1958.

The Anglo-American Invasion of Jordan and Lebanon 215

77. PREM 11/2381, Johnson to Foreign Office, Telegram no. 1268, Secret, 12 August 1958.
78. PREM 11/2381, Dixon to Foreign Office (Lloyd to Foreign Office), Telegram no. 847, Secret, 14 August 1958.
79. PREM 11/2381, Dixon to Foreign Office (Lloyd to Macmillan), Telegram no. 929, Secret, 20 August 1958 d 21 August 1958.
80. PREM 11/2381, Bishop to Macmillan, 22 August 1958; Minute by Macmillan, 22 August 1958.
81. PREM 11/2381, de Zulueta to Macmillan, 4 September 1958.
82. CAB 128/32 pt. 2, fol. 399, CC67(58)1, Secret, 12 August 1958.
83. Harold Macmillan, *Riding the Storm 1956–1959* (London, 1971), p. 532.
84. PREM 11/2388, T400/58, Foreign Office to New York (Macmillan to Lloyd), Telegram no. 1654, Confidential, 13 August 1958.
85. CAB 128/32 pt. 2, fol. 445, CC73(58)2, Secret, 29 September 1958.
86. DEFE 6/52, JP(58)169(Final), Top Secret, 17 December 1958.
87. PREM 11/2389, VL1015/596, Middleton to Lloyd, no. 129, Confidential, 27 August 1958.
88. FO 371/134159, VL1092/48, I.D. Scott to R.M. Hadow, Confidential, 17 September 1958.
89. PREM 11/2389, T565/58, American Embassy London to Macmillan (Eisenhower to Macmillan, 3 November 1958), Confidential, 4 November 1958.
90. PREM 11/2389, T567/58, Foreign Office to Washington (Macmillan to Eisenhower), Telegram no. 7865, Confidential, 7 November 1958.

9

The Defence of Kuwait

The crises of July 1958 led to Britain raising the issue of military consultation and planning in the Middle East with the United States. In response, Dulles proposed that the two countries should examine urgently the situation in the Gulf, Libya, Sudan and Jordan. The existing liaison should be developed in London between the British military, and Admiral James L. Holloway, the Commander-in-Chief of United States Naval Forces, Eastern Atlantic and Mediterranean.[1] The agreed planning studies were to take into account the special relationship London enjoyed with the Sheikhdoms in the Gulf, and the special relationship the United States enjoyed with Saudi Arabia. Consequently any study was to be confined to 'the co-ordination of independent national operations'. Eventualities to be prepared for included: the Ruler of Kuwait announcing adherence to the United Arab Republic; a coup against the Ruler supported by the bulk of the Kuwait armed forces and the police; a coup in favour of the United Arab Republic and opposed by the Kuwait forces; the direct intervention of Iraqi forces.[2] The Foreign Office preference was for 'individual plans fully co-ordinated' in some areas, particularly the Gulf and Libya where it was in the interests of both Washington and London that Britain should shoulder the main burden.[3]

An American National Intelligence Estimate of 28 October 1958 acknowledged that for some time in the future Britain would probably try to retain its position intact in the Gulf and the Arabian peninsula. This would be done through tactical adjustments and compromises, but Britain would be ready to use force. In the long run, however, Britain would probably be compelled to accept the elimination of its political control, and also the curtailment of its economic prerogatives. Any serious interruption to the availability of oil from the Gulf, on terms favourable to Britain and Western Europe, would have important implications for the United States. It was possible that Washington would find itself facing a Soviet threat aimed at frustrating British action. The loss of the British position would adversely affect the operation of American oil companies, as well as the use by the American navy of British facilities in the area. American air force facilities in Saudi Arabia would also be adversely affected.[4]

Later that year, in November, the Ruler of Kuwait who, as the Cabinet was told, had been assuming progressively greater responsibility for the internal administration of his country, suggested that Kuwait should adhere to certain maritime conventions and the International Telecommunications Union. The Cabinet was warned that if London opposed this it would forfeit the Ruler's goodwill and would appear to be attempting to impose its authority on a country legally independent, although it enjoyed British protection. If Britain allowed the Ruler to develop an international personality of his own 'we could hope to retain his confidence without modifying the substance of our relationship with him'.[5] In January 1959, the Ruler warned that he would have to yield to internal pressures for the establishment in Kuwait of Consuls from Arab states. The balance of opinion of the Middle East Committee of the Cabinet was that it would be less objectionable if Kuwait were to take a more active and independent part in its relations with other Arab states than for it to join the Arab League. The common oil policy of the League could weaken Britain's bargaining position with Kuwait, but the alternative was consuls from states like Egypt and Iraq, and the opportunity for those countries to intervene in Kuwait's internal affairs and to indulge in subversive activities.[6]

In November 1958, the Official Committee on the Middle East considered the paper that the Foreign Office had been instructed to prepare on long-term policy in the Middle East. The second part of that paper emphasized how Britain could not successfully use force in the Middle East without at least moral support from the United States. That support would probably be forthcoming for a bloodless police operation, but it was not certain whether it could be obtained and kept for serious fighting and lengthy occupation. During the crisis over Lebanon and Jordan Dulles had taken 'a strong line about the justice of intervention in Kuwait', and he would probably still support Britain if it took forcible action to defend an important Western interest. But there was the danger that if there were not parallel American involvement, say over the air base at Dharan in Saudi Arabia, and there were a long military occupation, Dulles' personal inclinations could be overridden by pressures from advisers, congressional and public opinion, and the danger of isolation in the United Nations.

This Foreign Office paper, though emphasizing that no order of priorities could be rigid, singled out areas of direct and very great importance to Britain. Kuwait, the largest single source of sterling oil and the holder of considerable reserves of sterling, was listed first; the only other country in this primary category being Turkey as the eastern bastion of NATO. Libya, Sudan, the Horn of Africa, Aden and the Protectorates, Iraq, Iran and the remainder of Britain's position in the Gulf were classed as a direct interest but short of first importance. Lowest in the order of priority and not of direct interest to Britain were Lebanon and Jordan.

The first challenge to British interests the Foreign Office considered was a Nasserite coup in Kuwait with the overthrow of the Ruler and the loss of oil supplies. The paper argued that Britain would have to be able and willing to occupy Kuwait for long enough to secure a political settlement which guaranteed oil supplies on reasonable terms not only from Kuwait but also from the rest of the Middle East. The terms would need to be more favourable than those available before intervention, and it was noted that even permanent occupation of Kuwait, which was not realistic, would necessitate agreement with other oil producing states. Failure to protect important British interests by force would involve a heavy blow to British prestige. The Foreign Office pointed to the wisdom of guarding against this in advance 'by seeking to reduce our obvious involvement in Kuwait, by appearing to take a back seat and encouraging the Ruler to show his independence in various ways'. Britain had an obligation to protect the Ruler in the event of external attack, and it was this obligation which prevented Kuwait from being absorbed. Britain would have to intervene unless an Iraqi occupation had been so swift and the Ruler so slow to ask for help, that Kuwait had ceased to exist before British assistance arrived. There was the important caveat that a prolonged British occupation to preserve the Ruler against a hostile population, involving possibly considerable bloodshed, would exacerbate Britain's relations with the rest of the Arab world and make any satisfactory settlement after withdrawal impossible. There was also the possibility, in the event of Western Europe being starved of oil, of a Western occupation of Kuwait in which Britain, as the power with the nearest available forces, would have to play the principal part. In such a contingency Britain would need to proceed with the full and active support of the United States and the European allies.[7]

A revised version of the first part of the Foreign Office's paper pointed to the need for Britain to adopt a benevolent attitude towards Arab solidarity. But this did not mean Britain should abandon its friends or relinquish its position in the Gulf. Britain should insist that Arab solidarity rested on a relationship between equal and independent partners and not one that was imposed by force or subversion. Following comments by the Chiefs of Staff and Ministers, the areas of primary concern to Britain in the Middle East were extended from Kuwait and Turkey to include Iran and Aden. Britain, in the long term, should take steps towards establishing a relationship with the Middle East which would rest upon mutual cultural and commercial benefits, and should work for increased United Nations involvement in the area.[8]

There were increasing indications of a difference in London and Washington as to whom to back in the Middle East. When the British ambassador at Baghdad, Sir Michael Wright, warned Qasim about the possibility of a Nasserite coup against him, a State Department official seemed annoyed that Britain appeared to be backing Qasim against Nasser. The British view was that Qasim was the lesser evil, but that should Qasim fall further under Communist influence, the situation would have to be reviewed again. London concluded, after Viscount Samuel Hood, the Minister at the British embassy at Washington, had talked to William M. Rountree, the Assistant Secretary of State, that there was not any serious divergence between Washington and London. Should the Americans conclude, however, that Qasim would not be able to maintain his independence against the Communists, then Washington would prefer the success of pro-Nasser forces.[9]

Just before Christmas a meeting of ministers addressed, inconclusively, Britain's position in the Middle East. There was speculation as to advantages of a communist controlled Iraq, against which American help could be rallied alongside Arab nationalist sentiment, over a Nasserite controlled Iraq, which together with Arab nationalism could threaten Britain's interests in Kuwait. The meeting favoured Anglo-American talks on these matters with a view to formulating a joint policy.[10] Indeed, when Macmillan referred the Foreign Office documents to the Middle East Committee, after they had been endorsed by the Official Committee on the Middle East, the Prime Minister emphasized how the Foreign Secretary was anxious it be clear that the Foreign Office had not abandoned the idea of using force in Kuwait if the necessity should arise: provided London acted in full consort with Washington, Lloyd 'did not think that the consequences of using force would necessarily be worse than those of failure to act'.

The preliminary view of the Middle East Committee was that Britain should consider adopting a creative approach as an alternative to disengagement in the Middle East. This would necessitate taking into account the attitude of the oil companies to widening the bases of Arab benefits from oil, and the extent to which the West could support a movement towards Arab unity. It was first necessary to discuss these questions with the Western allies and in particular the United States.[11] The Middle East Committee thought that countries like Egypt would not be willing indefinitely to contemplate small territories like Kuwait accruing vast oil revenues, and that a wider distribution of the revenues might promote stability. Such a plan would need to be prepared by Arab countries, and this might not be in Britain's interests as it could encourage Arab states to create a distribution and marketing system of their own. There were, however, possible advantages in taking more oil from Iran and less from Kuwait, not only to help maintain the present regime in Iran but also because that country might use the revenue to buy goods from Britain whereas Kuwait would just increase its sterling balances.[12] To all this Macmillan insisted that it was not possible to reach decisions in advance about specific action: Britain had to maintain a flexible approach and he favoured joint studies with the American authorities about the aims in the Middle East.[13]

Sir Humphrey Trevelyan, the new British ambassador at Baghdad, wanted Britain to establish, as soon as possible, full diplomatic relations with the United Arab Republic and Saudi Arabia as a means of improving Britain's general position in the Middle East. But he did concede how it was important that it was not thought Britain had switched to a policy of friendship with Nasser to defeat an Iraq which seemed to be going Communist. The Cabinet Defence Committee, on 23 January 1959, favoured meeting Iraq's requests for heavy weapons valued at between £7 and £8 million, as there was the danger that Iraq would turn to the Soviet Union if Britain refused. Macmillan, however, thought it important to secure American concurrence for this move.

Alan Lennox-Boyd, the Secretary of State for Colonies, on 4 February 1959, placed the case before the Cabinet Middle East Committee that the British policy pursued in the Middle East since the Suez crisis of 1956 of two elements – seeking to coexist with Cairo and Baghdad, and at the same time trying to safeguard British oil interests and military facilities and to defend Britain's remaining Middle Eastern friends and allies – made no attempt to fill the power vacuum which had developed in the Middle East with the British withdrawal from Egypt and Iraq. Furthermore, Egypt and Iraq showed little sign of wanting to coexist with Britain or British friends in the Middle East. Lennox-Boyd argued that Arab opinion was formed and led by Cairo, Damascus and Baghdad. Britain could not have forces everywhere all the time, and there was the danger that friendly Arab governments could be overthrown before Britain could come to their rescue. Britain had to have a 'creative approach', in the words of Macmillan, and develop a policy which, while safeguarding its existing interests on the periphery of the Arab world, would also fill the vacuum in the centre. Lennox-Boyd wanted a study made of the likely use of force in the Middle East. He concluded that Britain's policies there needed to be buttressed by a readiness to do a deal with Nasser should he be prepared to accept British terms, and to destroy him if he pursued his career of aggression against Britain's friends.[14]

That same day Lloyd spoke to Dulles about these matters. Dulles explained that Washington had improved its relations with Nasser and thought he was a lesser evil than the Communists, but he was still an evil. The Israelis had accused Washington of wanting to back Nasser, and they felt that a Communist Iraq was less of a threat than the hegemony of the United Arab Republic in the Arab world. Washington wanted to see Iraq pursue an independent line. But the situation was confused, and the State Department favoured a 'hands off' policy.[15]

The Cabinet Defence Committee on 17 February 1959 raised the issue of an approach to Washington about possible joint action in the furtherance of mutual Anglo-American interests in Iraq. Military intervention could jeopardize the supply of oil from Iraq, and possibly the rest of the Middle East, but such action taken in conjunction with the Americans could exercise a favourable influence on the position in Iraq. Britain had still not concluded an agreement with Iraq about staging and overflying rights, and 400 RAF personnel were being kept in unsatisfactory conditions on the base at Habbaniya. The Chiefs of Staff view was that Anglo-American military intervention in Iraq could succeed, provided that it enjoyed Turkish goodwill. The Americans, however, should not be pressed on the matter.[16]

The American National Intelligence Estimate of the same day, 17 February, pointed to Britain's awareness of the danger a Communist-controlled Iraq would pose to Western access to Middle Eastern oil. But British hostility to Nasser had led London to hope that Qasim would be a feasible alternative between a Nasser-dominated and a Communist-dominated regime in Iraq, and an effective rival to Nasser for influence in the Arab world. But there were indications that some parts of the British government were realizing these were futile hopes. The further consolidation of leftist forces in Iraq could increase British sentiment in favour of an effort by Nasser to stop the Iraqi Communists.[17]

The Middle East Committee of the Cabinet, on 11 March 1959, considered Britain's future policy in the Middle East as a prelude to Macmillan's visit to the United States. It was suggested that Britain should adopt a policy of not taking sides in inter-Arab disputes, but should instead rest its association with the Arab world on commercial and cultural links rather than on political and military alliances. Britain needed to reduce its dependence on oil in the Middle East and find alternative sources of supply. Discussion emphasized that the concept of disengagement in relation to Arab countries generally, did not mean that Britain should necessarily remain indifferent if particular countries were threatened. Indeed the British attitude to developments in countries like Jordan and Lebanon, which were of little direct concern to Britain, would be an important factor in retaining British influence in other parts of the Middle East such as the Aden Protectorate and Colony, and the Gulf states, where Britain had important strategic interests. Macmillan pointed to the need for talks with Washington about aims in the Middle East, and military plans for dealing with situations which could arise, particularly in Iraq and Iran. It was necessary to formulate a common policy with Washington on the supply of arms and the provision of aid. Britain had to be ready to face the changes that would come over oil policy. Britain's principal interest in negotiations with the oil producing states would be to retain control of distribution and refining processes.[18] The Americans wanted to continue their 'hands-off' policy towards the Middle East, to wait on events in Iraq, and normalize relations with Nasser. Washington also wanted Britain to improve its relations with Saudi Arabia.[19]

London was becoming increasingly worried that the United States would not continue to support Jordan financially. It was thought that British and American aid would see Jordan through the financial year 1959–60, but Rountree had spoken of Jordan's only hope being in developing relations with its Arab neighbours. The Foreign Office did not hold out much hope of that, and was worried that any act which 'threw the Jordan question into the already troubled witches' brew of inter-Arab relations could well be disastrous'. It could bring about another Arab–Israeli war. Britain had borne the burden of Jordan for many years in the interests of peace and stability in the Middle East and realized how irksome this burden could be. London and Washington had to co-operate on aid proposals 'to keep a friendly and independent Jordan afloat'. From Amman the British ambassador, Sir Charles Johnston, warned that Washington was so preoccupied with the Berlin crisis, and so impressed by Nasser's anti-Communist stand, that the Americans could be expected to follow a 'take it or leave it line' in their talks with the Jordanians. Rountree explained to Hood on 17 March that it was not an acceptable premise on the American side that the independence of Jordan was an essential interest of the United States, and the Americans would not be able to promise any additional funds for Jordan. Jordan, Rountree thought, should be encouraged to improve its relations with its Arab neighbours.[20]

During Anglo-American talks at the end of April Christian A. Herter, who had just become Secretary of State, commented that British and American policies towards Nasser were identical. Both London and Washington would try to regularize their relations with Nasser, but would not try to run after him. There was no question of the Americans discussing massive aid for Egypt. Lloyd was worried that Britain and the United States could drift apart in the Middle East: there was a danger of this if Washington came to regard Nasser as the champion of the anti-Communists in the Middle East. Nasser was more anti-Qasim than anti-Communist. Caccia insisted that he doubted whether the Americans had ever seriously contemplated a policy of embracing Nasser. The State Department, however, was inclined to think that the British outlook on Iraq coloured the British view of Nasser. The Americans had not pressed Hussein to mend his fences with Nasser, and were intending to be generous in their gift of equipment for the Jordanian army.[21]

There was a change of government in Jordan. This brought to the surface resentment on the part of at least one American military official who complained to the British ambassador at Amman, Johnston, that the British had removed a friend of the United States and replaced him by their own man. The American ambassador at Amman, Sheldon T. Mills, proffered the explanation that 'frankly some of his military people were rather "burned up" to see the way the British ran things in the military field here while American paid'. Mills went on to say that he had pointed out to them how the arrangement suited American interests well: the British had 'certain experience and connections here which it was valuable for them to use in the common cause'. If American advisers took over from the British the training of the Jordanian armed forces, this would cost the United States even more. Some American military complained that the British were 'sticking their chests out'. Mills offered to send the complainants to Greece, South Korea or somewhere where the American missions played the leading part, and the British were in a secondary role. Mills, however, explained that Washington's view was that the role of Jordan's army was to maintain internal security. Jordan's protection against external aggression had to be assured by diplomatic means.[22]

Initially the problems of the Gulf were to be considered by the Defence Committee. Lloyd suggested that Britain needed a smaller version of the United States' Sixth Fleet, which was stationed in the Mediterranean, and was capable of deploying its striking power within hours. Arab nationalist sentiment prevented Britain from maintaining adequate troops on land, but nobody minded ships sailing about on the sea. A similar American striking force in addition to the

British one would be better still. The Americans needed to be brought in.[23]

On 13 May 1959 Lloyd discussed the position in Kuwait with Herter. Lloyd thought that the Ruler was more ready to look to Britain for military assistance and, if there were a real threat from Iraq, would ask Britain in even before an attack took place. Washington and London needed to act together, not necessarily in terms of mounting a joint expedition, but in the sense that the British action should be backed immediately by American public support, and Washington should make forces available elsewhere in the Gulf should they be needed, for example in Saudi Arabia. The Anglo-American experience in Jordan and Lebanon of 1958 had to be repeated. Though wary, Herter agreed to give the joint planning on the American side a kick.[24]

Macmillan secured Eisenhower's agreement, at a time when the British Chiefs of Staff were reviewing plans to meet a threat to Kuwait from Iraq, to initiate joint planning along the lines of the contingency plan prepared for Lebanon in 1958.[25] The State Department consented to Britain informing the Deputy Ruler that Britain was in touch with the United States about plans for the defence of Kuwait provided that Kuwaitis understood there was no specific American commitment to Kuwait.[26] Herter was advised that Washington could give assistance to Kuwait in terms of the Eisenhower Doctrine for the Middle East.[27]

The Ruler, shaken by public demonstrations in Kuwait in February which proclaimed the revolution, seemed more sensitive to the need to clean up his administration and to check apparent corruption and inefficiency. He was also more alive to the need for reassurances from Britain about guarantees to meet a potential Iraqi attack. On 25 May the official responsible for defence in Kuwait, Sheikh Abdullah Mubarak, met British military representatives in Bahrain under the chairmanship of Sir George Middleton, the Political Resident in the Gulf. Mubarak was told that Britain needed a four-day warning period; any call for assistance had to come at the earliest possible time so Britain could reach Kuwait before the Iraqis attacked. The beneficial effect of Britain being able to stockpile weapons in Kuwait was touched on.[28]

Duncan Sandys, the Minister of Defence, pointed out that at that time it would take 24 days to assemble the necessary forces and thus it would not be practicable to reconquer Kuwait by direct assault if it were suddenly invaded and occupied. In the last resort Britain would have to try regaining Kuwait by an air attack on Iraq. Even with the support of the Americans that would be a risky operation, and, as pointed out by the Commonwealth Secretary, Lord Home, it would be difficult to carry world opinion. Britain needed to adopt measures to act quickly in the Gulf, and this was seen as a 'higher priority than anything else'. Air-conditioned quarters might be needed at Sharjah, which would be a considerable expenditure. It might be a precaution to provide the Kuwaiti government with tanks, but the tanks would have to remain in hands friendly to Britain.[29]

Britain needed to stockpile ammunition and some heavy equipment in Kuwait, and have some troops there to form the basis of an intervention force.

The Ruler was sensitive to the political implications for the Arab world of such a British presence. He questioned A.S. Halford, the British Agent, about the number of experts needed to service tanks. Halford doubted whether the Ruler knew what a Centurion tank was.[30]

British efforts to involve the Americans met with limited success. Macmillan wanted vigorous action to lead the American authorities to be prepared gradually to participate, if necessary, with Britain in joint operations in the Middle East, particularly in Kuwait and Iran.[31] As the American planning staffs were not, initially, authorized to participate in the preparation of joint plans, Lloyd raised the matter with Herter at Geneva on 28 August, the result of which was an agreement that both sides should prepare independent national plans in the first place, and then compare and modify them. An annex would be produced outlining facilities which each side had that they could offer to the other.[32]

Following the collapse of the Baghdad Pact when Iraq withdrew in March 1959, Washington's relationship with its successor, the Central Treaty Organisation (CENTO) made up of Turkey, Iran, Pakistan and Britain, remained equivocal. The same reasons were given for not joining CENTO as had been given for not joining the Baghdad Pact. With Pakistan moving closer to the Soviet Union, the original political intention of CENTO receded, and the organization concentrated more on economic planning and co-ordination.[33]

In October 1959, a paper on the future of Anglo-American relations drawn up by the Permanent Under-Secretary's Department, pointed to potential differences between London and Washington in the Middle East. It was argued that the American interest was overwhelmingly absorbed by the Communist threat, and how they tended to regard everything else of subordinate importance. Two other problems figured large in British thinking: radical nationalism and the security of oil supplies. These differences were reflected in the attitudes towards Nasser and Iraq. It was also latent in the attitudes on Yemen, and could affect views on Syria, particularly if Syria resumed its historic role in Egyptian–Iraqi rivalry. It also affected views on the future of Jordan. Other sources of difference were: the American involvement with Saudi Arabia; Britain's special responsibilities in the Arabian Peninsula; and the relative weights of financial responsibility for keeping Jordan afloat. But the experience since the Bermuda conference of March 1957 had shown that these differences of emphasis, if carefully handled, need not result in fundamental policy divergences. London and Washington had 'a common interest in stability, in checking the growth of Communism, the survival of Israel, peaceful evolution rather than violent change, stable relations between oil companies and producing countries, access to oil on acceptable terms, and the economic development of all countries in the area'. It was also thought safe to forecast that the Arab–Israeli problem need never in the future be a source of Anglo-American friction.[34]

In November 1959 the Chiefs of Staff revised the plans for intervention in Kuwait, and this was known as Operation Vantage. With the inclusion of a parachute battalion, increased air transport capability, and better stockpiling arrangements, the speed of intervention and the rate of the build-up were improved. The plan, however, did require contingent authority in the event of Iraqi aggression against Kuwait for action against targets between Basra in Iraq and the Kuwaiti border, and also on the airfields at Basra and Shaiba. As the parachute battalion was to be based at Cyprus, this obviated the envisaged expensive construction of quarters at Sharjah.[35] There were, however, no plans for re-entering Kuwait should it be occupied by Iraq: at a meeting at Chequers in October 1960 it was pointed out that the British plans envisaged intervention in Kuwait only by invitation of the Ruler, and that British forces were not designed to recapture it after a successful Iraqi occupation.

In February 1961 Macmillan referred this matter to the Defence Committee. Lord Home, who had replaced Lloyd as Foreign Secretary, thought that, as any such operation would need at least the agreement of the Americans, this was a chance to encourage Washington to be more forthcoming than it had been the previous year and to agree to joint planning rather than co-ordinated planning in the Middle East. Home and Watkinson, the Minister of Defence, had altercations over the matter. In April Home agreed that work could be deferred on plans to reconquer Kuwait from the Iraqis until plans for prior intervention had been completed. Watkinson insisted that an assault on Kuwait, following an Iraqi occupation, would take at least eight, and in some circumstances 16 to 25 days to mount. It was suggested that if it remained the military view that plans to dislodge the Iraqis by British forces alone would be unrealistic, and as Home did not want to drop his proposal, then the right course was for him to persuade the Americans, possibly more amenable to the idea after the Bay of Pigs fiasco, of the advantages of joint planning.[36]

In July 1960 the Defence Committee raised the issue whether Britain should maintain a capacity to intervene in Kuwait and elsewhere in the Gulf if Britain lost Aden as a base. The Ministry of Defence advised that if it were thought that Aden would be lost in the last few years of the 1960s, detailed plans for an alternative strategy would have to be worked out.[37]

From the British Residency at Bahrain, Sir George Middleton recommended a new approach: the future of the Western Gulf seemed to lie in Saudi Arabia. British policy:

> should be political rather than military and be designed as a holding operation and a period of preparation for the time when the old Saudi Arabia emerges as a more modern Arab state to take our place in the Gulf; and during this interim period we should concentrate on developing the Gulf States politically and economically so that their people can be first and not third class citizens in the new Arabia.

Middleton's views were scorned in the Foreign Office. A.R. Walmsley commented on the Resident's assumption that Britain could leave behind it a friendly and well-organized Arabia:

> If we could be confident that this was possible we should revise our thinking

fundamentally on Anglo-Saudi relations, starting with Buraimi. Hitherto we had taken the view that our departure from the Gulf would be comparable to that of the departure of the Romans from Britain, and that there is no parallel with our departure from the Indian sub-continent or parts of Africa where we were able to count on friendly and viable successor states. I still fear that this sombre comparison is nearer the truth than the Political Resident's rosy picture.

Any reliance on the United Nations would be both unsound and dangerous. Walmsley thought it dangerous to even think of telling the Ruler of Kuwait that he would have to rely on help other than British.[38]

At this time the Ruler of Kuwait showed further restlessness over the apparent British tutelage and, following the British agreement in 1959 to Kuwait applying to join the Arab League, pressed for the reduction or termination of British jurisdiction. In Kuwait, as in the other Gulf states, Britain had the right of jurisdiction over British subjects and almost all other foreigners. The Cabinet agreed that there was little alternative to Britain accepting a gradual reduction of its jurisdiction, but hoped that this would be in step with the introduction of reforms.[39] London began to prepare for initiatives to modify the 1899 Agreement, something it increasingly conceded was 'anachronistic' – the words of Norman Brook, the Secretary of the Cabinet – but there was some concern as to whether other Gulf states might want to follow Kuwait's example.[40]

J.C.B. Richmond, who had served as the Political Agent in Kuwait since October 1959, was an Arabist, a man who respected the Ruler's own views and who kept interference by the Agency in Kuwait's affairs to a minimum. Richmond, in March 1961, warned the Foreign Office against a British policy in Arabia that could be construed as divide and rule in the Arab world, and hoped that it was still London's intention to give cautious encouragement to efforts to unify the Arab world, and that the sooner that happened the greater the chance of the area remaining outside the Iron Curtain. Richmond doubted a reading of the Ruler's intentions which suggested that he attached primary importance to British military protection of Kuwait. The Political Agent, looking back to the role of Sir Percy Cox in 1923 in ameliorating border disputes, suggested that the Ruler was thinking more in terms of a visit 'by a new Sir Percy Cox to settle (this time in Kuwait's favour!) a frontier dispute with the Saudis, than of a successful military operation like the airborne landing in Jordan in 1958'. Given also his contacts with other officials in Kuwait, Richmond insisted that it was misleading to suggest that the British decision to maintain its military capability to intervene in defence of Kuwait's independence was a response to Kuwait's wishes. He also pointed out that Kuwait was already aligning its oil policy with those of other oil-producing states. It was deceptive therefore to suggest that, provided Kuwait's political independence was preserved, the flow of oil to Western markets and also the continued investment of Kuwaiti financial surpluses in London were assured.

In the Foreign Office A.R. Walmsley doubted whether Richmond understood the difference between a relationship of military protection, and one, however friendly, lacking the military element. A shift from one to the other would involve a fundamental review of British policy in the area.[41] London largely ignored the views of its man on the spot. After all Kuwait was seen as being of the utmost importance for Britain, indeed listed as an area of great interest in the Middle East in envisaged long-term policy.

Edward Heath, the Lord Privy Seal, when informing the Cabinet on 13 April of the Ruler's request that the Exclusive Agreement of 1899, under which London had assumed responsibility for the external affairs of Kuwait, be replaced by an instrument reaffirming friendship and support, said that there would be no change in the military and financial arrangements. Heath explained that there were three possible alternatives: first, the exchange of notes abrogating the 1899 Agreement which would be accompanied by an oral and unpublished assertion that Britain recognized its continuing obligation to assist in maintaining Kuwait's independence; secondly, an exchange of notes which stated that the abrogation of the 1899 Agreement did not affect Britain's obligation to maintain the independence of Kuwait; thirdly, a formal treaty recording the same obligations subject to ratification. Macmillan was worried that other Arab states could be offended by the conclusion of a formal treaty between Britain and Kuwait.

In the paper he submitted to the Cabinet, Heath acknowledged that the agreement of 1899 did not itself establish that Kuwait was under British protection. That had been first stated in a letter from the Political Resident in the Persian Gulf to the Ruler of Kuwait of 3 November 1914 that 'conveyed the recognition of the British Government that the Sheikhdom of Kuwait was an independent Government under British protection'. This was reaffirmed in an unpublished letter of 21 October 1958 from the Political Agent in Kuwait to the Ruler that Britain would 'continue to be ready, as in the past, to provide any support which may be necessary in connexion with Kuwait's relations with other countries'.[42] Britain did not have the right of uninvited intervention, and it was thought that the Ruler would not agree to any such suggestion.[43]

The Ruler, with an eye to criticism from Arab states, insisted that a form of words which Heath regarded as 'less consistent than was customary in instruments constituting a defence commitment' be used: 'nothing shall affect the readiness of Her Majesty's Government to assist the Government of Kuwait, if the latter request such assistance'. The Ruler further suggested that the title Political Agent in Kuwait be changed to that of Consul-General. The Ruler would be able to apply for membership of the United Nations, an application which Britain had undertaken to sponsor, and to join the Arab League.[44]

Letters were exchanged between the Political Resident in the Gulf, Sir William Luce, and the Ruler on 19 June 1961. The four points of these letters – abrogation of the 1899 Agreement, reaffirmation of close friendship, consultation on matters of mutual interest, and the terms of British assistance – did not change Kuwait's international status. A public statement had been made in March 1960 that Kuwait was fully responsible for the conduct of its international relations. But 19 June was celebrated as Independence Day.[45]

In Iraq the leader, Qasim, reacted. Until that time the revolutionary government in Iraq had given every indication that it recognized the separateness of its 'brotherly' neighbour; indeed this had been the term used in connection with the signing of a trade agreement between Iraq and Kuwait in May 1961. Iraq had welcomed Kuwait's membership of the International Labour Organisation, and acknowledged its foundation membership of the Organisation of Petroleum Exporting Countries. In April 1961, however, Qasim, scorning a rumour that Kuwait would join the Commonwealth, had spoken of there being no boundaries between Iraq and Kuwait. Then, on 25 June, at a press conference in Baghdad, Qasim announced, in effect, his claim to Iraqi sovereignty over Kuwait, appointing the Ruler as Qaimmaqam (prefect) of the district of Kuwait in the Basra province. If the Ruler misbehaved he would be considered as a rebel: 'Kuwait was part of Iraq and no one could behave despotically with the rights of the Iraqi people.'

Commenting on Qasim's motives, the British ambassador at Baghdad, Sir Humphrey Trevelyan, speculated that he had probably hoped to manoeuvre Kuwait into joining Iraq but that his hand had been forced by the 19 June agreement. Initially Trevelyan reported that although he could not rule out military action, Iraqi opinion held that peaceful action would be tried first by Qasim. But, later, when considering whether Qasim did have plans for mounting an internal coup in Kuwait, and in view of the Arab reaction supporting the Ruler, initially from Saudi Arabia, and then later from the United Arab Republic and Jordan, it would be difficult for Qasim to send troops into Kuwait without an invitation. But Trevelyan stressed that 'we should leave Qasim in no doubt that if he attacks Kuwait, he will have to deal with our forces'.

Trevelyan, however, thought that it was preferable, from a political point of view, that Arab States should take the lead in defending Kuwait. If Britain sent troops into the Sheikhdom as a precautionary measure, there was the danger that Iraq could penalize British interests. There was every reason to defer putting British troops into Kuwait 'provided we are satisfied we can get them there in time if Qasim attacks', and Trevelyan acknowledged how that last possibility could not be excluded.

On 28 June, Trevelyan, alarmed by developments including press campaigns, was firm: Britain had to be sure that Qasim realized if he attacked he would meet British forces in strength; those British forces had to be there to meet him. Later that day Trevelyan reported information revealing Qasim's intention to build up in Basra a striking force suitable for an attack on Kuwait. He acknowledged that military requirements might make it necessary to put British troops into Kuwait for deterrent and defensive purposes, and asked for warning of such a move.[46]

From Kuwait Richmond, on 26 June, warned that British moves to defend Kuwait could give Qasim a propaganda advantage and win him the support of

Arab states, but if his intentions were military there was a danger in the British government failing to take precautions early enough. London asked Richmond to counsel the Ruler that it seemed unlikely Iraq would fight, but provocative statements should be avoided.

The Ruler asked for a formal assurance of support. London sent a message reaffirming its determination to carry out all the obligations entered into with the exchange of letters of 19 June 1961. If thought essential by the Ruler this message could be published, though there were worries that Qasim could regard such a move as provocative. The Ruler was anxious that HMS *Bulwark*, fortuitously in the area, should be seen to be visible in Kuwaiti territorial waters. On 29 June Richmond was instructed to inform the Ruler that the latest information showed that Qasim was preparing for an early military attack. The Ruler should make a formal request for British assistance. Tank crews would then be sent to activate the eight Centurions in Kuwait. HMS *Bulwark* would arrive off Kuwait on 1 July.[47]

Macmillan was advised that an armed clash with the Iraqis could lead to the loss of British oil interests in Iraq. If Qasim were defeated he could be overthrown, but it was difficult to tell whether a successor regime would be better or worse from the British point of view. If Britain allowed Kuwait to go, the other Sheikhdoms would no longer rely on Britain. It was not in the interests of the Egyptians or the Saudis to allow Iraq to annex Kuwait.

Home told the Cabinet on 29 June that in response to the possibility that Qasim would shortly move armoured forces to Basra, precautionary measures by British forces were already underway. Discussion in the Cabinet stressed the need for the clear and public support of the American government. The previous day Home had reminded Dean Rusk, the American Secretary of State, of action which Britain and the United States could take separately or together in an area the security of which was crucial to both countries. Home was able to tell the Cabinet on 30 June that Washington would give full political support if military action by British forces became necessary. The Ruler had made the formal request for assistance and so the plans for providing military support could go ahead.[48] Sir H. Caccia, the ambassador at Washington, reported that the State Department was anxious 'to keep out of the matter so far as possible'. The department felt that London was better qualified to give private advice to the Ruler and that the situation was also best kept in an inter-Arab context.[49]

After seeing the Ruler on 30 June, Richmond reported that the Kuwaitis were 'clearly anxious that British moves should go ahead as quickly and openly as possible'. At the same time Trevelyan warned from Baghdad that Qasim, if he could not get Kuwait easily by military measures, could decide to do just enough to make Britain put troops into Kuwait 'in order to convert an inter-Arab quarrel into a first-class anti-British issue'.[50]

Macmillan later, on 3 July, informed the Cabinet that during 30 June 'information had been received which indicated that Iraqi forces were making preparations which would enable them to launch an attack on Kuwait at short notice'. As Prime Minister, he had consulted the ministers most directly concerned, and decided that Britain should place certain forces at the disposal of the Ruler of Kuwait. The first contingent, including No. 42 Royal Marine Commando, a squadron of Centurion tanks and ten Hunter aircraft had arrived in Kuwait on the morning of 1 July. Over the ensuing weekend the build-up of forces had continued. There was thought to have been a serious risk that the Iraqis might have occupied the city of Kuwait on the night of 30 June. The position of the British forces had remained precarious until 3 July. Initial refusal of the Turkish government to allow aircraft to overfly Turkey, and then the permission given on 31 June for night flights only, had resulted in delays. Macmillan reported, however, that British forces had reached a strength which should enable them to deal with the likely scale of attack, and would be reinforced over the following few days. HMS *Bulwark* would provide logistic support. There was, however, the danger of it being exposed to attacks by Iraqi motor torpedo boats. The aircraft carrier HMS *Victorious* was due in the Gulf on 7–8 July and would provide improved air cover. The services, the Prime Minister observed, had adapted prearranged plans. Indeed the revision of Vantage, the plan code named Bellringer, was still under preparation.

Home speculated further. Should Iraq not use force, the affair would become the subject of international debate. Britain would have to retain its force in Kuwait pending suitable arrangements for Kuwait's security which might mean the provision of a United Nations force. It was possible that Iraq could strike on 14 July, Independence Day, and there was some evidence that Qasim had originally intended an attack on that day before the 19 June notes of exchange.[51] Home also pointed out that Commonwealth countries and the United States, informed in advance of British action, had supported the British action.[52]

Washington had offered more. On 1 July Rusk told Caccia that a small United States task force, Solent-Amity, was steaming northwards off the East African coast near Mombasa. The force comprised two destroyers and small landing craft including one LST (Landing Ship Tank) loaded with equipment but not tanks, and carried 500 marines. The force could be ordered to Bahrain to join an American destroyer already there, and could arrive by 5 July. Rusk explained that the State Department had doubts over the introduction of an American force into an area where there was no American commitment and would appreciate British views on this. The next day Rusk telephoned to say that on the prevailing evidence a United States staff study suggested that Solent-Amity need not proceed to Bahrain.

Macmillan responded gratefully mentioning 'the comfort which we draw from the knowledge that the United States has forces in the area'. But Home elaborated on 'nicely balanced' considerations: the presence of Solent-Amity in the area of Kuwait could show 'the solidarity of American support in a manner which we would greatly welcome'; on the other hand the Kuwaiti case would already be before the United Nations, and an American force especially sent to the area as distinct from the American destroyers already there, could make it easier for the Arabs and Soviets to argue that this was 'a joint imperialist manoeuvre'. Home hoped that Solent-Amity would continue to steam north, and that the situation could be reviewed before the force reached Bahrain. Indeed, it had already been noted in the press that Solent-Amity had changed course, and was proceeding towards the Gulf. London thought that the most useful help Washington could provide would be for the destroyer at Bahrain to proceed to the north of the Gulf and make a reconnaissance there of possible Iraqi maritime activities. There were reports of 12 Motor Torpedo boats – some of which had Soviet crews – at Basra, and suggestions of Iraqi troops being sent to Fao, all of which could indicate an intention to mount a maritime adventure. British naval forces were 'thin'. This reconnaissance would help, particularly if, in addition, the second American destroyer in the area could be moved from Aden to Bahrain.

Rusk, however, wondered whether the proposed destroyer reconnaissance might not be regarded 'as a blatant United States intrusion into affairs in which they were not as yet directly involved'. He felt that the Soviets should not be encouraged in any way to escalate the affair. After consulting President J.F. Kennedy at Hyannis Port by telephone, Rusk reported that Solent-Amity would continue steaming northwards for the next 24 hours by which time it was hoped there would be an agreed decision about its destination. In addition it was felt that the suggested naval reconnaissance would have to be at very close quarters, and aerial means would be preferable both from a military and political point of view. Macmillan thought there was no need to press the Americans on this.

Following discussions with Harold Watkinson, the Minister of Defence, and the Chiefs of Staff, he suggested to Rusk that as Qasim had not attacked the previous evening, and as the build-up of British forces was proceeding satisfactorily, to avoid giving the Soviets and Arabs the pretext of making accusations of joint imperialist manoeuvres and even the opportunity for Russian intervention in some form, it was no longer necessary to suggest that Solent-Amity should continue to approach the Gulf. The Prime Minister also understood the American hesitations about reconnaissance and, in any case that situation had been improved by the arrival of another Royal Navy frigate in the area. Britain had been 'greatly heartened' by the renewed offer of American support. Washington had independently reached the same conclusions, and orders were given to Solent-Amity to resume normal operations.[53]

The Arab response to Kuwait's plight was later described by Richmond as 'sluggish'. Only Saudi Arabia offered military assistance, and its motives could be described as questionable in view of the border disputes. On the other hand Trevelyan, the ambassador at Baghdad, had suggested on 29 June the despatch to Kuwait, at the Ruler's request, of a token force of Saudi Arabian troops so that Qasim would have to fight Arabs. As London did not have diplomatic relations with Saudi Arabia, as a consequence of the quarrel over the Buraimi oasis, it asked Washington on 29 June to urge King Saud to help restrain the Iraqis. This Washington did at the same time as giving its full political support to Britain.

Sir William Luce, the Political Resident in the Gulf, who arrived in Kuwait from Bahrain on 1 July and effectively took over from Richmond, saw the Ruler that same day, and gave his personal opinion that the acceptance of a token Saudi Arabian military force might have some political value as proving that Kuwait had Arab support and was not totally dependent on Britain. Luce said that a contingent of any size could present military difficulties, and the Ruler was insistent that overall command should be British. A military mission of around six Saudi Arabian officers had arrived earlier that morning. Further reinforcements arrived on 7 July.[54]

Before its military operation Britain was worried that the Security Council could be approached to prevent it from taking precautionary action in Kuwait. In the view of Richmond, Kuwait acted 'prematurely' on 1 July in asking for a meeting of the Security Council. London had reservations about a possible United Nations presence in Kuwait. There were attractions in that, if the Iraqi threat were sustained, Britain would not want to maintain its forces in Kuwait indefinitely. But the United Nations presence could lead to a situation where the Rulers of the Gulf were no longer dependent on Britain for their defence, with implications for Britain of loss of access to oil and the subsequent financial implications. That had dictated Britain's reluctance to accept a United Nations presence at Buraimi. If Britain withdrew its forces under pressure from the General Assembly, the Ruler's confidence in Britain could be damaged. Trevelyan argued for a political settlement in accordance with Arab ideas. A United Nations force in Kuwait could fill the gap between the point at which the presence of British forces became a political liability, and the point at which Kuwait could safely be left without foreign forces. While Watkinson urged that Kuwait build up its own forces, Macmillan agreed with the suggestion that it might be better for the Ruler to pay British troops.

The Cabinet was warned on 6 July of increasing criticism, especially from the Arab countries, of the British forces in Kuwait, and also of the strain on Anglo-Kuwaiti relations. Watkinson referred to plans for the gradual withdrawal of British forces from Kuwait, and suggested that while equipment and heavy weapons could be left in the Sheikhdom, British forces could be limited to one battalion to guard the airfield. This, together with a token United Nations force, and an increase in the Kuwaiti forces, could maintain the integrity of the territory.

The Foreign Office insisted that any United Nations arrangements had to ensure Kuwait's independence, and that the Ruler needed to be satisfied with the defence arrangements. These arrangements should be broad based and include Britain. Implementation of them by the Arab League was to be avoided: their defence arrangements would be inadequate and efforts to make the League improve such arrangements would just be characterized as an attempt to divert them from Israel; they were interested parties either wanting a share of Kuwaiti oil revenues or jockeying for position in the Arab world.[55]

In the Security Council, on 5 July, the delegate from the United Arab

Republic asserted that differences between Kuwait and Iraq should be settled by Arabs in the Arab League. He said further that his government insisted on the instant withdrawal of the British forces, and introduced a draft resolution to that effect on 6 July. It, and a resolution by Britain asking all states to respect the independence and territorial integrity of Kuwait, were both lost on 7 July.[56]

On 6 July, London asked Richmond to see the Ruler and explain that it did not want to embitter inter-Arab relations by maintaining troops on Kuwaiti territory longer than necessary, and there were advantages in broadening the responsibility for Kuwait's defence. The Ruler's reaction to a possible Arab League solution was to be sought. From Baghdad, Trevelyan urged a solution whereby Kuwait's membership of the United Nations, tied to physical arrangements for its future defence, could guarantee its independence. Macmillan wondered whether thought was being given to how or to what extent Britain could withdraw, and whether Kuwait's security could be entrusted to the Arab League and the United Nations.

From Cairo, Harold Beeley, the head of the British mission, reported that Nasser had been curiously passive about the whole affair. Should, however, British forces remain in Kuwait the improving Anglo-Egyptian relationship could be harmed.

The Ruler himself, in an interview with Richmond, insisted that his ultimate reliance was on the British government. The Ruler would not require a British component in any United Nations force, but he would insist that the British government was satisfied with the effectiveness of the arrangements. He was sceptical of an Arab League solution.

Richmond, himself, warned that if British troops remained for some time that would do Britain harm and the Soviet Union good in the Arab world. The Political Agent in Kuwait was thinking along the lines of 'doing without troops altogether and having an observer corps under the auspices of the United Nations, perhaps in conjunction with the Arab League'.[57]

The thrust of this advice was summed up by Philip de Zulueta of the Prime Minister's office in a minute to Macmillan. Britain could maintain a military presence in Kuwait at a minimum level for as long as was necessary. Alternatively, Britain could hand over its responsibilities to some international force – United Nations, Arab League, or other. It was suggested that an Arab League force would in effect mean a partition of Kuwait between various Arab countries. Britain's position in the Gulf would be undermined. And it looked as if the Soviet Union would not acquiesce in a United Nations force. Macmillan put de Zulueta's suggestion for achieving a breathing space to Home: Britain should say that it was prepared to withdraw its forces from Kuwait provided that Kuwait were admitted to the United Nations and the Arab League, and Qasim's claim to annex it were withdrawn.[58]

Washington remained supportive. It was sympathetic to Britain's difficulties. While inclining to the idea of a United Nations observer corps, the State Department accepted that this might need to be backed up with stiffened

Kuwaiti forces assisted by seconded British personnel. The Bureau of Near Eastern Affairs thought that a token garrison of about a company each of British and Saudi troops might be safer. Washington waited on a British initiative.[59]

The initiative came with the Ruler's memorandum to the Arab League of 12 July, following the suggestion put to him by Richmond, in which Kuwait agreed to request the withdrawal of British troops if either Qasim withdrew his claim or the Arab League provided alternative protection. Assessing this move several months later Richmond described it as 'sensible'. The Political Agent observed that during July Kuwait began to realize that it was not 'whole-heartedly liked and admired' by the countries of the Arab League. A mission by Sheikh Jabir to the Arab capitals revealed hostility and jealousy. It was felt that Kuwait intended to use its new found wealth selfishly, and not for the benefit of Arabia. But Richmond observed with approval that, nevertheless, Kuwait 'did not allow her disillusionment with the Arab countries to turn her back to complete reliance on British military protection and she did not lose sight of the need to seek an Arab political solution'. This Richmond argued gave Kuwait a chance to polish its image; as well as British military protection Kuwait realized that it needed wide recognition in the United Nations, and, through investment, to give other Arab countries an interest in preserving its independence.[60]

Home was initially attracted to the idea of a 'holding force' of troops from Tunisia, Morocco and Sudan. He advised his Prime Minister that although Kuwaiti forces could not be relied upon to defend their country for any length of time, with expansion, 'stiffening' provided by a British training mission which could also look after stockpiled equipment, they might be able to delay an Iraqi advance for 36 hours and allow time for British reinforcements to arrive. Home thought this scheme, developed by authorities in the Gulf, would provide the best long-term solution. It was effectively later endorsed by the Official Middle East Committee. Luce had warned how a permanent British unit would prove unacceptable to Kuwaiti and Arab opinion. This line of thinking was reinforced by Trevelyan who advised that British relations with Iraq would go sour unless British troops left Kuwait: 'Our public line should be that we are concerned to prevent the rape of Kuwait and not to enforce its perpetual spinsterhood.'

Home subsequently pointed to the need to improve relations with Iraq in view of the likelihood of important oil negotiations. Macmillan noted that the sooner Britain could withdraw altogether the better. The State Department remained supportive: it would understand if a small British element had to remain alongside an Arab force.[61]

On 12 August the Ruler signed an agreement with the Arab League and requested the withdrawal of British forces 'upon the arrival of Arab forces', envisaged for around 10 September. Alan Rothnie, who was temporarily replacing Richmond, commented that the Ruler had 'chosen a queer way of "consulting" us'. The Ruler insisted that this measure in no way affected the Exchange of Notes of 19 June 1961.[62]

Richmond warned about the danger of the Sheikhs reverting to their origins, and using British support to rule a population of townsmen, many of whom were educated, by methods appropriate to the rule of illiterate tribesmen. Britain could find itself in the position of 'having come to protect the oil fields and stayed on to protect the Sabah'. When Watkinson, the Minister of Defence, outlined to the Cabinet the military dispositions needed in Kuwait – the stockpiling of equipment and a small number of technicians to maintain it – he reflected Richmond's way of thinking in emphasizing that Britain would have increasingly to rely on political methods to secure its interests in Kuwait: 'while it would continue to be necessary to maintain some military presence in the Persian Gulf in order to safeguard our oil interests generally, a fresh political assessment might show that it was unnecessary to maintain a military deployment on the full scale envisaged' earlier that year. The Middle East Committee warned that the military plans depended on maintaining strategic reserves in Kenya which would not be possible after the end of 1962.[63]

Norman Brook, however, reiterating a policy of which he had reminded Eden in 1956 and that he had developed as Foreign Secretary in 1953, warned against the traditional policy of extracting oil concessions from an autocratic ruler in return for military protection. There were fewer and fewer places where foreign troops were tolerated. British policy took 'no account of the rising tide of nationalism in these countries, and, so long as it forces us to support the Sheikhs and Rulers, we are bound to find ourselves, in the end, on the losing side'. If Britain continued to take the line 'that our only course is to prop up the existing regimes for as long as they will last and get the oil while we can', as this depended on the inhabitants remaining 'fairly primitive', Britain needed to get the oil companies to investigate the possibility of transferring the sources of supply from Kuwait to the next primitive territory down the coast. If there were substance in the argument, Brook observed that Britain should not look at Kuwait as a long-term commitment. T.J. Bligh of the Prime Minister's Office agreed: he pointed to the need for a constructive political plan with which Britain could supplement its dependence on a military policy, and observed that it was strange how the Foreign Office should 'imagine that they can rely indefinitely on a purely military strategy in the Middle East'.[64]

In the short term there was no practical alternative to a British policy towards Kuwait which relied, in the end, on British military measures as a means of safeguarding it independence, and with that the protection of British economic and political interests in the Gulf.[65] But the crisis of 1961 led to Kuwait sending goodwill missions around the world, to the establishment of the Kuwait Fund for Arab Economic Development, and to diplomatic relations with Saudi Arabia, the United Arab Republic, Lebanon and Jordan. Richmond, who returned as the first British ambassador at Kuwait, astutely observed in his survey of the year 1961 that although Anglo-Kuwaiti relations were better than they had been since the Suez crisis of 1956, they were changing with Kuwait's evolution and were no longer those of exclusive intimacy. The Ruler was likely to accept British advice, but Kuwait was 'bound to seek closer and closer relations with her Arab sisters and she must be circumspect in parading her friendship with Her Majesty's Government'. Richmond observed that Kuwait's eventual salvation had to be sought in the Arab world and that most younger and some older Kuwaitis realized that. Richmond concluded: 'The events of 1961 have laid on Kuwait the difficult task of showing the world that she is more than a collection of oil wells sheltering under British military protection. If she is to succeed in this she will need from her British ally steady nerves and accurate timing even more than readiness to go to battle on her behalf.'[66]

It has been argued that Britain's military support of Kuwait in July 1961 was not the success it seemed, that the operation had the makings of a military disaster and would have been an embarrassment to Britain had there been an Iraqi attack.[67] In October 1961, A.R. Walmsley of the Foreign Office also warned that, legally, it might be unprofitable to dispute with Iraq its claims over Kuwait on the basis of the pre-1914 documents, and, furthermore, when looking at the period between 1914 and 1932 he thought there was advantage in Britain not taking the initiative. Britain was on debatable ground on aspects such as Article 16 of the Treaty of Lusanne which left the future of the ex-Ottoman territories to be settled by the parties concerned. There were doubts as to whether Sir Percy Cox had the right in 1923 to make a declaration on the frontier between Kuwait and Iraq.[68] But these are, in the end, comparatively minor and side issues.

What the 1961 operation did mark was both a vindication of the British policy which had evolved towards safeguarding British interests in the Middle East with the development of the defence strategy which no longer saw the Middle East as one of the three cardinal pillars, and the application of a new and more sophisticated policy, originally outlined by Eden as Foreign Secretary in a Cabinet paper of 16 February 1953 in which Eden had observed that Britain, in the second half of the twentieth century could not hope to maintain its position in the Middle East by the methods of the nineteenth century. Commercial concessions 'whose local benefit appears to rebound mainly to the Shahs and Pashas no longer serve in the same way to strengthen our influence in those countries'. In 1953 Eden had observed:

> In most of the countries of the Middle East the social and economic aspirations of the common people are quickening and the tide of nationalism is rising fast. If we are to maintain our influence in this area, future policy must be designed to harness these movements rather than to struggle against them.

Britain's strategic purposes in the Middle East, the then Foreign Secretary argued, could no longer be served by arrangements which local nationalism would regard as military occupation by foreign troops. In April 1956, Norman Brook wondered whether Britain had discovered how to apply these principles in practice.[69] Perhaps the experience of the Kuwait crisis, and its outcome, suggested that Britain finally had.

The Cabinet and Defence planning committees in 1958 confirmed a policy, already evident in 1956, that Britain's 'great' interest in the Middle East lay in Kuwait with its oil and sterling reserves. Initially it was listed above the only other 'great' interest, Turkey, and later Iran and Aden were added.

At a time when Britain moved towards an Anglo-American policy for the Middle East,[70] Kuwait and the Gulf were initially seen as areas of predominant British interest, though it was throughout acknowledged that Britain could not act forcibly without American support, which did not have to be military. Attempts to involve the Americans in joint planning for protecting Kuwait were unsuccessful, but the Americans did agree to a form of side-by-side planning. During the actual crisis Washington not only gave diplomatic support, but allowed for the contingency of possible military support as well, and throughout refrained from trying to impose any policy on the British.

It was during the crisis itself that Macmillan and other British officials increasingly accepted that there had at least to be the appearance of an Arab solution to an Arab question. Many British officials, particularly those serving in Arabia, welcomed this development, and the move away from the methods of the last century. There was a renewed awareness that British policy, as Eden's papers for the review of policy initiated in the middle of 1956 observed, had to transfer effort from military preparations to improving Britain's economic and political position.

Notes

1. Public Record Office, London, PREM 11/2399, fos 27–9, T355/58, Macmillan to Dulles, Top Secret, 27 July 1958; fol. 16, R.J. Ballantyne to de Zulueta (Dulles to Macmillan), Top Secret, 2 August 1958.
2. PREM 11/2399, fos 10–12, Note by the Chief of the Defence Staff on United States–United Kingdom Studies on the Middle East, August 1958.
3. PREM 11/2399, fos 5–6, D.C. Symon (Foreign Office) to F.A. Bishop (Prime Minister's Office), Secret, 25 August 1958.
4. *Foreign Relations of the United States* (hereafter cited as '*FRUS*') 1958–60(12), pp. 781–2, Special National Intelligence Estimate on the British position in the Gulf–Arabian peninsula area, 28 October 1958.
5. Public Record Office, London, CAB 128/32 pt. 2, fol. 497, CC80(57)7, Secret, 11 November 1958.
6. CAB 134/2230, ME(M)(59)2nd Meeting, Secret, 28 January 1959.
7. CAB 134/2432, OME(58)46, Points for a Middle East Policy Part II, Secret, 19 November 1958.
8. CAB 134/2434, OME(58)53, Points for a Middle East policy; proposed Ministerial Paper, secret, 10 December 1958; OME(58)56, Note by the Foreign Office on Points for a Middle East Policy, Secret, 15 December 1958. The initial and final versions of the papers Points for a Middle East Policy, Parts 1 and 2 remain closed for 50 years.
9. Public Record Office, London, FO 371/133074, EQ1015/388/G, Minute by

Stevens, Top Secret, 29 November 1958; EQ1015/381/G, Foreign Office to Washington, Telegram no. 8516, Secret, 30 November 1958; Hood to Foreign Office, Telegram no. 3247, 1 December 1958.
10. PREM 11/2735, Extract from Meeting of Ministers at 10 Downing Street on 21 December 1958.
11. CAB 134/2230, ME(M)(59)1st Meeting, Secret, 16 January 1959.
12. CAB 134/2230, ME(M)(59)3rd Meeting, Secret, 9 February 1959.
13. CAB 134/2230, ME(M)4th Meeting, Secret, 11 March 1959.
14. FO 371/141831, V1051/5, Humphrey Trevelyan to Sir R. Stevens, Confidential, 22 January 1959; CAB 131/21, D(59)1st Meeting, Cabinet Defence Committee, Top Secret, 23 January 1959; CAB 134/2230, ME(M)(59)4, Memorandum by Lennox-Boyd on a Middle East policy, Top Secret, 4 February 1959.
15. FO 371/141841, V1074/1 G, Record of conversation between Lloyd and Dulles, Secret, 4 February 1959.
16. CAB 131/21, D(59)4th Meeting, Cabinet Defence Committee, Secret, 17 February 1959; FO 371/140956, EQ1071/13 G, Cabinet Defence Committee, Secret, 17 February 1957.
17. *FRUS* 1958–60(12), pp. 381–8, Special National Intelligence Estimate on the Communist threat to Iraq, 17 February 1959.
18. CAB 134/2230, ME(M)4th Meeting, Secret, 11 March 1959.
19. FO 371/141841, V1074/4, Caccia to Foreign Office, Telegram no. 684, Secret, 12 March 1959 d r 13 March 1959; Eisenhower Library, Abilene, John Foster Dulles Papers, 1951–9, Series White House Memoranda, Box no. 7, File Meetings with the President 1959(1), Memorandum by Dulles of Conversation between Eisenhower and Macmillan, Personal and Private, 22 March 1959; Ann Whitman File, International Series, Box no. 24, File Macmillan Visit 20–2 March 1959 (4), Memorandum of Conference with President on 22 March 1959, 27 March 1959.
20. PREM 11/2735, V1074/5, Record of conversation between Lloyd and Herter on 29 April 1959; FO 371/142130, VJ1072/1/G, Foreign Office to Washington, Telegram no. 1346, Secret, 14 March 1959; VJ1072/2, Johnston to Foreign Office, Telegram no. 251, Secret, 17 March 1959; VJ1072/3, Hood to J.G.S. Beith, Secret, 18 March 1959.
21. FO 371/114830, V10345/4, Caccia to Foreign Office, Telegram no. 1072, 24 April 1959 recd. 25 April 1959; V10345/5, 10419/9/59G, Caccia to Stevens, Secret, 29 April 1959.
22. FO 371/142130, VJ1072/5, C.H. Johnston to J.G.S. Beith, Confidential and Guard, 29 May 1959; VJ1072/7/G, C.H. Johnston to Sir Patrick Dean, Top Secret, 19 June 1959.
23. PREM 11/3427, PM/59/52, Lloyd to Macmillan, Top Secret, 9 May 1959.
24. PREM 11/3427, Lloyd (Geneva) to Foreign Office, Telegram no. 31, Secret, 13 May 1959.
25. PREM 11/3427, T255/59, Macmillan to Eisenhower, Telegram no. 2312, Top Secret, 14 May 1959; T258/59, Eisenhower to Macmillan, Secret, 15 May 1959.
26. PREM 11/3427, Caccia to Foreign Office, Telegram no. 1244, Top Secret, 22 May 1959 recd. 23 May 1959.
27. *FRUS* 1958–60(12), pp. 786–7, Memorandum from the Legal Adviser (Becker) to Herter, 15 May 1959.
28. PREM 11/3427, Foreign Office to Bahrain (Lloyd to Middleton), Telegram no.

755, Secret, 24 May 1959; Middleton to Foreign Office, Telegram no. 417, Top Secret, 25 May 1959.
29. PREM 11/3427, BF11/6/59, F. Bishop to Macmillan, Top Secret, 8 June 1959.
30. PREM 11/2437, Halford to Foreign Office, Telegram No 411, Secret, 24 June 1959.
31. PREM 11/2753, Bishop to Macmillan, Anglo-American Planning in the Middle East D(59)25, Top Secret, July 1958; Foreign Office to Geneva (Profumo to Lloyd), Telegram no. 669, Top Secret, 31 July 1959.
32. PREM 11/2753, WG1016/318G, Record of a Conversation between Lloyd and Herter on 28 August 1958, Top Secret; GM14, British Joint Services Mission Washington to Ministry of Defence London, Top Secret, 14 August 1959.
33. FO 371/140716, EB1017/29, Washington to Foreign Office, Telegram no. 471, Secret, 29 August 1959 recd. 31 August 1959.
34. FO 371/143672, ZP1/26/G, SC(59)27(Final), The future of Anglo-American relations, Secret, received in registry 13 October 1959.
35. PREM 11/3427, Watkinson to Macmillan, Top Secret, 4 January 1960; Watkinson to Macmillan, Top Secret, 7 April 1960.
36. PREM 11/3427, Watkinson to Home, 17 January 1961; FS/61/11, Home to Watkinson, Top Secret, 8 February 1961; W. Geraghty to Macmillan, 26 April 1961.
37. FO 371/152118, ZP15/44/G, F. Bishop to Stevens, Top Secret, 2 August 1960; FO 371/152119, ZP15/49/G, Comments by Ministry of Defence on draft report by Middle East working group, 31 August 1960.
38. FO 371/152120, ZP15/51/G, Middleton to Stevens, Secret, 10 September 1960; Minute by A.R. Walmsley, 23 September 1960.
39. PREM 11/3427, Bishop to Macmillan, 30 November 1959; CAB 128/33, CC61(59)9, Secret, 3 December 1959.
40. PREM 11/3427, Norman Brook to R.A. Butler, 16 May 1960.
41. FO 371/156834, BK1051/10, Richmond to R.S. Crawford, Secret, 9 March 1961; Minute by Walmsley, 17 March 1961; Mustafa M. Alani, *Operation Vantage: British Military Intervention in Kuwait 1961* (Surbiton, Surrey, 1990), pp. 178–81.
42. CAB 128/35 pt. 1, fos 120–1, CC20(61)4, Secret, 13 April 1961; CAB 129/104, C(61)49, Memorandum by Heath on Kuwait's future relations with Britain, April 1961.
43. PREM 11/3427, PM/LPS/61/46, Heath to Macmillan, Secret, 21 April 1961; Minute by Macmillan, 23 April 1961.
44. CAB 128/35 pt. 1, fol. 190, CC31(61)5, Secret, 13 June 1961.
45. FO 371/162879, BK1011/1, Richmond to Home, Kuwait: Annual Review for 1961, Confidential, 11 January 1962.
46. Humphrey Trevelyan, *The Middle East in Revolution* (London, 1970), pp. 182–92; Hussein A. Hassouna, *The League of Arab States and Regional Disputes* (New York, 1975), pp. 91–4; PREM 11/3427, Trevelyan to Foreign Office, Telegram no. 624, Secret, 25 June 1961; Trevelyan to Foreign Office, Telegram no. 635, Secret, 26 June 1961; Foreign Office to Baghdad, Telegram no. 769, Top Secret, 26 June 1961; Trevelyan to Foreign Office, Telegram no. 639, Top Secret, 26 June 1961; Trevelyan to Foreign Office, Telegram no. 640, Secret, 27 June 1961; Trevelyan to Foreign Office, Telegram No 644, Secret, 27 June 1961; Trevelyan to Foreign Office, Telegram no. 658, Secret, 28 June 1961.

47. PREM 11/3427, Richmond to Foreign Office, Telegram no. 273, Secret, 26 June 1961; Foreign Office to Kuwait, Telegram no. 366, Secret, 26 June 1961; Richmond to Foreign Office, Telegram no. 281, Secret, 27 June 1961; Richmond to Foreign Office, Telegram no. 281, Secret, 27 June 1961; Foreign Office to Kuwait, Telegram no. 377, Secret, 27 June 1961; Foreign Office to Kuwait, Telegram no. 378, Emergency Confidential, 27 June 1961; Richmond to Foreign Office, Telegram no. 292, Secret, 28 June 1961; Foreign Office to Kuwait, Telegram no. 413, Emergency Secret, 29 June 1961.

48. PREM 11/3427, P. de Zulueta to Macmillan, Secret, 29 June 1961; Foreign Office to Washington, Telegram no. 4308, Top Secret, 28 June 1961; CAB 135/28 pt. 1, fos 222–3, CC36(61)3, Secret, 29 June 1961; fol. 237, CC37(61)2, Confidential Annex, 30 June 1961.

49. FO 371/156845, BK1083/9, Caccia to Foreign Office, Telegram no. 1556, Secret, 27 June 1961; Telegram no. 1563, Secret, 27 June 1961.

50. PREM 11/3427, Richmond to Foreign Office, Telegram no. 316, Emergency Top Secret, 30 June 1961; Trevelyan to Foreign Office, Emergency Top Secret, 30 June 1961.

51. See PREM 11/3428, Trevelyan to Foreign Office, Telegram no. 762, Top Secret, 4 July 1961 for an assessment of Qasim's intentions.

52. CAB 128/35 pt. 1, fos 237–8, CC38(61), Secret, 3 July 1961; for an account of the military preparations and operation see David Lee, *Flight from the Middle East* (London, 1980), pp. 166–83.

53. PREM 11/3428, Caccia to Foreign Office, Telegram no. 1606, Top Secret, 1 July 1961; Caccia by telephone, Unnumbered, 1 July 1961 recd. 2 July 1961; Foreign Office to Washington, Telegram no. 4452, Emergency Top Secret, 2 July 1961; Caccia to Foreign Office, Top Secret, 2 July 1961; Washington to Foreign Office, Telegram no. 1612, Top Secret, 2 July 1961 d r 3 July 1961; T.J. Bligh to Macmillan, 3 July 1961, Minute by Macmillan; Foreign Office to Washington, Telegram no. 4483, Emergency Top Secret, 3 July 1961; Caccia to Foreign Office, Telegram no. 1621, 3 July 1961 d r 4 July 1961; *FRUS* 1961–3(17), pp. 176–7, Home to Rusk, 2 July 1961; p. 178, Editorial note.

54. FO 371/162879, BK1011/1, Richmond to Home, Kuwait: Annual Review for 1961, Confidential, 11 January 1962; PREM 11/3427, Trevelyan to Foreign Office, Telegram no. 676, Top Secret, 29 June 1961; Foreign Office to Washington, Telegram no. 4344, Secret, 29 June 1961; PREM 11/3428, Richmond to Foreign Office, Telegram no. 331, Secret, 1 July 1961; Foreign Office to Washington, Telegram no. 4424, Top Secret, 1 July 1961; Richmond to Foreign Office, Telegram no. 340, Emergency Secret, 2 July 1961.

55. PREM 11/3427, Foreign Office to Washington, Telegram no. 4344, Secret, 29 June 1961; PREM 11/3428, Richmond to Foreign Office, Telegram no. 328, Emergency Secret, 1 July 1961; Foreign Office to New York, Telegram no. 2569, Emergency Confidential, 2 July 1961; Trevelyan to Foreign Office, Telegram no. 763, Secret, 4 July 1961; PREM 11/3429, Watkinson to Home, Top Secret, 5 July 1961; de Zulueta to Macmillan 5 July 1961, Minute by Macmillan; Foreign Office to New York, Telegram no. 2679, Secret, 6 July 1961; CAB 128/35 pt. 1, fol. 241, CC39(61)2, Secret, 6 July 1961.

56. PREM 11/3429, Sir P. Dean (New York) to Foreign Office, Telegram no. 1094, 5 July 1961 d r 6 July 1961; Hassouna, *League of Arab States*, pp. 98–9.

The Defence of Kuwait

57. PREM 11/3429, Foreign Office to Kuwait, Telegram no. 644, Secret, 6 July 1961; Trevelyan to Foreign Office, Telegram no. 849, Secret, 7 July 1961; Macmillan to de Zulueta, undated; Richmond to Foreign Office, Telegram no. 421, Secret, 8 July 1961; Richmond to Foreign Office, Telegram no. 432, Secret, 9 July 1961; FO 371/156851, BK1083/125, Beeley to J.G.S. Beith (Foreign Office), 8 July 1961.
58. PREM 11/3429, de Zulueta to Macmillan, 9 July 1961; T226/61, Macmillan to Home, 9 July 1961.
59. PREM 11/3429, Caccia to Foreign Office, Telegram no. 1685, Secret, 11 July 1961 recd. 12 July 1961; Telegram no. 1696, Confidential, 12 July 1961 d r 13 July 1961.
60. FO 371/162879, BK1011/1, Richmond to Home, Kuwait: Annual Review for 1961, Confidential, 11 January 1962.
61. PREM 11/3429, PM/61/97, Home to Macmillan, Top Secret, 14 July 1961; Trevelyan to Foreign Office, Telegram no. 939, Secret, 17 July 1961; PM/61/99, Home to Macmillan, Secret, Minute by Macmillan, 23 July 1961; Caccia to Foreign Office, Telegram no. 1789, Secret, 25 July 1961. PM/61/102, Home to Macmillan, Secret, 28 July 1961.
62. PREM 11/3429, Rothnie to Foreign Office, Telegram no. 591, Secret, 12 August 1961; Rothnie to Foreign Office, Telegram no. 438, Immediate, 12 August 1961; Rothnie to Foreign Office, Telegram no. 603, Secret, 14 August 1961.
63. FO 371/156885, BK1193/227, Richmond to Sir Roger Stevens (Foreign Office), Secret and Personal, 16 August 1961; CAB 128/35 pt. 2, fol. 309, CC49(61)5, Secret, 5 September 1961; CAB 129/106, fos 210–11, C(61)140, Memorandum by Heath on Kuwait, Top Secret, 2 October 1961.
64. PREM 11/3430, Brook to Macmillan, 13 September 1961; T.J. Bligh to Macmillan, Top Secret, 4 October 1961.
65. CAB 128/35 pt. 2, fos 338–9, CC53(61)5, Secret, 5 October 1961.
66. FO 371/162879, BK1011/1, Richmond to Home, Kuwait: Annual Review for 1961, Confidential, 11 January 1962.
67. D.E. Russell, 'Kuwait 1961: The War that never Happened' (M.Sc. dissertation, University of Wales, Aberystywth, 1993); TS.5450/18/CDS, Report by the Commander-in-Chief Middle East on operations in support of the State of Kuwait in July 1961, Top Secret, 30 September 1961.
68. FO 371/156854, BK1083/152, Submission by Walmsley on publication of White Paper on the Iraqi claim to Kuwait, 10 October 1961.
69. PREM 11/1457, fos 2–4, Norman Brook to Eden, 14 April 1956.
70. See Wm. Roger Louis and Ronald Robinson, 'The Imperialism of Decolonization', *The Journal of Imperial and Commonwealth History*, 22 (1994), pp. 462–511 at p. 483.

10

Conclusions

In October 1961 the Defence Committee of the British Cabinet was instructed to reassess defence policy and strategy in the Middle East in accordance with the newly defined political assumptions as to why Britain had a presence there. The political assumptions outlined were: first, the safeguarding of Britain's stake in the oil of the Gulf and support for the independence of Kuwait that this entailed; secondly, Britain had to discharge its obligation to protect the states in the Aden Protectorate and the Gulf; thirdly, to preserve the countries of the area from Communist influence. To achieve this Britain should try to retain its air staging facilities in Kenya if possible. Future plans, however, were to be framed on the assumption that Kenya would not be available as a military base after 1963, the date of its envisaged independence.[1]

American policy, although similar in orientation, had a different emphasis. The Planning Board recommended to the National Security Council on 7 July 1960 that the paramount objective of American policy in the Middle East should be 'the continued denial of the area to Soviet domination'. The next objective, to maintain the continued availability of sufficient Middle Eastern oil to meet vital Western European requirements on reasonable terms, was restated by the Planning Board so as to downgrade the relative importance of Middle Eastern oil for the United States, and to remove the implication that Washington acting alone would be prepared to use force to maintain Western access to it.[2] By February 1960 the Operations Co-ordinating Board felt that there had been an expansion of American and Free World influence in the Middle East. It viewed what it saw as a widening gulf between the two principal political forces in the area: communism and Arab nationalism. Arab nationalism seemed increasingly aware of the threat of international communism. Although the revolution in Iraq and the civil war in Lebanon in 1958 had removed the Western leadership in those countries, the perceived increasing strength of communism in Iraq had been opposed by Nasser and there was discernible 'a steady growth toward more normal relations between the Western powers and the United Arab Republic, a significant relaxation in tensions among the Arab countries themselves (with the exception of Iraq) along with a relaxation in the unifying urge of Arab nationalism itself'.[3]

British policy in the Middle East, following the military support of Kuwait in 1961, confirmed what statesmen regarded as the reality of the British position in the Middle East that had evolved in the decades following the end of the Second World War: one in which Britain was no longer the paramount power. In effect, Britain had conceded its position to the United States. Washington was the dominant Western power in the area.

Official British policy for the Middle East in September 1945 reflected the view that other powers were, if possible, to be excluded from the area and that American penetration, even commercial, was to be resisted. As the Americans assumed increasing responsibility for Greece and Turkey with the evolution of the Truman Doctrine in 1947, and as British paramountcy in the area was eroded when London surrendered the Palestine mandate in May 1948, Britain found itself in a position where, with Washington showing an interest in the Middle East in the late 1940s, it had to welcome what it increasingly saw as a necessary support for its position. With the joining of the Cold War as Britain and the United States divided the world between themselves, Britain was left with responsibility for the Middle East in war. This was something that Britain tried to resist. It was in a position where it had to do everything it could to encourage the American interest, and play down divergences of policy over Iran and Saudi Arabia. At the time of the fall of the second Labour government in October 1951 Britain could still be regarded as the paramount power in the Middle East. But its position was being steadily eroded and some British officials thought that Britain's leadership of the Arab world, secure since 1918, had been successfully challenged by the United States and France from 1945, and doubted whether either of those countries was capable of taking Britain's place in the Middle East. The Middle East in 1951 remained one of the three cardinal pillars of British defence.

Washington, on the whole, did support the British position in Egypt. This new American interest in the Middle East uncovered divisions between the State and Defence departments, and rivalries between the armed services. While there was a realization in Washington that the British influence in the Middle East was declining, and that many countries in the area were looking more towards the United States, Washington remained reluctant to commit its forces there in time of war. The United States was, however, prepared to increase its economic stake in the area.

It was Churchill's peacetime administration which oversaw the dramatic change in British defence policy, the move away from considering the Middle East as one of the three cardinal pillars of British strategy towards the conclusion that it was an area of more limited significance in the age of thermo-nuclear weapons and at a time when Britain's financial strictures meant a limitation of its world role. Churchill personally felt that the Americans should become involved in an area for which Britain had undertaken responsibility in the agreement made between the two countries at the end of 1947. Dulles decided on his visit to the Middle East in 1953 that Britain could no longer be entrusted with the responsibility, on behalf of the West, for the defence of the Middle East. Following this, the National Security Council concluded that Washington would have to assume more and more of Britain's responsibilities in the area and in doing this would have to act increasingly on its own rather than alongside London.

At the end of Churchill's period of office the image of Britain in the Middle East — through its negotiation of withdrawal from the Suez Canal base, the weakened position it had in Iran's oil exploitation, the challenge its faced to its traditional base in Iraq and the difficulties with Saudi Arabia and that country's American ally over territorial disputes in the oil-rich Gulf — was that of a declining role in an area which had been largely a British preserve since the time the modern Middle East had been created by the Western powers in their own interests in the settlements that followed the end of the First World War.

The declining British influence in the Middle East matched London's revised defence policy. British officials, particularly those in the Middle East, did not always like the growing American involvement in the area, but it was something that Britain had to accept with as good a grace as possible. Indeed, towards the end of Churchill's period of office, the views of London and Washington on the Middle East were close enough to enable the consideration of a joint plan to impose a settlement of the Arab–Israeli dispute.

This situation changed. Eden, when he became Prime Minister, shifted British policy towards an emphasis on a more direct British role in the Middle East. This was seen as being necessary to preserve British oil interests. To implement this policy Britain also had to be prepared to act in the Middle East without the close concurrence or agreement of the United States. Perhaps it is ironical that the basis of the more independent British policy was the Northern Tier concept, as it took form in the Baghdad Pact (initially called the Turco-Iraqi Pact). This idea, in origin, was American. Initially, Britain saw the Northern Tier concept as a means of renegotiating the Anglo-Iraqi Treaty of 1930. London always insisted that it wanted Washington to adhere to what became known as the Baghdad Pact.

Washington, however, when confronted with the reality of the Baghdad Pact did not want to accede. It had reasons: first, the Zionist lobby in the United States, perceived as being powerful at election time, could demand that if the United States joined the Pact it should give Israel a security guarantee; secondly, Washington did not want to provoke the Soviet Union into action in the Middle East. Against this background Eisenhower kept reiterating that it was his policy to allow Britain to take the lead in the Middle East, and to leave it with the principal responsibility for the area's defence. The American president was determined that Britain should have to pay as much as possible for the defence of the Middle East at a time when Britain was drastically reducing its defence expenditure to sustain the domestic economy, and when British forces in the

Middle East were scheduled to be run down in accordance with the new strategy based partly on thermo-nuclear weapons.

The Middle East by the end of 1955 was no longer one of the three pillars of British strategy. The area was important for Britain because of the vital British oil interests there. This realization meant an emphasis on the British position in Iraq and the Gulf. In effect Britain decided to work with its friends in the Middle East. This meant a policy based on links with the pashas and not the peasants. And it was this policy that brought London into conflict with the friends of Washington, and in particular those in Saudi Arabia, a country over which Washington was seen as exercising paramountcy. From London's perspective Washington seemed unable to understand the importance for Western interests of the Gulf states. Washington appeared to think they could be sacrificed to Saudi Arabia if that would keep Saudi Arabia on the side of the West.

Some American officials thought that, at the end of 1955, the British were 'flexing their muscles' in the Middle East: there had been the British pressure on Iran to join the Baghdad Pact; the quarrel with the Saudi Arabians in the Buraimi area; and the efforts to push Jordan into the Baghdad Pact. There was an American suspicion that the British were trying to restore some of their lost prestige in the Middle East. At this time London was infuriated over what it saw as an ambivalent American policy, difficult to discern and continually changing, and one which appeared in part to be dictated by American oil interests.

As Prime Minister, Eden enforced a distinctly British policy in the Middle East. He insisted that the British dependence on Middle East oil, together with the experience the British had of the area, meant that London had to be willing to pursue a policy in the Middle East without the full agreement and support of Washington. Where Washington and London did agree was over the conclusion that Moscow had opened up another front in the Cold War by supplying the Egyptians with arms. Where they differed was in their diagnosis of how to deal with the Arabs over this. London thought that its Arab allies might react favourably to firmness. Washington believed that shows of force would drive the Arabs to Moscow. Throughout Eden's premiership the main objective of British policy in the Middle East was to ensure the flow of oil in Iraq and the Gulf. This policy led to head-on clashes between London and Washington.

Eisenhower, and many of his officials, could not grasp the importance of the Gulf for Britain. Eisenhower chose King Saud as his man in the Middle East. The president confessed that he knew little about Saud, and in 1958 acknowledged that this policy had been a mistake and that Britain's choice of Nuri had been a wiser one. But in 1955 ARAMCO and American oil interests dictated that Saud should be humoured. Eisenhower could not understand why Britain was not prepared to allow Saud to take over Buraimi, and effectively Muscat and Oman as well. To Eisenhower this seemed a small sacrifice to pacify Saud. Britain refused to co-operate and make this sacrifice. Eisenhower was aided in his assessment of British motives by Hoover.

Britain chose Iraq and Nuri. Iraq saw Egypt as its rival for the leadership of the Arab world. Britain saw Nasser challenging Britain's position not only in the Middle East, but in Africa and in the Muslim world. Nasser had to go. The Americans agreed with this. Anglo-American differences during the Suez crisis of 1956 hinged on the timing of this in relation to Eisenhower's presidential election.

By December 1956 British and American officials saw the need to re-establish the close relationship between London and Washington. Throughout the first Eisenhower presidency that relationship had not been 'special': Eisenhower had insisted from the outset that Britain was only one among a number of allies. Close advisers like Humphrey and Hoover disliked the British and often viewed them as colonialists who wanted the Americans to pay for the safeguarding of British interests in the Middle East while leaving the British in command. That changed with the second Eisenhower administration. Eisenhower revived the 'special' relationship with Britain during the meeting with Macmillan in Bermuda in March 1957 and, although the Eisenhower Doctrine initially seemed like American unilateral action in the Middle East to fill the vacuum left by Britain's withdrawal, what evolved by the time of the Syrian crisis of August 1957 was a willingness on the part of Washington to consult intimately with Britain over policy in the area. And by the time of the crises in Lebanon, Jordan and Iraq in July 1958 the United States had, in effect, acknowledged that it had assumed the leadership of the 'Free World' in the Middle East. Washington's actions during the Anglo-American invasion of Jordan and Lebanon showed the extent to which it had taken over Britain's place in the Middle East, and filled the vacuum left by the British decline in the area, evidenced in the aftermath of the Second World War, particularly with the end of Britain's mandate over Palestine.

In 1958 the British Cabinet and Defence planning committees confirmed a policy, already evident in 1956, that Britain's 'great' interest in the Middle East lay in Kuwait with its oil and sterling reserves. Initially, this was listed above the only other 'great' interest, Turkey, and later Iran and Aden were added. As Britain moved towards an Anglo-American policy for the Middle East, Kuwait and the Gulf were initially seen as areas of predominant British interest. It was, however, acknowledged that Britain could not act forcibly without American support, and this support did not have to be military. London could not persuade Washington to embark on joint planning for the protection of Kuwait. When Iraq seemed to threaten the invasion of Kuwait in 1961 Washington, however, not only gave diplomatic support, but allowed for the contingency of possible military support as well, and throughout refrained from imposing a policy on London.

The Kuwait crisis of 1961 forced the acceptance on Macmillan and other British officials that there had at least to be the appearance of an Arab solution to an Arab question. This constituted a move away from the methods of the previous century, and an acknowledgement of the value of the policy outlined by Eden for the Cabinet in 1953 of the need to harness the social and economic aspirations of the common people of the Middle East at a time when the tide of nationalism was rising fast. It had also been Eden's government, just before the start of the Suez crisis of 1956, that had initiated the review of British policy to transfer effort from military preparations to that of improving Britain's economic and political position.

Britain's policy for the Middle East that evolved throughout the 1950s was, in many ways, initiated with the change in military strategy and straitened economic circumstances. That policy was also, in effect, helped by Washington's assumption of an increased responsibility in the area. Eisenhower, during his first presidency, had not wanted this. He preferred to leave Britain in the lead in the area, and had wanted Britain to pay as much as possible for the defence of the area. It was, however, Eisenhower's policy during the Suez crisis of 1956 that led, as Henry Kissinger later observed, to the United States having to take over Britain's burdens in the Middle East.[4]

Notes

1. Public Record Office, London, CAB 131/126, D(61)65, Note by Brook enclosing Macmillan to Watkinson, Top Secret, 23 October 1961.
2. Eisenhower Library, Abilene, White House Office Central Files 1953–61, Series Special Staff File, Box no. 6, File Near East (1), Briefing note United States policy towards the Near East for National Security Council meeting on 7 July 1960, Top Secret, 6 July 1960.
3. Eisenhower Library, Abilene, White House Office, Office of the Special Assistant for National Security Affairs Records 1952–61, OCB Series Subject Subseries, Box no. 4, File Near East (Middle East) (1), Operations Co-ordinating Board Report on the Near East, Secret, 3 February 1960.
4. Henry Kissinger, 'Suez weakened Europe', *The Listener*, 20 May 1982, pp. 9–11.

Bibliography

AUSTRALIA

Canberra

Australian Archives
(a) *Cabinet*
A4638
(b) *Defence Committee*
A2031, A5799
(c) *Department of External Affairs*
A1838
(d) *Prime Minister*
A426
(e) *Shedden Papers*
A5954

National Library of Australia
(a) Sir Frederick Eggleston Papers
MS423
(b) Sir John Latham Papers
MS1009
(c) Sir Robert Menzies Papers
MS4936
(d) Sir Percy Spender Papers
MS4875

BRITAIN

Cambridge

Churchill College, Cambridge
Alexander of Hillborough Papers
Attlee Papers
Halifax Papers

British Library of Political and Economic Science
Dalton Papers

Public Record Office
(a) *Bevin Papers*
    FO800
(b) *Cabinet*
    CAB 41; CAB 42; CAB 65; CAB 66; CAB 128; CAB 129; CAB 131; CAB 133
(c) *Colonial Office*
    CO 537; CO 733
(d) *Defence*
    DEFE 4; DEFE 6
(e) *Dominions Office (Commonwealth Relations Office)*
    DO 35
(f) *Eden Papers*
    FO 800
(g) *Foreign Office*
    FO 371; FO 381; FO 954
(h) *Lloyd Papers*
    FO 800
(i) *Prime Minister's Office*
    PREM 4; PREM 8; PREM 11

Oxford

Western Manuscripts Department, Bodleian
Attlee Papers

UNITED STATES

Abilene, Kansas

Eisenhower Library
John Foster Dulles Papers, 1951–59
Christian A. Herter Papers, 1957–61
C.D. Jackson Papers, 1931–67
White House Office Central Files Confidential File 1953–1961

White House Office, National Security Council Staff Papers, 1948–61
White House Office, Office of the Special Assistant for National Security Affairs, 1952–61
White House Office, Office of the Staff Secretary, 1952–61
Ann Whitman File (Papers of Dwight D. Eisenhower as President, 1953–61)
Oral Histories

Burlington, Vermont

Guy W. Bailey Library, University of Vermont
Senator Aiken Papers
Governor Ernest Gibson Jr Papers
Warren R. Austin Papers

Charlottesville, Virginia

Aldeman Library, University of Virginia
J. Rives Childes Papers
Louis Johnson Papers

Independence Missouri

Harry S. Truman Library
Dean Acheson Papers
Clark M. Clifford Papers
Jonathan Daniel Papers
Elsey Papers
Edward Jacobson Papers
Herschel V. Johnson Papers
Howard McGrath Papers
Harry S. Truman Papers
Oral Histories

Lexington, Virginia

George C. Marshall Library, Virginia Military Institute
Marshall S. Carter Papers
George C. Marshall Papers
Kenneth W. Condit, *The History of the Joint Chiefs of Staff. The Joint Chiefs of Staff and National Policy, 1947–1949* Vol. 2 (Historical Division, Joint Secretariat, Joint Chiefs of Staff, 22 April 1976) Record Group 59, General Records of the Department of State, Records of Charles E. Bohlen 1942–52
Record Group 59, Department of State, Policy Planning Staff
United States National Security Council: Papers of the National Security Council
United States Joint Chiefs of Staff, White House Records of Fleet Admiral William D. Leahy, 1942–49.

Princeton, New Jersey

Princeton University Library
Bernard M. Baruch Papers
John Foster Dulles Collection
Louis Fischer Papers
James V. Forrestal Diaries
George Kennan Papers
Arthur Krock Papers
Adlai E. Stevenson Papers
Harry Dexter White Papers
The John Foster Dulles Oral History Collection

Washington, District of Columbia

Georgetown University Library
Robert F. Wagner Papers

Library of Congress Manuscript Division
Emmanuel Celler Papers
Jessup Papers

National Archives
Record Group 59, General Records of the Department of State, Decimal Files 1945–9, 501.BB Palestine; 711; 741; 867N; OSS Bureau of Intelligence Research; Records of Charles E. Bohlen 1942–52; Office of Near Eastern Affairs Palestine; Records of Policy Planning Staff 1947–1953; Records Relating to Palestine, Palestine Reference 'book' of Dean Rusk, 15 February–19 April 1948

Washington National Records Centre (Suitland, Maryland)
Record Group 0000319 Entry 00082 Army Staff Intelligence (G2) Library 'C File' 1946–51
Record Group 84 Entry 57A-446 (Cairo Embassy)
Record Group 84 Entry 59A543 Pt. 5, 800 Palestine (London Embassy Files)
Record Group 162 G2 Regional File 1933–44, Palestine 2800–900

Published Primary Sources

Documents on British Policy Overseas
Foreign Relations of the United States

Books

Acheson, D., *Present at the Creation* (London, 1970).

Aitken, J., *Nixon: A Life* (London, 1993).

Alani, M.A., *Operations Vantage: British Military Intervention in Kuwait 1961* (Surbiton, Surrey, 1990).

Alteras, I., *Eisenhower and Israel: US–Israeli Relations, 1953–1960* (Florida, 1993).

Anderson, I.H., *ARAMCO. The United States and Saudi Arabia: A Study of The Dynamics of Foreign Oil Policy 1933–1950* (Princeton, NJ, 1981).

Anderson, T.H., *The United States, Great Britain, and the Cold War 1944–1947* (Columbia, Miss., 1981).

Aronson, G., *From Sideshow to Centre Stage: U.S. Policy Toward Egypt 1946–1956* (Boulder, Colorado, 1986).

Attlee, C.R., *As It Happened* (London, 1954).

Balfour-Paul, G., *The End of Empire in the Middle East: Britain's Relinquishment of Power in her Last Three Arab Dependencies* (Cambridge, 1991).

Barber, J., *South Africa's Foreign Policy 1945–1970* (London, 1973).

Barber, J. and Barratt, J., *South Africa's Foreign Policy: The Search for Status and Security 1945–1988* (Cambridge, 1990).

Barclay, R.E., *Ernest Bevin and the Foreign Office* (London, 1975).

Barker, E., *The British between the Superpowers* (London, 1983).

Bator, V., *Vietnam. A Diplomatic Tragedy: Origins of U.S. Involvement* (London, 1977).

Berridge, G.R., *South Africa, The Colonial Powers and 'Africa Defence': The Rise and Fall of the White Entente, 1948–60* (London, 1992).

Bethell, N., *The Palestine Triangle: The Struggle between the British, the Jews and the Arabs, 1935–48* (London, 1979).

Bialer, U., *Between East and West: Israel's Foreign Policy Orientation 1948–1956* (Cambridge, 1990).

Bill, J.A., *The Eagle and the Lion: The Tragedy of American-Iranian Relations* (New Haven, Con., 1988).

Bill, J.A. and Louis, W.R. (eds), *Mussadiq, Iranian Nationalism, and Oil* (London, 1988).

Blake, R., and Louis, W.R. (eds), *Churchill* (Oxford, 1993).

Brenchley, F., *Britain and the Middle East: An Economic History* (London, 1989).

Bullock, A., *Ernest Bevin, Foreign Secretary 1945–1951* (London, 1983).

Burrows, B.A.B., *Footnotes in the Sand: The Gulf in Transition. 1953–1958* (Wilton, Salisbury, 1990).

Cable, J., *Intervention at Abadan: Plan Buccaneer* (London, 1991).

Cairncross, A. (ed.), *The Robert Hall Diaries, 1954–61* (London, 1991).

Cobban, H., *The Making of Modern Lebanon* (London, 1985).

Cohen, M., *Churchill and the Jews* (London, 1985).

Cohen, M., *Palestine and the Great Powers 1945–1948* (Princeton, NJ, 1982).
Colville, J., *The Fringes of Power: Downing Street Diaries 1939–55* (London, 1985).
Copeland, M., *The Game Player: Confessions of the CIA's Original Political Operative* (London, 1989).
Cross, C., *The Fall of the British Empire: 1918–1968* (London, 1968).
Crystal, J., *Oil and Politics in the Gulf* (Cambridge, 1990).
Danchev, A., *Oliver Franks: Founding Father* (Oxford, 1993).
Deighton, A. (ed.), *Britain and the First Cold War* (London, 1990).
Devereux, D.R., *The Formulation of British Defence Policy towards the Middle East, 1948–56* (London, 1990).
Dilks, D. (ed.), *Retreat from Power; Studies in Britain's Foreign Policy of the Twentieth Century* (London, 1981).
Dixon, P., *Double Diploma: The Life of Sir Pierson Dixon, Don and Diplomat* (London, 1968).
Donoughe, B. and Jones, G.W., *Herbert Morrison: Portrait of a Politician* (London, 1973).
Eden, A., *Full Circle* (London, 1960).
Eisenhower, D.D., *The White House Years: Mandate for Change 1953–56* (New York, 1963).
Eisenhower, D.D., *The White House Years: Waging Peace 1956–1961* (London, 1966).
Epstein, L.D., *Britain – Uneasy Ally* (Chicago, 1954)
Evans, T.E. (ed.), *The Killearn Diaries 1934–46* (London, 1972).
Eveland, W.C., *Ropes of Sand: America's Failure in the Middle East* (London, 1980).
Fernea, R.A. and Louis W.R., (eds), *The Iraqi Revolution of 1958: The Old Social Classes Revisited* (London, 1991).
Ferrell, R.H. (ed.), *The Eisenhower Diaries* (New York, 1981).
Fitzsimons, M.A., *The Foreign Policy of the British Labour Government, 1945–1951* (Notre Dame, Ind., 1953).
Foot, M., *Aneurin Bevan: A Biography, 1945–1960* Vol. 2 (London, 1973).
Freiberger, S.Z., *Dawn over Suez: The Rise of American Power in the Middle East, 1952–1957* (Chicago, 1992).
Gallman, Waldemar J., *Iraq under General Nuri: My Recollections of Nuri al-Said, 1954–1958* (Baltimore, 1964).
Gasiorowski, M.J., *U.S. Foreign Policy and the Shah. Building a Client State in Iran* (London, 1991).
Gilbert, M., *Winston S. Churchill: 'Never Despair' 1945–1965* (London, 1988).
Gladwyn, H.M.G.J., *The Memoirs of Lord Gladwyn* (London, 1972).
Glubb, J.B., *A Soldier with the Arabs* (London, 1957).
Glubb, J.B., *Britain and the Arabs: A Study of Fifty Years, 1908–1958* (London, 1959).
Goldsworthy, D., *Colonial Issues in British Politics, 1945–1961: From 'Colonial*

Development' to 'Wind of Change' (Oxford, 1971).
Gorst, A., Johnman, L., and Lucas, W.S. (eds), *Post-war Britain, 1945–64 Themes and Perspectives* (London, 1989).
Hahn, P.L., *The United States, Great Britain and Egypt, 1945–1956* (Chapel Hill, 1991).
Harris, K., *Attlee* (London, 1982).
Hassouna, H.A., *The League of Arab States and the Regional Disputes* (New York, 1975).
Hathaway, R.M., *Ambiguous Partnership. Britain and America 1944–1947* (New York, 1981).
Hayter, W., *A Double Life* (London, 1974).
Horne, A., *Macmillan 1957–1986* (London, 1989).
Ismay, Lord, *The Memoirs of Lord Ismay* (London, 1960).
Jackson, W. and Lord Bramall, *The Chiefs: The Story of the United Kingdom Chiefs of Staff* (London, 1992).
James, R.R.J., *Anthony Eden* (London, 1986).
Jones, M., *Failure in Palestine: British and United States Policy after the Second World War* (London, 1986).
Kimche, J. and D., *Both Sides of the Hill: Britain and the Palestine War* (London, 1960).
Kuniholm, B.R., *The Origins of the Cold War in the Near East: Great Power Conflict and Diplomacy in Iran, Turkey and Greece* (Princeton, NJ, 1980).
Kunz, D.B., *The Economic Diplomacy of the Suez Crisis* (Chapel Hill, 1991).
Kyle, K., *Suez* (London, 1992).
Lapping, B., *End of Empire* (London, 1985).
Lee, D., *Flight from the Middle East* (London, 1980).
Lesch, D.W., *Syria and the United States: Eisenhower's Cold War in the Middle East* (Boulder, Colorado, 1992).
Lloyd, S., *Suez 1956 A Personal Account* (London, 1978).
Louis, W.R., *The British Empire in the Middle East 1945–51. Arab Nationalism, the United States, and Postwar Imperialism* (Oxford, 1984).
Louis, W.R. and Owen, R. (eds), *Suez 1956. The Crisis and its Consequences* (Oxford, 1989).
Louis, W.R. and Stookey, R.W. (eds), *The End of the Palestine Mandate* (London, 1986).
Lucas, W.S., *Divided We Stand: Britain, the US and the Suez Crisis* (London, 1991).
Lytle, M.H., *The Origins of the Iranian-American Alliance 1941–1953* (New York, 1987).
Macmillan, H., *Riding the Storm 1956–1959* (London, 1971).
Macmillan, H., *Tides of Fortune, 1945–1955* (London, 1969).
McGhee, G. *Envoy to the Middle World: Adventures in Diplomacy* (New York, 1969).
McNeill, W.H., *America, Britain and Russia. Their Co-operation and Conflict*

1941–1946 (London, 1953).
Meyer, G.E., *Egypt and the United States: The Formative Years* (London, 1980).
Monroe, E., *Britain's Moment in the Middle East 1914–1971* (London, 1981).
Montgomery, B.L., *The Memoirs of Field-Marshal the Viscount Montgomery of Alamein* (London, 1958).
Moran, C.M.W., *Winston Churchill. The Struggle for Survival, 1940–1965* (London, 1966).
Morgan, K.O., *Labour in Power 1945–1951* (Oxford, 1984).
Morris, B., *The Birth of the Palestinian Refugee Problem, 1947–1949* (Cambridge, 1987).
Morris, B., *Israel's Border Wars 1949–1956* (Oxford, 1993).
Mosley, L., *Dulles: A Biography of Eleanor, Allen, and John Foster Dulles and Their Family Network* (London, 1978).
Nicholas, H.G., *Britain and the United States* (London, 1963).
Northedge, F.S., *Descent from Power: British Foreign Policy 1945–1973* (London, 1974).
Ovendale, R., *'Appeasement' and the English Speaking World: Britain, the United States, the Dominions, and the Policy of 'Appeasement', 1937–1939* (Cardiff, 1975).
Ovendale, R., *Britain, the United States, and the End of the Palestine Mandate, 1942–1948* (Woodbridge, Suffolk, 1989).
Ovendale, R. (ed.), *British Defence Policy since 1945: Documents in Contemporary History* (Manchester, 1994).
Ovendale, R., *The English-Speaking Alliance: Britain, the United States, the Dominions and the Cold War 1945–1951* (London, 1985).
Ovendale, R. (ed.), *The Foreign Policy of the British Labour Governments, 1954–1951* (Leicester, 1984).
Ovendale, R., *The Longman Companion to the Middle East since 1914* (London, 1992).
Ovendale, R., *The Origins of the Arab–Israeli Wars*, 2nd edn (London, 1988).
Pappé, I., *Britain and the Arab–Israeli Conflict, 1948–51* (London, 1988).
Rendel, G., *The Sword and the Olive. Recollections of Diplomacy and the Foreign Service, 1913–1954* (London, 1957).
Reynolds, D., *British Policy and World Power in the 20th Century* (London, 1991).
Roberts, H.L. and Wilson, P.A. (eds), *Britain and the United States. Problems in Co-operation* (London, 1953).
Roosevelt, K., *Countercoup: The Struggle for the Control of Iran* (New York, 1979).
Rothwell, V.H., *Anthony Eden: A Political Biography 1931–57* (Manchester, 1992).
Rothwell, V.H., *Britain and the Cold War, 1941–1947* (London, 1982).
Rubin, B., *The Great Powers in the Middle East 1941–1947: The Road to the Cold War* (London, 1980).

Rubin, B., *Paved with Good Intentions. The American Experience and Iran* (New York, 1980).
Sayed-Ahmed, M., *Nasser and American Foreign Policy 1952–1956* (London, 1989).
Seale, P., *The Struggle for Syria: A Study of Post-War Arab Politics 1945–1958* (London, 1987).
Shinwell, E., *Lead with the Left: My First Ninety-Six Years* (London, 1981).
Shlaim, A., *Collusion Across the Jordan* (Oxford, 1988).
Shuckburgh, E., *Descent to Suez: Diaries 1951–56* (London, 1986).
Silverfarb, D., *The Twilight of British Ascendancy in the Middle East: A Case Study of Iraq, 1941–1950* (New York, 1994).
Spiegel, S.L., *The Other Arab–Israeli Conflict: Making American Middle East Policy, from Truman to Reagan* (Chicago, 1985).
Strang, W., *Home and Abroad* (London, 1956).
Sykes, C., *Crossroads to Israel* (London, 1965).
Trevelyan, H., *The Middle East in Revolution* (London, 1970).
Watt, D.C., *Succeeding John Bull. America in Britain's Place 1900–1975* (Cambridge, 1984).
Williams, F., *A Prime Minister Remembers: The War and Post-War Memoirs of the Rt. Hon. Earl Attlee* (London, 1961).
Williams, P.M. (ed.), *The Diary of Hugh Gaitskell 1945–1956* (London, 1983).
Wilson, M.C., *King Abdullah, Britain and the Making of Jordan* (Cambridge, 1987).
Woodhouse, C.M., *Something Ventured* (London, 1982).
Young, J.W. (ed.), *The Foreign Policy of Churchill's Peacetime Administration 1951–1955* (Leicester, 1988).

Articles

Aldrich, R., 'Intelligence, Anglo-American relations and the Suez crisis, 1956', *Intelligence and National Security*, IX (July 1954), pp. 544–54.
Ball, S.J., 'Bomber bases and British strategy in the Middle East, 1945–9', *Journal of Strategic Studies*, XIV (1991), pp. 515–33.
Brands, H.W., 'The Cairo-Tehran connection in Anglo-American rivalry in the Middle East, 1951–1953', *The International History Review*, XI (1989), pp. 434–56.
Brown, M.E., 'The nationalization of the Iraqi Petroleum Company', *International Journal of Middle Eastern Studies*, X (1970), pp. 107–24.
Cohen, S.A., 'A still stranger aspect of Suez: British operational plans to attack Israel, 1955–1956', *The International History Review*, X (1988), pp. 261–81.
Dooley, H.J., 'Great Britain's "Last Battle" in the Middle East: notes on Cabinet planning during the Suez Crisis of 1956', *The International History*

Review, XI (1989), pp. 486–517.

Fry, M. and Hochstein, M., 'The forgotten Middle Eastern crises of 1957: Gaza and Sharm-el-Sheikh', *The International History Review*, XV (1994), pp. 46–83.

Gasiorowski, M.J., 'The 1953 *coup d'état* in Iran', *International Journal of Middle East Studies*, XIX (1987), pp. 261–86.

Gormly, J.L., 'Keeping the door open in Saudi Arabia: the United States and the Dhahran Airfield, 1945–46', *Diplomatic History*, IV (1980), pp. 189–205.

Gorst, A. and Lucas, W.S., 'Suez 1956: strategy and the diplomatic process', *Journal of Strategic Studies* XI (1988), pp. 391–436.

Hahn, P.L., 'Containment and Egyptian Nationalism: the unsuccessful effort to establish the Middle East command, 1950–53', *Diplomatic History*, XI (1987), pp. 23–40.

Heiss, M.A., 'The United States, Great Britain, and the creation of the Iranian Oil Consortium, 1953–1954', *The International History Review*, XVI (1994), pp. 511–35.

Jalal, A., 'Towards the Baghdad Pact: South Asia and Middle East defence in the Cold War, 1947–1955', *The International History Review*, XI (1989), pp. 409–33.

Kent, J., 'The Egyptian base and the defence of the Middle East, 1945–54' *The Journal of Imperial and Commonwealth History*, XXI (3) (1993), pp. 45–65.

Kissinger, H., 'Suez weakened Europe', *The Listener* (20 May 1982), pp. 9–11.

Little, D., 'The making of a special relationship: the United States and Israel, 1957–68', *International Journal of Middle East Studies*, XXV (1993), pp. 563–85.

Louis, W.R., 'The imperialism of decolonization', *The Journal of Imperial and Commonwealth History*, XXII (1994), pp. 462–511.

Mason, M., '"The Decisive Volley": The battle of Ismailia and the decline of British influence in Egypt, January–July 1952', *The Journal of Imperial and Commonwealth History*, XIX (1) (1990), pp. 45–64.

Morsy, L.A., 'The Role of the United States in the Anglo-Egyptian Agreement of 1954', *Middle Eastern Studies*, XXIX (1993), pp. 526–58.

Oren, M.B., 'A winter of discontent: Britain's crisis in Jordan, December 1955–March 1956', *International Journal of Middle East Studies*, XXII (1990), pp. 171–84.

Ovendale, R., 'Great Britain and the Anglo-American invasion of Jordan and Lebanon in 1958', *The International History Review*, XVI (1994), pp. 284–303.

Ovendale, R., 'Macmillan and the Wind of Change in Africa, 1957–60', *The Historical Journal*, **38** (1995), pp. 455–77.

Petersen, T.T., 'Anglo-American rivalry in the Middle East: the struggle for the Buraimi Oasis, 1952–1957', *The International History Review*, XIV (1993), pp. 71–91.

Podeh, E., 'The struggle over Arab hegemony after the Suez Crisis', *Middle*

Eastern Studies, XXIX (1993), pp. 91–110.
Raad, Z., 'A nightmare avoided: Jordan and Suez 1956', *Israel Affairs*, I (1994), pp. 288–308.
Ruehsen, M. de M., 'Operation "Ajax" revisited: Iran, 1953', *Middle Eastern Studies*, XXIX (1993), pp. 467–86.
Shlomo, S., 'Origins of the 1950 Tripartite declaration on the Middle East', *Middle Eastern Studies*, XXIII (1987), pp. 135–49.
Warner, G., 'Review article the United States and the Suez Crisis', *International Affairs*, 67 (1991), pp. 303–17.

Theses

Ashton, N.J., 'British Strategy and Anglo-American Relations in the Middle East, January 1955–March 1959' (Ph.D. thesis, University of Cambridge, January 1992).
Owen, T.H.A., 'Britain and the Revision of the Anglo-Egyptian Treaty, 1949–1954' (Ph.D. thesis, University of Wales, Aberystwyth, 1991).
Russell, D.E., 'Kuwait 1961: The War that never Happened' (M.Sc. dissertation, University of Wales, Aberystwyth, 1993).

Index

Note: ME stands for Middle East.

Abdullah 3, 6, 7, 14, 18, 25, 26
Acheson, Dean: and British arms exportation 31; and Iran 70, 71; on Morrison 46; and Northern Tier 33–4; and US-Anglo relations 24–5, 36
Aden Protectorate 87, 124, 125, 141, 149, 225
Africa 7–8, 9, 19–20
Alanbrooke, Viscount (formerly Alan Brooke) 5, 9–10
Allen, George V. 115–16, 123, 143–4, 146
'Alpha' 115–17, 131, 133
American Christian Palestine Committee 30, 61
Anglo-Egyptian Treaty (1936) 7–9, 99
Anglo-Iranian Oil Company 3, 43; Iran's dissatisfaction with concession issue 30, 32–3, 45; nationalization of 46–7, 58, 70; negotiations over 73–4
Anglo-Iraqi Treaty (1930) 26, 97, 108; negotiation of 15, 91–2, 111, 112, 134, 244
Anglo-Jordanian Treaty (1948) 97, 98, 101–2, 170; Jordan's abrogation of 185; Jordan's desire to terminate 181–2
Anglo-Turkish agreement (1913) 191
Arab–Israeli conflict 102, 111, 131, 150, 167; Anglo–American policy for solution 115–20, 133–4, 244
Arab–Israeli War (1948–9) 18, 27, 84, 133
Arab League 27, 65, 94, 111, 112; formation 4; and Israel 100; and Kuwait 217, 226, 232, 233, 234
Arab Union 190–1, 192–3, 201
Arabism *see* nationalism, Arab
ARAMCO (Arabian-American Oil Company) 86, 91, 172; Anglo-US differences over 43, 44, 45; benefit of to Saudi Arabia 27, 42; and Buraimi 85, 88–9, 125, 126, 127, 145, 146
arms: British exportation of to Arabs 30–1; British supply to Israel 119–20
Aswan High Dam project 131, 132–3, 144, 146, 148, 151, US-Anglo withdrawal 155–6
Atlantic Pact 34
Attlee, Clement 6, 11, 48, 62, 102; and Africa 7, 9

Baghdad Pact (1955) 64, 91, 129, 155; and Britain 60, 141, 142, 149, 153, 167, 179, 183, 184, 244; collapse of 224; and Egypt 111–12, 113, 143; and Iran 114, 130, 131, 146; and Jordan 113, 114, 131, 134, 147; origins see Turco-Iraqi Pact; and US 122–3, 124, 131, 132, 134, 145, 147–8, 150, 155, 169–70, 180, 191, 193, 244
Bahrain 85–6, 148–9, 179, 190
Balfour Declaration (1917) 2
Belgrave, Sir Charles 148
Ben-Gurion, David 17, 18, 117, 133–4; relations with Britain 41, 96–7, 98, 100, 103; and US-Anglo invasion of Jordan 204, 207, 208
Bermuda Conference: (1953) 76–7; (1957) 184–5, 186, 246
Bevin, Ernest; and Africa 7–8; on Arab nationalism 61; and Egypt 8–9, 39; ME policy 3, 4–5, 39; and Palestine 11, 12, 14, 15, 16, 60–1; and US 15, 24–5, 28
Britain: clashes with US over ME policy 168–9, 170–1, 172, 245; and communist

threat 18–19; concentration on establishing friendly relations with Arab states 84, 93, 95–6, 236; decrease in importance of ME in global strategy 178, 211, 236; differences/common interests with US policy and (1959) 224; diminishing of influence in ME 52, 53, 64, 103, 179–80, 243, 244; early flexible policy 1–2; importance of ME 2, 4, 9, 10, 12, 18, 20; importance of protecting oil interests 130, 131, 134, 135, 141, 145, 148, 152, 172, 183, 184, 244; joint US-Anglo planning of protection of oil resources 186–7, 189; military expenditure 153, 154; military presence in ME 2–3; need for co-ordination of Anglo-US policies 28–30, 31–2, 35–7, 40, 153, 154–5; need for mutual defence arrangements with Arab states to defend oil 63–4; need for US co-operation and support to maintain position in ME 47, 53, 122, 141–2, 167, 168, 181, 183, 184, 237, 243–4; new economic and social policy under Bevin 4–5, 6–7, 39; objectives of policy (1956) 152; objectives of policy (1961) 242; post-Suez revision of policy 181–2; principles of policy (1951) 31–2; reasons for decline in influence 67; reassessment of defence policy in light of financial considerations, 58, 65, 102, 109, 152, 178, 243, 247; redeployment and reduction of forces 50, 66, 153–4, 181; reduction in defence expenditure 109, 134; revision of global strategy under Churchill 58–9, 102–3, 243–4; security of ME position through alliances with Arab states 15, 19; talks with US on defence 120–3
Brook, Norman 101, 182, 235, 236
Brooke, Sir Alan *see* Alanbrooke, Viscount
Buraimi 90; British conflict with Saudi Arabia over 87, 125–30, 143, 151; US view of Britain's situation 90, 143, 144, 145, 146, 161, 169, 172, 245
Burrows, Bernard 28, 34, 86, 87, 127
Butler, R.A. 58, 59, 116

Caccia, Sir Harold 199, 222, 229
Caffery, Jefferson 35
Caltex Agreement (1950) 43
Canal Zone *see* Suez Canal
CENTO (Central Treaty Organization) 224

Chamoun, Camille 193, 198–9, 200, 201, 203, 211
Chapman-Andrews, E.A. 52
Chehab, General Faud 203, 204, 210
China 130, 151
Churchill, Winston 58; Egyptian policy 62, 68, 74–8, 100, 102–3; on importance of US involvement 62, 66, 68, 102, 171, 243–4; and Iraq 91, 92–3; and Israel 96–7, 98, 99–101, 103, 118; and Jordan–Israeli conflict 101–2; and Palestine 60–1; on Soviet threat 68–9, 102; support of Zionism 60–1, 62, 96, 103; and US involvement in Iran 70–4
Cold War 6, 24, 31, 59, 183, 243
command arrangements *see* Middle East Command
Commonwealth: conference on ME (1951) 37–40
communism: effect of on policy 18–19, 29, 242
Cyprus 4, 5, 181, 187
Cyrenaica 9, 14, 19, 39

Damascus: French bombing of (1945) 1
'Defence Policy and Global Strategy' papers: (1950) 31; (1952) 59; (1951) 51
Dickson, Sir William 149, 150, 199, 201
Dixon, Sir Pierson 47, 201
Dodds-Parker, A.D. 152–3
Duce, Terry 126
Dulles, Allen 108, 126, 127
Dulles, John Foster: and 'Alpha' plan 115, 116–17, 133; and Aswan Dam 155; and Baghdad Pact 110, 112, 123, 131, 132, 134, 150, 168, 171, 180; and Buraimi 90, 126, 127, 128, 145, 146, 151; and Iran 73–4; and Jordan 203, 204, 205, 206, 209, 217; and Kuwait 217; and Lebanon 202, 217; and Nasser 130, 148, 149, 151, 155; and Northern Tier 92, 94, 102, 110, 132; and Suez crisis 157, 159, 164–5; and US-Anglo relations 62–3, 69, 180, 185, 216, 244

Eden, Anthony 46, 144; and Aden 125; and Anglo-US relations 50, 62–3, 108, 140–1, 171, 172, 245; and Arab–Israeli relations 115, 133–4; and Aswan Dam 132; background 62; and Baghdad Pact 112, 113, 148; and Buraimi/Saudi Arabia conflict 89, 90, 91, 125, 145, 146; conflict with Churchill over Suez 75–6,

Index

77–8, 103; emphasis on more direct role in ME 108, 244; health 160; and Iran 70, 71, 73; and Israel 93, 98; and Jordan–Israeli conflict 97, 101; and Libya 59; and Macmillan 129, 171; and Nasser 108, 151, 181; and Northern Tier 108; objectives of policy 152, 172, 245; policy based on mutual assistance to Arab allies 65–6, 108, 236; request to US for Centurion tanks for Iraq 123–4; retirement 183; and Suez crisis 129–30, 156–60, 160–1, 163, 166; and Turkey 92–3

Egypt 4, 35; arms deal with Soviet Union 120, 130; and Aswan Dam 131, 132–3, 144, 146, 148, 151, 155–6; and Baghdad Pact 111–12, 113, 143; and blockade of Israel 101; and Britain 130–1, 148, 149, 150, 156; Churchill's policy towards 62, 74–8, 100, 102–3; coup (1952) 75; importance of as base in war 19, 20, 37, 38, 39, 40; and Iraq 167, 172, 181, 242, 245–6; Israeli attack on Gaza (1955) 117, 119; and Kuwait 185; and Middle East Command 51, 52, 69; need for joint Anglo-US policy over 142; negotiations over revision of Anglo-Egyptian Treaty 7–9; significance of Britain's position in 32, 48–9; union with Syria 190 *see also* United Arab Republic; and US 131–2, 148; *see also* Nasser, Gamal Abdul; Suez Canal; Suez crisis

Eilat, Elihu 118, 119

Eisenhower, Dwight D.: and Anglo-US relations 67–8, 75, 77, 123, 134, 171, 211, 244–5, 246, 247; and Buraimi/Saudi Arabia conflict 146, 169; and Egypt 76, 77, 150; health 130, 155; and invasion of Jordan 186, 207, 208, 209; and invasion of Lebanon 201, 202, 211; and Iran 72; and Kuwait crisis 223; and Macmillan 184–5, 188, 198, 211; and 'Omega' policy 149; and Saudi Arabia 149, 169, 172, 245; and Suez crisis 140, 156, 157–8, 159, 160, 161, 162–3, 165–6; and Syria 188

Eisenhower Doctrine 178–94; becomes law 184; difficulties encountered in Congress 184; origins and reasoning behind 182

Farouk, King 6, 69
Fawzi, Dr. Mahmud 111–12, 161
'Fertile Crescent' scheme 3, 6, 111

France 96, 167; bombing of Damascus 1; interest in ME 65; and Israel 117, 120; and Suez crisis 157, 158, 161–3; and Syria 111; US–Anglo resistance to involvement of in ME 50, 51–2
Franks, Sir Oliver 33, 46, 47, 65–6
Furlonge, G.W. 64

Gaitskell, Hugh 48
Gaza Strip 117, 119
Glubb, John 3, 15; dismissal 147
Grady, Henry F. 44–5
Greece 37, 40, 66
Gulf: Anglo-US differences over policy 84–5, 87–8, 135, 245; British interests in 85, 129, 135, 179, 184, 185, 189, 216; *see also* individual countries

Hare, Raymond 88
Heath, Edward 227
Henderson, Loy 71
Herter, Christian A. 222, 223, 224
Home, Lord 225, 229, 230–1, 234
Hoover, Herbert 121–2, 126, 129, 132, 170, 246
Hussein, King 134, 147, 185; and Anglo-US invasion of Jordan 201, 202–3, 206, 209–10
hydrogen bomb *see* nuclear weapons

Ibn Saud, King 26, 27, 30, 42, 87, 88, 90
India 5, 7, 34, 41
Iran 64, 95, 110, 167; Anglo-US conflict over 44–8; Anglo-US talks on 32–3; and Baghdad Pact 114, 130, 131, 146; and Britain 30, 46, 93, 113, 178–9; overthrow of Mossadeq 72–3; and Pakistan 41; question of armed intervention by British at Abadan 46–7, 48; and US 25, 30, 122; US pursues independent policy to Britain's detriment 70–4; *see also* Anglo-Iranian Oil Company
Iraq 3; and Britain 93–6, 131, 152–3, 183, 207, 219, 245; Britain's new defence agreement with 64, 93–5, 111, 112–13, 114; coup (1958) 193, 201, 207; and Egypt 167, 172, 181, 242, 245–6; and Kuwait 191–2, 193, 223, 225; and Kuwait crisis (1961) *see* Kuwait; and renegotiation of Anglo-Iraqi Treaty 15, 91–2, 111, 112, 134, 244; supply of Centurion tanks from US 123–4, 147; and Syria 26, 111, 126; and Turco-Iraqi

Pact 109, 110, 111–13, 114; union with Jordan (Arab Union) 190–1, 193, 201; and US 26, 92–3, 95, 120–1, 122

Israel 25, 34; arms supply by Britain 119–20; and Arab–Israeli war 18; Arabs dislike of 19, 84 *see also* Arab-Israeli conflict; blockade by Arab League 100; blockade by Egypt 101; Britain's concern about internal developments 118–20; and Britain's invasion of Jordan 204, 205–6, 207, 208, 209; British relations with after creation 19; Churchill's support of 96–7, 98, 99–101, 103, 118; and Commonwealth issue 118, 120; conflict with Jordan 97–8, 100, 101–2; development of relations with Britain 41, 64, 98–9, 103, 208; French support for 117, 120; moves towards activist policy and war against Arabs 117; and Gaza Strip 117, 119; proclamation of state (1948) 17; raid on Qibya 97, 101, 103; and Suez crisis 158, 161–3, 164; and Turco-Iraqi Pact 118

Jordan 116, 144; and Anglo-Jordanian Treaty 97, 98, 101–2, 170, 181–2, 185; [Anglo-US invasion of 193, 202–11: British intervention 205, 206–7; invasion 207–9; planning 199; request from Hussein to intervene 202–3; request to Israel for overflying rights 204, 205–6, 207, 208, 209; US logistic support 206, 207, 208; US reluctance to proposed military intervention 203, 204–5; withdrawal from 210]; and Baghdad Pact 113, 114, 131, 134, 147; British relations with 25–6, 64; conflict with Israel 97–8, 100, 101–2; crisis in (1957) 185–6; reduction in British commitments 154, 180; and Soviet Union 144; 'Unified Plan for the Jordan Valley' 114; union with Iraq (Arab Union) 190–1, 193, 201 *see also* Transjordan

Kenya 242
Khan, Liaquat Ali 34
Khrushchev, Nikita 150–1, 188
Killearn, Lord 4, 5, 7
King David Hotel: bombing of 10, 11, 61
Kirkpatrick, Ivone 111, 128, 140
Korean War 32
Kuwait 86, 167, 207; and Arab Union 190–1, 192–3; British interests in 64, 85, 123, 178, 179, 185, 190, 191; challenge to British interests by coup 218; contingency intervention plans 218, 223–4, 224–5; [crisis (1961) 228–37, 246: agreement with Arab League 234; Arab response to 231–2; Britain's wish to withdraw troops from 233–4; British precautionary methods on possible Iraqi attack 229–30; consequences of 235–6; Qasim's claim to sovereignty 228–9; and United Nations 232, 233, 234; US naval reconnaissance 230–1]; and Egypt 185; importance to Britain 185, 187, 217, 246; and Iraq 191–2, 193, 223, 225; need for joint Anglo-US planning 223, 224, 225; request for and abrogation of Exclusive Agreement (1899) 226, 227–8; wanting more independent role in relationship with Arab states 217; US-Anglo oil interests 154

Lampson, Sir Miles *see* Killearn, Lord
Lebanon 113, 193, 242; blockade of Israel 100; crisis (1958) 198–204, 208, 209, 211: Anglo-US contingency intervention plans 198–9, 200; deterioration of situation 199; US to intervene alone 201–2; US landings 203–4; US revision plan for joint military action 201–2; US withdrawal from 210
Lennox-Boyd, Alan 220
Libya 148; and Britain 59, 96, 152, 183; joint Anglo-US co-operation over 154–5, 182
Lloyd, Selwyn 129, 182; background 63; on British ME policy 64, 185; and Buraimi 90, 145, 146; on defence expenditure 109; and Egypt 148, 151; and Israel 119, 147; and Jordan 180, 210; and Kuwait 222, 223, 224; and Lebanon 100, 210; and Libya 96, 152; and Suez 157, 158, 161, 162, 164–5

McGhee, George 28–9, 34, 35, 45, 48–9, 50
McMahon Act (1946) 189
Macmillan, Harold 116, 155; and Arab Union 192–3; and Buraimi 126; and defence of Kuwait 219, 220, 223, 224, 225, 229–30, 232, 233, 234; and Eden 129, 171; and Egypt 130–1; and Eisenhower 184–5, 188, 198, 211; and Iraq 193, 207, 220; and Israel 119; and Jordan 203, 205, 206–7, 208, 209–10; and Lebanon 200; and Saudi Arabia 128–9; and Suez crisis 157, 158, 159,

160, 170–1, 183; and US–Anglo relations 187, 188, 211
Makins, Sir Roger 47, 85, 86, 122, 123
Manila Pact 110
Massigli, R. 111
MEDO (Middle East Defence Organization) 69
Menderes, Adnan 110
Middle East Command 48, 50, 51–2, 69, 98
Middle East Co-operative Defence Board 51
Middleton, Sir George 179–80, 199, 211, 225
Morrison, Herbert 41, 46, 48, 49, 63, 72
Mossadeq, Dr Muhammad 45, 46, 48, 64, 70, 71–2; overthrow of 72–3
Moyne, Lord 42, 101, 103
Muscat 129, 141, 188; British support for Sultan of 127–8, 130, 143, 187

Nabulsi, Suleiman 185
Nasser, Gamal Abdul 77; and Arab–Israeli conflict solution 115, 117, 133; and Aswan Dam 132, 133; and Baghdad Pact 112, 143; and Britain 108, 147, 148, 150, 151, 172, 181, 186, 220, 222; and Kuwait 185; nationalization of Suez Canal 140, 155, 156–7; and Soviet Union 123, 130, 150, 151; US policy towards 116, 148, 156, 181, 187, 221, 222
nationalism, Arab 3–4, 61, 64–5, 66, 67, 84, 193, 210, 242
National Military Organization 10
NATO (North Atlantic Treaty Organization) 32, 40
Neguib, Muhammad 75, 76, 77, 100
New Zealand 52
Nicholls, J.W. 118
North Atlantic Treaty 24, 25, 31
Northern Tier strategy 131; and Britain 108–9, 109–10, 132, 134, 171; development of idea 33–4, 37–8, 91, 92, 94–5; Turco-Pakistan Pact 92, 93, 94, 110, 169; and US 84, 92, 94, 108–9, 109–10, 113, 134, 171; *see also* Baghdad Pact
nuclear weapons 58, 68; effect of emergence on British defence policy 59–60, 78, 94, 102, 111, 243; US–Anglo co-operation over 188–9
Nuqrashi, Mahmud Fahmi al- 6
Nuri al-Said 3, 147; and Arab Union 190, 192; and Britain 26, 91, 92, 121, 245; and Nasser 181; and Northern Tier 94–5; overthrow of 193; and Turco-Iraqi Pact 110, 114
Nutting, Anthony 63, 78, 114

Oman 141, 143, 187–8
Oman, Imam of 127–8, 187
'Omega' policy 149

Pakistan 25, 113, 224; and Britain 120, 122; defence role in ME 25, 41; and Northern Tier 34; and Turco-Pakistan Pact 92, 110
Palestine 1, 4, 154, 243; Anglo-US differences over 9–10; and Balfour Declaration 2; British policy 5, 10, 11–14; British withdrawal 14–15, 17; and Churchill 60–1; debate over partition 5, 10–11, 13–14, 16; General Assembly vote for partition 16–17; Jewish immigration into 2, 6, 9–10; and United Nations 12, 13, 16; and Soviet Union 13, 14, 15, 16, 17; *see also* Zionists
Pelham, G.C. 88–9
Portsmouth, Treaty of (1948) 15
President Warfield 13

Qasim 218–19, 221, 228, 229, 230
Qatar 85, 86, 179
Qibya: massacre at 97, 101, 103

Richmond, J.C.B. 226–7, 232, 233, 234, 235–6
Roosevelt, Kim 72, 124, 125
Roosevelt, President F.D. 5, 61, 72
Rowan, Sir Leslie 70
Rusk, Dean 229, 230, 231

San Remo Conference (1920) 1
Saud, King: and Buraimi 125, 146; and US 149, 169, 172, 245
Saudi Arabia 1, 142; Anglo-US conflict over interests 41–4, 84–5, 87–91, 123, 135, 143–4, 245; and Britain 26, 27–8, 42, 89, 141, 189, 225–6; British conflict with over Buraimi 87, 125–30, 143, 146, 151; development of US interests 25, 26–8, 41–2; Eisenhower's support of King Saud 149, 169, 172, 245; and Kuwait crisis 231–2; and Oman 187; plan for detachment from Egypt 149–50, 151; US oil interests in *see* ARAMCO; US position over Buraimi 90, 143, 144, 145, 146, 161, 169, 172, 245

SEATO (South East Asia Treaty Organization) 168
Shah of Iran 72–3, 110, 146
Sharett, Moshe 101, 119
Shepherd, Sir Francis 44–5, 48
Shuckburgh, Evelyn 63, 77, 95, 109–10, 113, 115, 119, 120–1, 133, 143–4, 149
Sidky, Ismail 8, 9
South Africa 20, 52, 123
Soviet–Iranian Treaty (1921) 25
Soviet Union 58, 65, 150–1; Churchill on military threat of 68–9, 102; and Egypt 8, 123, 130, 150, 151, 159; and Jordan 144; and Palestine 13, 14, 15, 16, 17; security of ME as defensive base against 2, 5, 7, 9, 10, 24, 32, 33; and Syria 188
Sputnik 188
Stevens, Sir Roger 178–9
Stevenson, Sir Ralph 52, 113
Stokes, Richard 47
Strang, Sir William 18, 19, 20, 51, 89, 91
Sudan 14, 40
Suez Canal 5, 32, 52, 77; and Anglo-Egyptian Treaty 7; Churchill's policy towards 62, 68, 74–6, 77–8; evacuation of 63–4, 77–8, 155; importance to Britain 156–7; withdrawal proposals 8, 12, 39, 49, 62; *see also* Suez crisis
Suez Canal Users' Association 159, 160, 161
Suez crisis 140–72; Anglo-French intervention plan 161–3; attack mounted 163; Britain prepared to use force 157, 158–9; Britain's reaction to nationalization 156–7; ceasefire 166; consequences of 167; demand for British/French withdrawal by Arab states 168; effect of US presidential elections 160, 163, 165, 170–1; and Israel 158, 161–3, 164; nationalization by Nasser 140, 155, 156–7; origins 140; reaction of US to invasion 163–4; US economic sanctions against Britain 166–7; US reluctance to use military force 140, 156, 157–8, 159–60 Syria 224; and Britain 52, 148; foiled coup 164; and France 111; and Iraq 26, 111, 126; union with Egypt 190 *see also* United Arab Republic; US and 25, 131, 140, 188

Tedder, Lord 10, 11, 33
Transjordan 4, 7, 12, 14–15, 18, 19 *see also* Jordan
Tripartite Declaration (1950) 31, 50, 119, 147, 148, 150, 161
Trott, A.C. 41, 42, 43, 44
Troutbeck, Sir John 91–2, 95, 103
Trucial Sheikhdoms 85, 86, 89, 129, 154
Truman, Harry S. 24, 68; and Iran 71; and Palestine 5–6, 11, 16–17
Truman Doctrine (1947) 243
Turco-Iraqi Pact 109, 110, 111–13, 114, 115, 118, 121, 122 *see also* Baghdad Pact
Turco-Pakistan Pact 92, 93, 94, 110, 169
Turkey 10, 25, 34, 38, 39, 59, 66, 188; and NATO 40; and Turco-Pakistan Pact 92, 93, 94, 110, 169; *see also* Turco-Iraqi Pact

United Arab Republic 191, 193, 216, 242; and Britain 219; creation 190; and Jordan 205, 206; and Kuwait crisis 232–3; and Lebanon 199, 200
United Nations 210; and Kuwait 232; and Lebanon 201; and Palestine 12, 13, 16; and Suez crisis 168 United States: agreement that ME is responsibility of Britain 3; development of relations with Britain over ME 20, 24–5; influence of communist threat on policy 224; need for review of policy in light of Britain's declining influence 66–7, 77, 102; defence talks with Britain 120–3; objectives of policy (1961) 242; pursual of more independent policy 69, 77, 102; reluctance to relieve Britain of ME responsibilities 32, 34–5, 37, 50, 53, 67–8; support needed for Britain to maintain position in ME 47, 53, 122, 243–4; takes on major responsibility for defence of ME 178, 189, 193–4, 244; unwillingness to make military sacrifices 34–5, 37, 50, 53, 243; *see also* Britain (for Anglo-US policy); individual countries
UNSCOP (United Nations Special Committee on Palestine) 13–14

Wilson, Evan 109
Wright, Sir Michael 28, 29, 30, 113, 114

Yemen 26, 87, 125, 224

Zahedi, General Fazullah 72, 73
Zionists 119; Churchill's support of 60–1, 62, 96, 103; lobbyists in Congress 30, 61; and Palestine 2, 6, 9, 10, 11, 13, 17